England's Landscape

The North East

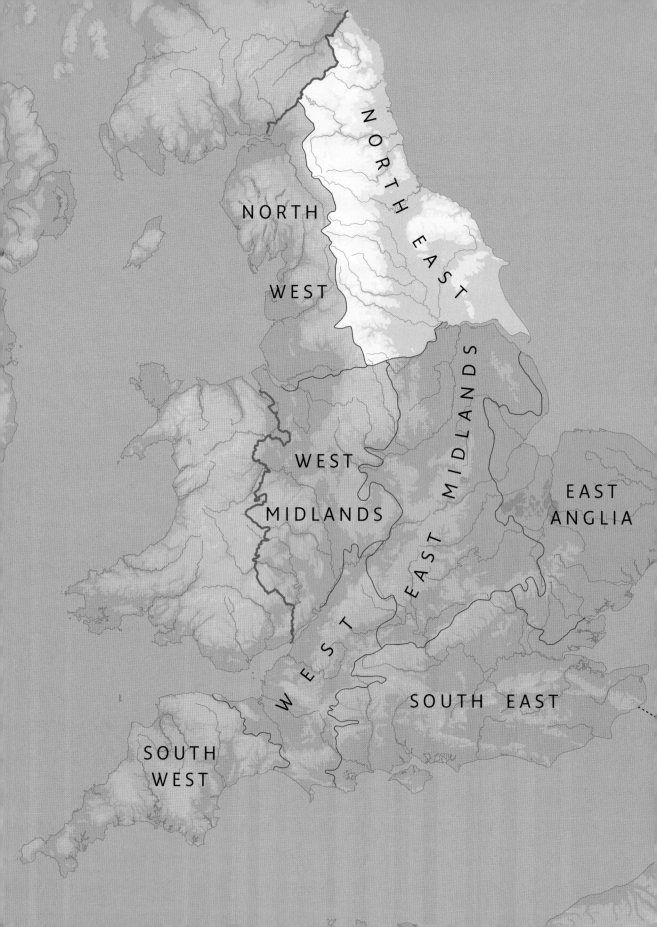

NORTH
WEST

NORTH EAST

WEST
MIDLANDS

EAST MIDLANDS

EAST
ANGLIA

W E S T

SOUTH EAST

SOUTH
WEST

Collins

England's Landscape

The North East

EDITED BY F H A AALEN WITH COLM O'BRIEN

F H A AALEN
THOMAS FAULKNER
ANDREW GREG
RICHARD LOMAS
D M MACRAILD
RICHARD MUIR
LINDA POLLEY
A W PURDUE
CHRISTOPHER TOLAN-SMITH

SERIES EDITOR NEIL COSSONS

ENGLISH HERITAGE

First published in 2006 by Collins, an imprint of
HarperCollins*Publishers*
77–85 Fulham Palace Road, London W6 8JB

www.collins.co.uk

10 9 8 7 6 5 4 3 2 1
10 09 08 07 06

ISBN 10 – 0 00 715576 X
ISBN 13 – 9 78 0 00 715576 7

British Library Cataloguing in Publication Data
A CIP catalogue record for this book is available from the
British Library.

Map on previous page:
The regions: the red lines bound the general area covered by
each volume.

Volume Editor's Acknowledgements
The volume editor would like to thank the following individuals
for their help with the preparation of this volume: Tony Hopkins,
photographer; Professor Melvyn Jones, Sheffield Hallam
University; Ged Lawson, Durham County Council Planning
Department; Roger Mercer, RCAHM Scotland; Professor Brian
Roberts, Durham University; and Robert White, Yorkshire Dales
National Park.

Publisher & Commissioning Editor Myles Archibald
Production Director Graham Cook
Edited by Colm O'Brien and Adele Campbell
Designed by D & N Publishing, Hungerford, Berkshire
Indexed by Sheila Seacroft

Printed in Italy by LEGO SpA, Vicenza

ACKNOWLEDGEMENTS

SERIES EDITOR
Sir Neil Cossons OBE, MA, FSA
Chairman, English Heritage
President, Royal Geographical Society
The series editor would like to acknowledge the contribution of
the following people:

EDITORIAL BOARD:
Professor David Cannadine MA, LittD, DPhil, FBA, FSA
Queen Elizabeth the Queen Mother Professor of British History,
University of London

Professor Barry Cunliffe CBE, LittD, DPhil, FBA, FSA
Professor of European Archaeology, University of Oxford

Professor Richard Lawton MA, Hon DLitt
Professor Emeritus, Department of Geography, University of
Liverpool

Professor Brian K Roberts PhD, FSA
Professor Emeritus, Department of Geography, University of Durham

ENGLISH HERITAGE EXECUTIVE EDITORS:
Dr Paul Barnwell, *Head of Medieval and Later Rural Research*
Dr Martin Cherry, *Former Chief Buildings Historian*
Humphrey Welfare, *Northern Territory Director*
Graham Fairclough, *Head of Characterisation*

ENGLISH HERITAGE PROJECT MANAGERS:
Val Horsler, *former Head of Publishing*
Adele Campbell, *Commercial Publishing Manager*

Special thanks to Angus Lunn for his editorial help on the
geological and geographical sections of this volume. All new
ground and air photography was taken specifically for this series.
Thanks to: Damian Grady, Senior Investigator of English
Heritage Aerial Survey and Investigation Team, and to the
photographic and dark-room teams in Swindon; Steve Cole,
Head of Photography, and the staff of the English Heritage
Photography team. Archive material from the National
Monuments Record was researched by the Enquiry and
Research Services teams led by Alyson Rogers (Buildings) and
Lindsay Jones (Archaeology/Air Photos). Graphics lists were
managed by John Vallender and Bernard Thomason. Graphics
were produced under the management of Rob Read of 3's
Company (Consultancy) Ltd, by Steve Cheshire, John Hodgson,
Martyn Norris and Drew Smith. All other images were
researched by Jo Walton and Julia Harris-Voss.

Contents

CONTENTS

Foreword

The landscape of England evokes intense passion and profound emotion. This most loved of places, the inspiration for generations of writers, poets and artists, it is at once both the source of the nation's infatuation and the setting for grievous misunderstanding. For people who visit, the view of England offers some of their most lasting images. For exiles abroad the memory of the English landscape sustains their beliefs and desire for a homecoming.

But for those who live in England the obsession is double edged. On the one hand we cherish the unchanging atmosphere of a familiar place, and on the other make impossible demands of it, believing that it will always accommodate, always forgive. Only in the last half century or so have we started to recognise the extreme fragility of all that we value in the English landscape, to appreciate not only that it is the metaphor for who we are as a people, but that it represents one of our most vivid contributions to a wider culture. At last we are beginning to realise that a deeper understanding of its subtle appeal and elusive character is the key to a thoughtful approach to its future.

The unique character of England's landscape derives from many things. But nowhere is the impact of human intervention absent. If geology and topography set the scene, it is the implacable persistence of generations who since the end of the Ice Age have sought to live in and off this place that has created the singular qualities of the landscape we have today. Not, of course, that the landscape before people was in any sense a static thing; on the contrary, the environment untouched by mankind was and is a dynamic and constantly changing synthesis. Every layer of that complex progression can still be found somewhere, making its own peculiar contribution to the distinctiveness of today's England. It is a compelling narrative. Through this series of regional studies our distinguished contributors – as authors and editors – have distilled something of what has created today's England, in order to decode that narrative.

Unique is an overused term. But it has a special resonance for the landscape of England, both urban and rural. What we hope readers of this series will begin to feel is the nature of the qualities that define the English landscape. Much of that landscape has of course been inherited from cultures overseas, as conquest and migration brought here peoples who have progressively occupied and settled Britain. They created what might be called our shared landscapes, defined as much by what links them to the wider world as through any intrinsically native characteristics. The peoples whose common bonds stretched along the Atlantic seaboard have left a legacy in Cornwall more akin to parts of north-west France or Spain than to anywhere else in England. There are Roman roads and cities and medieval field systems that have their closest parallels in the European plains from whence they derived. Great abbeys and monasteries reflected in their art and architecture, their commerce and industry, a culture whose momentum lay outside these islands. And when disaster came it was a pan-European epidemic, the Black Death, that took away between a third and a half of the people. England's are not the only deserted medieval villages.

And yet, paradoxically, much of what today we would recognise as the quintessential England is only some two or three centuries old. Parliamentary enclosure, especially of the English lowlands, was itself a reaction to an even greater economic force – industrialisation, and the urbanisation that went with it. It has given us a rural landscape that epitomises the essence of Englishness in the minds of many. The fields and hedgerows surrounding the nucleated villages of the pre-existing medieval landscape are of course quite new when set against the timescale of human occupation. Indeed, when the first railways came through there remained, here and there, open fields where the rows of new hawthorn hedges were still feeble whips scribing lines across a thousand years of feudal landscape.

As Britain emerged to become the world's first industrial nation, its astonishing transformation was at its most visible in the landscape, something new, indigenous and without precedent. It fuelled the debate on the picturesque and the sublime and was a source of wonder to those who visited from overseas. But in its urban and industrial excesses it soon came to be detested by aesthetes, social commentators and a burgeoning class opposed to the horrors of industrial capitalism. What was perhaps the most decisive contribution of Britain to the human race provoked a powerful counteraction reflected in the writings of Ruskin, Morris, Octavia Hill and the Webbs. It was this anguish that a century ago energised the spirit of conservation in a growing band of people determined to capture what was left of the pre-industrial rural scene.

Today the landscape of England is, as ever, undergoing immense change. But, unlike the centuries just past, that change once again draws its energy and inspiration from forces overseas. A new form of global economy, North American in flavour, concept and style carries all before it. The implications for the long-term future of the landscape and the people who live in it are difficult to predict. The out-of-town shopping malls, the great encampments of distribution warehouses crouching like so many armadillos across the rural shires, the growth of exurbia – that mixed-use land between city and country that owes nothing to either – are all manifestations of these new economic forces. Like the changes that have gone before, they have become the subject of intense debate and the source of worrying uncertainty. But what is clear is that a deeper understanding of the landscape, in all its manifestations, offers a means of managing change in a conscious and thoughtful manner.

This was the inspiration that led to this new regional landscape series. To understand the language of landscape, to be able to interpret the way in which people make places, offers insights and enjoyment beyond the ordinary. It enables us to experience that most neglected of human emotions, a sense of place. These books set out to reveal the values that underwrite our sense of place, by offering an insight into how the landscape of England came to be the way it is. If understanding is the key to valuing and valuing is the key to caring, then these books may help to ensure that we can understand and enjoy the best of what we have, and that when we make our own contribution to change it will not only reinforce that essential distinctiveness but will also improve the quality of life of those who live there.

Neil Cossons

1

North-eastern Landscapes

F H A AALEN

What is a north-eastern landscape? There is no simple answer to this question, for the interplay between the physical structure of the land and human activity has given rise to countless different landscape forms, yet time and again the land presents a scene that somehow seems to typify the regional character. This book looks at geological structure, land-forming processes, vegetation, natural resources and 10,000 years of human activity, to examine how together these have given rise to the North East's varied landscapes. The character of the North East can be summarised in four landscape types, each apparent many times over: open moorland; enclosed lowlands with village settlements; part-rural/part-industrial areas; and the towns and cities. By way of an introduction to the more detailed aspects of the volume, each of the following four scenes tells a story of the interaction of natural and human processes, and each offers a description of a landscape type in the North East.

ON TOP OF THE PENNINES – BOLLIHOPE COMMON

No trees grow on Bollihope Common (Fig. 1.1). Nothing stands high in the face of the wind, save a row of painted poles that mark the line of the road against the risk of winter snows drifting across land where no field-walls run to break their flow. But in August the scene is benign, as hardy sheep graze on patches of short grass around the edges of soft, bushy Pennine heather blazing purple in late summer sunshine. Bees, from hives carried out on to the hill for the season, busy themselves making honey that will later be sold in the dale in Stanhope or Wolsingham.

Even at this dry time, from the base of the peat exposed in small erosions, brown-stained water seeps and trickles into burns, which finger their way across the plateau. Bollihope Burn collects these strands as it tumbles down to the Wear, cutting a gorge where trees do find sufficient shelter to grow and where, on the grassy paddocks of Bollihope Shield, sheep are brought together. Sunday picnickers relax by their cars while their children play in the water.

This quiet and emptiness are deceptive, for all around are signs that this was once a busy landscape. By the crossing of the burn, a vertical face of grey stone, left from some long-disused quarry, stands out in contrast to the rounded forms of these north Pennine hills. Veins of lead run through here and Weardale was once busy with lead-working; roadside notices, warning of the dangers of the mine shafts scattered about the hillside, pick out the lines of the mineral. The road that served a former mine-head at the east edge of the Common is now a grass-covered track hugging the side of the hill. To the west of the road untidy mounds, now softened with heather cover, are spoil tips from a quarry nibbled into the hill.

On the slope north of the burn the straight drystone walls of a rectangular field plot seem out of place on these open hills; but the snaking courses of low embankments of stone, now grass-covered, along with small cairns and other features, are fragments of a more distant past and a more intensive use of the

FRONTISPIECE OPPOSITE:

An aerial view looking to the south of Bamburgh castle (foreground). *The open, lightly wooded and intensively farmed landscape of the level coastal lowland of north Northumberland can be seen. The coastal fringe is characterised by a succession of sweeping sandy bays backed by dune belts ('links') and separated by rocky promontories; the special visual qualities of the coast and the richness of its habitats led to it being designated as an Area of Outstanding Natural Beauty.*

land. Where archaeologists have stripped off the turf cover, prehistoric features have been revealed.

Back on the Common, strike out south up the hill towards the high point on the skyline, the Raven Seat. A pair of grouse rise clucking from the heather, startling walkers. Across the hill, ascending in single file, is a line of shooting butts, each cut into the slope and neatly finished with drystone retaining walls and a turf top, well camouflaged. This, not mining, is the modern industry on these hills. In Roman times the game was different. Micanus, a Prefect of Cavalry, had set up an altar hereabouts to Silvanus in thanks for the capture of a boar of outstanding size which, as he wrote on the dedication, many of his predecessors had been unable to take. Silvanus was a god of woodland; the boar a woodland animal: how the vegetation has changed since then. Micanus and his colleagues were not the first hunters on these hills. Six thousand years before, Stone Age people shot arrows whose flint tips became lodged, and are occasionally found, beneath the peat.

Reaching the Raven Seat, stand on the watershed nearly 600m above sea level. A partly derelict fence makes its crooked way along the top and on its other side the burns flow south into the Tees. Down on the Common, more visible here than from below, are stripes and chequer patterns in the heather where patches have been burned in recent years as part of the careful management of this not entirely natural scene. Into the distance the vistas are wide all round the compass: to the west, still higher ground; east into the lower dales; north and south to two more distant watershed ridges, beyond the Wear and beyond the Tees. Purple heather carpets these high tops of England.

Fig. 1.1 Bollihope Common.

IN THE VALE – SHERIFF HUTTON

Coming through the wooded Howardian Hills on the way from Hovingham to York, the road rises to a sharp left bend. At the crest of the hill, the Vale of York below surprises you. The horizon is suddenly distant; ahead towards Selby, towards Leeds to the right. Pasture-green enclosure fields are separated by low, darker-green hedges, while elsewhere these have been removed to create vast areas of modern agricultural land. Clusters of trees punctuate the landscape, as do the harsh inorganic sheds on some of the scattered farmsteads, their clean lines and unweathering surfaces catching the eye and the light.

Trees line the slightly hollowed road as it descends steeply into the greenness of the Vale, opening abruptly at the bottom of the slope. The road twists over Ings Beck: 'Ing' meaning damp pasture. By the bridge is North Ings Farm, its 19th-century grey stone buildings lurking within asbestos and corrugated iron sheds of the early post-war years.

Then, in front, the first distant silhouetted glimpse of the jagged corner towers, which are almost all that remain of Sheriff Hutton castle, the bright sky shining through the few remaining windows. It disappears. Round some long gentle bends, it is there again, straight ahead, suddenly seeming much closer, dominating a low ridge, which crosses the Vale. It remains in sight as you approach on the now straight late 18th-century wide-verged enclosure road, its hedges punctuated by once evenly spaced trees (Fig. 1.2).

Up the scarp of the ridge and into the village centre, turning left, you drive as far as you can go, well beyond the now curiously invisible castle. Ahead lies the church with its squat tower and flat-roofed aisles, an agglomeration of different periods, styles and building stones; some bright white, others a dark sandy brown. To the right the view south is blocked by the mounds of a 12th-century motte-and-bailey castle. It overlies the ridge and furrow of earlier agriculture visible to the south and, though only faintly, in the heavily ploughed field to the east. Beyond, glimpsed from the far end of the churchyard, is Sheriff Hutton Hall, nearly hidden in a belt of trees. To the north, the churchyard is enclosed by brick cottages of the 18th or 19th century, some rendered and painted; they may be the much rebuilt descendents of longhouses.

Returning along the main street to the village, the form of the settlement emerges. In front of the church is a triangular 'green', the partly infilled remnant of an early market place. The village street is hollowed out by centuries of human and animal traffic. On the right, short terraces are irregularly set back from what is now a service road, separated from the lower street by a grassy bank. Eighteenth- and 19th-century cottages are interspersed with much more modern but traditionally proportioned houses. Tucked back at the end of the green on the left, a small estate of council houses is a reminder of mid-20th-century rural poverty and of the welfare state, their uniform pink brick having a starker appearance than the hand-made bricks of the older dwellings. Ahead, the older houses, some painted, closely flank the road; built above it they create a hemmed-in feeling.

A road, marking the end of the original village, goes off to the right. Opposite, a break in the houses opens into an unexpected sloping green square surrounded by more spaciously placed houses. It is a second market-place, created a few years after the 'new' castle was built at the end of the 14th century. The castle would once have dominated this part of the village but the view is now obscured by a clutter of small buildings on the far side of the square and by what is now Castle Farm; the view from the main street is similarly obscured. On the other side of the road, the pattern of building observed nearer the church continues, but the plots on which the houses stand are longer. They have been subdivided, their backs now built up with 20th-century houses facing the road to Bulmer, formerly 'Back Lane'.

The junction with the road to York is now the main public focus of the village, attracting passing car-borne trade. A post office, the Highwayman pub and a

Fig. 1.2 Sheriff Hutton.

couple of small shops are nearby, and a small brick garage with an old diamond-shaped blue and white metal RAC sign projecting above the entrance.

Across the York road the historic village continues for a short distance, though with late 20th-century housing increasing the density of the buildings. Then another small council estate, a school and several generations of 1960s, 1970s and 1980s retirement homes and houses for people who commute the 20km to York. Turning down the main road towards York, and looking back, you see the castle more clearly than before, separated from the car park of the modern parish hall by a moated boundary. Then the road bends away round the side of the former late-medieval castle park before a straight stretch, then a twist down to the enclosed fields of the floor of the Vale.

A COUNTRYSIDE OF COAL – EARSDON, SEGHILL AND BACKWORTH

Earsdon sits on top of a hill, a small but prominent feature on this coastal plain, and the blackened sandstone tower of St Alban's church catches the eye from afar. At the edge of the Tyneside conurbation it is not quite a country village, yet its wide, straight front street hints at its medieval origins. Come here for a panorama: east to the sea, south to the urban area, west and north the views are long – 60km to Cheviot on a clear day.

A bridleway leads the eye down the slope, alongside horses cropping the grass on the broad ridges of former medieval ploughland. A line of trees picks out the course of Briar Dene Burn and Fenwick's Close Farm is glimpsed beyond: a rural scene. But close by is a stark intrusion: a pit-heap, high, grey and raw in the landscape. For this is a coalfield and though the seams are long-since worked out, here at Fenwick's Pit and all around are tell-tale signs of how the industry insinuated itself into the countryside. Down the hill and across the burn the path runs alongside the pit-heap. Its steep edge, perhaps 12 or 15m high, is becoming colonised by self-seeding pioneers: brambles, rosebay willowherb and hawthorn. It gives off a gaseous smell. The top is bare of plant or soil cover and boys have created a track for motor bikes.

Round the north side of the tip the path cuts west across tidy fields where kale is growing and next year's cereals are already showing through. A hedgerow, set on an embankment and curving off northwards, stands out among the mostly straight boundary lines, a reminder that monastery tenants at Holywell Grange worked this land before enclosure and before the pit-men came. Rooks and gulls circle another pit-heap which now looms in front; this one reworked as a land-fill site. To the north-west is Seghill, once a colliery village but now neither rural nor urban.

West along the main street is the old village core, by the Mining Institute and the Primitive Methodist chapel, and a left turn from here takes you south-east along the West Cramlington Wagonway. These precursors of the railways were the arteries along which horses pulled wagons of coal from the pits to staiths on the Tyne and Blyth rivers. They criss-crossed the coalfield; some became incorporated into railways; some have been lost in redevelopment; others, as here, have found new use for walkers, cyclists and horse riders. The land is low-lying as you head out of Seghill and from the wagonway's high embankment it is easy to see the pools of standing water in the fields on both sides, where the surface has subsided into old coal workings. Cattle graze on the rounded slopes of a hill; it takes a moment to realise that this is not a natural feature – it is another pit-heap, now softened and greened. The wagonway runs alongside on its way to Backworth. From here, a left turn takes you through the part of the village that grew in the coal age – redbrick terraces, vegetable gardens, post-war replacement of older houses – and across the railway line again.

In front of the Fenwick Pit the scene is squalid. Unkempt paddocks, their patchy hedges running wild; secret compounds, shuttered behind high rusty steel panels; dumped cars; cannibalised wagons; and, incongruously, flags fluttering in front of a second-hand car lot. It is difficult to characterise, yet across the whole of this landscape there is a sense that tumultuous events happened here, that brutal forces set themselves down and then moved on. The costs were high, in lives as in landscape; a monument in Earsdon churchyard lists the 204 names of the men and boys as young as 10 and 11 killed in Hartley Colliery in 1862. Throughout all this time, farmers have cultivated the land.

A footpath leads through this chaos, past more subsidence ponds. A boundary fence disappears into one, almost a small lake in its own right: the migrating birds treat it as such and the bulrushes are spectacular. Then back up the hill to Earsdon where the horses, returned from their rides with suburban daughters, have earned their hay.

THE CITY

Green fields give way to houses. The Flying Scotsman drops speed as, high above on the right, the *Angel of the North* spreads wide its rust-red wings over the valley below. Grey slate roofs over redbrick walls step down the steep slopes and here yellow earthmoving machines, fresh from manufacture, wait silently in rows.

Fig. 1.3 Newcastle, looking downriver below the Tyne Bridge to the Millennium Bridge.

Gateshead disappears from view as now the train enters a cutting, passing the site of the silent workshops where Robert Stephenson once built locomotives. A sharp curve left and again the engine points north, as it approaches the gorge. Thirty metres above the waters of Tyne, the train eases on to the bridge and comes to a stop, held by a signal light. Look right over the full-tide water glinting in the morning sunlight at the high arch of Tyne Bridge, icon of the city and region, and beyond to the new, steel-grey arch of the Gateshead Millennium Bridge, the latest addition to a famous set (Fig. 1.3). From the valley sides where once a chemical works exploded, industry and its chimneys have disappeared as hotels rise up to cater for visitors to the crisp steel and glass spaces of the Sage Music Centre and the flour mill which is now an art gallery: the Tyne's South Bank.

Ahead is Newcastle: a changed city. No ships now stand at the quay where merchants, brokers, chandlers and ships' masters once did business; instead young Geordies, short-sleeved, short-skirted, drink and dance. To the left, the Dunstan Coal Staith is a relic and reminder of how this all began; when ships from Gdansk and Lübeck in the Baltic, from Kampen, Nieuport and Cherbourg in Zeeland, Flanders and France, from King's Lynn and London in England, sailed into the Tyne with timber, bricks or grindstones and left carrying the coal that became synonymous with the city. Today, ro-ro car ferries bring cargoes of people to and from Amsterdam and Bergen, docking down-river in deep-water installations near the mouth of the Tyne.

Back in the city, above the river bank, is the castle; its square stone keep hemmed in tight by railway arches, reminds of distant times when this place was a frontier, on the edge of William the Conqueror's England. In 1080 Walcher, the Conqueror's Norman bishop and unwelcome in these parts, had been done to death outside his church by a mob in Gateshead. The lantern of St Nicholas Church stands proud on the skyline; Scottish prisoners were once held here to dissuade their friends from bombarding the town. Time and growth have pulled the axis of the city away from its riverside and the Town Hall which once stood across the street from St Nicholas has gone and civic administration moved to a newer centre north of here. The shopping streets of the upper town are beyond your immediate field of view, but obliquely in the distance are the suburbs that sprang up as the city outgrew its medieval core during the past 200 years. Highest on the skyline in front, the exoskeleton of steel trusses at St James' Park, the football stadium where, in the season, 50,000 of the passionate and the committed know agony or ecstasy in black and white.

The signal turns green and you are again on the move, leaving behind the river, and to the left you see the Centre for Life, which nurtures biological technologies. Finally the train glides towards the station and the concourse comes into view. You have arrived in the city.

2

Environmental Setting and Regional Landscape Forms

F H A AALEN

Northern England is a long belt of mainly hilly country linking the wider, lowland territory of central England to the Southern Uplands of Scotland. Although a relatively narrow tract, reduced at its narrowest point to only 100km from sea to sea, it nevertheless embraces strong contrasts: physical, climatic and cultural. The North East region is the eastern flank of this diverse territory, dominated by the Pennines and the Cheviot Hills but containing various smaller, upland areas along with productive and well-populated lowlands.

On the east, the region is bounded by the North Sea coast, while its western limits follow roughly the Pennine watershed and, north of the Tyne, Northumberland's borders with Cumbria and Scotland. The wide Humber estuary forms part of the southern boundary, however, further inland there is no easily agreed frontier; a boundary running south-westwards along the Don valley through Doncaster and Sheffield to the edges of the Peak District has been adopted, though references are made to more southerly places where this contributes to full understanding of landscape features.

The physical environment of the North East can be austere and sometimes dramatic, with wide tracts of treeless moors exposed to the winds; but gentle dales with stone-walled fields and clustered villages can show a softer face. Solid geology, relief and superficial glacial deposits, climatic conditions and soils have all combined to produce diverse sub-divisions within the region, each evoking particular human responses and, thereby, the creation of distinctive cultural landscapes which are a combination of natural and human features (Figs 2.1 and 2.2).

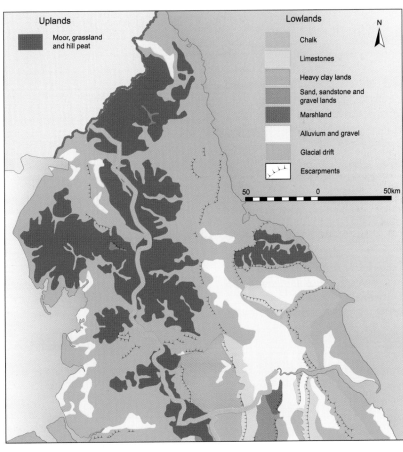

Fig. 2.1 Human settlement has been strongly influenced by the region's varied physical background. *Drift-covered lowlands in the north of the region contrast with southern areas near or beyond the ice limits where the underlying rocks have a more direct influence on land-use or are submerged by beds of alluvium or gravel. For long periods, however, northern communities have had to relate to humanised rather than wholly natural settings. The extensive upland moors, for example, often regarded by visitors as 'natural', are largely the product of clearance by prehistoric communities and were once covered by natural woodland.*

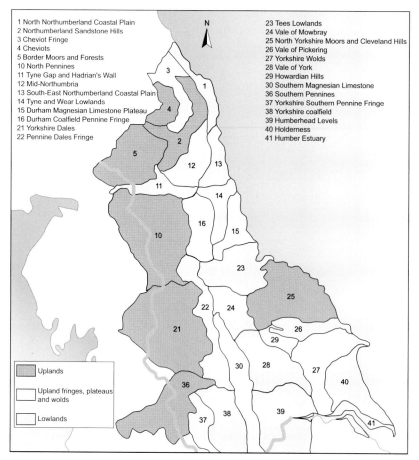

1 North Northumberland Coastal Plain
2 Northumberland Sandstone Hills
3 Cheviot Fringe
4 Cheviots
5 Border Moors and Forests
10 North Pennines
11 Tyne Gap and Hadrian's Wall
12 Mid-Northumbria
13 South-East Northumberland Coastal Plain
14 Tyne and Wear Lowlands
15 Durham Magnesian Limestone Plateau
16 Durham Coalfield Pennine Fringe
21 Yorkshire Dales
22 Pennine Dales Fringe

23 Tees Lowlands
24 Vale of Mowbray
25 North Yorkshire Moors and Cleveland Hills
26 Vale of Pickering
27 Yorkshire Wolds
28 Vale of York
29 Howardian Hills
30 Southern Magnesian Limestone
36 Southern Pennines
37 Yorkshire Southern Pennine Fringe
38 Yorkshire coalfield
39 Humberhead Levels
40 Holderness
41 Humber Estuary

Uplands

Upland fringes, plateaus and wolds

Lowlands

Fig. 2.2 In a study of England's landscape diversity, the Countryside Commission identified 'character areas', each with a distinctive natural and man-made landscape. Forty-one of *these areas lie within the North East region or substantially overlap it. The areas are here grouped together in three broad categories: uplands; upland fringes, plateaus and wolds; and lowlands.*

A continuous process of landscape transformation flows from the changing interactions between human society and its habitat. Cultural changes constantly influence human assessment of environmental resources and the ability to exploit and modify them, and the natural environment itself is continually changing with independent, long-term rhythms such as climatic changes and shifts in sea-level. Landscapes can therefore be seen as the products of communities adjusting to their intimate habitat and adapting it to their needs, and this entails constant changes in settlement and land use as well as repeated manipulation of the physical environment itself. Periods of concerted landscape change can be identified, through extensive woodland clearance, for example, or drainage and flood-control works, but most modification was gradual and partial and much of the inherited fabric remained intact. Thus, present-day landscapes are not simply products of modern activities, but bear the imprint of a range of past cultures and patterns of land use and settlement. A sequence of superimposed landscape patterns can often be identified, because each time the landscape was remodelled, fragments of the earlier system tended to survive in undisturbed places or to show through the newer patterns, albeit in a subdued, less legible way.

THE PHYSICAL BACKGROUND

Rocks and ice

There are some limited outcrops of Lower Palaeozoic rocks in the uplands west of the Cheviots and in upper Teesdale, and the Cheviot Hills consist of Devonian volcanic rocks and granite. A large part of the uplands, together with the lowlands of Northumberland and central Durham, are underlain by Carboniferous sedimentary rocks. These are, variously, sandstones (sometimes, where coarse-grained, called grits), shales or other fine-grained rocks, limestones and coal seams. In the uplands it is normally older strata, including more limestones and fewer and thinner coals, that crop out, while in parts of the lowlands thick Coal Measure coals were a basis of the industrial development of the region. On higher ground, where the strata are more or less horizontal, wide, rolling plateaux occur, usually capped by sandstones, but where the beds are tilted tougher rocks form alignments of scarped ridges, or cuestas, separated by vales in the weaker shales. This latter type of landscape is found in the Barnsley coalfield, and north of the Tyne Gap in west Northumberland. On the coalfield of south-east Northumberland such scarped topography is largely concealed by thick glacial deposits.

Away from the Pennines, the Carboniferous and younger strata tilt gently to the east. Erosion, cutting across the dipping strata, has exposed an eastwards succession of progressively younger rocks, including Permian magnesian limestone, Triassic mudstone, Jurassic limestone and sandstone and, ultimately, Cretaceous chalk. This structure gave rise to a series of topographic belts in which the resistant rock sequences form escarpments facing westwards, for example in east Durham (magnesian limestone), the North York Moors (Jurassic rocks) and the Yorkshire Wolds (chalk), while the weaker rocks form depressions and vales, such as the Vales of York and Pickering and the lower Tees valley.

A prominent feature of the landscape in Northumberland and Durham is the Great Whin Sill. This is a somewhat complicated sheet of igneous rock, intruded (like a sandwich filling) into the Carboniferous strata, and which, being very hard, forms a striking cuesta across Northumberland. Hadrian's Wall used this to dramatic effect, as did the castles at Dunstanburgh and Bamburgh. It is also responsible for the spectacular waterfalls on the Tees at High Force and Cauldron Snout.

During the Quaternary Era (roughly the last 2 million years) the region experienced a sequence of glaciations, the most recent of which, the Late Devensian, ended about 20,000 years ago. More southerly parts of north-east England lay beyond the ice sheet limit – the North York Moors, the higher parts of the Wolds, the southern part of the Vale of York and much of the old West Riding of Yorkshire.[1] Thus there is a contrast between the widespread glacial deposits and fresher landforms north of

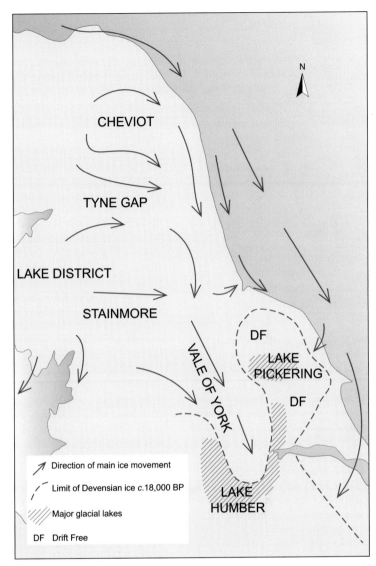

Fig. 2.3 Sources and general direction of major Devensian ice-flows, *southern limits of drift and sites of major pro-glacial lakes.*

the ice-limit and the more patchy deposits (from earlier glaciations) and maturer landforms to the south. The ice originated on higher ground within the region and also forced its way in from the Southern Uplands of Scotland and the Lake District through the Tyne Gap and over Stainmore. The various ice masses merged in the lowlands into a massive south-moving sheet, reaching down the coast far beyond the Humber and into the Vale of York as far as the huge York and Escrick moraines, and possibly to Doncaster. Ice from local caps in the Pennines flowed down the Yorkshire dales, joining from Swaledale, Wensleydale and Nidderdale the main ice sheet in the Vale of York. The ice moving parallel to the coast made incursions onshore (Fig. 2.3).

The ice sheet left behind an extensive blanket of drift deposits, consisting of till (laid down directly by the active or melting ice) and a variety of water-laid deposits (laid down by meltwater in contact with the ice or beyond its margins). Drift, more than 60m thick in places, underlies much of the lowlands within the glacial limits. This is enough to muffle the solid face of the countryside and generally soften the contours of its topography. Till forms an almost continuous mantle over the Northumberland coastal plain, the magnesian limestone plateau in eastern Durham, the lower Wear and Tees valleys and Holderness, and it is widespread in the Vale of York. It also covers the lower slopes and floors of upland valleys, but is thinner and patchy as higher levels are reached. For reasons which are not completely understood, the till in some areas forms rather featureless terrain, but elsewhere was moulded by the ice into prominent drumlins – streamlined oval hills generally around 10m high and 500m long, notably in Wensleydale, parts of the Vale of York, the Tyne Gap and on lower Tweedside.

Glaciofluvial sands and gravels from meltwaters are also widespread, often overlying tills. Where they were deposited in contact with melting ice the topography is often hummocky, and where deposited as outwash, down-valley away from the receding ice, they often form wide terraces above the modern rivers. In either case the freely draining soils that have developed on these deposits have long been favoured for agricultural activity. In fact most of the region's farmland, except for the high moorland rough grazings, makes use either of glacial tills (which, being usually heavy and poorly drained, require efficient field-drainage systems) or the glacio-fluvial sands and gravels.

In the uplands, where the drift cover is incomplete, the drainage has largely retained its pre-glacial pattern. But on lower ground some of the pre-glacial valleys were partly or completely buried by glacial drift. Such buried valleys were a bugbear to miners, where a coal seam ceased abruptly at a 'wash-out' which, moreover, could lead to mine flooding. Some rivers, like the Wear in its lower course, were sharply and permanently diverted. The meandering gorge of the Wear at Durham City is probably the result of such a diversion, and so also the gorge cut through the limestone plateau to the estuary at Sunderland. Other rivers, however, re-established themselves close to their pre-glacial course (Fig. 2.4).

Meltwater channels, cut by water flowing beneath or along the margins of ice bodies, are very numerous, with impressive examples around the Cheviots, North Pennines and North York Moors. In many places meltwater was impounded in short-lived pro-glacial lakes, dammed along the receding ice edge. Lake Humber, in the Vale of York, was vast, and others included lakes Pickering, Tees, Wear and, in north Northumberland, Lake Milfield. Once the ice had completely retreated, clay and silt was deposited in these former lakes to form difficult ground, awaiting modern land drainage. More permanent ponds and lakes formed in the irregular

Fig. 2.4 a. Valley systems formed mainly by pre-glacial rivers but buried by glacial deposits are a widespread feature in County Durham.
b. Numerous and striking gorge-like sections occur along the river courses in Durham where post-glacial rivers, diverted by drift-infilling of the valleys, have cut down into the rock of the pre-glacial valley sides (based on Dewdney 1970).

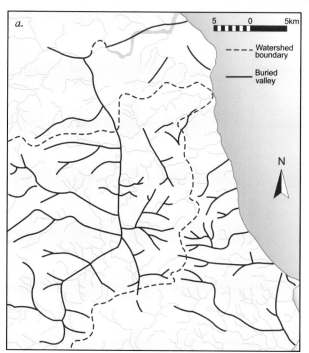

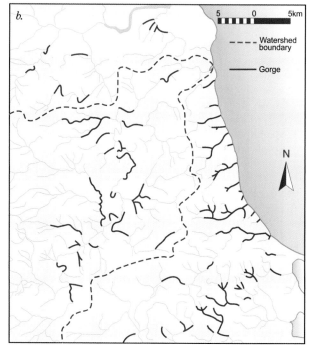

terrain left by the melting ice, and became important habitats for early post-glacial hunting groups. Sea-level fell during the Late Devensian glaciation and, as the ice retreated, much of what is now sea-bed in the southern part of the North Sea was exposed as dry land connecting Britain to the continent of Europe. The subsequent rise in sea-level, culminating about 6,000 years ago, drowned river valleys and created the modern estuaries, but evidence of former lower sea-levels can be seen even now, when submerged peats and tree trunks are exposed at low tides at Hauxley in Northumberland and elsewhere.

There are thus broad scenic contrasts between uplands with ice-smoothed, relatively drift-free slopes and the lowlands which, even where they are underlain by a variety of rocks, are physically unified by the drift blanket and the smothered solid geology finds only muted expression in the landscape. In the south of the region, beyond the main Late Devensian ice advance, the drift cover thins or is absent and the solid geology finds more direct expression in the landscape, fragmenting it into a patchwork of distinctive terrains, which include the North York Moors, the chalk Wolds of east Yorkshire, and the Barnsley coalfield area with its complex terrain of cuesta ridges.

Western uplands

The uplands in the west of the region form an almost continuous belt of bleak, relatively level moorlands used mainly as rough grazing and grouse moors. These moors are interrupted by numerous dales, which contain improved land and scattered settlement. Eastwards, the moorlands slope gradually downwards into the farmed lowland areas of Northumberland and Durham and, further south, into the Vale of York and the coalfield areas of the old West Riding.

East–west passes, which provide routeways across the country, cut the uplands into blocks, each with its own distinctive character. Of these, the Northumberland uplands, between the Scottish border and the Tyne Gap, are geologically the most heterogeneous and include the rounded Cheviot Hills and the striking sandstone ridges that sweep round in a great semi-circle to the east and south. There is also a belt of rounded fells, now heavily afforested, which stretches south-westwards from the Cheviots into Cumbria and the spectacular terrain of scarped ridges on either side of Hadrian's Wall. Collectively this upland area forms a vast territory of exceptional solitude and beauty; much of it lies in the Northumberland National Park (Fig. 2.5).

South of the Tyne Gap, the Pennine range breaks into three distinct upland units. The North Pennines, or 'Alston Block', forms a vast plateau some 300–600m above sea-level lying between the Tyne Gap and the Stainmore Pass, spectacularly defined to the west by the Cross Fell escarpment above the Eden valley and deeply dissected by dales radiating to the north, east and south-east. The smooth moorland surfaces of the plateau, much covered either by blanket bog or upland heath heather, provide almost 100,000ha of common grazing land (Fig. 2.6). The 'Askrigg Block' lies west of Leeds between the Stainmore Gap and the Aire Gap, and much of it is now embraced within the Yorkshire Dales National Park. This area is again dominated by high moorland but with much varied and dramatic scenery closely related to the succession of Carboniferous rocks in the area. The limestones of the Great Scar Limestone Group are outstanding for their limestone pavements around Ingleborough and Malham; the Yoredale beds of Swaledale and Wensleydale form distinct stepped topography with steep cliffs (scars) on hill and dale sides produced by the alternating horizontal bands of hard limestones and sandstones and weak mudstones, and the Millstone Grit underlies the moorland ridges between the dales and also caps some of the highest hills (Fig. 2.7). Further local variation results from glacial features, including U-shaped valley troughs such as Wharfedale, drumlins, drift and alluvial deposits, and also from human activities such as mining and regular burning of moors (Fig. 2.8). The Carboniferous rocks are fringed to the east

ABOVE: ***Fig. 2.5 Cheviot Hills, north Northumberland, with Breamish valley in the foreground and extensive rolling hills to the south***, *their steep smooth slopes carrying well-drained soils and a light green, semi-natural grassland ('white country'). Bracken has spread on the lower slopes and there is a scatter of small, geometrical coniferous plantations. This is a multi-period landscape, with hillforts such as Ewe Hill and Brough Law (right foreground) and a profusion of prehistoric and medieval settlements, cultivation ridges and terraces (left foreground) recording the ebb and flow of settlement.*

LEFT: ***Fig. 2.6 Cow Green Reservoir and Widdybank Fell, County Durham, with higher summits of the western Pennines on the horizon.*** *The reservoir lies in the upper reaches of the Tees, surrounded by relatively level, bleak fells blanketed with peat (now much reduced by draining and burning) and heather and bilberry moorland used for sheep grazing and grouse shooting. Widdybank Fell is one of the outstanding botanical areas of the north, containing rare Arctic and Alpine communities.*

LEFT: *Fig. 2.7 While many uplands discourage close human settlement, the dry limestone plateau of the Malham area,* developed on the Great Scar Limestone, has provided an attractive environment for farming communities from early times. The large and regular walled fields are mainly of early 19th-century origin, but they overlie remnants of earlier cultural landscapes (Iron Age, Romano-British and medieval), which include field systems, lynchets, cultivation ridges and clearance cairns. The extensive rock exposures may be partly attributable to soil erosion induced by sustained land use.

BELOW: *Fig. 2.8 This stretch of upper Wharfedale (Kettlewell in foreground) is characteristic of the deep, sheltered dales that dissect the elevated, level moorlands of the Askrigg Block.* The stepped profile of the dale sides is related to the succession of rock types in the Yoredale series; limestone bands, for example, produce steep cliffs (scars), with sandstones often concealed under limestone scree. The dale bottom was deepened by moving ice and covered by boulder clay. This range of environments is reflected in altitudinal zonation of land use: narrow walled fields and field barns on the fertile valley bottoms and lower dale sides; scar woods on slopes; large, rectangular parliamentary enclosures on the fell sides; and common pasture on moorland tops.

by a narrow belt of Permian magnesian limestone along the edge of the Vale of York. Although partially covered by drift, it forms a ridge of well-drained, fertile soils dissected by dry valleys and also by river valleys, whose landscape has been strongly influenced by mining and industrial development (Fig. 2.9).

The Pennines, to the south of the Aire Gap, are more complicated geologically and penetrated by numerous river valleys, including the Wharfe, Aire and Calder to the east and the Ribble to the west: the range thus loses much of its coherence and allows relatively easy communications from east to west. Glacial drift in any appreciable amount is confined to the north, particularly to the valleys of the Aire and Wharfe and the Bradford basin, while further south, beyond the Late Devensian glacial limit, the drift is patchy and the relief sensitively reflects the underlying geology. Strong traditions of manufacturing and mining have led to intense settlement in the narrow valleys and on the coalfield areas. The high, exposed moorlands to the west are formed on Millstone Grit, with acidic grasslands and heath and extensive blanket bog; they have been heavily

LEFT: ***Fig. 2.9 Halifax lies on the western slope of the River Hebble, a tributary of the Calder.*** *A centre of the cloth trade for many centuries, the settlement grew strongly in the industrial era and its main buildings in local sandstone and gritstone date largely from the 19th century. The urbanised area expanded considerably in the 20th century. Proximity of dense population to moorland plateaus is a distinctive feature of the southern Pennine slopes. While constraining settlement growth, the upland surrounds are important for recreational activities, quarrying, reservoirs and wind turbines.*

BELOW: ***Fig. 2.10 Heptonstall Moor lies towards the Pennine watershed, west of Hebden Water.*** *The Millstone Grit moors of heather and bent grass are separated from the winding, steep, wooded valleys by shelves of improved land with roadside dwellings, dispersed farms and a neat rectilinear pattern of small, walled fields. The upper reaches of the valleys contain the Gorple and Widdop reservoirs.*

quarried for sandstone building stone and are important water-catchment areas with numerous reservoirs. The narrow, steep-sided valleys of the Pennine slopes contain bands of dense settlement, with particular concentrations at valley junctions. On the Coal Measures to the east, differential erosion of alternating hard sandstones and weak shale bands has produced numerous low, rounded 'cuesta' ridges with a predominantly north-west to south-east trend; they are a feature of the Barnsley coalfield and dominate the landscape further south around Sheffield and as far west as the impressive west-facing escarpment along the east side of the River Derwent in Derbyshire. An effect of the ridges is to complicate the flow of Pennine streams from east to west (Fig. 2.10).

Lowlands and eastern upland blocks

A belt of lowland runs through the region from north to south, linking the Tweed basin with the English Midlands. The Tweed lowland, between Berwick and Cornhill, is one of the most extensive drumlin zones in Britain and its confusion of south-west to north-east mounds and sodden hollows formed a barrier to movement and presented difficulties for farmers until the environment was transformed in the 18th and 19th centuries by drainage ditches, lime application, shelter belts, field enclosures and a grid of roads. Dominated by its large dispersed farms, this area has remained deeply, resolutely rural.

The long coastal lowland of Northumberland has distinctive northern and southern portions. In the north, where the plain is narrow and bounded inland by fell sandstone ridges, its surface is formed by gently undulating glacial drift. The coastline here is varied, with the extensive inter-tidal mud flats of Holy Island and Budle Bay, a series of rocky headlands, some formed by the Whin Sill, and long beaches backed by sand dunes (Fig. 2.11). South of the River Coquet, the fell sandstone ridges trend markedly inland and the plain broadens to encompass the south-eastern coalfield area of Northumberland and a wide tract of gently rising country inland. The coalfield is a relatively flat lowland, except for the steeply-cut valleys of the rivers Wansbeck and Blyth, deeply blanketed by glacial deposits and strongly influenced by coal mining in the 19th and 20th centuries.

Fig. 2.11 The drift-covered coastal plain of north Northumberland with its comparatively light rainfall is an area of large farms and productive agriculture. There is a variety of coastal features, including alluvial flats and sheltered bays and accumulations of blown sand and dunefields. Lindisfarne lies in the foreground, with Guile Point and the rectangular Budle Bay to the south. Bamburgh Castle is visible on the coastline, and beyond it a succession of sandy bays and rocky headlands.

Deep mining has now ceased but extensive open-cast coal-working continues and the high embankments of excavated and stored over-burden dominate local landscapes between Morpeth and Warkworth. Along the coasts of the coalfield, long belts of sand dunes fringe a series of broad, drift-backed bays separated by rocky sandstone headlands, contrasting strongly with the high, rocky, cliffs that prevail further south in Durham and most of Yorkshire. The higher hill country, broken only by Whin Sill crags and low sandstone ridges, is transitional in physical character between the coalfield and the interior moorlands and still rural, although with an increasingly Tyneside-looking commuter population.

As the land mass broadens southwards, the coastward tract is interrupted by three contrasting elevated areas and the main lowland belt assumes an enclosed, inland character. In County Durham only the coastal plateau of drift-covered magnesian limestone separates the Wear lowlands around Durham City from the sea, but the sense of enclosure is accentuated south of the Tees as the lowlands pass into the Vale of York. There the coastline veers eastwards and the Vale is separated from the sea by the imposing North York Moors and further south, beyond the wide Vale of Pickering, by a distinctive belt of chalk wolds, which also separates the Vale of York from the low, level coastal peninsula of Holderness (Fig. 2.12).[2]

Fig. 2.12 Farndale, North York Moors.
The landscape of the North York Moors is dominated by broad ridges of resistant Jurassic sandstone clad with heather and some peat and still used as common land. Where south-flowing streams have cut into the underlying shales, broad steep-sided dales such as Farndale have been formed, with a landscape of dispersed farms and small fields bounded by stone walls and scattered hedgerows, in strong contrast to the surrounding moors and often separated from them by a belt of bracken on better-drained slopes.

The North York Moors, formed chiefly of resistant Jurassic sandstones and siltstones, is a conspicuous, somewhat isolated hill mass in the north-east corner of Yorkshire, which lacks a continuous coastal plain and is therefore bypassed by the major routeways from north to south. This upland (which contains the North York Moors National Park) has a distinctive landscape with large expanses of level heather moorland and is impressively defined by a steep escarpment to the Tees lowlands and the Vale of York: it is, moreover, the only upland region in England that extends to the eastern seaboard and its coastline exhibits a series of magnificent cliffs with fishing villages such as Staiths and Whitby clinging to their bases. The Hambleton and Howardian hills, south-west of the North York Moors between Thirsk and Helmsley, are of limestones and calcareous sandstones, with good-quality agricultural land on the plateaux and woodland on the slopes. During the Late Devensian glaciation the centre of the upland area was not actually over-ridden by the ice sheets, but the higher parts experienced severe frost conditions and snow-cover fed powerful torrents that deeply eroded the river valleys. The Vale of Pickering to the south of the Moors, inland from Scarborough, is a very low-lying alluvial plain surrounded by hills which, during early prehistory, was strewn with large lakes whose sites are now marked mainly by peat deposits. Much of the traditional village settlement here is peripheral, most markedly in the eastern portion of the Vale known as 'the Carrs'.

The drift-free, chalky outcrop of the Yorkshire Wolds, the northernmost portion of the main chalk belt of England, forms an island surrounded by wet, low-lying territories and the North Sea, and the history of its cultural landscape differs markedly from the surroundings. On the north and west, the Wolds, like the North York Moors, present a marked escarpment to neighbouring lowlands, from which the chalk surface dips gradually to the south-east to be eventually overlain by the glacial and alluvial deposits of Holderness. The characteristic rolling topography of the Wolds is attributed partly to meltwater streams when the subsoil was frozen, with winding, dry and partially dry valleys of varying size. Surface water is absorbed by the pervious chalk and accessible only by deep wells. With a shortage of standing or running water, prehistoric and historic settlements have been focused around springs, wells and dewponds (Fig. 2.13).

Fig. 2.13 The large township of Warter, lying on the western edge of the Yorkshire Chalk Wolds, is divided and given some shelter by a network of dry valleys: much of the farmland, however, with its large fields and widely spaced steadings, shares the characteristic openness and exposure of the Wolds as a whole. Warter village, in the foreground, is a shrunken medieval village, replanned as an estate village in the late 19th century.

The Vale of York, between the Pennines on the west and the scarped uplands on the east, owes much of its subdued relief and varied soils to the diverse cover of glacial and post-glacial deposits, which includes belts and islands of boulder clay and considerable tracts of water-sorted sands and gravels. Farming in the Vale has been hampered by low wet ground and the flood plains of major rivers liable to flooding, especially the Ouse and Derwent, and efficient land drainage is needed to avoid waterlogging of the soils. Swamps and floods also impeded land communications, although terminal moraines left at the limits of the Late Devensian ice provide some dry routeways. The rivers, however, were widely used as routeways. York indeed, at the junction of the Ouse and Foss rivers, was the capital of a Viking kingdom in the north of England and flourished as a medieval maritime port; the rivers of the Vale have continued to have commercial significance and were partly canalised in the 19th century (Fig. 2.14).

The Humberhead Levels is an extensive tract of low, level landscape which occupies part of the site of the former pro-glacial Lake Humber and embraces the wide flood plains of several streams draining into the Humber estuary from north and south. Much of the present fertile, arable land here has been won since the 17th century from bogs (which survive at Thorne and Hatfield), marsh and areas liable to seasonal flooding, through the construction of drainage dykes and embankments, the redirection and regulation of rivers, and warping – the impounding of tidal silts to enhance soils. Holderness is another distinctive landscape, much influenced by reclamation, drainage and other improvements. The chalk underlying the peninsula is concealed by an uneven blanket of varied glacial deposits, which today forms productive soils and is intensively farmed. Before the improvements of recent centuries, however, much of the area, although long settled, was ill-drained and peaty. A different type of landscape, flat and lightly settled, has been developed in the south of the peninsula by reclamation of former salt marshes along the shores of the Humber between the Hull valley and Spurn Point.

The Humber, with its fringing tidal flats, is so vast that it perhaps merits consideration as a distinctive landscape in its own right.[3] Along with its navigable tributaries, such as the River Hull up to the port of Beverley, it has been a principal commercial waterway from early medieval times, an outlet for trade with the Low Countries and with the Baltic through Kingston upon Hull. It was also significant for fishing, as well as the reclaimable tidal deposits on flatlands fringing the estuary. For land transport, however, the Humber and its marshy surrounds was a major physical impediment, especially in the 19th century as road and rail transport developed. Only in the 1970s with the Humber suspension bridge was a direct estuary crossing built.

Fig. 2.14 Much of the Vale of York had been enclosed by the early 18th century, but on the Humberhead Levels to the south there remained large areas of peaty, poorly drained common pasture and the present landscape there is largely the product of recent artificial drainage and embankment. This view over Holme-on-Spalding-Moor towards the Humber shows the new pattern of dispersed farmsteads and large regular fields divided mainly by ditches and dykes. There is some evidence of Iron Age and Romano-British settlement on the dry sandy ridges of the area, but uncertainty as to the degree of continuity between these early sites and present-day settlements.

CLIMATE

Along with the northerly latitude, the two dominant influences on the region's climate are the shelter against moist westerly winds provided by the Pennines and Cheviots and the presence of the lengthy North Sea coastline. Late, chilly springs and cool, unconvincing summers feature throughout the region, with spells of fine autumn weather often providing some modest compensation. Uncongenial onshore winds in spring and early summer bring mists, known locally as sea-frets, or low stratus cloud to the coasts. However, persisting fogs are most common in the Vale of York and the North Riding. Snowfall is very variable from year to year: heavy falls are associated with north-easterly winds off the North Sea and the upper reaches of Weardale and Teesdale are among the snowiest areas in England (Fig. 2.15).

Within the region, variations are brought about by local differences in altitude, aspect and shelter. Rainfall distribution relates very closely to altitude and the higher ground in the west of the region produces a marked rain-shadow effect. Rainfall totals are much lower than in the Lake District to the west, the wettest area in England. Indeed, the north-east coasts record some of the lowest rainfalls in Britain (less than 635mm) and, throughout the region, low-lying sheltered areas, such as the Milfield basin in the lee of the Cheviot hills, the lower Tees valley and the Vale of York,

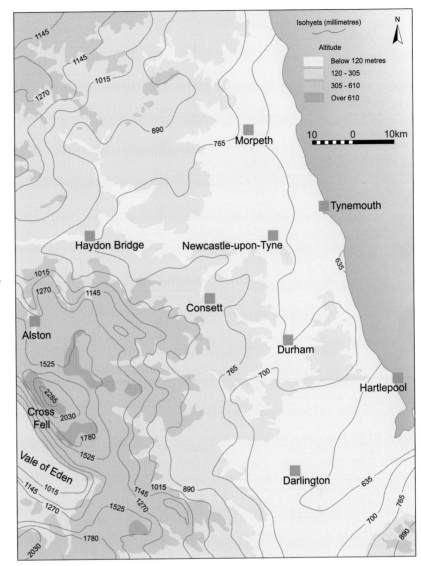

Fig. 2.15 The rain-shadow effect over the North East is most marked in south Northumberland and Durham *where average annual precipitation and altitude are mirror images. Rainfall is highest over Cross Fell on the western edge of the Alston Block and the driest area is the Tees lowlands.*

especially south of York itself, are appreciably drier than adjacent uplands. Proceeding inland from the coast, the rise in ground levels is generally gradual but, nevertheless, precipitation, frost and cloudiness increase noticeably and there is a significant decrease in sunshine. In the deeply dissected uplands of this most northerly region of England, local conditions of aspect and shelter assume particular importance, especially in the dales and valleys that are aligned east–west and where south-facing slopes are warmer and drier and the narrowness of the dales can funnel and intensify westerly air streams.

Climate influences not only vegetation and land-use patterns but also the way we see landscapes; the impression that a landscape conveys, its character and hues, are constantly affected by weather conditions. The generally good visibility of the Northumberland uplands is attributed to exceptionally clear air as well as to its varied topography. In Northumberland and Durham smoke pollution was never too serious, away from the immediate coalfield, since much of it was carried out to sea by prevailing westerly winds. Smoke hazes, however, were once general over all the coalfields, exacerbated by drifts of smoke from the Midlands and Lancashire, but these problems have reduced in recent decades.

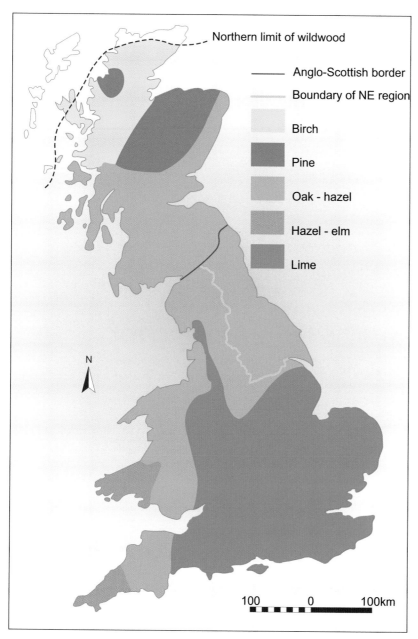

Northern limit of wildwood

Anglo-Scottish border

Boundary of NE region

Birch

Pine

Oak - hazel

Hazel - elm

Lime

N

100   0   100km

Fig. 2.16 Before the early and comprehensive forest clearance by farmers and their livestock, almost the whole of northern England, as well as a large part of Scotland and Wales, was covered by broad-leaved deciduous woodland composed mainly of oak and hazel. The boundary between the oak–hazel woodland and the lime-dominated province of lowland England corresponds closely with the southern boundary of the North East region.

VEGETATIONAL HISTORY

Following the ice retreat and continuing climatic amelioration, the North East was re-colonised by trees that eventually formed a dense cover of deciduous woodland, dominated by oak and hazel just as in Scotland and Wales (Fig 2.16). Indeed, the southern boundary of our region corresponds roughly with the frontier between the oak–hazel wildwood province and the lime-dominated province characteristic of the south of England. Thus, old woods in the Sheffield area are not dissimilar to woods in the Lake District, while those just to the south-east of the city are more akin to the woods of Suffolk or Kent.[4]

Vegetational history in the North East, as elsewhere in Britain, is essentially a lengthy story of human clearance of the woodland and increasingly intensive land-use. Inhabited for millennia by only a small population of mobile Mesolithic hunters, the tree cover remained largely intact. It was, however, locally interrupted by the use of fire to drive game and enlarge the forest glades, and it is possible that the tree-line on the Pennines and other hill areas was lowered in this way and permanent moorland initiated. The presence of Neolithic farmers is evident from the mid-5th millennium BC, but the Mesolithic/Neolithic transition may have been prolonged and the impacts of either community on the woodland thus difficult to distinguish. Much of the woodland removal and creation of agricultural land that shaped the landscape of the North East seems to have happened in the first millennium BC, with the woodland cover reduced to perhaps a half by the Pre-Roman Iron Age.[5] At this stage the wider landscape became essentially a human artefact that would be constantly modified by successive societies, each reacting to and reshaping the landscape that it inherited.

The natural resources that the landscape offers and the transforming effects of human exploitation of the land and its resources are explored in following chapters.

NOTES

1   Teasdale & Hughes 1999.
2   de Boer 1964, 212–29.
3   Jones 1988.
4   Jones 2003, 6–7.
5   Dark 2000, 57–63, 100–107.

3

Landscapes of the Prehistoric and Roman Period in the North East

CHRISTOPHER TOLAN-SMITH

HUNTING AND GATHERING LANDSCAPES

The earliest evidence for the presence of humans in the North East during the late-glacial era comes from a group of bone and antler tools found in Victoria Cave near Settle in North Yorkshire. Small bands of hunters began to shelter in the cave from about 12,000 BC, during a milder interstadial stage late in the glaciation. This was not an isolated case but part of a wider movement, for similar finds have been recovered from Kinsey and Kirkhead caves to the west while an antler spear point from Gransmoor to the east comes from about the same date.[1] Stone tools of this period, at the very end of the Old Stone Age (Late Upper Palaeolithic) have been found as far north as the valleys of the rivers Tees and Tyne. The spread of population northwards in the British Isles was part of a movement taking place on a continental scale, with similar trends in the Low Countries and Scandinavia. At this time the low sea-levels meant that Britain remained joined to the continent by a vast area of low-lying ground consisting of gravel ridges, wide estuaries and salt marshes, which now forms the bed of the North Sea. From time to time trawlers fishing on the Leman and Ower Bank recover implements similar to those found on land.

In north-east England the landscape at this time was mainly open, with grasses and shrubs such as crowberry being dominant, and in certain locations, such as on the coastal plains, around the margins of late-glacial lakes and in sheltered valleys, birch woodlands were becoming extensive. Evidence for past vegetation comes from pollen grains that have settled on boggy ground or in lake sediments. As the levels of peat or sediments built up, so, season by season, the pollen grains fell and fossilised and were held within the deposits. In this way they preserved a record of the plant life of the area and the changing proportions of species of trees, shrubs and grasses.

The first arrivals moving into this landscape were pioneers in the true sense of the word, entering an unfamiliar world whose opportunities and dangers they had to recognise and learn. Their impact on the landscape was probably in the temporary disturbance of game herds and the more long-term disruption of vegetation around their campsites. Their need for firewood to provide warmth, light and protection from predators determined where a band of hunters could halt and exhaustion of supplies was a strong incentive to move on. Their impact on the vegetation of these sparsely wooded landscapes, though slight, may

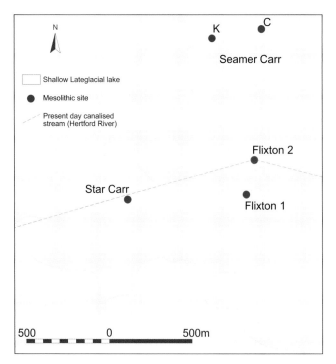

ABOVE: *Fig. 3.1 Diagram of Mesolithic sites, Late-glacial Lake Pickering (North Yorkshire).*

BELOW: *Fig. 3.2 By the Early Postglacial much of the landscape of the North East was mantled in light woodland*, at first consisting mainly of birch and pine but, with the rising of temperature, becoming dominated by oak, elm and hazel. Mesolithic hunter-gatherers pursued their prey through these forests and erected their encampments in clearings, often situated beside open water.

nevertheless have been noticeable. We may be certain that areas with a good supply of firewood would become well known and would have quickly emerged as specific named places to which groups would return at intervals. It is also likely that areas of disturbance would be recognisable to other groups.

One such area was that around Lake Pickering – a Late-glacial and early postglacial lake occupying the Vale of Pickering, an attractive locality offering a wide range of resources (Fig. 3.1) and with Late Upper Palaeolithic and Early Mesolithic (Middle Stone Age) sites scattered about its shores. The best known of these is Star Carr where excavations offer a vivid picture of the life of these early inhabitants of the North East.[2] They manufactured stone tools on the dry slopes immediately above the lake margins, which they kept open by frequently burning the reeds, to aid hunting or simply to improve visibility and access to the open water. This is one of the earliest known examples of people deliberately modifying the landscape. A walkway of split aspen and birch logs enabled access to the lake, while part of the lake margin may have been deliberately consolidated with dumps of logs and brash, perhaps the debris from clearing trees for the encampment. Here people made spear points from antlers, of which nearly 200 examples have been recovered. Animal bones found suggest that they hunted a range of species, in particular wild cattle, elk, red and roe deer. The animal skeletons are incomplete and this suggests that this was a site for butchery, with the main meat-bearing joints eaten elsewhere. The animal remains also indicate that most of the activity here took place during the summer and that Star Carr is unlikely to have been occupied year-round. The study of plant remains has produced evidence for occupation during two distinct episodes of 80- and 130-years' duration, from about 8770 BC and 8590 BC respectively and separated by an interval of several decades. Perhaps a band of hunter-gatherers made regular visits to Star Carr over a period of several generations and these visits were interrupted before being resumed again about a generation later. The reason for this interruption is unknown but the dating suggests that it may have occurred within the span of a single lifetime and the return to Star Carr may have been initiated by an individual, or individuals, who remembered having visited the site in their childhood. This is, of course, all speculation but it is very rare in Mesolithic archaeology that we are able to consider events at this level of detail. The broader evidence from Star

Carr provides an excellent indication of how the activities of the early hunter-gatherer inhabitants of the North East articulated with the landscape, and the pattern established there can be extrapolated throughout the region, at least on the coastal plains and in the main river valleys (Fig. 3.2).

The sources of the raw materials used by these hunter-gatherers give an insight into the extent of their mobility. Over 70 per cent of the raw material used for flint working on Mesolithic sites in the Wear valley originated in the Yorkshire and Lincolnshire Wolds, while at Deepcar, near Sheffield, 95 per cent came from sources up to 80km away in east Yorkshire.[3] Although situated at only 150m above modern sea level, Deepcar is surrounded by upland fells and is one of the earliest sites of human penetration into the Pennines. Its seems to have been a temporary encampment at which parties of hunters made brief halts in order to repair their equipment before moving deeper into the uplands to sites at significantly higher levels such as Warcock Hill at 380m and Lominot at 426m above modern sea level, both in the Pennines west of Huddersfield, and around Malham Tarn where some of the richest assemblages of Mesolithic material in the Yorkshire Dales have been found. The finds from these high-level sites are mostly of hunting equipment, or the debris produced in its manufacture. Given the hostility of the climate on such upland fells, and it would have been even more rigorous at times of low sea-level, it is assumed that these sites were occupied during the summer by groups who spent other times of the year in the river valleys or by the coast.

Today, the uplands of the Pennines and North York Moors are open landscapes where broad expanses of heather extend from horizon to horizon. At the time the Mesolithic hunter-gatherers of Deepcar were probing the tributaries of the upper Calder and others camped around Malham Tarn, these fells were less open and were being aggressively colonised by scrub vegetation consisting mainly of hazel and birch. There is good evidence from the study of pollen in both the Pennines and the North York Moors, that hunter-gatherers were taking steps to check this development, using fire to create and maintain clearings and suppress the tree line.[4] This may seem destructive, but the vegetation quickly recovers after burning and the fresh new growth is highly nutritious (Fig. 3.3). Such areas of new growth would undoubtedly have been attractive to the hunters' prey animals where they would have been easily identified and culled. It is also the case that burning stimulates the hazelnut crop and this is one of the few plant foods regularly recorded on Mesolithic sites.

In the uplands, as in the lowlands, the pattern of land use during the Mesolithic was one of the seasonal movement of mobile bands exploiting a range of resources as they became available. In both settings landscapes were modified and manipulated but, whereas in the lowlands the cycle of clearance was matched by one of regeneration, in the uplands, with their thin soils, degeneration followed. In many of these areas, the tree cover, once removed, was unable to re-establish itself. Against a background of a

Fig. 3.3 In all but the most destructive of forest fires regeneration is rapid and prolific, providing an abundance of new growth for browsing animals. This illustration, from a site in Spain, shows regeneration after an extensive fire in oak woodland.

Fig. 3.4 Open heather moorland,
so admired today as Areas of
Outstanding Natural Beauty,
are in fact an artefact of human activity,
Mesolithic hunter-gatherers having initiated a
process of deforestation which, on the thin soils
of the uplands, was irreversible.

generally deteriorating climate after about 8000 BC the long-term trend was the development of heather-grass moorland on mor humus soils. These upland landscapes, so admired today for their openness, are partly artefacts of human endeavour (Fig. 3.4).

LANDSCAPES OF EARLY FARMING: THE NEOLITHIC AND EARLY BRONZE AGE

Two of the most far-reaching developments that have affected the landscape over the past 10,000 years are the Industrial Revolution of the 18th and 19th centuries AD and the adoption of farming, during the 4th millennium BC. At 5000 BC England was a land of hunters and gatherers and had been so for at least 7,000 years. Over those millennia the landscape had evolved into a mosaic of open uplands, areas of regenerated woodland and primeval wild wood, although by the end of the 6th millennium the latter may have been in short supply. Dotted across this landscape were clearings at various stages of regeneration, some freshly cleared others reverting to impenetrable scrub, but all clearly bearing the signs of human activity. A view towards the horizon in any direction would have revealed columns of smoke, either from camp fires or from areas of woodland being cleared, perhaps for a second or third time. However, by recent standards, the population was sparse. Precise figures are unattainable but a reasonable estimate would place the population of the North East between 250 and 500 people living in groups of various sizes, which probably fluctuated throughout the year.[5] By 4000 BC food production, or farming, had been adopted in many areas and the old symbiotic relationship of the hunter-gatherers and their landscape was to change for all time.

At one time it was generally assumed that arable farming and animal husbandry, along with other aspects of the Neolithic, or New Stone Age, were introduced into Britain by colonists from continental Europe. This view now has little support. Although the species of crops and domestic animals involved were not native to Britain and had to be introduced from outside, this was a piecemeal process and farming spread mainly through indigenous hunter-gatherer communities selectively adopting novel resources and practices. Some population movement and displacement probably did occur as groups adopting new ways sought the most favourable land, but this was a gradual process spanning generations. Hunting and gathering continued long after the end of the Mesolithic era with some practices such as forest clearance, the stimulation of the hazelnut crop through burning and the selective culling of herds of grazing animals, having already prefigured primitive farming in their impact on the landscape. Sources of raw materials used in the Neolithic era were widely scattered, as they had been in the Mesolithic era. For example, 45 per cent of the stone axes found in Yorkshire are made from material quarried at Great Langdale in the Lake District while small numbers come from as far afield as North Wales and the Whin Sill in Northumberland. This period continues to be one of mobility, of communities continuing to hunt and gather but also beginning to practise some herding and possibly sowing a few crops in small clearings.

There is little direct evidence for farming practices in the North East during the Neolithic and Early Bronze ages. Some pollen studies show disturbance of the vegetation but it is not known whether this was to create primitive fields or simply a continuation of Mesolithic woodland management, though the locations in question are mainly in uplands, which are unlikely to have been particularly attractive to early farmers. The Late Neolithic and Bronze Age trackways of Holderness provide a rare example of evidence from the lowlands.[6] These were built out of hurdles of coppice wood and imply a degree of woodland management more advanced than the simple creation of clearings. Stone axes also imply woodland management or clearance; although also found in Mesolithic sites, they are a key artefact type of Neolithic societies. In Northumberland and County Durham few stone axe finds have been made either on the heavy boulder clay soils of the coastal plain or in the uplands above 300m. The most favoured locations appear to have been the upland fringes around the 120m contour and the south-facing slopes of the main river valleys.[7] These axe finds may document the main areas of Neolithic agriculture. One development, which has been noted throughout England, is the marked decline in elm pollen after about 3000 BC. There has been a lively debate about the cause of this decline, whether it results from the use of elm leaves as fodder for domestic cattle, or whether there is a natural cause such as an early outbreak of Dutch elm disease. As elms were not the only trees to suffer, some human agency is the most likely. At Linton Moss, Eshton Tarn and White Moss in Craven, the elm decline is followed in pollen records by evidence for an increase in grassland, which would support the case for a growth in pastoralism.

In the Tyne valley there is widespread evidence for activity from the period of late hunter-gatherers, around 6000 BC, to the Early Bronze Age around 2000 BC. Two interesting, albeit tentative, conclusions have emerged from the analysis of survey data. First, that whereas traces of hunter-gatherers could be found almost anywhere, evidence for early farming communities was more restricted. Typically, the foci of activity during these later periods tended to be in locations with a south-easterly aspect at altitudes of between 100m and 130m above sea level and between 1.5 and 2.5km from the River Tyne. Secondly, there was a less than expected degree of overlap between Mesolithic and Neolithic activity. As communities began to invest increasing effort in food production they will have become more sedentary; crops take months to ripen and herds need to be closely controlled or confined for their own security. It is also the case that whereas during the Mesolithic it was possible to hunt and gather widely, some parts of the landscape, in soil type, drainage and aspect, are more suited to farming than others. Areas in which the primeval wild wood had been replaced by impenetrable secondary scrub would be particularly unattractive to early farmers. These factors explain the more concentrated nature of evidence for the early farmers.

Fig. 3.5 The Devil's Lapful at Kielder in Northumberland consists of an elongated mound of stones. It has never been excavated but is assumed to mark the site of burials of Neolithic date. Before being engulfed by modern forestry plantations it commanded wide views across the valley of the North Tyne, now occupied by the Kielder Reservoir.

OPPOSITE PAGE:

TOP: *Fig. 3.6 The tiny 4m-wide cairn on Birkside Fell, situated at 380m above sea level in the North Pennines, was excavated in 1997.* It covered a single pottery urn containing a cremation. Radiocarbon dates suggest the burial occurred in the earlier part of the second millennium BC.

BELOW: *Fig. 3.7 Location of Neolithic henge monuments and standing stones at Milfield,* north Northumberland.

Notwithstanding these distinctions, the landscapes of the early farmers differed little from those of the Late Mesolithic hunter-gatherers. Except in the uplands, which remained open, the country was still mainly wooded, though most of this woodland was now secondary and some areas were probably choked with scrub. Browsing and grazing animals were making inroads into the woods and clearings, made by human endeavour, were kept open for longer periods until soil exhaustion brought about their abandonment. In some favoured areas clearings became more numerous and coalesced to former larger open spaces, and the investment of labour involved in clearance will have encouraged communities' sense of ownership. Whereas hunter-gatherers worldwide express a sense of identity with the landscape and see themselves as part of it, in the case of farmers this identity is developed through territory: farmers own land, hunter-gatherers dwell in it.

Where there is a clear distinction between hunter-gatherers' and later use of the land, it is in the construction of ritual or symbolic landscapes, a wholly new phenomenon in the Neolithic. While we know that hunter-gatherers imbue their landscape with deep symbolic significance, it was not until the Neolithic and Early Bronze Age that communities began to modify the meaning of their landscapes through the construction of ritual and symbolic monuments, sometimes on a vast scale. Burial monuments were perhaps one way in which communities demonstrated their ancestral ties with the land. Initially they accommodated multiple burials, but by the end of the 3rd millennium they often contained just a single interment, probably of a high status individual. In the North East the early stage in these developments is best represented by the earthen long barrows of eastern Yorkshire, of which at least 23 are known. Willerby Wold and Kilham are the best-known examples. Both were elongated trapezoidal mounds of chalk rubble 37m and 58m long respectively, covering multiple burials, with cremations and disarticulated inhumations. Both mounds incorporated timber structures, which seem to have been the scene of funerary rituals preceding the act of interment. The same is true of the cairn at Street House, Loftus on the Cleveland coast, dated to *c.* 3600 BC.[8] Further north, the stone-built long cairns of Northumberland, such as the Devil's Lapful at Kielder (Fig. 3.5), are probably equivalent structures, though none of these has been studied in recent decades. Round mounds of stone, or earth and stone, are also known from the Neolithic though they are more a feature of the Early Bronze

Age. Duggleby Howe in North Yorkshire is a striking example. This immense mound, 36m in diameter and originally over 6m high, covered the remains of about 60 individuals including both inhumations and cremations deposited at various times during the 3rd millennium BC. Round mounds or cairns of Early Bronze Age date are widespread in the North East, occurring singly or in groups. Size varies considerably, some being little smaller than Duggleby Howe while others are tiny by comparison, such as the recently excavated ring cairn at Birkside Fell in the North Pennines which is only 4m in diameter and covered a single cremation in a pottery urn (Fig. 3.6). Soils and pollen buried beneath these mounds and cairns suggest that they were erected in open country, or at least in substantial clearings, and that they were often sited in prominent positions along the skyline where they were intended to be seen from afar and become notable features in the landscape.

Prominent also were the henge monuments of the Neolithic and Early Bronze Age. These consist of circular or oval enclosures surrounded by a bank and a ditch, which is usually on the inside of the bank, indicating that a defensive function is unlikely. They can have one or two entrances and in their interior can include a variety of structures in either stone or timber. Stonehenge is, of course, the most famous example, though it is unique in the elaboration of its internal structures. Most henges incorporated simple circles of undressed stones, timbers or even pits. Henge sizes vary enormously with diameters ranging from over 500m to a little over 10m and they are commonly associated with monuments of other kinds including burial mounds and the enigmatic cursuses, pairs of parallel

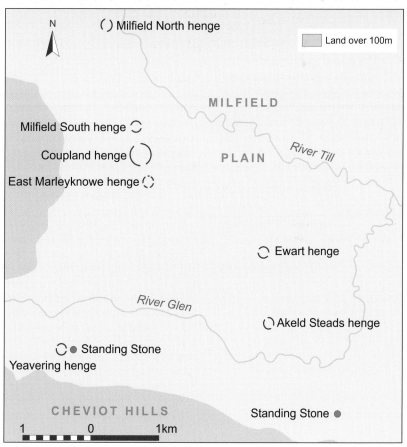

ditches running for hundreds, and sometimes thousands, of metres across the landscape, which seem to mark out avenues of some sort.

Two particular groupings of henge monuments are known in the North East: in the Milfield Basin in Northumberland and in the Vale of Mowbray in North Yorkshire. In the Milfield Basin six henges were arranged in a line extending for 2.5km down the western side of the basin with a seventh 2km to the west in the valley of the River Glen at Yeavering (Fig. 3.7).[9] These were all earthworks, now

*Fig. 3.8 Ploughing in recent centuries
has removed most traces of the seven
Neolithic henge monuments at
Milfield in Northumberland, though
most can still be identified as concentric crop
marks on aerial photographs.*

mainly ploughed flat, and they incorporate arrangements of posts and pits within
their interiors (Fig. 3.8). They vary in size, with overall diameters ranging from
100m at Coupland to 35m at Milfield North, and it appears from radiocarbon dates
that the complex was at its most developed during the mid-3rd millennium BC,
when settlement was expanding out of the basin into the surrounding landscape,
though Coupland has earlier dates. They are also associated with other monuments
including burial monuments, alignments of pits which may be boundary markers
and a possible processional way linking the henges. The extent and inter-related
nature of the Milfield complex implies that these monuments were erected in an
open landscape, a view supported by pollen analyses from the area.

In the Vale of Mowbray, six large henges lie on a roughly north-west/south-east
alignment extending for 12km along the land between the rivers Ure and Swale.
Three lie close together at Thornborough (Fig. 3.9) while the others, south-east
at Nunwick, Hutton Moor and Cana Barn, are more scattered. A further 7km to
the south-east, and on the same alignment, lie the Devil's Arrows, three immense
standing stones beside a crossing of the River Ure at Boroughbridge (Fig. 3.10).
The three monuments at Thornborough, which are evenly spaced at 550m
intervals, are almost identical, with diameters of approximately 240m. Each was
surrounded by an internal ditch and bank with two entrances facing each other,
though aerial photographs and recent excavations have revealed traces of
additional outer ditches and banks at two sites. The other henges in the Vale of
Mowbray are very similar to those at Thornborough. Their date range is likely to
be broadly contemporary with the Milfield henges. The central henge at
Thornborough is built over a cursus, which runs for more than 2km on an
alignment at right-angles to that of the henges. A double line of pits and several
round barrows have also been identified from aerial photographs. As at Milfield,
the extent and interrelationships of the complex imply that these monuments
were erected in an open landscape. A study of flints from the plough soil
suggests a decline in normal land-use practices during the period in which
the henges were at their most fully developed, and that the landscape around
the monuments was afforded a special, perhaps sacred, status. Another
possibly sacred Neolithic landscape has been identified on the Yorkshire
Wolds, centred on the village of Rudston where at least three cursuses converge.

ABOVE: **Fig. 3.9 The three henge monuments at Thornborough form part of a group of six sites in the Vale of Mowbray, in North Yorkshire.** *Viewed from the south the henges at Thornborough can be seen to be equidistant and lie virtually on a straight line. The most northerly is today obscured by trees while the southern henge, albeit damaged by ploughing, can be seen from crop-marks to have consisted of a series of concentric ditches and earthwork banks, while the bank of the central henge still stands 3m high.*

LEFT: **Fig. 3.10 Fifteen kilometres to the south-east of the Thornborough henges, and on the same alignment, lie the Devil's Arrows at Boroughbridge.** *Today this group consists of three immense standing stones, though antiquarian writers recorded more stones on the site in the 16th century. Each is about 6m high and made from stone quarried 10km away at Knaresborough. The surviving three stones are aligned at right angles to the River Ure and probably mark a crossing place.*

In the churchyard is a 7.7m-high slab of gritstone, England's tallest standing stone. Like the Devil's Arrows at Boroughbridge, the Rudston monolith was dragged several kilometres across the landscape before being erected.

The great age of henge-building had passed by the end of the 3rd millennium in the North East, as elsewhere in England, and other ceremonial structures had begun to take their place. The best known are the stone circles, some of which were erected within earlier henges. However, they are rare in this region and most, or perhaps all, of the 24 Yorkshire examples might really be parts of robbed-out round barrows. In Northumberland there are five stone circles around the margins of the Milfield Basin – Duddo and Threestone Burn are perhaps the best known. They are positioned so as to overlook the primary routes in and out of the valley and perhaps, in the case of Hethpool, the route on to Cheviot itself.

Throughout the sandstone areas of Northumberland and on Rombald's Moor, near Ilkley in Yorkshire, numerous rock surfaces have been carved with motifs: groups of semi-circular hollows known as cup-marks, which are often surrounded by one of more rings, giving rise to the term cup-and-ring marks (Fig. 3.11). No convincing explanation has been suggested for the meaning of these carvings and in recent years research has tended to focus on their settings within the landscape. They are not randomly scattered but are usually sited at significant or prominent places such as on scarp lines, on cols or at positions where several valleys converge. One idea is that these designs encoded messages for people traveling through the landscape; alternatively, they may have been territorial markers or recorded a mythological dimension to contemporary communities' experience of the landscape

Fig. 3.11 This striking example of a Bronze Age cup-and-ring carving lies on Doddington Moor in Northumberland. *Here a simple cup is surrounded by four concentric rings cut as grooves into the rock surface while a further groove partly bisects the design. A second, more weathered carving can be seen in the bottom right of the photograph. No convincing explanation has been offered as to the meaning of carvings of this type though it has been noted that many occupy prominent positions in the landscape and are numerous on the high ground of north Northumberland and the North York Moors.*

LANDSCAPES OF THE LATER BRONZE AGE AND THE IRON AGE

By the middle of the 2nd millennium most of the great henge monuments were in decline or had been abandoned to become overgrown by scrub. From this we can infer that the focus of spiritual activity had shifted, although we have little evidence as to where. There certainly seems to have been an increasing interest in natural places such as bogs and rivers on the evidence of finds of high-status metalwork, which are assumed to have been ritually deposited. However, the archaeological evidence for activity during this period, the Middle and Late Bronze Age and into the Iron Age, consists of the remains of settlements and field systems marked out by permanent boundaries. Whereas during the Neolithic and Early Bronze Age the landscape remained mainly open, by the middle of the Bronze Age we have evidence for the beginnings of an enclosure movement.

Most of the available evidence comes from the uplands, but this is an accident of survival, for similar evidence from the lowlands has often been destroyed by later cultivation or other developments. Conditions for agriculture in the uplands remained good until the middle of the 2nd millennium and the huts and fields we can see today, on the ground and in aerial photographs, mark the high-water mark of prehistoric agricultural expansion. Houses, or huts, survive as roughly circular banks of stone 3–8m in diameter, though the evidence of excavation is that they were originally built of timber and were later rebuilt in stone, perhaps because of a shortage of timber once the initial phase of expansion had passed. Hundreds have been recorded in Yorkshire, Durham and Northumberland on isolated hillsides where they can occur singly or in groups of up to 20, within simple farmyard enclosures, where livestock could be corralled or produce stored (Fig. 3.12). The field boundaries are made up of stones cleared from the surface, and in some cases these amount to little more than lines of clearance cairns. Sometimes the fields are irregular in outline and the system as a whole appears to have grown piecemeal from an original focus. Elsewhere the fields are more regular, consisting of groups of oblong enclosures. It is usually assumed that the irregular fields were intended to accommodate livestock and that the shape did not matter, whereas the more regular fields were given over to cultivation; as all allotment holders know, it is easier to dig over a patch of ground by working systematically in straight lines. Further evidence for crop cultivation comes from the development of lynchets – steps formed as soil creeps down slope – and from hand mills for grinding grain.

Few of these hut-circles and field systems have been directly dated and as a type they span a long period. The climate had begun to deteriorate by the middle

Fig. 3.12 This agglomeration of hut circles and curvilinear enclosures on Burton Moor in Wensleydale *is typical of the kind of remains associated with stock management during the Bronze Age. Situated at about 500m above sea-level the site is above the viable limit for crop cultivation even during the relatively benign conditions of the early second millennium.*

of the 2nd millennium and by its end temperature had fallen by $2°C$, the growing season had contracted by five weeks and the altitude limit for crop ripening had been lowered by 150m. Even in the absence of radiocarbon dates we can assume that many hut-circle settlements at higher altitudes must date from before this deterioration for them to have been viable.

The deterioration in the climate seems to have had serious consequences for the prehistoric communities of the North East. At one time it was thought that there may have been a wholesale abandonment of the uplands; and indeed there is something of an hiatus in the settlement record in the centuries on either side of 1000 BC. However, it is more likely that communities dealt with the changing conditions by modifying their economies and social organisation. Some of the higher level settlements were abandoned and the communities involved moved to lower and more sheltered places. This is, after all, why the high level evidence survives, being above the limit reached by all subsequent developments. However, the high moors and fells probably continued to be used, but for pasture rather than crop cultivation, with flocks and herds being moved between lowlands and uplands on a seasonal basis. Such livestock management may provide a context for some of the extensive linear boundaries and the dykes that run across moorland tops. In the lowlands, communities had to respond to the effects of rising sea levels. In Holderness, for example, they built hurdle trackways to facilitate the movement of people and livestock as access to grazing land in the salt marshes became increasingly difficult.

Another response to the stresses caused by deteriorating climate was a move towards a greater nucleation of settlement with groupings of circular huts frequently clustered within walled perimeters, some of which take on a defensive aspect. The defences in question very often consisted initially of no more than one or two timber palisades, such as those at Alnham High Knowes in the Cheviots. As time passed these were replaced, first by timber-framed ramparts of earth and stone and later by substantial drystone walls or concentric banks of dump construction of the typical hillfort (Fig. 3.13). Where ground conditions allowed, ditches were included in the defensive circuits. The replacement of wooden structures by others built wholly of stone may be a further indication of dwindling supplies of suitable timber. The move to defended sites began early in the 1st millennium BC, in the Late Bronze Age, and developed through the Iron Age. The hillfort at Easton Nab, overlooking the Tees valley, began life as a small Bronze Age palisaded enclosure, while excavations at Grimthorpe on the Yorkshire Wolds have dated the origins of that hillfort to around 800 BC.

The need for elaborate and extensive defences during the 1st millennium BC suggests a level of social unrest not hitherto encountered and the construction of the defences themselves required a massive input of labour, implying a level of social organisation only previously seen in henge building two millennia earlier. The population of the hillforts is difficult to estimate and depends on whether the hut-circles within were occupied contemporaneously. The sites themselves vary greatly in size. The multiple ramparts of the small hillfort at Dod Law West, near Wooler in Northumberland, enclose an area about 60m across, with nine hut-circles of which six may have been occupied at any one time.[10] At the much larger 5.2ha site of Yeavering Bell, 8km to the west, a single stone wall encloses about 130 hut platforms, while 20 hut-circles have been identified within the rampart enclosing the 300m wide summit of Ingleborough, in the Yorkshire Dales.

We know from writers in the Classical world that society in the North East during immediately pre-Roman times was organised on tribal lines, dominated by warrior elites, and it was such high-status individuals who could command the input of labour required for large-scale building projects. We also know from the same sources the names of the tribes in question: the Parisi in east Yorkshire and the much larger grouping of the Brigantes to the west and north. With these names the region begins to emerge from the shadowy anonymity of prehistory.

Not everybody lived in hillforts and from the middle of the 1st millennium BC numerous smaller farmsteads begin to appear. These consist of groups of hut-circles within enclosures, which can best be described as farmyards rather than defensive works. Many show development through time, often from initial timber phases to rebuilding in stone and usually involving an increase in the number of huts; and many were occupied into the earlier part of the Roman period. They are particularly numerous in Northumberland where groups of generally between two and six circular huts lie within stone-built enclosures, with a stone causeway leading to the huts from a single simple entrance and yards either side of the causeway.[11] In the North Tyne area these are broadly rectilinear, while in the Cheviots they tend to be curvilinear. These differences in plan are probably a simple reflection of the prevailing topography; in the Cheviots they are often built on hillsides with the huts terraced into the upslope end to assist drainage.

Farmsteads are often associated with field systems, many of which include terraces formed by lynchets, which implies a return to crop cultivation at relatively high altitudes. A marked improvement in the climate occurred between

Fig. 3.13 The hillfort on Brough Law in the Ingram valley in Northumberland is dated to c. 200 BC. *With its stone ramparts enclosing a cluster of hut circles it is a classic example of an Iron Age defended site. Steep slopes add to the protection on the north and west sides while the slopes to the south and east are covered with traces of prehistoric agriculture and contemporary, non-defensive settlements.*

about 200 BC to AD 500 and farming settlements appear in the Pennines up to about 300m above sea level, while in the Cheviots there is crop cultivation up to 400m. The evidence here takes the form of parcels of very narrow parallel ridges, known as 'cord-rig', usually no more than 1.4m apart and easily distinguished form later medieval ridge-and-furrow (Fig. 3.14).[12] These ridges were probably dug with spades whereas ploughs created the lynchets of the larger terraced fields. Most dated examples of cord-rig belong to the immediately pre-Roman period but some, such as those on Snear Hill in Northumberland which are associated with circular huts and other clearance cairns, may be much earlier.

The field systems associated with terraces or cord-rig often extend over several hectares but are usually focused on one or more farmsteads. However, in the Yorkshire Dales and the Tyne valley there are much more extensive systems running to tens or even hundreds of hectares.[13] In the Dales these systems are characterised by groups of parallel boundaries, 30–50m apart, often extending for several kilometres oblivious of the terrain, up hill and down dale. The areas in between are divided by shorter boundaries running at right-angles, giving rise to the term 'co-axial' field systems. The major boundaries are sometimes aligned on pre-existing features such as Bronze Age barrows and systems can incorporate both curvilinear and rectlinear farmsteads. The absence of evidence for crop cultivation suggests that these systems were designed with livestock management in mind. Co-axial field systems have been identified in Swaledale, Wensleydale, Ribblesdale and Wharfdale (Fig. 3.15). They are generally dated to the latter part of the 1st millennium but realignments and adjustments suggest that some could

Fig. 3.14 Some of the evidence for Iron Age and Romano-British arable cultivation takes the form of small parcels of hand-dug ridges known as cord-rig, *easily distinguishable from later medieval ridge and furrow by its diminutive size. Cord-rig can be more easily identified on aerial photographs than at ground level. The parcels of cord-rig adjacent to the hut-circle settlement at Crindle Dykes in Northumberland lie 1.5km south of the Roman fort at Housesteads on Hadrian's Wall.*

have had earlier origins. Hints of a co-axial system have also been identified in the Tyne valley between Newcastle and Corbridge. Here, parallel boundaries run upslope for about 3.5km from the edge of the valley to the upland fell, while other boundaries running at right-angles sub-divide the area into a brick-like pattern. The main elements are up to 200m apart and thus more widely spaced than the systems in the Dales. This Tyne valley system can be dated to the late 1st millennium BC by the fact that several farmsteads of Iron Age or Romano-British date have been built onto its main elements and similar systems near Doncaster have been dated to the 4th and 3rd centuries BC.

In the Yorkshire Wolds linear earthworks divide the landscape into blocks and corridors. These were developed piecemeal over long periods but they appear to be based on frameworks laid down early in the Late Bronze Age, perhaps as territories extending from defended enclosures such as Staple Howe and Devil's Hill on the north edge of the Wolds and Paddock Hill at the junction of the Great Wold Dyke, which runs for more than 10km on the south side of the Gypsy Race waterway. These early enclosed zones seem to have been used in cattle rearing and for stock management. They made use of rectangular paddocks strung out in lines along trackways. A number of areas without any sort of enclosure are approached by trackways with funnel-shaped endings, suggesting that here the droveways guided animals from paddocks and through cultivated and inhabited land onto open pasture.

The systems established here in the Late Bronze Age were further developed during the 1st millennium BC with more enclosed spaces created, settlement complexes growing up along the trackways and fields formed for arable cultivation. This subdivision and infilling was probably a response to the increasing pressures on land of a rising population. It was also at this time, from about the 4th century BC, that a new tradition of burial under square barrows evolved. In the Great Wold valley of the Gypsy Race in particular, these occur in cemeteries of up to 100 and more or stretched out along trackways and other linear features. One of the best known is the Arras cemetery near Market Weighton, which when first investigated contained over 100 barrows, though ploughing has now levelled most of them. All the recorded barrows were small, less than 10m across and no more than 1m high. At least three barrows were erected within square, ditched enclosures 9–12m across. Most covered pits were dug into the chalk, and contained simple inhumations accompanied by a limited range of personal ornaments, though in the case of the so called 'Queen's' barrow the accompaniments were more lavish. Three burials, the

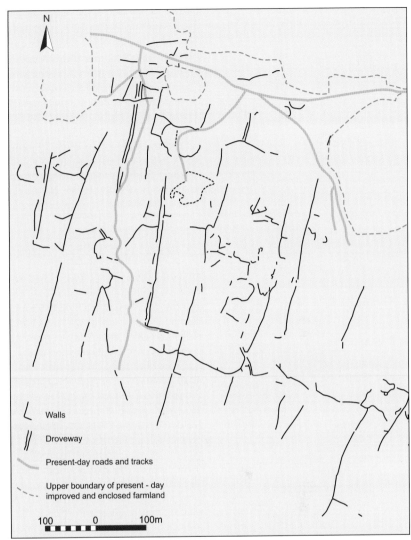

Walls

Droveway

Present-day roads and tracks

Upper boundary of present - day improved and enclosed farmland

100 0 100m

Fig. 3.15 Harkerside West, Swaledale.
Remains of an extensive late-prehistoric co-axial field system (land division system) on moorland at Harkerside West on the southern side of Swaledale, north Yorkshire. The roughly parallel walls and lanes slope down northwards to the edges of the enclosed land flanking the River Swale.

colourfully named 'Lady's', 'Charioteer's' and 'King's' barrows, were particularly noteworthy in that they were accompanied by dismantled carts or chariots, while the latter also included the skeletons of two horses. Dismantled carts or chariots have also been found in cemeteries at Wetwang Slack and Garton Slack, near Driffield. This funerary rite is unknown elsewhere in Iron Age Britain but was practiced in the Champagne and Marne area of eastern France.

Field systems and their associated settlements imply widespread clearance, and throughout the region, the pollen record documents inroads into the remaining woodland. For example, pollen studies at Roxby on the North York Moors indicate that only 12 per cent of the landscape remained wooded by the late Iron Age, while those from Fellend and Steng Moss in Northumberland show massive clearance from the first century BC onwards, a finding repeated at the Harkerside co-axial system in Swaledale. By the end of the 1st millennium BC, many areas in the North East were as open as they are today.

LANDSCAPE AND EMPIRE: THE ROMAN PERIOD

When the Roman legions marched into north-east England in AD 69–71 they beheld a landscape that was mainly open. Most of the lowlands were divided into small fields defined by ditches and earthwork banks, which were probably surmounted by hedgerows. In the uplands the boundaries consisted of stone walls. There was still plenty of woodland, but this was on slopes that were too steep to clear and cultivate and in the damp valley bottoms. Most of it was managed as a source of raw materials, probably under coppicing regimes, or as wood pasture for stock. Amongst the fields were farmsteads linked by droveways along which livestock moved between pastures and areas of fallow. In most areas fields were grouped into a patchwork of enclosures focused on a farmstead or group of settlements, but in some areas co-axial field systems indicate a more wide-ranging pattern of organisation. Whether such developments reflect the exercise of coercive authority or community effort is unknown.

At Stanwick, north of Richmond in North Yorkshire, a tribal capital was established. Occupation here began with an undefended site of the Iron Age and from about AD 50 a 240ha enclosure developed out of existing boundaries, with an inner area of 52ha within ditch-and-rampart defences. Stanwick can be considered as a town, or *oppidum*, and as such the only true example in the North East. The inner area represented the main focus of settlement and finds from the excavations include numerous exotic trade goods from the Romanised parts of Britain and further afield in the empire.

Although most of lowland Britain was overrun within a few months of the invasion of AD 43, Roman governors at first made no attempt to bring the north within the realm of the empire. Instead, following a policy widely used elsewhere, they negotiated alliances with native leaders. In the case of the North East the alliance was with the Brigantes, and in particular with the matriarchal head of the royal family, Queen Cartimandua. For nearly three decades in the middle of the 1st century AD the Brigantes enjoyed both their continuing independence and many of the material benefits of peaceful relations with the empire.

As the Roman authorities were well aware, alliances with fickle tribal leaders were fragile affairs and when the Roman army finally moved into the north it was to put down a revolt by a faction of the Brigantes. The phase of conquest was relatively short-lived with few implications for the landscape. As the legions advanced, they dug ditches and threw up earth banks to create temporary marching camps such as the one at Malham Moor, which had an area of 8.2 ha. These embankments may have been surmounted by palisades constructed from trees felled in the immediate vicinity, though the legionaries may have carried timber stakes with them for this purpose.

These camps were temporary features and, in the longer term, the army maintained control through a system of garrison forts. Most were new constructions, sited according to strategic requirements rather than the tactical considerations of a military campaign. Most were built to a standard pattern to house units of 500–1,000 auxiliary troops. Each consisted of an oblong enclosure about 2ha in extent, with gates on each side and rounded corners giving rise to a standard 'playing-card' shape. The interiors were occupied by barrack blocks and stores, with stables in the case of cavalry units. The commander's house, built on the lines of a civilian town house, and a headquarters building for administration of the garrison, were prominently positioned in the centre of the fort. Latrines were provided at suitable locations where the slope of the ground facilitated flushing. Bath blocks, which presented a fire hazard, were usually built outside the main area of the fort. Initially, these garrison forts were built of earth, turf and timber and the quantities required must have been considerable, while there was a continual demand for fuel for heating. By the 2nd century most of the forts that continued in use had been rebuilt in stone. This probably implies both recognition of the need to maintain permanent garrisons in the Brigantian area and a diminution of available supplies of building timber.

Between AD 78 and 85, the provincial governor Julius Agricola attempted to conquer the rest of mainland Britain with the legions pushing into the far north of Scotland. Many of the garrison forts in the north-east of England were first established at this time, including the line of nine forts built in the Tyne–Solway gap, which formed a strategic system extending from Corbridge in Northumberland to Kirkbride on the Solway shore and which were linked by the Roman road known as the Stanegate. Agricola's conquest of Scotland was a failure and in the reign of Hadrian, possibly on his direct initiative, a new frontier emerged just north of the Stanegate. Although the frontier works underwent many developments over the following 250 years, the initial phase from coast to coast was completed by the time of his death in AD 138.[14]

The Hadrianic frontier consisted of a number of elements, of which the wall itself was just one. Immediately to the north of the wall, except where it followed the precipitous crags of the Whin Sill in mid-Northumberland, there was a substantial ditch with the excavated material dumped as an irregular discontinuous mound to the north. Two techniques were used in the construction of the wall. East of the River Irthing, in Northumberland, the wall was built with a rubble core and stone facing, which may have been rendered. It stood about 4m high and was possibly surmounted by a wall-walk and parapet. To the west, in Cumbria, the wall was initially built in turf though it was later rebuilt in stone. Every Roman mile (1,686 yards or 1.54km) there were small fortlets known as milecastles, which provided access through the wall, and between adjacent milecastles were two turrets. Although not part of the initial plan, from an early stage in the development of the system, forts were added to the line of the wall at about 10km intervals (Fig. 3.16). To the south, the frontier zone was marked by the construction of the *vallum*, a deep flat-bottomed ditch between parallel banks of upcast. The *vallum* is regarded more as a formal line of demarcation than a component in the defensive system. Nevertheless, it could only be crossed easily at a series of purpose-built causeways protected by gates and giving access to each of the forts. The forts themselves were joined by a road known as the 'Military Way'.

The construction of Hadrian's Wall and its associated features was a massive undertaking comparable to the major civil engineering works of the present day and its impact on the landscape was similar. Except in the central zone, where the wall follows the precipitous crags of the Whin Sill, almost every excavation has recorded ploughmarks directly beneath the wall foundations. This alone is good evidence that the frontier works were built in a cleared and farmed landscape; that in the initial build it was a turf rampart for nearly half its length implies vast

Fig. 3.16 The Roman fort at Housesteads is the best preserved along the line of Hadrian's Wall and is a classic example of military works of this type, the oblong, 'playing card' shape being evident in this aerial photograph. Excavations in the interior have revealed the remains of barracks, granaries, the headquarters building and the commandant's house, while outside the south and west gates are clear traces of the associated civilian settlement or vicus. To the north, Housesteads looks out over the crags of the Whin Sill, the crest of which is followed by the line of Hadrian's Wall, which joins the north-east corner of the fort towards the bottom of the photograph and leaves again at the north-west corner, though this is mostly obscured by shadow. Beyond the shadows and in the centre of the photograph can be seen the remains of Milecastle 37 and the line of the wall can be followed westwards to Crag Lough and beyond.

extents of open pasture and studies of fossil pollens confirm this. Many Romano-British farmers must have found their lands cut in two by the frontier works and faced difficulties over gaining access to their lands. In the Tyne valley, construction of the wall completely disrupted the Late Prehistoric co-axial fields (Fig. 3.17).[15] Even in the rocky central zone the impact must have been acute and the settlement at Milking Gap near the fort at Housesteads found itself hemmed in between the wall and the *vallum* (Fig. 3.18).

The impact of the frontier on the pre-existing landscape must have been exacerbated by the construction works themselves and in particular by the demand for timber, vast quantities of which were used in the forts and other works. Given that much of the landscape at the time was open, some of this building material must have been imported, but attrition of the local woods continued apace. Pollen residues from Fozy Moss near Sewingshields, east of Housesteads, document rapid forest clearance and an almost totally deforested landscape at about AD 130.[16]

The landscape impact of Hadrian's Wall continued beyond the initial phase of disruption and construction. It has been estimated that, when fully manned, the frontier works may have housed up to 30,000 troops who would have consumed up to 10,000 tons of wheat a year – the yield of about 12,000ha. It seems inconceivable that the garrison could have been supplied from within the immediate vicinity of the frontier zone, or even from within the region as a whole. In a short space of time most forts acquired civilian settlements, or *vici*, outside their gates, such as that at Housesteads. While some of the residents were probably farmers, others were merchants or worked in the service industries, such as bar and brothel keepers: a non-productive part of the regional population that still needed to be fed.

The Hadrian's Wall complex was part of an infrastructure of military control established throughout the north of England, with hinterland forts connected to the centre of the military command in York by a network of roads. York itself was in between the two main north–south roads, linked by connecting roads. Ermine Street entered the region at the fort of Brough on the Humber crossing, passed east of York and continued on to the fort of Chester-le-Street, County Durham, reaching the River Tyne at Newcastle. Dere Street came through the fort of Doncaster in the south, passed west of York to forts at Catterick in north Yorkshire, and Binchester, Lanchester and Ebchester in County Durham, en route to the River Tyne crossing at Corbridge. The fort of Bowes, north Yorkshire, protected the road going west from Dere Street across Stainmore and on to the west end of the frontier at Carlisle. North of the frontier, Dere Street, as it continued on towards the Cheviots and into what is now Scotland, had garrison forts at Risingham and High Rochester in Northumberland. Never before had the landscape been brought under control in such a systematic way over so wide an area.

Hinterland forts, no less than those along the wall, attracted civilians to their gates. The civilian settlement at Catterick in north Yorkshire, where Dere Street crosses the River Swale, grew to cover an area of 10ha.[17] It contained an inn, or *mansio*, richly appointed with painted wall plaster and an extensive bathing suite and was provided in the 3rd century with its own defensive wall. Aldborough and

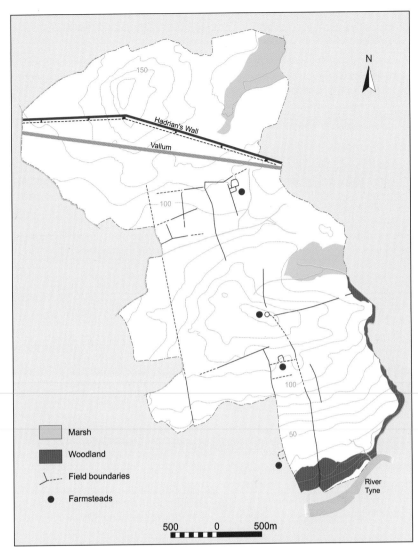

Fig. 3.17 Relationship between late-prehistoric co-axial fields and Hadrian's Wall (between Milecastle 15 and Turret 16B). *Iron Age and Romano-British farmsteads are marked while the extent of woodland and marsh is estimated. Contours are at 10m intervals.*

Fig. 3.18 If the Iron Age 'North Tyne'-type farmstead at Milking Gap was *still occupied in the third decade of the second century AD the occupants would have found themselves in the unenviable position of living between Hadrian's Wall and the* vallum. *This would certainly have led to their eviction and is one of many examples where the construction of the Roman wall can be shown to have disrupted an existing agrarian landscape.*

Brough on Humber, which were founded as forts, became towns in their own right as the administrative centres for the Brigantes and the Parisi. At York, across the river from the legionary fortress, a colony of veterans was established: a status shared with Lincoln, Gloucester and Colchester.

As in the frontier zone, the implications for the landscape of these developments were twofold. First, the building works involved produced a demand for raw materials. Building stone had to be quarried and clay dug for floor and roofing tiles. Above all there must have been an almost insatiable demand for timber, both for construction works and to fuel the hypocausts of the central heating systems and bath blocks. Fuel was also a requirement of industrial developments such as the major pottery works at Crambeck, 30km north-east of York. Pollen records throughout the region document further major inroads into the remaining woodlands. Secondly, the growing urban communities and the military garrisons produced a demand for food, which could only be met by an increase in production. Throughout most of the region the late prehistoric system of mixed farming remained unchanged during the Roman period, though the reorganisation of some field systems may have been a response to the increased demand. The co-axial fields around Doncaster, which were established in the Iron Age, continued in use, as did many of the ditched enclosures of the Yorkshire Wolds, and the Pennine dales also show intensive usage in the Iron Age and Roman periods with ditched trackways and co-axial fields. The relationship of the Romano-British subsistence farmers to the market economy of the empire is most clearly documented by discoveries of exotic trade goods such as pottery, beads and brooches, on native sites. These were presumably obtained through trade at the *vici* and small towns.

In some cases reorganisation went beyond the adjustment of field boundaries. At Gargrave, on the edge of the Yorkshire Dales, a cluster of round timber and turf hut-circles was replaced in the second half of the 2nd century by a rectangular, stone villa consisting of a number of rooms opening off a corridor (Fig. 3.19). Other rooms were provided in wings at either end of the main block and there were mosaic floors and both internal and external bath blocks, while over time further ranges of ancillary farm buildings were added to the site. The Gargrave villa sat at the centre of a 40ha field system, while the discovery of pig bones during the excavations implies the use of wood pasture beyond the delimited fields. Similar villas were established elsewhere on good soils in the Tees valley, in the Vale of York and on the Wolds around Malton, with that at Beadlam sporting one of the most northerly mosaics in the empire.[18] However, the North East lay at the very margins of sustainability for this type of villa-oriented farming economy and such establishments can only have played a minor role in developing agricultural production. Throughout much of the region, the pattern of the landscape continued to develop as it had done for millennia. Woodland was further reduced in extent and what remained was probably more intensively managed. Most of the population lived in farmsteads that, though sometimes grouped in loose clusters, could not be described as villages in the sense in which that term is used in later periods.

Around and beyond the frontier, the rural population did not develop the sort of villa estates with the trappings of the Roman Classical world that emerged in Yorkshire; but it was nevertheless drawn to some extent into the economy of the Roman province, as finds of industrially-produced pottery, glass beads, brooches and other ornaments demonstrate. The hillfort at Dod Law West remained in use until the second century AD but in most cases the hillforts were abandoned and their populations moved elsewhere.[19] The same sorts of settlement enclosures that accommodated people before the Roman era continued to be built, though their houses were now more likely to have stone walls, and the countryside north

Fig. 3.19 A reconstruction drawing of the Roman villa at Gargrave as it may have appeared in the 3rd century AD. The main residential block, the 'winged-corridor building', is shown lying at the centre of the complex, with various subsidiary buildings on either side along with a kitchen garden and a wood store. Livestock graze in a mainly open landscape.

of Hadrian's Wall was dotted with these farmsteads throughout the coastal plain from Kennel Hall Know near the Tyne to Doubstead by Berwick, just south of the Tweed. The same is true of the valleys leading into the Cheviot Hills, North Tynedale and Redesdale and the valleys of the Till-Breamish and Bowmont. Along the coastal zone the settlements have been identified in air survey but little is known of the fields they cultivated; the extensive co-axial fields of Yorkshire seem not to have been created here. In the hill country where ruins still survive at ground level, as at Coldberry Hill close to Wooler and Brands Hill to the south, small settlement compounds are set within field plots and served by droveways. In most cases the settlements are small with no more than three or four huts, but in the Breamish valley above Ingram 34 huts were tightly clustered in a settlement enclosure at Greaves Ash, which replaced a small Iron Age defended site; it is possible that this well-favoured area supported a larger population in Roman times than it does today. A traveller north of the frontier in the 3rd century would have seen a busy landscape with a population living in dispersed settlements and occasional larger clusters, cultivating field plots that were separated from one another by areas of open heath and moorland and small wooded areas. This scene would have differed from that of two or three centuries earlier in degree more than in its fundamentals.

The Roman world in Britain was in decline from the middle of the 4th century. This was due in part to the inroads of restless peoples from beyond the frontiers; but a phase of deteriorating climate in the 4th century, which made it difficult to sustain the levels of production that had been attained during the 2nd and 3rd centuries, must also have contributed. The effects of rising sea-levels were felt far upstream in most river valleys and threatened the economic viability of centres such as York, where flooding of the River Ouse destroyed riverside facilities and the bridge. The landscape legacy of 350 years of Roman occupation consists mainly of the towns, many of which have survived to the present day, and the road network which, until the advent of motorways and by-passes, continued to provide the infrastructure of the region. In the frontier zone today Hadrian's Wall and its associated features again exercise an influence with the designation of the area as a World Heritage Site. In the history of landscape as a whole, the Roman period was an interval during which the indigenous prehistoric system was brought, probably prematurely, within the realm of a wider market economy. When access to those markets was withdrawn production fell back to something approaching pre-Roman levels. Secondary woodland regenerated over Romano-British fields in the Tyne valley and seven centuries were to elapse before the relics of these early fields emerged from the woods once more to provide the underlying structure to the medieval open-field system.

NOTES

1   Tolan-Smith & Bonsall 1999.
2   Mellars & Dark 1998.
3   Radley & Mellars 1964.
4   Simmons 1996, 5.
5   Smith 1992.
6   Van der Noort & Ellis 1995;
     Van der Noort & Fletcher 2000.
7   Burgess 1984, 133–7.
8   Viner 1984.
9   Harding 1981; Waddington 1999.
10   Smith 1990.

11   Burgess 1984, 164–73.
12   Topping 1989.
13   Fleming 1998; Tolan-Smith 1997;
     White 1997.
14   Johnson 1994.
15   Tolan-Smith, M 1997.
16   Dumayne & Barber 1994.
17   Wilson 2002.
18   Neal 1996.
19   Smith 1990.

4

The North East in the Medieval Period

RICHARD LOMAS and RICHARD MUIR

By the medieval period we mean the centuries that began with Britain's severance from the Roman Empire. The date usually given for this is AD 410, but it seems likely that the Empire's capacity to manage its northern frontier had been deteriorating over a generation or more before that date. Nor is there a hard and fast definition of the end of the medieval period; but the effects of the Reformation and the closing of the monasteries and friaries in the reign of Henry VIII brought about far-reaching changes, and so the failure of the northern protest against these changes – the Pilgrimage of Grace in 1536–7 – can serve as a marker, particularly in Yorkshire. Further north, though, disturbed conditions on the Anglo-Scottish border continued to affect the lives of people of every social class for over 60 years. Only after the Union of the Crowns in 1603, when James VI of Scotland succeeded Elizabeth I in England as James I, did it become possible for the nation to move on from the instability and social conflict that had been endemic for over 300 years on both sides of the border (Fig. 4.1).

NORTHUMBRIA

In the earliest post-Roman phase, the Kingdom of Northumbria gave political unity to the North East, but this remained fully effective for only two and a half centuries, from the reign of Aethelfrith (592–616) until the Viking capture of York in 866–7. Aethelfrith, the great warrior king, emerged as the ruler of Bernicia, a kingdom centred on Bamburgh (now in north Northumberland), which comprised the modern counties of Durham and Northumberland – the land between the rivers Tees and Tweed – as well as the parts of what is now Scotland between the rivers Tweed and Forth. South of the Tees, the Kingdom of Deira, occupying what is now Yorkshire, was a separate political entity with its own ruling house, until Aethelfrith merged the two by force at the beginning of the 7th century to create Northumbria.

In Deira, as in most English realms, communities of several households buried their dead over several centuries in communal cemeteries. But no such cemeteries have been discovered north of the Tees valley: the cemetery of some 120 individuals at Norton on the north bank of the Tees and possibly one at Darlington are the northernmost examples. Added to these original differences, from the mid-9th century three further factors come into play that make it appropriate to consider the land north of the Tees, the former Bernicia, separately from the former Deira, between the Tees and the Humber.

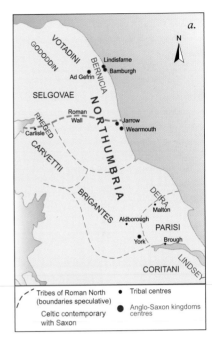

Fig. 4.1 a. *Romano-British tribes and Anglo-Saxon kingdoms.*
b. *Political divisions in the mid-11th century.*

The first was the creation of the Norse Kingdom of York, consequent upon its capture by a Viking army in 867. This led to extensive Norse settlement in what is now Yorkshire, which formed part of a region in central England known as the Danelaw. Norse colonisation is clearly revealed in the place-names of Yorkshire, which abound in Norse elements, such as the place names ending in *by* (farm or village) and the use of the word *beck* to denote a tributary stream. There are very few Norse elements in place names north of the Tees and such as there are, are largely confined to the far south of County Durham.

The second factor is the remarkable and very durable institution known as the Community of St Cuthbert. This was a body of monks, headed by a bishop, which was the guardian and trustee of the saint's shrine at the monastery of Lindisfarne on Holy Island. This role acquired heightened significance in 698 when, 11 years after his death, the monks exhumed Cuthbert's remains and found that the soft tissue of his body had not decayed: proof they believed of Cuthbert's exceptional holiness. This, and the stories of the miracles he performed in life and posthumously, underpinned the cult of the saint, assiduously promoted by the Community, which attracted deep and widespread veneration (Fig. 4.2). The Community remained at Lindisfarne until 875, when danger from sea-borne raiders drove them off the island. After seven years, during which they had several temporary homes, they settled in 883 on the site of the Roman fort at Chester le Street, where they remained until 995 when once again the problem of security led them to move 10km further south to a more defensible location at Durham. All the while, by means of purchase for, and gifts to, St Cuthbert, the Community assembled a landed estate of such an immense extent that by the early years of the 11th century the Bishop of Durham, the elected head of the Community of St Cuthbert, wielded political authority in the Tees–Tweed region alongside and on an equal footing with the Earl of Northumbria, whose family probably descended from the royal house of Northumbria.

The third factor was the Anglo-Scottish border, which remained profoundly influential from the 10th to the 17th centuries. Military activity in the 10th century gradually created the kingdoms of England and Scotland, one consequence of which was the dismemberment of Northumbria, with Lothian (the land between the Tweed and the Forth) being lost to Scotland. This gain did not satisfy the ambition of the Scottish kings, who strove to reunite the territory of ancient Bernicia under their rule by extending their southern boundary to the Tees. They were thwarted by the Norman King of England, William II, who in the early 1090s forced his Scottish counterpart, Malcolm III, to accept the Tweed boundary. This has remained unchanged, except for the transfer of

Fig. 4.2 Reconstruction of a Saxon settlement at Lindisfarne. Excavations at Greenshiel on the north side of Lindisfarne (Holy Island) in Northumberland have revealed a medieval settlement probably in use in the 9th century but later buried by shifting sand dunes. The site consists of a small cluster of elongated rectangular buildings, two of which are similar to medieval longhouses; remains of ridge-and-furrow cultivation nearby may be associated with the settlement. Small informal nuclei of this kind were probably widespread in the North East before the introduction of organised street and green village forms.

Berwick upon Tweed from Scotland to England in the 14th century. By the Treaty of York in 1237, the Scottish crown finally and formally renounced its claim to land south of the Tweed. In 1296, however, war broke out between the two countries, and truly peaceful conditions did not return until after 1603.

From Romans to Normans: 410–1066

Though the early years of the Kingdom of Northumbria were a time of religious fervour, which produced such masterpieces as the Lindisfarne Gospels, the Ruthwell Cross and the Venerable Bede's *The Ecclesiastical History of the English People*, our knowledge of the landscape and land ownership is minimal and tentative. An added frustration is the region's omission from the Domesday survey, the source of much information about conditions in England south of the Tees prior to the Conquest. The reason for this omission was that at the time the survey was commissioned in 1085 the new Norman regime had only recently suppressed native resistance north of the Tees and had yet to undertake any land redistribution.

What is certain is that the bulk of the population lived in the countryside and was engaged in farming, but whether in family farms or in more communal arrangements is a major uncertainty. The basic social unit was the township, a defined and named area of land worked by its inhabitants. It is not certain how many of these farmers were English immigrants and how many were native Britons, who had simply exchanged a native for a foreign master. On balance, it seems more likely that Bernicia at least was not a kingdom of mass migration and that a high percentage of the farming population was of native origin. Nor is it clear whether these tillers of the soil were legally free or in a state of servitude. What is known is that in return for their land they paid rent in the form of food renders and services.

Townships were grouped into units known as *shires*. These districts, comprising up to two-dozen townships, were both landed estates and units of local government; and, after Christianity had been adopted, they were parishes. Within these shires were two other classes. *Drengs* were men who, amongst other things, were supervisors of the farming population of their shire, for which service they were given the tenancy of one township or part of a township. Still more socially elevated were *thanes*, who in addition to duties related to the shire, probably constituted the warrior elite of the kingdom and almost certainly were of immigrant English stock.

Though not certain, it is likely that all of Northumbria was divided into shires. A sufficient number survived into later centuries as ecclesiastical parishes to give some idea of their structure. The clearest evidence of pre-Conquest arrangements, albeit derived from an early 13th-century source, is that from Islandshire in north Northumberland, which was also the parish of Holy Island. Of its 22 townships Fenwick was retained as the estate headquarters, while Fenham was assigned to the parish church for the support of the parish clergy. A further two, Beal and Goswick, and part of another, Buckton, were *drengages*, whose tenants owed money rents and unspecified services at Fenwick, while the townships of Kyloe, Low Lynn and Berrington comprised a *thanage*. It is likely that the remaining townships were occupied by tenant farmers, whose rents and services were owed at Fenwick.[1] A thanage would normally comprise three townships, for example Halton near Corbridge, which consisted of the contiguous townships of Halton, Great Whittington and Clarewood.[2] In the post-Conquest years some of these three-township thanages appear to have been converted into Norman-style military tenures known as knight's fees. One likely example is the cluster of Yeavering, Coupland and Akeld, which may well have constituted a thanage within the shire of Yeavering, within which was an important Bernician royal palace. The recent 'reconstruction' of this shire has shown how it is possible to identify past landscape structures beneath more recent forms.[3]

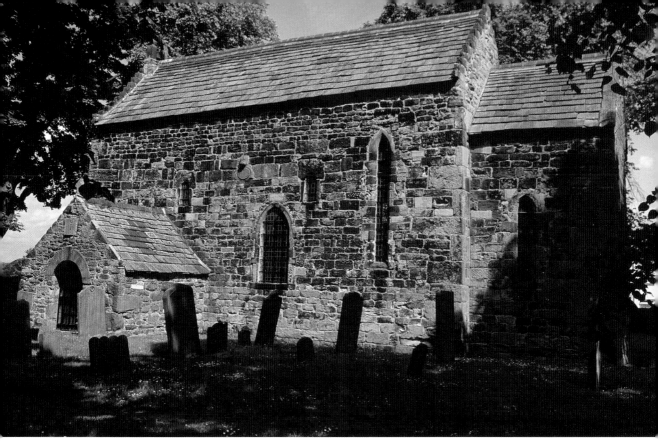

Fig. 4.3 The 7th-century stone church at Escomb, Co. Durham, with its long, high and narrow nave, is one of the few near-complete Anglo-Saxon churches left in England. Constructed with stone from the ruins of the nearby Roman fort at Binchester, it stands in a roughly circular churchyard, a feature that suggests Celtic rather than Roman Christianity.

Two other developments in landholding of this period are noteworthy: the proliferation of monasteries following hard upon the programme of conversion launched in 635 by St Aidan and his Irish monks from their Lindisfarne monastery on Holy Island; and Lindisfarne itself and the double monastery of Wearmouth-Jarrow, became institutions of international standing in the fields of art and scholarship. Monasteries were handsomely endowed, particularly by the royal family. King Ecgfrith (670–85) provided Wearmouth with 70 hides of land and Jarrow with 40; a hide was probably 120 acres, which means that Wearmouth had nearly 8,500 acres (3,440ha) and Jarrow nearly 5,000 acres (2,025ha). Not to be outdone, Ecgfrith's first wife, Aethelthryth, gave 240 square kilometres of land (much of it unsettled moorland) to St Wilfrid to support the monastery he founded at Hexham. Her gift was, or came to be, Hexhamshire. In less than 100 years, a sizeable amount of the kingdom had passed into the hands of the church. However, none of these monasteries, and also those at Tynemouth and Hartlepool, survived the catastrophic disruption of Northumbrian life by the 9th-century Viking raids and invasions. Sadly, nothing of the early fabric of Lindisfarne, and little of that at Jarrow and Monkwearmouth, has survived, while the only extant part of Hexham is the crypt in which relics were housed and displayed for the veneration of pilgrims. The most complete physical evidence we have of Northumbrian stone churches of this period is at Escomb, near Bishop Auckland, which, curiously and as yet inexplicably, appears not to have been monastic and never became a medieval parish church (Fig. 4.3).

The one monastic institution that not only survived but flourished spectacularly was the Community of St Cuthbert, which, as already noted, finally settled in Durham in 995. By that date its estate was immense. The core was the land between the Tyne and its tributary the Derwent in the north, and the Tees in the south, except for three small enclaves on the north bank of the Tees centred upon Hart, Gainford and Sadberge and known collectively as the Wapentake of Sadberge. This anomaly was part of the County of Northumberland until Hugh of le Puiset, Bishop of Durham from 1154 until 1195, bought it from Richard I in 1189. The Community's estate also included Ryton, occupying the angle between the north bank of the Derwent and the south bank of the Tyne. Together these properties were simply known as the Land of the Haliwerfolc (the people of the Holy Man). Only later did they come to be called County Durham, which remained unchanged until it was truncated by the creation of the new counties of Tyne and Wear and Cleveland in 1974. The Community also possessed Norhamshire and Islandshire (from the outset) and Bedlingtonshire (from *c.* 910). These were classed as parts of County Durham until the mid-19th century: it was not until 1844 that an act of Parliament made them parts of Northumberland.

Medieval expansion, 1066–1296

For the 230 years after 1066 we have a clearer idea of the shape and development of the landscape. The determining factors were twofold. One was the change in landownership wrought by the post-1066 Norman regime. In this, Northumberland was affected more radically than Durham. Between 1095 and 1135, most of the land in Northumberland (including the Wapentake of Sadberge) was redistributed to 25 men, all but one of Norman or Anglo-Norman stock, by William II (1087–1100) and Henry I (1100–1135). Most of them in their turn devolved parts of their estates on to men prepared to be their feudal tenants. Some of these too were Normans, but others were clearly native English.

Unlike most of its secular counterparts, the Community of St Cuthbert was not dispossessed. For its members the major change came in 1083 when the new Norman bishop, William of St Calais (1081–96), replaced them with a priory of Benedictine monks, all of whom were English. He also divided the hitherto monolithic estate into two unequal portions, the smaller for the monks, who were to constitute the cathedral chapter, the larger for the bishop. Thenceforth, the Land of the *Haliwerfolc* had two landlords, but with political and administrative authority retained by the bishop.

The difference between the two counties is reflected in the number of castles built by Norman incomers. In County Durham there were, strictly speaking, only two – Durham, built by the bishop, and Brancepeth – as Barnard Castle, which was built by the Balliol family, was at that date in Northumberland. In contrast, 12 were built in Northumberland: Alnwick, Bamburgh, Harbottle, Mitford, Morpeth, Newcastle, Norham, Prudhoe, Wark on Tweed, Wark on Tyne, Warkworth and Wooler, with Barnard Castle making a 13th (Figs 4.4 and 4.5).

The other determining factor was the increase in population. Though circumstantial, evidence clearly points to rising numbers, albeit from a low-level base: until the great surge in industrial expansion in the 19th century, the region remained one of the most thinly populated in England.

Perhaps the most outstanding feature of the landscape was the planned townships. They ranged in area from 500 to 4,000 acres (200 to 1,600ha). In most cases the land under cultivation was less than half the total size; at Longhoughton in Northumberland, for example, cultivated land accounted for 43 per cent of the township's 2,472 acres (496ha), the remainder being uncultivated moorland and ox pasture (Fig. 4.6).[4] At a township's centre was a nucleated village, with farmsteads clustered in orderly fashion around an open space, the green. Greens varied in shape but many were half elliptical, a good example being Shincliffe, near Durham. Most are still clearly identifiable.

The core of every township community was its bondmen, of whom there were usually somewhere between 12 and 30. All had the same quantity of arable land: usually 24 acres (9.7ha) though in a significant number of places 30 acres (12ha) was the standard. Broadly speaking, 24-acre (9.7ha) holdings predominated in Northumberland and on lay estates, while most 30-acre (12ha) holdings were in Durham and on ecclesiastical estates.[5] These arable acres were distributed in the

ABOVE: **Fig. 4.4 The numerous medieval castles of Northumberland and Durham vary in their location and design.** *Bamburgh Castle stands on a spectacular narrow ridge of Whin Sill, which overlooks the extensive coastal dunes and tidal flats and the village of Bamburgh and has been the site of pre-Roman Iron Age and Saxon fortifications. The substantial mid-12th-century keep and three baileys are the main relics of a large Norman castle, considerably modified by 18th- and 19th-century renovations.*

BELOW: **Fig. 4.5 Harbottle is a small, isolated village strategically located above the River Coquet and close to Clennell Street, a major medieval route over the Cheviots.** *The outstanding feature here is a mid-12th-century motte-and-bailey earthwork constructed on the instigation of Henry II; from the late 15th century it was the centre for the organisation of the Middle Marches and thus a key element in the defence and control of the Borders. Fell sandstone hills lie on the horizon.*

form of rigs (in the south the word used is ridge), which were long, narrow, inverted 'S'-shapes, in a series of fields known as flatts, the size and shape of which was dictated by the lie of the land. The flatts were grouped into two, three or four large fields. Rigs varied in area, but half an acre was common. Possession of these farms entitled their holders to a share of hay produced by the township's meadowland and the right to pasture a specified number of animals on the township's common. In return for the arable land and attendant rights, tenants paid rent in the form of cash, produce and service.

In addition, there were cottage tenants or cottars, often the same number as there were bondmen, and with arable holdings of standard size, ranging between 1 and 6 acres (0.4 and 2.4ha). Since their land was insufficient to support them, they supplemented their income by working for the bondmen or on the landlord's home farm or demesne. Most townships also had a small number of freehold tenants, whose arable holdings were in many cases the same size as those of the bondmen but whose rent was small and fixed. In essence, the arrangement was individual possession of land, which was operated communally.

It is self-evident that the symmetry of these townships was not organic, but the result of decisions that only landowners could have taken and enforced. When this restructuring took place is uncertain. Archaeological evidence from Thrislington in County Durham points to the 12th century, which would indicate that pre-Conquest townships were less systematically organised and that the Norman incomers radically reconstituted rural arrangements.[6]

But no sooner had these new arrangements come into being than they were subject to the pressure of population growth. The response was threefold. The first was the founding of new townships, made possible by the abundance of moorland; clear evidence of this is the place-name element *New*, as in the Teesside township of Newsham.[7] Similarly, large townships were split into two or even three, identified by the prefixes North and South, East and West and Upper and Nether. For example, the Durham township of Rainton was divided into East Rainton and West Rainton in the late 12th century, each with a different but clearly planned tenurial structure.[8] Thirdly, but less radical, was the creation of additional holdings within existing townships. The survey of the episcopal estate commissioned *c.* 1380 by Bishop Thomas of Hatfield (1345–81) shows that in 58 townships in Durham around 1,600 new tenements were created, which brought nearly 4,000ha into cultivation. In some places, these holdings were clearly the outcome of landlord planning; but elsewhere the evidence indicates that they were the product of a more piecemeal and perhaps unlicensed process.[9]

In addition, discrete farms were created, which from the outset resembled those of today. For example, the huge expanse of moorland between Durham and Chester le Street was probably empty in 1100, apart from the small townships of Plawsworth, Old Durham and Kimblesworth (Fig. 4.7). (By 1311, six substantial farms – Crook Hall, Dryburn House, Cater House, Earl's House, Hagg House and Harbour House – had been carved out of it, as well as a new village with the giveaway name of Newton, and the demesne farm at Finchale, the cell established by the cathedral

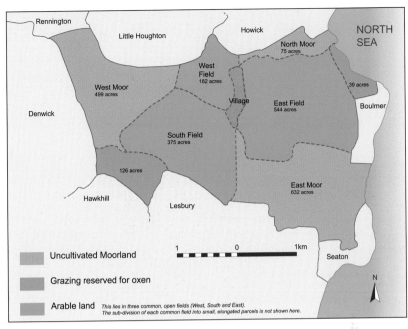

Fig. 4.6 Longhoughton. *Longhoughton, a township of above average size, was one of the 66 townships that comprised the barony of Alnwick, the largest of the 20 baronies created in Northumberland between 1095 and 1135. All but 17 of the townships were held by 22 feudal tenants, but Longhoughton was among those retained in demesne. Evidence from 1353 shows that it was unusual in having no freehold tenants, but there were 28 bondmen, each with 24 acres (9.7ha) of arable land, and 29 cottars. There was a manor house from which the demesne farm of 240 acres (97ha) of arable and 24 acres (9.7ha) of meadow was run, and also two water mills. The annual value then was just over £25, compared with £92 in 1289, before the depression caused by the Scottish wars and the Black Death.*

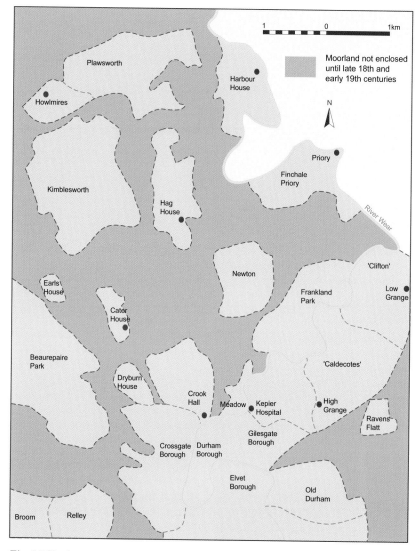

1   0   1km

Moorland not enclosed
until late 18th and
early 19th centuries

N

Plawsworth

Harbour
House

Howlmires

Priory

Kimblesworth

Finchale
Priory

Hag
House

River Wear

Newton

'Clifton'

Earls
House

Frankland
Park

Low
Grange

Cater
House

Beaurepaire
Park

'Caldecotes'

Dryburn
House

Crook
Hall

Meadow

Kepier
Hospital

High
Grange

Ravens
Flatt

Gilesgate
Borough

Crossgate
Borough

Durham
Borough

Elvet
Borough

Old
Durham

Broom

Relley

Fig. 4.7 Enclosures around Durham.
*Apart from the three villages of Old Durham,
Kimblesworth and Plawsworth, it is fairly
certain that all other settlements were enclosed
from the moor between c. 1100 and 1311,
when Harbour House was created. Three were
hamlets (Newton, Relley and Broom); two
were parks (Frankland and Beaurepaire);
the rest were farms. At this time, what is now
the City of Durham comprised four separate
boroughs: Durham belonged to the bishop;
Elvet and Crossgate to the cathedral priory;
and Gilesgate to Kepier Hospital. Within
their bounds were numerous small closes.*

priory in the 1170s. The vast stretch of
moorland south of Hexham underwent
a very similar development. Three
hamlets were created – Dotland,
Yarridge and Coastley – and about 50
small farms, consuming between a
quarter and a third of the available
land.[10] These new farms and villages
were the consequences of formal acts by
the great landlords who owned the
moorland, in these cases, respectively,
the Bishop of Durham and the
Archbishop of York. Most of these
various forms of colonisation were most
numerous in the central and western
parts of the region, where unsettled land
was most abundant. It is important to
remember, however, that despite these
substantial and impressive inroads into
these tracts of moorland, large areas
remained unenclosed and uncultivated
until the late 18th and 19th centuries.

This period, particularly the first
three-quarters of the 12th century, was
the great age of monastic foundation.
In this region, however, the pattern is
skewed by the great influence of
Durham Cathedral Priory as the
trustees of St Cuthbert. The only other
monastic house in County Durham
was the tiny nunnery at Neasham in
the far south, founded in the
Wapentake of Sadberge while it was
still part of Northumberland. The
Priory's ability to defend St Cuthbert's
land is well attested by its victory over
Bishop Hugh of le Puiset's son, Henry,
whom it persuaded not to found a cell of Guisborough Priory on moorland just
outside Durham.[11] Thereafter, the only other monastic houses in the county were
the Priory's own cells at Finchale, Jarrow and Monkwearmouth.

The situation in Northumberland was different; between 1085 and 1165 six
monasteries and three nunneries were founded, giving representation to three of
the new monastic orders. The earliest of these foundations was Tynemouth
(c. 1090), a cell of the Benedictine abbey of St Albans; then came Hexham 1114
(Augustinian Canons), Brinkburn 1135 (Augustinian Canons), Newminster
1138 (Cistercian Monks), Alnwick 1147 (Premonstratensian Canons) and
Blanchland 1165 (Premonstratensian Canons). The nunnery of St Bartholomew
in Newcastle was probably founded by King Henry I, but the origins of the other
nunneries at Holystone and Lambley are obscure. In addition, Durham
Cathedral Priory had cells on Holy Island and the Inner Farne and Tynemouth
Priory maintained one on Coquet Island.

Monasteries contributed to the number of discrete farms that existed by 1300.
Durham Cathedral Priory had 22 scattered around the county, while in
Northumberland 15 belonging to Hexham and Newminster can be identified.
That at Sturton Grange near Warkworth belonging to the latter is particularly
interesting in that its boundaries, which can be traced from the charter evidence,

still survive.[12] Most were carved out of moorland but there were instances of village destruction to make a farm. For example, the Cathedral Priory appears to have turned Ketton into a farm and resettled the village as Newton Ketton on the adjacent moorland. Similarly, Kepier Hospital near Durham converted the neighbouring villages of Caldecotes and Clifton into farms, High Grange and Low Grange respectively.[13]

Monasteries were not the only additions to the landscape. In 1100, there were around 130 parish churches, a very small number considering that the number of townships was close to 1,000. To cater for the growing population (and also for the convenience of landlords) around 160 new churches came into being. They did not enjoy parochial status, however, but were 'chapels of ease' catering for outlying parts of larger parishes and very much subordinate to the parish church. Good early examples have survived at Seaton Delaval and Old Bewick in Northumberland.

Moorland was also enclosed to create parks, which served a variety of purposes, some economic and some recreational, as well as being status symbols. They were the work of the region's greatest landowners, since only they had the necessary land and wealth. The largest was Beaurepaire (now Bearpark), owned by the Cathedral Priory, at the centre of which the priors built a palatial manor house. Covering over 600ha, it was one of the largest in England. Assembled in the 13th century, it comprised the land of a village named 'Crukton', which the monks depopulated, and tracts of adjacent moorland gifted by the bishops. When complete, it was surrounded by a wall. There were at least 15 other major parks within the region, among the most notable being: Auckland Park (next to Auckland Castle) and Stanhope Park (within the Forest of Weardale) belonging to the bishop; the East and West Parks attached to Brancepeth Castle; and Hulne Park and Cawledge Park belonging to the lords of Alnwick (Fig. 4.8).

The third major aspect of landscape development in this period was the borough. Indeed, the most prominent Norman settlers acted in accordance with

Fig. 4.8 Beaurepaire. Durham Cathedral Priory's enclosed park of Beaurepaire comprised the village of 'Cruckton' (which the monks depopulated), given by Gilbert de la Ley, Lord of Witton Gilbert, before 1213, and blocks of moorland granted by bishops Nicholas Farnham (1242 and 1248), Robert Stichill (1267) and Richard Kellaw (1311). The manor house was built by Prior Bertram Middleton in 1258, but needed extensive rebuilding after the Scottish raids of 1315 and 1346. Before the Dissolution of the priory in 1539, 26 closes were created for growing cereals and hay and for controlled grazing; the rest of the land was rough pasture and woodland. In the 150 years after the Reformation, the Dean and Chapter (which replaced the monastery in 1541) gradually divided the park into farms.

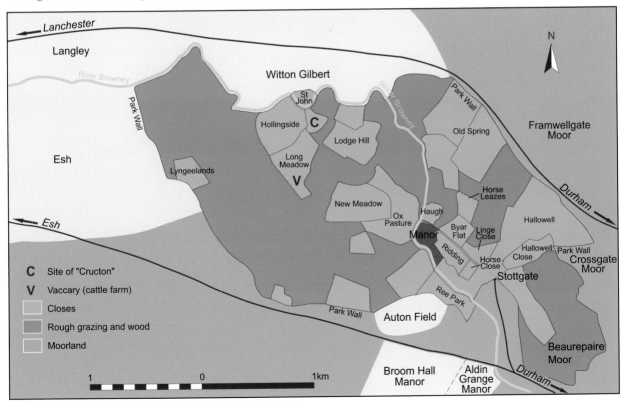

Fig. 4.9 'Forests' and territorial divisions (counties, wards, liberties and debatable grounds) in northern England. *In the medieval period the term 'Forest' was applied to large territories legally reserved as hunting grounds for the king and Border lords such as the Bishop of Durham. A Forest could include farmland, moor and settlements as well as woods; the term, however, often led historians to an inflated idea of the extent of woodland in the medieval landscape. There were Forests in lowland areas, but most lay in upland dales and moors, delaying the expansion of peasant settlement there. In the 13th and 14th centuries many of the Forests were progressively settled by farmers and miners, with fragments surviving into modern times as deer parks (based on Smailes 1960).*

what appears to have been a widely accepted development formula: castle or manor house + borough + church (parish church or chapel or monastery). In County Durham, 11 boroughs can be identified. Seven – Durham, Gilesgate, Sunderland, Gateshead, Bishop Auckland, Stockton and Darlington – were episcopal foundations, while two, Crossgate and Elvet, located on the outside of the loop of the River Wear at Durham, belonged to the Cathedral Priory. The others were founded in the Wapentake of Sadberge before it was sold to Bishop Hugh of le Puiset: Hartlepool, by the Bruces, and Barnard Castle, by the Balliols.

The last neatly illustrates the formula and also the comprehensive scope of Norman landscape restructuring. The centre of the pre-Conquest estate granted by William II to Guy de Balliol was at Gainford. His decision to move it 13km upstream was dictated by the ideal site for his castle, the vertical rock overlooking the river. The borough, created by his immediate successors in front of the castle, took the form of a wide street suitable for a market, at each end of which streets branched off at right angles. At its eastern end a church was built, but without parochial status: it remained a 'chapel of ease' within the ancient parish of Gainford until the 19th century. The original burgesses were probably drawn from the neighbouring township of Marwood, which the Balliols destroyed to create a park (Fig. 4.9).

Eleven boroughs also came into existence in Northumberland, although the war-torn conditions in the county meant that not all were successful. The most notable was Newcastle upon Tyne, which grew from the settlement by the castle, founded

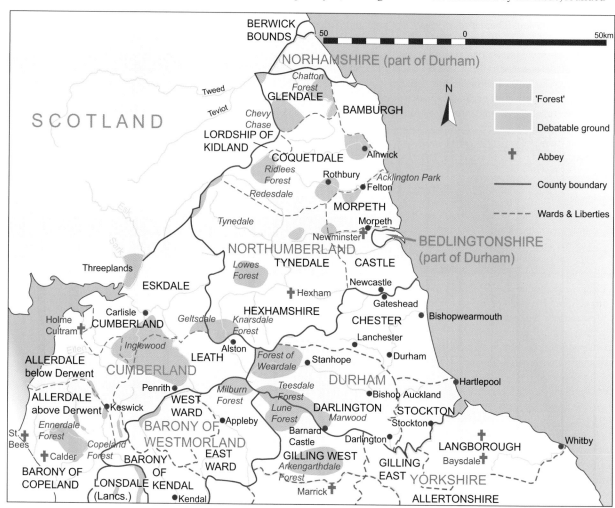

in 1080, to be one of the largest and most important boroughs in England, a fact demonstrated by its elevation to county status in 1400, only the fourth borough to be so honoured. It was of royal foundation, as was Bamburgh, which never prospered, allowing its skeletal topography to reveal the original concept. The same can be said of Wooler, Corbridge, Norham, Alnmouth and Newbiggin, but Alnwick, Morpeth and Hexham did develop into recognisably urban settlements.

Boroughs had three significant landscape features. Universal was the layout of the burgage plots, long and narrow in shape and set end-on to the street, and the vennels that broke them up into blocks and allowed access to the back lanes. A detailed study of Alnwick revealed that the town was laid out with the use of standard measures, so that the tenemental structure was in no way haphazard or casual.[14] The original form of burgage plots is most clearly evident at Warkworth and at the north row at Rothbury, especially when viewed from the back lanes. Warkworth, which can be described as a 'failed' borough, is another good illustration of the Norman formula. At the bottom of the hill stands the ancient parish church, in front of which was a triangular market place, now partly built over. From this the main street extends southwards up the hill to the castle, with the burgage plots abutting it at right angles (Fig. 4.10).

All the region's boroughs had burgages but only four had walls. The earliest was Durham, where there were wooden walls by 1006. They were rebuilt in stone by Bishop Ranulf Flambard (1099–1128) to enclose the castle and cathedral, but were only extended around the market place after a devastating Scottish raid in 1312. Newcastle's wall was much longer – about 3km – and was built in the hundred years after 1260. The wall at Hartlepool, which cut off the peninsula on which the town stood, was a response to Scottish raids in the early 14th century. The same reason applied at Alnwick, though its wall was not built until the mid-15th century. Sections of wall are still extant and visible at all four boroughs.

The third of the boroughs' notable landscape features was the bridge, the building and maintenance of which was a pious act. Because the region's seven main rivers flowed from west to east and were sufficiently wide to constitute serious obstacles to movement, the need for bridges was urgent. In the course of the medieval period at least 16 were built in stone, starting with Framwellgate Bridge over the Wear at Durham built by Bishop Ranulf Flambard in the second decade of the 12th century. The most complete is that at Warkworth, which has retained its defensive tower. In fact, there were only two places where a needful bridge was not built, Norham and Stockton on Tees, where the river crossing was by ferry.

One borough, Berwick upon Tweed, requires separate mention. Founded by the Scottish king, David I (1124–53), it became the principal port of Scotland and at the height of its prosperity towards the end of the 13th century it was probably larger than Newcastle upon Tyne and was dubbed the 'Alexandria of the North'. In March 1296, however, it was devastated by the army of Edward I,

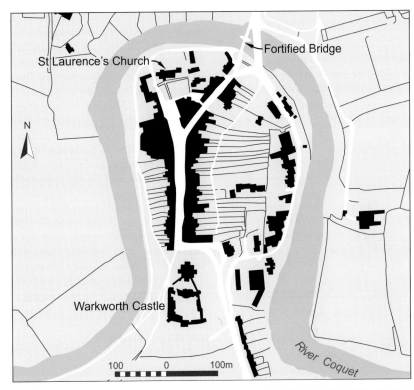

St Laurence's Church

Fortified Bridge

N

Warkworth Castle

100   0   100m

River Coquet

Fig. 4.10 Warkworth was a planned medieval borough located within a loop of the River Coquet close to the Northumbrian coast, and laid out along a single, broad street between the massive castle and the church of St Laurence. Expansion of the town has been checked by the surrounding river and the medieval lay-out remains largely intact; its narrow properties derive from the original burghal plots and the fortified bridge (1379) over the Coquet is still in place.

a catastrophe from which it never fully recovered. Although it was to change hands several times thereafter, from 1347 it was effectively an English town: its retention by England was in the end the issue that prevented peace between the two kingdoms. Its contraction due to its frontier situation is graphically illustrated by its Elizabethan ramparts, which encompass an area only two-thirds of that enclosed by the earlier wall.

Contraction, 1314–1600

Between 1296 and 1314 the region's prosperity and population were at their greatest, but in the following decades it suffered a series of calamities – failed harvests, plague and Scottish raids – from which it did not recover until the late 16th century.

The three disastrous harvests of 1315–17 were caused by atrocious weather and followed by extensive animal mortality, which continued until 1322. This resulted in severe economic depression, exacerbated by the almost constant Scottish raids. It is likely that the population declined, since it is clear that economic recovery in the 1330s and 1340s was only partial.

Then, in the summer of 1349 the region was devastated by the plague. Analysis of detailed evidence relating to 28 Durham townships reveals an aggregate mortality of around 50 per cent.[15] It is not unreasonable to assume the same elsewhere in the region. Subsequently, the plague returned on at least four occasions during the rest of the century, and in the last 20 years of it Scottish raids were again severely damaging, especially in Northumberland. The long-term consequence was a drop in population of about 40 per cent by 1400, and possibly more by 1450. Not until the last years of the 15th century are there even the faintest signs of an upturn.

This reduction in population inevitably had an effect on the landscape. Most obvious were deserted villages, which must include those where the site is occupied by just one or two farms as well as those with a total absence of habitation. An example of the latter is Woodham, now bisected by the A167 north of Darlington, where until recently there was nothing but fields. Woodham was one of the largest villages in the parish in 1340, but by 1426 it was deserted. Six kilometres away at Newton Ketton, the outline of the village green can be discerned, at either end of which is a farm, an arrangement that was in place by 1396.

Apart from the sheer reduction in population, another reason for desertion, clearly recognised at the time, was that many landlords found that arable farming no longer paid, expelled their tenants and turned the land over to grazing. Throughout the region, as elsewhere in England, the consequence was fossilised rig and furrow, most clearly seen in low light or light snow. The final total of medieval desertions has yet to be calculated, but research in County Durham has identified 59, while a survey of southern Northumberland has brought to light 30 examples. The Durham figure is reckoned to be 18 per cent of the total, that for Northumberland 14 per cent, the figures being close enough to give a fairly accurate erosion rate for the region.[16]

Falling population also meant that most of the chapels of ease built in the 12th and 13th centuries had become redundant by the time of the Reformation. Many have left no trace but in some cases parts of the fabric have survived, as at Wallsend (Holy Cross), or foundations are still visible, as at North Gosforth (St Nicholas) in the Melton Park housing estate.

But war did have some positive consequences for the landscape. From around the middle of the 14th century the gentry of Northumberland built towers, usually three storeys high and with walls 2.2m thick. Some are still occupied, but those in ruins appear to have been free-standing buildings. However, the excavations at Edlingham suggest that this was not normally the case and that most, if not all, towers were additions tacked on to an existing hall house.

The restored hall house at Aydon, near Corbridge, is a splendid example of this 13th-century style of gentry residence. Although the Crown jealously guarded its right to control castle building by means of licences to crenellate, it appears tacitly to have waived this requirement for towers, probably thankful that the leaders of Northumbrian society were prepared to see to their own defence. Henry V's survey of Border defences, made in 1415 as he prepared to invade France, lists 78 such towers, to which a further 35 were subsequently added.[17]

These towers were affordable by the gentry, even though their income from land was diminished by war. There were, however, a few castles of greater substance and cost for which licences were obtained, such as Chillingham in Northumberland and Lumley in County Durham, both comprising four towers linked by curtain walls (Fig. 4.11). The most spectacular, however, was the huge gatehouse castle at Dunstanburgh, built in the 14th century by the royal dukes of Lancaster. A similar castle, but on a smaller scale, was built in the 15th century by the Neville family at Bywell.

In complete contrast were the bastles, the vast majority of which were built in north Northumberland. Essentially farmhouses, they were modified versions of the traditional farmhouse, known as the longhouse, a two-room building, one for humans, the other for cattle. Bastle builders put one room above the other instead of side by side: cattle on the ground floor, humans on the upper floor. Bastles were built of stone and where possible roofed with slate, with access to the upper floor by either a retractable ladder or, later, an external stone stair. Bastle building began in the mid-16th century and was confined to a zone extending 32km in from the border, the maximum distance a raiding party could penetrate in one night.[18] They were a response to the difficult years of the reign of Elizabeth I, when the Scottish government declined to control the nefarious activities of its own Borderers. The accession of James VI to the English throne did not immediately end bastle building, however, which continued until the mid-17th century: clearly old fears died hard. Many still exist, some in use as outbuildings, some incorporated into larger houses, and others are in ruins, such as the conserved Black Middens, far up the North Tyne.

The medieval landscape remained basically unchanged until well after 1600. Not until after the Civil Wars did radical change come to the North East.

Fig. 4.11 Ford castle, controlling a fording point on the River Till, is of early 14th-century date and of the quadrilateral type with corner towers and strong curtain walls. The northern range was rebuilt as a mansion in the 16th century and there has been considerable later restoration and rebuilding on the site. St Michael's church (with the stump of a vicar's pele tower nearby) is older than the castle. In the 19th century a small, model village was built by Lady Waterford east of the castle to replace an older settlement.

YORKSHIRE

For Yorkshire, the medieval period began with the political and economic set-back of the end of Roman rule; its post-Conquest subdivision opened with the Harrying of the North in 1069–70, and the era eventually terminated in another social and political upheaval, the Pilgrimage of Grace in 1536–7. Between these watersheds, the region gradually recovered from post-Roman collapse and gradually adopted the systems of communal, open-field farming that were transforming the lowland English landscape, and experienced the establishment of a fully-developed system of feudal overlordship. As the centuries rolled on feudalism decayed and the open fields were dismantled. Often perceived as an era of stability and conservatism, this long medieval period was a time of immense transformation, the marks of which remain prominent in townscapes, countrysides and communities across the region.

Despite severe setbacks, the medieval centuries witnessed the growth of Christianity from a minority cult that barely survived the Roman departure to a religion of immense power and influence, as expressed in the magnificence of York Minster and the ruined Cistercian, Benedictine and Augustinian houses. It also saw the collapse of the kingdom of Northumbria and the absorption of the north by the greater entity of England. Northumbria had but a brief lifespan, though in the 8th century the light of its Christian scholarship shone beyond the North Sea.

Few eras are as opaque as the 'Dark Ages' that followed the Roman departure; evidence for flourishing communities in this period becomes very hard to find. Pottery, once so abundant, may have ceased to be made and settlements, once so close together, are hard to detect, indicating pronounced population retreat. Romanised patriachs or warlords may have managed to preserve a shell of civilisation, while the great estates of the Roman era perhaps only gradually fragmented into their local components. York, the great fortress and *colonia*, had been in an advanced state of decay before the Roman departure and it did not revive until the late 7th century. However, a less spectacular legacy of Roman rule gave Yorkshire a rather special place in the restoration of civilisation; the *eccles* place-names associated with the lost kingdom of Elmet in the south of Yorkshire derive from the Latin *ecclesia*, signifying 'a church'. Places like Ecclesfield and Eccleshill seem to have sustained Christian congregations in the period between the departure of Rome and the eventual re-conversion to Roman Christianity in the middle of the 7th century.[19]

Christianity in Yorkshire

Christianity seems to have maintained a lingering presence in Elmet. Meanwhile, the Irish church was developing in the west. In 563, Columba established a monastery on Iona in western Scotland and about 70 years later Christianity was transplanted to Lindisfarne in present-day Northumberland. Whatever the circumstances of indigenous Christian survival may have been, these developments would place Yorkshire at a cultural cross-roads. About 600, the Anglo-Saxons appear to have defeated British forces at a battle near Catterick, and north-east England could then have turned towards a pagan, Nordic, North Sea trading arena. The missionaries of the Irish church had become active in northern England, however, and the upland fringes of England could have become allied to that esoteric realm of wild seas, saints and romantic legend. But again, many lands to the south of Yorkshire looked more readily towards Rome, the lost centre of authority and now the focus of religious orthodoxy. These issues were decided at Whitby in 663 by King Oswy of Northumbria, who adjudicated on the rival claims of Colman, Bishop of Lindisfarne, who spoke for the Irish church, and Wilfrid, Abbot of Ripon, who presented the Roman case. The judgement, in favour of the latter, certainly reflected the *realpolitik* of the issue.

It is unlikely that the Synod of Whitby produced instant transformations in the physical landscape of religious worship. Sometimes, the springs, wells and ponds that were central to pagan worship were commandeered by the clergy. Much early missionary activity was focused on the social elite, while early churches are very difficult to identify, particularly since, if successful, their fabric tended to be incorporated into subsequent enlargements. While services held beside preaching crosses may have provided many communities with their first exposure to Christian worship, early church foundations were on royal estates. These churches were minsters, bases for bodies of clergy who were active in the surrounding area, and places which provided the king with literate clerics who could record the affairs of the royal estate. Many minsters can no longer be identified, but probable examples include Ledsham, retaining its 7th-century nave, Sherburn in Elmet, Bramham and Kirkdale. In subsequent generations of church establishment, the founders were the owners of estates who created places of worship for their families and their retainers; and then for their tenants, converting the estate into the parish in the process.

Paralleling the provision of Christian worship for aristocrats and then for lay folk was a process of monastic foundation. Essentially it was a story of two parts separated by the interregnum of plundering and decay associated with the Viking raids. The first phase was set in train by Bishop Wilfrid in the mid-7th century, while the phase following the Norman Conquest involved numerous orders, though in terms of wealth and impact the Cistercians were dominant in Yorkshire. Indeed, the Cistercian influence upon the landscape is a defining aspect of Yorkshire's heritage. The conversion era was quite strongly established in Yorkshire by the time that a formalised monastic movement was established. Wilfrid, influenced by a youthful trip to Rome, re-formed the former Irish monastery at Ripon in 661, under the patronage of the sub-king Alchfrith. The old minster church at York was renovated, while Whitby developed a cult of the Deiran king Edwin (616–33) and one of its monks wrote a life of Pope Gregory, whose Roman missionaries had brought Edwin and his kingdom to Christianity. This chapter of optimistic religious expansion ended with the onset of Viking raids from 793, targeted on affluent churches. In 865 this periodic raiding ended when Ivar the Boneless sailed his fleet up the Ouse to take York, the Northumbrian capital, in 866 (Fig. 4.12).

Paganism once more dominated society in the north-east of England and though Christianity was generally restored after Alfred's defeat of Guthrum in 878, the monastic impetus was lost. It was not really regained until after the Norman Conquest, when continental orders vied to gain the favour of the Norman king and his supporters. The initiative might have been regained by the Benedictines, or by the favoured Cluniacs, with their appetite for ceremony. In the event, it was the Cistercians, austere and uncompromising, who gained the most. They showed little interest in mission, removing villages such as Herleshow or

Fig. 4.12 Major Benedictine and Cistercian monasteries. Numerous medieval monastic orders influenced the North East and its landscapes. Up to the 10th and 11th centuries Benedictines were prominent, especially around York and in coastal areas. In the first half of the 12th century Yorkshire became primarily Cistercian territory, with new monasteries influencing the wider landscape through a network of large outlying farms (granges and vaccaries). A group of important Cistercian houses (Rievaulx, Fountains, Jervaulx and Byland) was established on the eastern and western fringes of the northern Vale of York. In the same period, major Cistercian monasteries were founded at Kelso, Melrose, Jedburgh (all Cistercian) and Dryburgh (Praemonstratensian) in the dales of Tweed and Teviot in southern Scotland, an outcome of the strong secular and religious linkages between Yorkshire and Scotland encouraged by King David I at a time when the division between Scotland and England was still fluid.

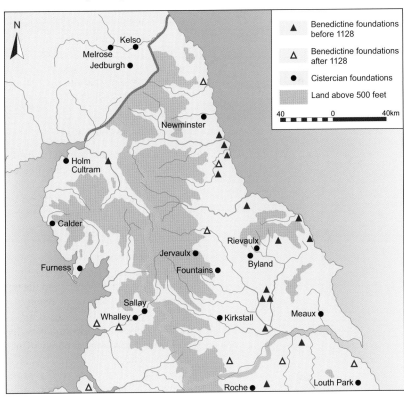

Melse that intruded on their solitude. It was their lust for isolation that positioned them to take the most advantage of northern territories, which were largely empty (or relatively easily emptied) of people. Dissidents from St Mary's, York, were adopted by the Cistercian Order and they established St Mary *ad fontes*, Fountains Abbey, and from then until the eruption of the plague the fortunes of the order in England grew and grew. By a piecemeal process of winning endowments from the devout, from nobles with souls that were far from secure, by bullying and by more blatant extortions, abbeys such as Byland, Kirkstall, Meaux and Jervaulx gained estates extending far beyond the abbey precincts. Two Cistercian abbeys, Fountains and Rievaulx, were immensely privileged and at the peak of monastic fortunes in the mid-12th century, Rievaulx supported 140 monks and 500 to 600 lay brothers (Fig. 4.13). The voracious appetite for territory and the use of work forces composed of semi-educated lay brethren provided the dynamic for Cistercian success. This concerned not only the raising of sheep and sale of fleeces to continental merchants, but also the breeding of other livestock, mining and the operation of smelters and forges. Numerous other orders were also active in Yorkshire's 70 or so monasteries: the Benedictines with new houses and refounded ones such as Whitby; the severe Premonstratensians at Easby and Coverham; the more approachable Augustinians with priories at Bridlington and Bolton in Wharfedale, who provided clergy for scores of churches; as well as various lesser movements (Fig. 4.14). There can be no more telling monument to the economic success of Yorkshire's medieval monastic movement than the echoing *cellarium* at Fountains, a vast cellar or storehouse, resembling some gigantic Gothic tunnel, where the produce of the estates was stored.

The arrival of the Black Death in 1349 was a landmark for monastic affairs as much as for others. When Fountains and Rievaulx were established, recruits thronged to take up the severe vocation. The plague hit the great abbeys as hard as other communities – Kirkstall was left with just 17 monks, less than half its previous total – and after the successive onslaughts of disease the stream of new recruits had dried to less than a trickle. The sense of vocation had withered. For those with futures to make, empty land-holdings were now available on attractive terms. The rise of monastic fortunes had been paralleled by a popular disenchantment with a movement that seemed to have lost its spirituality; the sleek abbot or prior with his hawks, his hounds and his deer park had become a target for contempt. When the Dissolution brought a formal end to the movement, the monasteries were near-empty echoing chambers: just 22 clerics at Rievaulx and 25 at Guisborough. Over-ambitious building programmes and poorly-costed pension schemes for maintaining elderly 'corrodians' could have contributed to the decline. Meanwhile, the abbey estates and granges had for long been let out to tenants, reducing the great colonising establishments of the 12th century to mere landlords.

For the lay people, the fortunes of the parish churches, which expanded gradually into the voids left by the monasteries, mirrored the prosperity of their communities. Where population growth was rapid and sustained, prosperity was reflected in new side aisles, lengthened chancels, heightened towers, battlements, clerestoreys to illuminate the interior and new, brightly glazed windows displaying the latest Gothic tracery. Yorkshire contains excellent examples of all the main styles in ecclesiastical architecture: Saxon Romanesque at Kirk Hammerton; Norman at Stonegrave; Early English, serenely displayed at Skelton; Decorated – terminated by the plague – at Patrington; and Perpendicular at Conisbrough. With about 500 medieval churches in Yorkshire, the list of showpieces could be far longer. One particular characteristic of Yorkshire to note is the fine Danish or Anglo-Danish hogback tombs in churches such as Brompton-in-Allertonshire and the gradually developing taste for buildings with excellent proportions and restrained decoration. It was exemplified in the late-medieval wool churches of the western uplands with their

OPPOSITE PAGE:

TOP: *Fig. 4.13 Rievaulx was among the most distinguished of Yorkshire monasteries* and the mother house of a family of monasteries that included Melrose in the Scottish Borders. Founded in Rydale (North York Moors) in 1132, Rievaulx had a strong influence on the cultural landscape of northern Yorkshire as a leading producer and exporter of wool and a major landowner with a score of outlying granges and extensive grazing on the surrounding moors.

BOTTOM: *Fig. 4.14 Bolton Priory, established in Wharfedale by Augustinians in 1154*, managed wide territories and traded in wool, horse breeding, lead-mining and ironworking. At the Dissolution the estate was purchased by the Earl of Cumberland who converted the gatehouse to a lodge, which was extended in the 18th century to produce the present Bolton Hall. The wooded parkland, painted by Turner and Landseer and acclaimed by Ruskin, is set against the background of Bardon Fell.

long, low naves built in the Pennine Perpendicular style, as it would be in the similarly simple 'churchwarden'-style churches of the Georgian era, which still echoed late-medieval Gothic influences.

Despite the growth of settlements and their associated churches, Yorkshire is to a considerable degree an upland area in which population is thinly dispersed. Many families lived in the outposts of gigantic parishes, and for them regular churchgoing was an impossibility, whatever the strictures of the church. Vast parishes, such as Grinton in Swaledale, reflect the thinly spread congregations. Chapels of ease, like Hubberholme in Langstrothdale, could be founded or elevated to fill spaces in the pattern of worship, while tortuous 'corpse roads' were used, at least in part, to convey the dead to a distant burial ground. Many voids were unfilled centuries after the end of the medieval period, and it fell to the Nonconformists to fill them when industrialisation began to quicken the commercial pulse.

Community and settlement

Just as the abundance of pottery and other artefacts tells of well-populated Roman countrysides, their absence suggests decline in the aftermath of Roman rule. Even after a century or more of active archaeological investigation and use of modern sophisticated technologies, our understanding of settlement in the six or so centuries preceding Domesday Book (1086) is sketchy at best and it seems safe to assume that population gradually recovered from its collapse. Though levels comparable to those of the Roman era would not have been attained until long after Domesday, archaeological studies at West Heslerton, on the north edge of the Wolds, are showing that locally at least the countryside could be densely occupied centuries before then.

In the past, our understanding of settlement has been clouded by an assumption that patterns of place-names demonstrate which 'nation' invaded, colonised and settled where, and when. In reality, place-names simply tell us that, in terms of language, cultural dominance was exchanged or shared among Old English, Old Danish, Old Norse and Celtic-speakers; they tell us nothing of conquests or evictions, and very little of villages. Some names, like Walden, by Wensleydale, the valley of the foreigners or British, suggest ethnic segregation. Others, like Yockenthwaite – 'Yocken's meadow' – combine elements from different languages and may imply integration. Many names which became attached to (much?) later villages have nothing to do with villages as such, but refer to solitary farmsteads or physical features of the farmland or wildscape.

Pre-Conquest 'villages' may well have been less tightly nucleated and generally smaller than later examples, rather than being organised settlements with greens, tofts, high streets and back lanes. Villages would very frequently develop from several co-existing nuclei, like hamlets, greens, manor houses or churches. For one of these 'polyfocal' villages to emerge, an injection of energy was needed to expand population and fuse the different elements into a single entity. This might come from the reorganisation of a manor, the winning of a market charter or from industrial developments – which continued to produce polyfocal villages through the Industrial Revolution. Close studies of rural townships in Yorkshire are very likely to reveal a mass of deserted settlements, mainly farmsteads and hamlets. These lesser settlements often disappeared before or at the time of the Black Death, with numerous small, straggling roadside hamlets apparently perishing. In the first stages of population recovery, settlements were liable to desertion for other reasons. This happened at Heslerton, where the waterlogging of the pagan Anglian settlement caused a move to a drier site nearby.[20]

Just as deceptive as place-names in the creation of village myths was Domesday Book, the Conqueror's inventory of his taxable assets. The names that appear are those of estates and townships and there was no attempt to record the names or sizes of villages – while the population recorded must be hugely underestimated for it would have been insufficient to keep the wildwood at bay. The Book is a fascinating review of the lingering damage resulting from the king's assault on the north. Insurrections, the assassination of Norman appointees and the ominous revival of Viking links provoked the Conqueror to impose the harshest of military solutions upon the dissidents of the north. This was the Harrying of 1069–70, the consequences of which, in terms of crippled and depopulated estates, would still be evident years later in the Domesday records of 1086. This distant event was extremely well documented, both by the testimony of near-contemporary chroniclers, such as Ordericus Vitalis and William of Malmesbury whose natural sympathies lay with the Norman dynasty, and in the terse but direct entries in Domesday. Though Ordericus's and Simeon of Durham's account is rhetorical at times, their evident revulsion at the evil perpetrated is genuine. All the evidence reveals a swathe of the north patterned with communities that had largely vanished, with gradually recovering estates and society, and others still that had been by-passed by the killing bands. Nidderdale was very badly mauled, with 13 of its 14 estates wasted according to Domesday, and here, and perhaps at some other places, there are strong suggestions that surviving feudal tenants were shifted from less-productive upland localities to re-populate lowland estates.

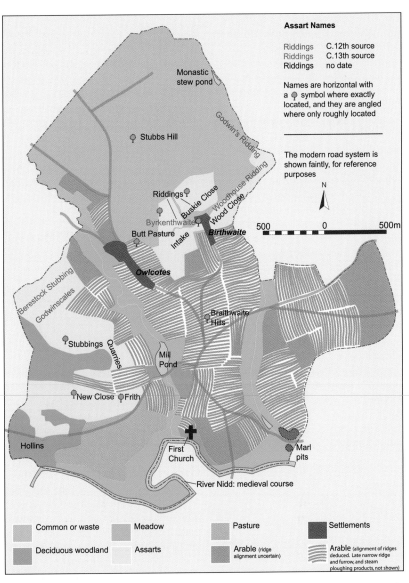

Fig. 4.15 A reconstruction of medieval land-use in the 12th and 13th centuries at Ripley, *north of Harrogate, north Yorkshire, showing the extent of arable land and alignment of plough ridges, as well as of the commons, woodland, meadow, pasture and assarts or 'riddings' (land reclaimed for cultivation).*

The landscape consequences of the Harrying extended far beyond desertion and decay. Where the pattern of settlement had been wiped bare, perfect conditions were created for the establishment of a great host of precisely planned villages, these being particularly numerous in the Vale of York. It might be an over-simplification to see these as purpose-built dormitories for the workers in a system of feudal estates, but the description is probably apt. Appleton le Moors is a good example, though there are many more, including those in the Dales, for example at East Witton and Arncliffe. Apart from late industrial settlements, few medieval villages have identifiable historical origins and those that have tend to be special cases. Kilnsey in Wharfedale and the nucleations of upper Nidderdale, for example, are descended from monastic granges, while Bainbridge and Buckden were forester bases in hunting country. The processes of village formation continued through the medieval period, with many examples, such as the well-known excavated example of Wharram Percy in the Yorkshire Wolds, resulting from the consolidation of several formerly discrete elements of settlement.[21]

Before the 14th century the physical and social climates favoured expansion to the very margins of the habitable area. Commons lost their trees, coppice woods

Fig. 4.16 Fieldscapes in many places record a long, gradual evolution from medieval open-field systems.
RIGHT: *a. At Clifton (near Dewsbury) the long, narrow S-shaped fields (the acres)* on lower ground near the village were formed mainly before the end of the 17th century by piecemeal consolidation of medieval open-field strips and eventually framed with drystone boundary walls. Wider elongated fields (doles) were made later by division of the common meadow, while rectilinear fields (crofts) were created further out on the poor soils of the common wastes at the township edges. Roads and lanes radiating from villages often perpetuate old tracks that gave access to the open fields and bounded the outer limits of the arable land.
OPPOSITE PAGE: *b. Following agreements between landholders, the medieval open-field strips at Middleton, North Yorkshire,* were gradually grouped together and defined by hedges to produce remarkably long, narrow fields running uphill and retaining the curving pattern of the earlier system. The sketch on the right shows how the medieval fields were formerly bounded by a dyke to the north and the wet, wooded land of Middleton Carr to the south (based on Raistrick 1970).

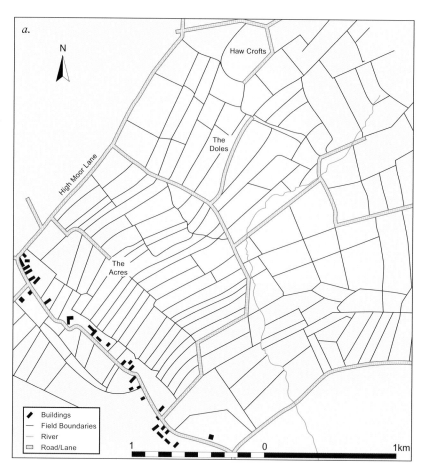

were established to meet timber demands and travellers must have heard axes ringing from every direction (Fig. 4.15). However, as the century ran its course, the climate deteriorated and families retreated from the impoverished margins. Disease spread among stock trampling mud in the sodden pastures and meadows, while the English defeat at Bannockburn allowed Scottish raiders to enter Yorkshire almost at will. By far the most devastating of the torments was the arrival of the Black Death in the middle of the century, with its several swift revisitations, which killed almost half the population in the course of a few years.

The 14th century was a watershed between expansion and retrenchment, but it also marked a gradual shift from the public to the private as feudal tenants became copyholders and communal lands were divided and hedged (Fig. 4.16). The difficulties of coping with tenants who had discovered the scarcity value of their labour, combined with the attractions of sheep rearing, gave many landowners a new perspective on the countryside. War and plague had totally extinguished relatively few villages in Yorkshire but the new surge in shepherding would empty strings of parishes, just as it was doing in the Midlands. Traditional sheep-rearing country, like the Dales, had come to terms with sheep and suffered less, but the High Wolds, the flanks of the North York Moors and the Vale contained much ploughland and suffered heavily as the new sheep-runs expanded. Wharram Percy was depopulated for the flocks of the Hilton family and by 1500 all that remained was a stranded church. Other villages were lost to the creation of aristocratic deer parks, like Wilstrop, while the post-medieval re-invention of the landscape park caused the removal of venerable villages, such as Hinderskelfe and Nidd.

Though deserted villages littered the medieval countryside, they were often juxtaposed with places experiencing modest prosperity and expansion. For any

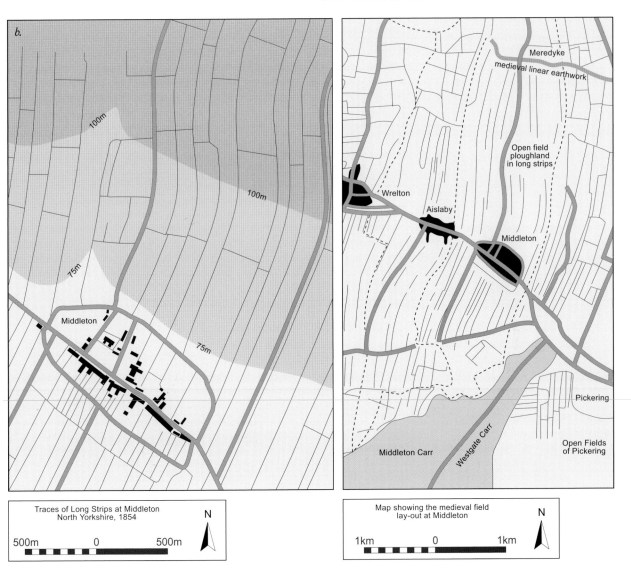

b.

Traces of Long Strips at Middleton
North Yorkshire, 1854

N

500m   0   500m

Map showing the medieval field
lay-out at Middleton

N

1km   0   1km

ambitious community the prerequisite for success was a market charter, normally
purchased from the monarch by lords keen to collect market tolls. Yet even with a
charter, the prospects for the average settlement were modest. Despite efforts to
regulate market numbers and competition, in areas like Wensleydale that had an
excessive number of markets there was insufficient trade to propel villages
towards true urban status. The great irony of medieval growth was that if a
settlement was exceptionally successful and became a town of some size, it would
have to suck a steady stream of immigrants in from its surroundings, for the
death rates in plague-ridden cities like York exceeded their birth rates. Where
industry existed, it was often practised as an adjunct to farming. Walk mills and
larger fulling mills punctuated the river banks, cloth would have been seen drying
on frames in 'tenterfields', and dyeworks and tanneries polluted the rivers.
Agricultural and forestry industries, such as bark stripping and charcoal-making,
were almost universal, but some specialisms were emerging, such as the linen of
Knaresborough and armaments-making in its satellite villages. By the end of the
medieval period a competent seer might have predicted that the area's long
experience of wool production and the abundance of swift little streams would
point the way to Yorkshire's industrial destiny.

The Yorkshire of the aristocracy

Whatever bonds of kinship and identity existed between the Yorkshire landholders and their tenants were broken after the Norman Conquest when the land was repartitioned between the king and his 26 tenants-in-chief. The largest of these held over 100 manors scattered within and between regions, so that the essence of aristocratic life involved frequent journeys between manors to consume the surplus production of one estate before moving on to the next. The span of affluence within the governing class was considerable, ranging from lesser knights, with estates sufficient only to provide them with arms and a mount, to the galaxies of scattered holdings held by the leading aristocrats. All these people shared the need for a secure home base, recreational facilities and for the confirmation and exaggeration of their status. Battlements and hunting rights went much of the way to meeting these needs.

As the members of the new aristocracy took over their estates, local labour forces must frequently have been called into service to raise castle mounds, or mottes, crowned with timber palisades. As fears of local insurgency receded, the timber house in the bailey might be abandoned in favour of a more commodious manor house. On the other hand, territorial ambition, wavering loyalties and distrust of powerful neighbours could develop the manorial bolt-hole into a credible castle. Yorkshire is home to a variety of Norman castle earthworks – the ringwork overlooking Middleham castle, the motte and bailey at Skipsea near Hornsea, originally with a tidal moat, and the unusual motte at Barwick that stands at the centre of its bailey. Enhancing such earthworks with thick-walled towers and curtain walls took castle-building out of the reach of the average lord, for the associated expenses could only be borne by the greater nobles; or by the monarch, who needed to maintain a martial presence among the fortifications of his barons. (York, Knaresborough and Scarborough were among the castles garrisoned by the king.)

Early castle-building was experimental, with emphases shifting between keeps and curtain walls. The triangular, curtain-walled enclosure at Richmond was an early innovation, built after 1071, with a stone keep being built over one of its entrances in 1150–70 (Fig. 4.17). Less vulnerable were designs without the corners that were easier to undermine. At Pickering, a royal hunting and administrative centre, a circular, stone shell keep was built on the motte, with wing walls linking it to the curtain that enclosed the bailey. At Conisbrough, the cylindrical keep of

*Fig. 4.17 **Built on a sheer rock at the entrance to Swaledale**, the tall, rectangular 12th-century keep of Richmond Castle, powerful and well preserved, dominates the old town clustered beneath it and is a focal point in one of the region's most picturesque and unspoiled urban landscapes.*

1185–90 was built on a huge splayed base which protected the foot of the wall. In several cases masonry additions developed the defensive concepts of earlier earthworks: in about 1250, Helmsley acquired massive D-shaped towers to guard the corners and entrance, while the Cliffords built a dramatic towered wall at their dynastic stronghold at Skipton. In the 14th century castles began to evolve in the direction of the palace rather than the citadel; Skipton castle had six gigantic, circular mural towers, a heavily-guarded inner gatehouse and four towers flanking its outer gatehouse.

By the end of the 14th century the quest for security had become so expensive that hardly any aristocrats could afford to build or even to undertake the modifications needed to create impregnable strongholds. Refinements in the arts of besieging castles and the appearance of mercenary forces resulted in the construction of a characteristically northern set of castles, which were castles in image rather than substance. They have been called the robber-proof palaces of the established nobility. Both Bolton-in-Wensleydale and Sheriff Hutton were palatial, built to the 'quadrangular palace castle' design of an enclosed courtyard with massive corner towers containing abundant accommodation for retainers, guests and their retinues. Their battlements suggested a martial status but their large windows, relatively thin walls and vulnerable angles of the square towers show these castles were about status, not defence (Fig. 4.18).

While the baronial castle in Yorkshire rose and then began the descent that would eventually lead to its becoming a stately home, the lesser aristocrats and country gentry sought to protect their goods and improve their status by imitating the works of the nobility. Among modest lords, homestead moats, with their references to the moats around the homes of the martial elite, were very popular, with more than 320 examples being recorded in Yorkshire. Markenfield Hall exemplifies the uppermost level of such developments, being built around 1318 when nearby Knaresborough was burned by the Scots. Spofforth Castle, a seat of the Percys, was in a different social league. The licence to crenellate the walls was gained in 1308, but it was probably more a palace and base for hunting than a castle. Similarly, Ripley Castle, with its late medieval gatehouse and keep, was more a fortified manor than a castle. The tower houses of the clergy and petty gentry that were scattered along the Scottish border zone were more defensive in character; Nappa Hall in Wensleydale, seat of the Metcalfes, was a southern outlier with two towers rather than one (Fig. 4.19).

Possession of one or more castles was an essential pillar supporting dynasties such as the Percys, Nevilles, Cliffords and Scropes. The medieval castle in Yorkshire was a defencework, but many castles never had to endure a siege and their day-to-day existence was as an administrative centre for the surrounding fiefdom, a social focus for the great families, their political allies and their guests, and a base for recreation, which usually concerned hunting in the adjacent chases and deer parks. Just as tastefully manipulated landscapes surrounded the great post-medieval mansions, so the countrysides around great abbeys and castles were likely to be embellished with artificially created sheets of water, surprise

Fig. 4.18 Castle Bolton in Wensleydale is a 14th-century castle of the 'quadrangular palace-castle' type, standing alongside a planned green village possibly older than the castle. The extensive ridge-and-furrow and lynchets close to the settlement are of uncertain date and perhaps partly post-medieval.

Fig. 4.19 Tower houses and pele towers, though not so numerous as in Northumberland, are found in small numbers in Yorkshire.

At Nappa Hall in Wensleydale, for example, the domestic accommodation is sandwiched between a greater and a lesser fortified tower of mid-15th-century date.

views, dramatically sited lists for jousting, vantage points and so on. Ravensworth Castle was surrounded by a great lake with an adjacent walled deer park and with formal gardens to grace the approaches. Another designed or ornamental medieval landscape was associated with the 14th-century castle at Harewood. It stood among gardens embellished with ponds and the upper rooms and rooftop walkway afforded views of the Wharfe valley and the nearby deer park.

The end of the medieval period is marked by the events of 1536, when 'pilgrims' from the north rallied at Market Weighton and marched south on what became known as the Pilgrimage of Grace. They were frightened, uneasy people, apprehensive that the Dissolution of the monasteries and the sale of their estates would put northerners at the mercy of southern speculators. The march failed and the retribution that followed changed the character of life in the North East. Their Yorkshire was far different from the Conqueror's realm and immensely changed from that which had existed at the time of the Roman departure. The great castles that had been built were now almost all decaying; the feudal peasantry of Norman times had become artisans, burgesses and copyholders; religion, once a source of unity, was now shrouded in schism, fear and secrecy. Villages had come and many of them had gone, while the land, once shared, was becoming privatised and parcelled up by unwelcoming hedgerows.

NOTES

1   Lyte 1920, 26–8.
2   Craster 1914, 389.
3   O'Brien 2002, 53–73.
4   Lomas 1996, 73.
5   Lomas 1992, 173–5.
6   Austin 1989, 164–7.
7   Pallister & Pallister 1978, 8.
8   Lomas 1992, 153; Fraser 1955, 53.
9   Lomas 1992, 152.
10 Lomas 1996, 84–7.
11 Scammell 1956, 110.
12 Hepple 2004, 89–115.
13 Lomas 1992, 142.
14 Conzen 1960.
15 Lomas 1989, 127–40.
16 Roberts & Austin 1975; Wrathmell 1976.
17 Bates 1891, 16–25.
18 Ryder 1992, 351–3.
19 Higham 1993, 99–101.
20 Powlesland 2003 .
21 Beresford & Hurst 1990.

5

The North East: Modern Period

D M MacRAILD and A W PURDUE

There can be no doubting the enormous impact of industrialisation and urbanisation on the economy and society in the late modern period[1] – roughly 1650 onwards – but perhaps an even greater influence on the landscape of the North East since the 16th century has been the development of agriculture. Even today, the greater part of the modern landscape owes more to agriculture than to any other human endeavour. Inseparable from this was the influence of the landed estate which, in the north-eastern counties, easily accounted for the largest proportion of the land, whether those of minor gentry or of great aristocratic proprietors. The influence of such estates upon the landscape went far beyond the utilitarian, as landowners shaped much of the countryside for aesthetic and sporting reasons.

This chapter traces the impact of human endeavour and economic development on both rural and urban landscapes in the North East in the modern period. Ranging from Yorkshire in the south up to Northumberland's border with Scotland, the following discussion emphasises the diversity of influences upon landscape.

CREATING THE EARLY MODERN LANDSCAPE: CONTEXTS AND CHANGES

To the eyes of later generations, much of the early modern landscape which had not yet been enclosed would have been unappealing, with its large open fields, its rather dreary villages often consisting of a line or two of cottages, and the general paucity of trees and hedgerows. Changes in farming practices and land tenure had been slow and incremental in the 16th and 17th centuries but quickened in the 18th, so that by the mid-1700s a rural landscape of farmhouses surrounded by consolidated farmlands with fields divided by hedgerows or stone walls, had largely been established (except in the uplands, which remained dominated by unenclosed commons). What constitutes a beautiful or pleasing landscape is notoriously subjective, but there can be little doubt that a combination of hard-headed commercial imperatives and the aristocracy's desire to sculpt the landscape to impress the viewer with their wealth and taste in the 16th–18th centuries, has resulted in a landscape that, for many people, is still the epitome of 'the English countryside'.

Enclosures and the cultivation of former wasteland produced the main changes to the rural landscape. Behind both were population increase, a prosperous agriculture and the gradual emergence of economic individualism that had previously been constrained by legal restrictions and military needs. In Yorkshire and Durham, the late feudal restrictions on the society and economy were eroding in the 16th century, but in the border county of Northumberland this only came with the end of border warfare and raiding in the 17th century, when a more peaceful and orderly society transformed retainers into tenants and encouraged both enclosures and the cultivation of waste, while enabling farming to become more productive.[2]

Although the manor house with its adjacent village surrounded by open fields was a standard unit in 1500, especially in Holderness, the Yorkshire Wolds and south Durham, there had always been many exceptions to this arrangement: dispersed farms with enclosed fields were not an innovation of the modern period. Though in many cases the demesne land lay intermingled with that of the tenants in strips, there were a number of demesnes in the North East where the land was enclosed and formed a discrete entity even in the late medieval period; a good example is Elvethall Manor on the edge of the Bishop's borough of Durham.[3] In the uplands of the Pennines and likewise in the Vale of York, extensive assarting (expansion into wasteland) had resulted in many isolated farms and small hamlets.[4] The old monastic lands were, for the most part, sold as estates or as parcels of discrete fields and there was considerable enclosure by agreement or sometimes by coercion in parts of the north-eastern counties during the 15th and 16th centuries. The impact on the landscape of Henry VIII's Dissolution of the monasteries was considerable. After the Dissolution many monastic buildings were simply left to decay, while others were adapted as houses by their new lay owners or had their stones used in the building of fine new manor houses, as in Yorkshire with Lord Fairfax's new house at Nun Appleton or Sir Stephen Proctor's Fountains Hall.

The amount of enclosed land had increased markedly by 1600 and, thereafter, the pace of enclosure quickened. The demise of subsistence farming in favour of commercial farming did not in itself create the pressure for enclosure for, though the balance between these altered, nearly all farmers had previously sought markets for some of their produce. Commercial pressures did, however, become more important with the end of the military dimension in the lord–tenant relationship. They led to the extension of pasture, especially for sheep grazing in the 16th century, and the subsequent move towards arable farming in the face of population increase. The commercial advantages that enclosures offered to farmers of more substantial consolidated holdings were obvious, as were the advantages for landowners of increased rentals from tenants working such holdings. Government, as ever, lagged behind the reality of economic change for it is clear that Tudor and even Stuart governments and parliaments retained an image of 'normal' England as that of manor house and dependent village surrounded by open-field systems, even when this world was being transformed by the sheep farming against which they vainly attempted to legislate. It was not by order of government but by individual agreement that most enclosures in lowland England were achieved.

By the end of the 17th century much of the land of the eastern coastal plain had been enclosed by agreement. The low-lying parts of the East Riding and North Riding were largely enclosed in the 17th century. In Durham, where the coal trade stimulated commercial attitudes, enclosures gathered pace from the Elizabethan period. Open fields had probably never been very common in the north and west of the county but the open fields of the south and south-east had nearly all been enclosed either by agreement or by agreement backed by decree from the Durham chancery by 1700 (see Fig. 6.12b). The village of Whessoe, near Darlington, disappeared and its common fields were replaced by separate farms, while on the lands of the Dean and Chapter of Durham, the 526ha Bearpark (formerly Beaurepaire) estate consisted by 1660 of 12 tenanted farms. In general, enclosure of open fields in lowland areas was accomplished by agreement and the enclosure of waste came later and was facilitated by Acts of Parliament, as in west and north Durham, where some enclosure of open moor and waste had taken

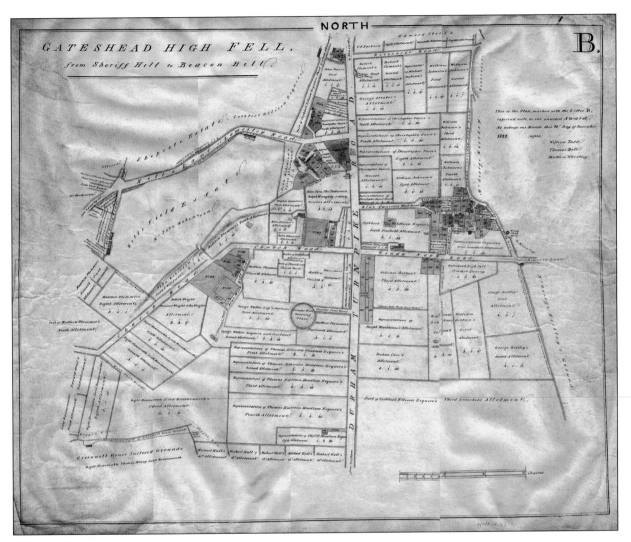

Fig. 5.1 Enclosure map of Gateshead High Fell, 1822. This is an unusually late enclosure map for an area so close to industrial Tyneside, but the land between Sheriff Hill and Beacon Hill had remained rather wild, common land as industrialisation and urbanisation proceeded nearby. The map depicts the meticulous work of the surveyors in their allotment of land to specific owners. Much of the area would soon be covered by buildings and become in practice part of Gateshead.

place by agreement but vast tracts were left to be enclosed by Acts in the 18th and 19th centuries as at Brancepeth (1758), Wolsingham (1755), Lanchester (1773) and Gateshead Fell (1822) (Fig. 5.1). By 1700 enclosed pasture was widespread in the Dales and the fields on the edge of the North York Moors had been enclosed. Many hectares of Holderness, the Vale of York and the Wolds remained unenclosed until a series of Acts between 1730 and 1810.

In much of Northumberland changes in agricultural practice and land tenure, which took place gradually in other counties, were concentrated into a much shorter period. In the uplands and the Middle Marches, open fields had never existed. Transhumance was still common in upper Tynedale as late as the early 17th century. In parts of the coastal plain a general rationalisation of manors by lords and tenants occurred in several instances, as at Chatton and Rock where the villages were divided into two during the 16th century and individual holdings were concentrated in one division rather than scattered over the whole area. However, defensive considerations in the lord–tenant relationship remained important in many parts of the county until the Union of the Crowns provided a fillip for enclosures and old patterns of tenure based on military needs gave way to commercial pressures. We can trace this rapid transformation in the sudden demise of the fortified farmhouses and bastles, still being built in the 17th century, and the appearance from the late 17th century of farmhouses designed to provide modest comfort. The declining need for armed tenants meant that landowners could alter the land use to sheep farming, evicting villagers and creating new single farms, which were then returned to arable use as the agricultural market swung back to favour corn.

In all three counties the enclosure of heath and moorland was in general a much later development and was facilitated by acts of parliament on a parish or area basis from the mid-18th century. The move to enclose wasteland seems to have spread northward from Yorkshire to Durham and finally to Northumberland. This resulted in the now familiar pattern of upland farms, their fields demarcated by stone walls, often encroaching on still-unwalled moorland where, as in most of the Dales, the adjacent farms had the right to graze sheep, cattle or horses upon stinted pastures.

Enclosures were instigated by landowners and more prosperous tenants for commercial gain, and these resulted in a social division of the countryside into three broad sections: landowners, farmers and landless farmworkers. The village unit was endangered by enclosures and many villages disappeared along with their open fields, as farmers moved out to new farmhouses, often building adjacent cottages for farmworkers among their enclosed fields. In Northumberland this process has been demonstrated at West Whelpington where the medieval village was abandoned and outlying farms established among their own fields. At Ogle, where there was demesne land of the Duke of Newcastle, a plan of the estate drawn in 1632 shows the state of the township just as the open fields were beginning to be enclosed and before the medieval village was abandoned as the inhabitants dispersed to outlying farmsteads. The actions of James Douglas, the Town Clark of Newcastle, at East and West Matfen and Clarewood in Northumberland illustrate the various ways in which a landowner could reorganise his estates: at Clarewood, where he was the sole freeholder, he was able to enclose all the land; in East Matfen he bought the principal estate from the Fenwick family but, as there were other freeholders who already had enclosed farms, he secured agreement among them for a division of the estate with the resultant disappearance of the already half-abandoned village; and at West Matfen, where there were eight other freeholders, he was unable to bring about an enclosure during his lifetime and, though this was achieved by Act in 1756–7, the village survived. Despite the phenomenon of the lost or abandoned village which has fascinated historians, many surviving villages display a continuity of the pattern of their original layout even as the very reason for it has passed.

In harness with progress in agricultural techniques, enclosures resulted in what has been seen as an agricultural revolution and great prosperity for landowners and more efficient farmers, a prosperity demonstrated by the many solid and even imposing farmhouses built in the 18th century. On the whole, agricultural change was characterised by new techniques rather than new technology and it has been claimed that the major innovation in implements, still not universal in the late 19th century, was the replacement of the sickle by the scythe. In areas of progressive farming, however, the land was improved by drainage and was, as for instance with Northumberland, dotted with lime kilns and designed farmsteads containing new barns, byres, stables and round sheds for horse-propelled threshing machines.

Though scenery was probably not a major consideration for most farmers, landowners and tenants did have aesthetic and stylistic concerns as well as economic ones. Aristocratic and, increasingly, gentry proprietors wished to display their wealth, position and taste to their neighbour, guest or passer-by and a great remodelling of the landscape resulted. Their houses, the view from the house and the stamp of their ownership upon even out-lying parts of their estates were important projections of themselves and their station. In the North East we can discern a gradual awakening, not just to influences from the south of England or the Scottish enlightenment, but to European influences as the wealth and prosperity of England and then Britain saw the provincial and the vernacular give way to the architect and the experience of the Grand Tour. The results of this development still constitute the bulk of what we term architectural and landscape heritage. In a sense this was Europeanisation, though the fervour for Chinoiserie in the late 18th century lent it an element of globalisation, but the movement remained very English in that it was lodged in the context of the landed estate.

MANAGING AND IMAGINING THE LANDSCAPE

As these influences took root, the epitome of fashion and good taste was to mould the landscape to imitate Italian art, in particular the paintings of Claude Lorraine. Freed from the last vestiges of the need for defence, fortified manors gave way to houses built purely for comfort and display, which became at once more imposing, more private and the centrepieces of man-made landscapes. This process occurred later in the North East than in the rest of England but we can discern its gradual northwards movement from the 16th century. In the East Riding, Burton Agnes Hall and Burton Constable Hall are examples of, respectively, early and late Elizabethan houses built (or in the latter case rebuilt) with little thought for defence. It was more than a century later, in 1622, that the outskirts of Newcastle felt safe enough for the Jacobean mansion of Denton Hall to be built. In rural Northumberland the gentry began to build Jacobean houses onto their sturdy towers, as at Belsay (1614) and Chipchase (1621). This slow move towards light and comfort rather than stout walls and defensive capability may well have been precipitate, for a large number of Yorkshire castles were defended during the Civil War. By the time that Capheaton Hall, to the west of Newcastle, was built in 1668, however, the need for defence was past. Newby Hall (1693), near Ripon, is a fine example of a late 18th-century mansion built to project wealth, leisure, display and taste with almost as much care lavished on the gardens and grounds as on the house itself, employing the foremost gardeners of the day (Fig. 5.2). Gardens could indeed become an obsession and at nearby Studley Royal, John Aislabie, once Chancellor of the Exchequer, retired in disgrace after the fall of the South Sea Company and devoted the rest of his life to creating a spectacular water garden with cascades and ponds interspersed with temples.

An increased desire for privacy led to internal arrangements, which kept servants and their quarters farther from the family, and to greater distances between the big house and the villages that had previously nestled close to the manor; gardens and parklands surrounded the house and roads that might bring passers-by too close were diverted. At Castle Howard, the Howards built a baroque masterpiece to replace the house that had been burned down in 1693 and the new mansion, the park and lake (Fig. 5.3) necessitated the demolition of the village. Often, however, the new villages were rather more pleasing and with better housing than their predecessors, partly because of philanthropy and partly due to a wish to enhance the appearance of the estates as a whole, examples being Capheaton in Northumberland, Sledmere House in the Yorkshire Wolds and Harewood House in the West Riding.

Pressures upon woodland in the late medieval centuries had resulted in a landscape increasingly denuded of tree cover, but this process was reversed from the early 18th century as landowners planted vast numbers of larch, pine, beech, ash, elm and oak in landscaped parkland and in small woods and copses, shelter belts and screens throughout their estates. Lord Ribblesdale was responsible for the planting of more than a million oak trees in the Ribble valley. Sir William Lorraine of Kirkharle in Northumberland planted 24,000 forest trees, 488,000 quicks and 580 fruit trees, while the first duke of Northumberland is said to have been responsible for 2 million new trees. On the Duke of Devonshire's Barden estate in Wharfedale

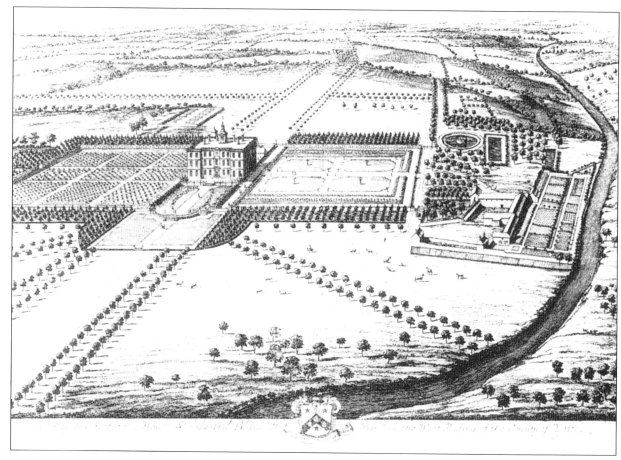

Fig. 5.2 Newby Hall. ABOVE: ***drawing by Kip** c. 1720;* BELOW: ***aerial photograph.*** *This North Yorkshire house, close to Ripon, is one of the finest houses in the North East. It was built for Sir Edward Blackett and completed in 1693. Redbrick and stone-quoined, it was built in the style of Sir Christopher Wren. The*

grounds and gardens were designed to complement the house and Blackett employed the leading gardeners of the day. Great changes were made when the house was sold by the Blacketts to William Weddell, who employed John Carr and Robert Adam to make the house a fitting context for the classical sculpture he had brought back from the Grand Tour and his set of Gobelins tapestries. The Kip drawing shows the west front and garden plan and the aerial photograph shows the developed relationship between house and grounds in the late 20th century.

nearly half a million trees, most of them broad-leaved, came to adorn the landscape.[5] Changing aesthetics and a persistent impulse to improve meant that the grounds of many great houses were re-landscaped again and again. At Belsay in Northumberland the appearance of the estate changed markedly in the mid-18th century and again in the early 19th century as one baronet opened up parkland vistas and a successor formed picturesque gardens and thick groves of rare trees to contrast with his new Doric house (Fig. 5.4).

Alexander Davidson, a great admirer of Nelson, planted trees at Swarland Park, north of Morpeth, to delineate the positions of ships in the fleets during the Battle of the Nile. The aesthetic imperative was important, but commercial and sporting aims also played their part. A ready supply of timber was important to estate management and copses and shelter were essential if the countryside was to provide good hunting and shooting. The influence of sport upon the landscape has been greatly underestimated and as hunting and shooting became more organised sportsmen proceeded to shape and nurture the land for the convenience of the fox, the partridge and the pheasant.[6]

ABOVE: *Fig. 5.3 Castle Howard. North Yorkshire, like Northumberland, has a large quantity of country seats still occupied by the aristocracy and landed gentry. Castle Howard and its extensive grounds were created between 1698 and 1738 for the great Whig magnate, the 3rd Earl of Carlisle. Along with Blenheim, it is seen as an outstanding example of the English baroque. Vanburgh and his assistant Hawksmoor were the architects. The grounds too are on a vast scale, with their rare trees and shrubs, towers and obelisks, the Mausoleum by Hawksmoor and the Temple of the Four Winds by Vanburgh.*

LEFT: *Fig. 5.4 Belsay. Belsay in Northumberland exemplifies the transition of great houses, with a Jacobean mansion built onto a medieval tower house, succeeded by Sir Charles Monck's new house some 320m away, built in the early 19th century in the Doric style. Belsay also demonstrates changes in landscape design and taste in gardens. Sir William Middleton, the mid-18th-century owner, provided walled gardens but opened up the surrounding landscape via hahas and designed eye-catchers to enhance the view, while Monck created densely wooded, Picturesque and Romantic gardens with lakes and cascades. A particular feature is the garden created in the quarry from which Sir Charles gained the stone for his Grecian temple of a house.*

Fig. 5.5 Gibside. *The partly demolished hall at Gibside lies on the south bank of the River Derwent in County Durham. Its extensive parkland setting was developed by George Bowes, an 18th-century coal magnate, and contains the 43m-high Column of British Liberty built in the 1750s at the end of the Grand Walk. The estate was later neglected and a considerable area reforested by the Forestry Commission. Old paths and rides were respected, however, and the estate, after long neglect, is now being restored by the National Trust.*

Romantic conceits and a desire for the picturesque resulted in follies and eye-catchers to enhance the view or to provide a curiosity for guests, such as the sham ruins built by Sir Walter Blackett on his Northumbrian estate at Wallington, the Gothic dog-kennels at Lancelot Allgood's nearby house at Nunwick, Robert Adam's Brizlee Tower at Alnwick Castle and the towering *Statue to British Liberty* built for George Bowes at Gibside near to Gateshead (Fig. 5.5). Such landmarks continued to be popular into the next century and the Penshaw Monument dedicated to the first earl of Durham has dominated the north Durham skyline since 1844 (Fig. 5.6). Even the most functional of farm buildings could be ornamented or disguised (Fig. 5.7).

Fig. 5.6 Penshaw Monument. *Dedicated to John George Lambton, 1st Earl of Durham, and based on the design of the Theseum at Athens, the monument was erected in 1844. This 'improbable blackened Parthenon' is sited on the edge of a magnesian limestone ridge and dominates the semi-urbanised surroundings of the Durham coalfield.*

Fig. 5.7 Ornamental features on farms and other rural buildings. *In both the 18th and 19th centuries there was a tendency to ornament farms and other rural buildings.* RIGHT: *Foal Park Farm, Constable Burton, north Yorkshire. The byres, barns and other functional farm buildings were constructed in the 1760s with rubble and are placed behind an architect-designed castellated façade in cut stone.* BELOW: *Deer shelter, Auckland Park, Bishop Auckland, County Durham. This Gothic-style arcaded enclosure was built in 1767 with a pinnacled tower designed for deer watching.* BOTTOM: *Horton Grange, Northumberland. A large model farmstead constructed in the 1850s on the estate of the Ridleys at Blagdon close to Newcastle. The building in the foreground with a substantial tower housed poultry and pigs.*

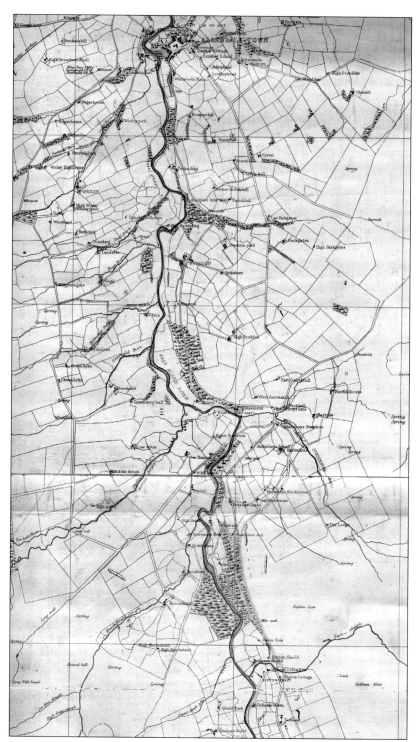

Fig. 5.8 Sopwith's map of the Allen Valley. This mid-19th-century map, a portion of which is reproduced here, was made by Thomas Sopwith, Chief Engineer of the Blackett-Beaumont mines. It reveals a landscape at once industrial and rural. Centuries of ever-more intensive lead mining had resulted in north Pennines valleys developing a unique landscape and economy where mines, smelting mills, chimneys and spoil heaps were interspersed among moorland and farmsteads. The number of farmhouses reflects the fact that lead-miners were also smallholders.

LANDSCAPE AND EARLY INDUSTRY

The countryside had never been solely agricultural, for the produce from agriculture needed processing. Flax was grown but also turned into linen, cattle were reared but skinners, tanners and glovers ensured that their hides were used for manufactured goods, while there were a host of cottage industries. Maltings and breweries were common features in towns and villages. Corn itself needed millers and wherever there were fast-flowing streams and rivers there were corn mills. Along the coast of the North Riding alum works were interspersed with farmland. In the East Riding, brick-making had a long history while the chalk pits of the Wolds provided the material for the manufacture of lime and whiting, and sand and gravel pits abounded in the lowlands. Landowners great and small were as concerned as farmers to maximise their incomes and sought to exploit the potential of their estates. This meant making the most of wealth that lay under the soil as well as profits from agriculture.

Coal mining had long been practised throughout the three counties wherever coal was close to the surface and grindstones had been extracted from northern quarries for centuries, but from the 17th century mineral extraction became more intensive. The rural landscape came to be dotted with coal and lead mines, lead-smelting plants and ironworks. In the dales of the northern Pennines a mixed agricultural and extractive economy resulted in small farmsteads, whose inhabitants worked in mines as well as fields (Fig. 5.8). Many of the unenclosed moors in the North East possess a striking legacy of the mining of lead and coal from the 17th century to the late 19th century, though some workings are much older. Marrick Moor, overlooking Arkengarthdale in north Yorkshire, is crossed by lines of derelict shafts, trenches and mounds, which follow the narrow, vertical veins of lead. Coal, generally extracted from shallow bell pits, was increasingly used from the 16th century as household fuel and dovetailed with lead-working in the Pennines where it was used for smelting. For the most part, mineral extraction and manufacturing were interspersed in a largely agricultural setting, but even in the 18th century there were hot spots, the area west of Gateshead being a good example. It contained many coal mines and was bisected by numerous wagonways (Fig. 5.9) along which coal was transported to the River Tyne. Cheap coal encouraged iron manufacturing along the Derwent valley, including German swordsmiths and Crowley's, the greatest ironworks in the country. Here, industry had a considerable impact on the landscape. Salt and glass works, also spin-offs from the coal trade, sprang up along the banks of the Tyne.

In Yorkshire, cottage-based weaving and spinning had complemented sheep rearing for centuries with fulling mills beating fuller's earth into the woven woollen cloth long before water-powered and then steam-

Fig. 5.9 Wagonways. *Stretches of old horse-drawn colliery wagonways linking mines to navigable water are still traceable in the landscape of the northern coalfield, often surviving as footpaths or raised grassy lanes. Risemoor Wagonway, constructed in the 1730s, was an extension of the old Crawcrook Wagonway, allowing coal from pits on Risemoor, Hedley Fell and Mickley Moor to the south of the Tyne to be brought down over the Stanley Burn and through Ryton to the staithes at Stella on Tyneside. The section shown in the photo runs close to Kyo Bog Lane to the west of Winlaton.*

powered mills were introduced. Knitting was an important supplementary occupation in the North Riding. By the early 17th century, Leeds was a major centre for the cloth trade and by 1800 the West Riding had become a major manufacturing region with woollen production concentrated around Leeds, Dewsbury and Halifax, and worsted production based around Bradford and Halifax (Fig. 5.10). Steel-making, which emerged later in the century, was largely confined to the Sheffield area. Before the woollen industry moved towards larger units of production, the productive process was sub-divided into a highly complex maze of specialities, which required organisation and management. It was not so much the size of the individual towns (for only Leeds and Bradford had over 100,000 inhabitants by 1881) that made the West Yorkshire wool industry such a phenomenon, but the archipelago of towns and villages (Fig. 5.11) engaged in different aspects of the same trade. The towns were already expanding rapidly, however, and the gradual introduction of steam power from the early 19th century gave an impetus to spectacular expansion. The change from cottage-based industry to large mills has left landscapes such as the Colne valley, where the survival of weavers' cottages and the now redundant mills which replaced their economic function demonstrate the development of industrialisation.

By later standards, neither industry nor towns dominated the landscape but rather intruded into it. Before the late 18th century, the port towns were most important but even the greatest of these, Newcastle and Hull (Fig. 5.12), were still largely confined within their medieval bounds. The basis for the growth of the North East ports was London's demand for coal, the greater part of which came from Newcastle though much of it was carried in ships from Hull and Whitby. Despite being denied the great boost that the Atlantic trade gave to west-coast ports, Hull became the third largest port in the country during the 18th century. Its trade was more diversified than Newcastle's but both towns were part of a complex trading network along the east coast and across the sea to the Netherlands, the

RIGHT: *Fig. 5.10 West Yorkshire, c. 1850–1980.* West Yorkshire conurbation grew as much inwards as outwards, absorbing outlying settlements at the same time as villages expanded towards the urban centres, from the mid-19th century. This area of sprawling urban settlement, roughly co-extensive with the old textile and coal-mining areas, has five major settlements (Leeds, Bradford, Halifax, Huddersfield and Wakefield) with many smaller towns and swollen villages between them.

BELOW: *Fig. 5.11 Hebden Bridge, west Yorkshire.* Hebden Bridge stands as a leitmotif for economic and industrial change. A crossing place for packhorses, its inhabitants were mainly handloom weavers and farmers until the early 19th century when the Hebden Water became part of the complex that powered the mills of the Calder and its tributaries, and factory spinning and weaving began. By the end of the 19th century the town was a centre for the manufacture of workers' clothing. Its architecture displays the distinctive feature of the 'top and bottom' house with the lower two storeys and the top two storeys as separate residences reached by the front or back doors. As its industry has declined, it has achieved a post-modern popularity as a desirable retreat, with artists replacing its former artisans.

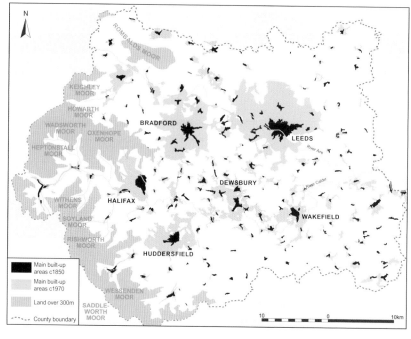

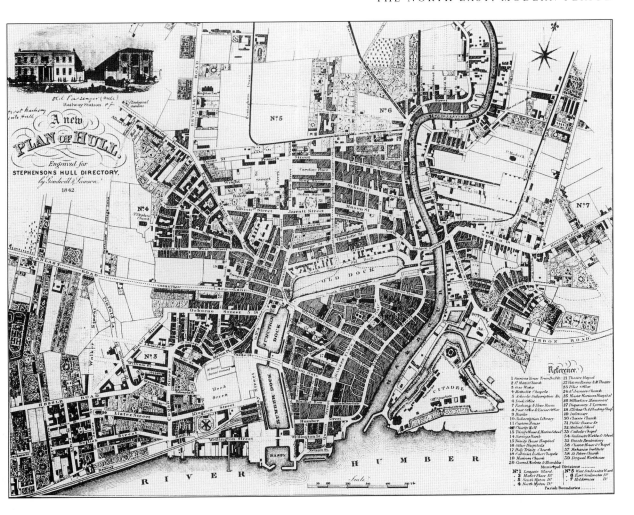

Fig. 5.12 Map of Kingston upon Hull, 1842. *This map of Hull demonstrates the considerable expansion of the docks that had taken place from the late 18th century. Though still compact by comparison with modern towns, Hull had already broken out of its medieval walls.*

Baltic and Iberia. Only in the last quarter of the 18th century did Hull move beyond its 14th-century defensive boundaries and it was not until the mid-19th century that Newcastle really expanded beyond its walls. Industrialisation and urbanisation can be too easily elided, especially before *c.* 1830; what was apparent to travellers passing through the environs of Newcastle or through the West Riding was the development of industrial areas, many of which were neither town nor country, characterised by the ubiquity of trade, manufacturing or mining, the growing population, the number of houses and the smoke.

Coal mining has had a decisive impact on the North East, in the Great Northern Coalfield of Durham and Northumberland and large areas of south Yorkshire. A mining community is by its nature ephemeral. Its first street, often Sinkers' Row, forecasts the fact that one day the last coal will be extracted. Most pit villages were an amalgam of the industrial and the rural, extractive industries set in the countryside (Figs 5.13 and 5.14), and their culture a hybrid of sectional workers' solidarity and rural sports. The life cycle of a single mine can stand for that of the industry as a whole. The modern period has seen the vast expansion of coal mining, accelerating during the 18th and 19th centuries, and then its decline and fall in the late 20th century. For at least 300 years, however, the coal industry dictated the economic rhythm of Durham and South Northumberland while it competed with textiles and iron and steel as the motive force for the South Yorkshire economy. Coal mining not only created villages and towns around the mineshafts, ranging from no more than a few rows of houses close to smaller and earlier pits (Fig. 5.15), larger

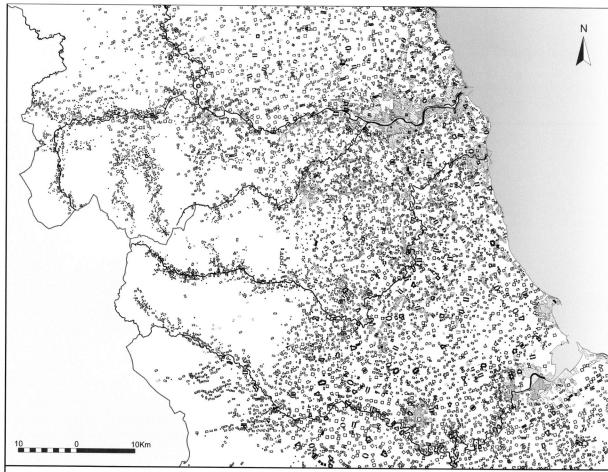

N

I. RURAL SETTLEMENTS

A. SMALL DISPERSED SETTLEMENTS
- 1. Detached building, country cottage, water mill, lodge, miner's cottage, etc.
- 2. Small or medium-sized farmstead.
- 3. Large farmstead.
- 4. Country seat with large ornamental garden or park.

B. SMALL NUCLEATED SETTLEMENTS (HAMLETS)
- 1. Irregular compact or loosely grouped hamlet of farmsteads and cottages.
- 2. Street hamlet.
- 3. 'Green' hamlet.
- 4. Hamlet suggesting former village green.
- 5. Hamlet form modified by country seat.

C. LARGE NUCLEATED SETTLEMENTS (VILLAGES)
- 1. Street village.
- 2. Street village suggesting former village green.
- 3. Other nucleated village suggesting former village green.
- 4. 'Green' village with :-
  - (a) triangular village green.
  - (b) spindle shaped village green.
  - (c) oblong village green.
  - (d) square village green.
  - (e) riverside village green.
  - (f) irregularly shaped village green.
- 5. Nucleated villages with pronounced 'row' development.
- 6. Village suggesting 18th century plan.

D. NUCLEATED NON-AGRICULTURAL SETTLEMENTS
- 1. Fishing village or small rural port.
- 2. Mining village with 'terraced' cottages in:-
  - (a) colliery estate (see also IICI(a)).
  - (b) ribbon development (see also IICI(b)).

II. URBAN SETTLEMENTS

A. EARLIER (GENERALLY MEDIEVAL) NUCLEI (in some cases with their urban functions decayed in modern times).
- 1. Narrow street.
- 2. Street market of -
  - (a) triangular form.
  - (b) spindle-shaped form.
  - (c) oblong form.
- 3. Square market-place.
- 4. Combined forms.

B. CENTRAL NEWCASTLE (associated with medieval plan features and superimposed development of the late 18th and earlier 19th century).

C. MODERN STREET PLANS
- 1. Built-up areas belonging largely to the Victorian era (ca. 1830-1920).
  - (a) Industrial 'grid-iron' plan (occasionally pre-Victorian with 'terraced' houses at high densities.

- (b) Uniform or complex ribbon development (the latter often pre-Victorian where associated with old arterials or country roads).
- (c) Open estate development (detached and semi detached houses).
- 2. Built-up areas belonging to the 'inter-war' period (ca.1920-1938) with detached or semi-detached houses at controlled low densities.
  - (a) Housing estates plans (geometrical or 'drawing-board' street patterns).
  - (b) Uniform or complex ribbon development.
- 3. Sea-front ('esplanade') development associated with seaside resorts.

III. SPECIAL SETTLEMENTS OR BUILDINGS

A. TRADITIONAL TYPES, either isolated or as dominant pre-urban nuclei of medieval towns.
- 1. Church or chapel (with or without vicarage).
- 2. Castle.
- 3. Pele tower or battle-house.

B. MODERN TYPES
- 1. Institution of relatively large extent (hospital, Public Assistance Institutions, etc.)
- 2. Colliery.
- 3. Other industrial establishments (lead mine, iron works, shipyard, etc.)

10   0   10Km

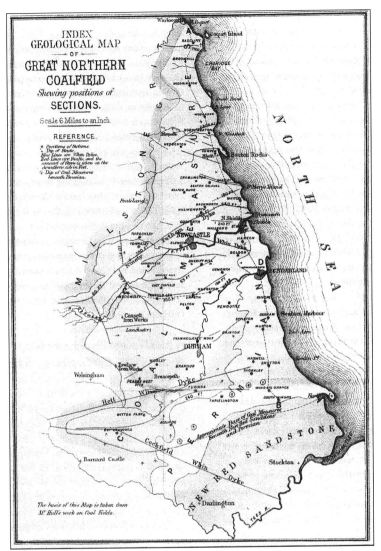

OPPOSITE PAGE:

Fig. 5.13 Rural and urban settlements in the area between south-east Northumberland and Teesside c. 1950. *This detailed map of the forms of rural and urban development in the section of the North East comprised of the riverside industrial and urbanised areas of the lower Tyne, Wear and Tees, the northern coalfield and the rural hinterland is part of a larger map compiled by the geographer M R G Conzen in the 1940s. A striking feature is the extensive, dense layer of coal-mining settlements (the great bulk of the settlements shown in red outside the major towns) superimposed on the rural pattern of villages and dispersed farmsteads (shown in black) of the coalfield areas between south-east Northumberland and the Tees lowlands. The oldest mining settlements, lying on the open coalfield to the west, were associated with numerous small pits and frequently formed distinctive straggling bands of small clusters and displaced settlement. On the concealed coalfield to the east the mines were deeper and the settlements on the colliery estates tended to be more compact and orderly. A comparable west/east contrast is found in the Yorkshire coalfields. The coal industry has declined to virtual extinction but the villages it created remain a significant element in the landscape.*

LEFT: **Fig. 5.14 Geological map of the Great Northern Coalfield (1850).** *Note how closely the map of settlements reflects the geology upon which mining villages were based.*

BELOW: **Fig. 5.15 Broomside Colliery.** *This County Durham colliery is shown by Thomas Hair (1810–75) in its pastoral setting with the pit-head contrasting with the fields and livestock around it. Wagons are being hauled up an incline by a stationary steam engine.*

communities such as that at Easington in County Durham (Fig. 5.16) and a medium-sized single-industry town as at Ashington in Northumberland, but played its part in the development of new towns dedicated to its export and the expansion of older ports. Coal mining was forever on the move: from the uplands to the coast and then beneath the sea; from shallow mines to deep; and from the exhausted pit to the newly sunk. Throughout the 19th century the most important mining area was the Great Northern Coalfield, but by the early 20th century its supremacy was challenged by the mines of south Yorkshire. After 1918, pits in Durham and Northumberland lost many of their lucrative export markets and by 1939 south Yorkshire had moved into the lead. Coal mining in both areas is now largely in the past but its mark on the landscape persists. Though the pit heads are dismantled, pit heaps are grassed over, and the lines of the wagonways fade, even villages whose raison d'être was their mine remain inhabited after its demise, while other villages with longer histories incorporate the buildings of their mining period as part of the physical embodiment of their pasts.

COMMUNICATIONS BEFORE STEAM[7]

Changes in communications change geography, or at least human perceptions of geography, making for new social and economic links and superseding old ones. In the modern period new means of transport also began to make a firmer mark on the landscape. Pathways for peddlers and shepherds and the packhorse ways and drove roads have left faint though distinct impressions, but the transport links of the late modern period have made bold marks, beginning with those of the canal systems developed in the southern parts of the region and the network of turnpike roads created throughout it during the 18th century.[8]

During the first half of the century even the Great North Road was poorly surfaced and deeply rutted in places and an uncomfortable journey from Berwick to Doncaster could take several days. Yet this same road had been subject to numerous improvements: it was, for example, the first in the country to have a turnpike, in 1663.[9] Though supervised by the Surveyor of the Highways, the task of maintaining and improving roads fell to parishes, who paid for the upkeep with horses, men or, in the case of the less wealthy, their own labour. Parish-level improvement systems ensured the effects upon the landscape varied; where commercial development was taking shape most quickly, roads were likely to be

Fig. 5.16 Easington Colliery, County Durham.

TOP: *Taken in 1992, when the colliery was still working, the photograph reveals the modern pit head and straight rows of miners' houses which are set close to it.*

ABOVE: *Unlike many mining villages, Easington is an old settlement with a Norman church and the core of an ancient village survives. An industrial enterprise was set amidst fields and close to the coast.*

better and most extensive. Even in the canal age, local manufacturers recognised the need for road haulage, especially for goods that might be damaged by bulk carriers or for goods that had a high value for their size and weight.

The needs of national security, law and order, agriculture and the demands of polite society for easier mobility between towns and between town and country added to manufacturers' requirements for an improved transport network. The difficulty of east–west communications was brought home during the 1745 rebellion when the state of the roads impeded a rapid cross-country march to intercept the Jacobite army as it made its progress down the west of England; but it was as much economics and the interests of landowners as military needs which brought about the Military Road between Newcastle and Carlisle. Communications between the East Riding towns of Beverley and Hull and the rest of Yorkshire were greatly improved by turnpikes linking them with York. Landowners were prominent in the setting up of turnpike trusts, which might prove shrewd investments in themselves and advantage their estates. Thus, by the end of the 18th century major roads were much improved and turnpikes provided new roads and improved old ones; with such improvements, journey times were cut, transport increased, and the economic activity focused along such arteries was growing.

From 1750 canals transformed the transportation of goods in the south of Yorkshire, connecting the county's burgeoning urban textile centres with markets and transport outlets. The availability of water transport had long been the major reason for the prosperity of many towns along navigable rivers and estuaries.[10] Rivers such as the Humber, the Ouse, the Don or the Calder were improved by canals which by-passed sections that were too shallow or rocky for boats, and further canals were dug to link these waterways. Then came the considerable feats of engineering as canals were dug across the Pennines. The Liverpool–Leeds canal (Fig. 5.17), which still snakes from Liverpool, was intended to open Yorkshire's mills to the growing Empire port on the Mersey. In the process

Fig. 5.17 Leeds–Liverpool Canal.
Approaching Gargrave and the Aire Gap, large areas of drumlins (ice-moulded oval hillocks) and stretches of river alluvium subject to flooding presented problems for communications. The Leeds–Liverpool canal (on the right), here at its most northerly point, winds elegantly through the landscape in comparison to the natural course of the River Aire which is marked by meander scars and levees and is intermittently straightened by artificial diversions. The railway, built in the 1840s, follows an uncompromisingly straight line across the floodplain on an embankment and cuts into the drumlins. A modern road (foreground) bridges river, canal and railway.

Fig. 5.18 Causey Arch (or Tanfield Arch), County Durham, was completed in 1727 as a single span of 32m to carry rails for horse-drawn wagons over the ravine of the Causey Burn and facilitate the transport of coal across the East Durham plateau to the coastal harbours. Among the earliest of all railway bridges, it is now scheduled as an Ancient Monument.

numerous locks were constructed to lift water-borne freight high over the Pennines, and tunnels – lower and smaller, but nevertheless impressive markers on the landscape – burrowed through hilly terrain, as at Batley. Canals made for commercial expansion and created new work opportunities and new habitats for nature. By meeting the needs of local commercialists they also shaped the urban landscape, just as railways would do later.

The profusion of canal building in Yorkshire and the absence of such waterways north of the Tees (despite an ambitious but still-born scheme in the early 1800s to link Carlisle and Newcastle via the Eden and Tyne rivers) tells us much about the nature and timing of economic development in the two spheres as well as the relative advantages of the landscape in the far North East. The first stage for increasing the possibilities of water-borne traffic was to widen and deepen rivers. With four such waterways mapping the landscape of the far North East – Tees, Wear, Tyne and Tweed – this region had an inbuilt advantage. Most mineral extraction and other commercial development focused on these rivers, reducing the need for canals. Moreover, that part of the North East had developed before most other regions rudimentary wagonways and primitive rail systems on which horse-drawn wagons carried coal along wooden and then iron lines to the nearest navigable rivers, and these would be the basis for one of the densest railway networks in the country. Even in the early days of these proto-railways, the impact upon the landscape was considerable. Causey Arch at Tanfield, near Stanley in County Durham (Fig. 5.18), is the oldest surviving single-span railway bridge in the world; built between 1725 and 1726, it typifies the early usage of primitive rails in the north-east coalfield. Standing some 24m above a woodland gorge it has dominated the local landscape for nearly three centuries.

The staithes at the riverside end of wagonways became equally noticeable and familiar features of the landscape. They developed from simple short piers from which small boats (keelboats on the Tyne) could be loaded with coal, which they then tendered to colliers (coal-carrying boats) (Fig. 5.19). In Durham and Northumberland, widened, deepened and dredged rivers had as fundamental an impact upon urban development, commercial growth and early industrialisation as any canal.

Fig. 5.19 Coal Staithes.

TOP: **Dunston-on-Tyne.** *Once a familiar sight on the banks of the rivers of the northern coalfield, coal staithes such as these at Dunston were where coal was loaded onto coal ships or colliers. On the Tyne above Newcastle much smaller staithes had previously enabled coal to be loaded onto keelboats and then taken to colliers below Newcastle's bridge. After the building of the High Level Bridge in the late 1840s, followed by the Swing Bridge of 1876, it was possible for larger ships to take coal on-board directly from large staithes. Only fragments of these impressive loading platforms now remain.*

MIDDLE: **Drops on the Tees at Middlesbrough.** *Thomas Hair's watercolour shows the 'drops' on the Tees at Middlesbrough. The Stockton and Darlington Railway (1825) terminated here and these staithes were huge enclosed structures, which had steam engines, enabling wagons to be lifted on to the staithes and then lowered on to the waiting colliers.*

BOTTOM: **Dene Staithe at Albert Dock.** *The history of coal mining in the North East is one of a move from mines near the surface to deep mines and an associated move towards mines nearer the coast. This aerial photograph taken in the 1970s by Norman McCord shows the impressive Dene Staithe at Albert Dock on the lower north bank of the Tyne, built to receive and transfer coal from the deep mines of north Tyneside. Coal was first shipped from this basically timber structure in 1884 and it was last used in 1943.*

THE LANDSCAPE AND TRANSPORT IN THE RAILWAY AGE

The pioneer Stockton to Darlington Railway of 1825, built by Newcastle engineer George Stephenson, essentially began as a wagonway with the addition of steam locomotives. Its economic effect was remarkable for it provided access to the sea for coal from the south-Durham collieries and, when extended, was responsible for one of the generally few new towns of the Industrial Revolution, Middlesbrough. It was followed in 1832 by the Hartlepool Dock and Railway Company, which revived the economy of Hartlepool by bringing coal to the port from inland collieries. In 1834 came the first railway in Yorkshire, linking Leeds to Selby and then to Hull. Thus, the spectacular innovation of railways grew out of the mining industry, bringing together the wagonway and the steam engine and resulting in armies of navvies constructing kilometres of rail-track and embankments, carving through the countryside and erecting often spectacular bridges and viaducts.

The 1840s and the 1850s saw a spectacular rate of development in the north-east rail system. By this time, York, Darlington and Newcastle were major railway hubs and Carlisle and Newcastle were linked by rail (Fig. 5.20). Such developments linked even the tiniest mining villages and all the major towns into a regional, trans-regional and then national network. Causey Arch had offered a foretaste of the feats of engineering that would enhance the northern landscape in the great age of railways. One of the most impressive is Ribblehead viaduct (Fig. 5.21), which spans Batty Moss with its 24 arches and connects Yorkshire and northern Cumbria on the Settle–Carlisle line. Constructed in the 1870s, its impact upon the landscape remains startling: not only on the land itself but also as an aerial viewpoint of dramatic scenery, which previously the Victorians could only have dreamed about. In the 19th century it provided jobs for hundreds of

Fig. 5.20 Newcastle–Carlisle Railway.
J M Carmichael is best known for his seascapes and maritime paintings but he depicted the Newcastle–Carlisle Railway even before it was completed. This view of Warden Bridge to the west of Hexham demonstrates the contrast between the new transport of the age of steam and the rural landscape it passes through. Within a few decades the railway would be seen as a familiar aspect of the landscape.

navvies and engineers, many of whom died during its construction. The effects of the railways were considerable, yet the horse and horse-drawn vehicles remained the essential means of local transport until the early 20th century.

Railway building was, of course, profit driven, but the pursuit of profit could cause one railway company to attempt to prevent a railway proposed by another company or to oppose bridges that might open up their lines to competition. For more than a century, the businessmen of Hull found plans to span the Humber with bridges or tunnels blocked by the interests of the North East Railway Company, which sought to protect shipping from the Tyne and Wear ports by charging tonnage rather than mileage rates for freight, and by the vested interests of west Yorkshire, Manchester and Goole. Equally the pursuit of profit did not invariably lead to profit. Many railways, such as the Northumberland Central Railway between Scots Gap and Rothbury, constructed with great expense in the 19th century and closed in the 20th, never made an annual profit, yet they have still left their mark on the landscape.

Fig. 5.21 Ribblehead Viaduct. Constructed in the 1870s, this impressive creation of the railway age is on the Settle and Carlisle railway. It is 400m long and is one of the many imposing viaducts crossing northern valleys. The remains of the builders' temporary camp, which included houses, shop, school and other services, are still traceable nearby. Stone for the piers of the viaduct were brought from quarries in Liddledale along a narrow-gauge railway.

WATER AND LANDSCAPE IN THE INDUSTRIAL AGE

Despite canals and railways, sea and river transport remained a central factor in urban and industrial development. In the mid-19th century, ships continued to provide the cheapest and most efficient means of carrying coal while, like the coal trade, the fish trade and the fishing fleets expanded in the early 19th century even as that relatively short-lived bonus to towns like Whitby and Berwick, the whaling industry, declined. Traditional trading links with London and with northern Europe expanded while markets further afield were found. The town of Seaham

Fig. 5.22 Seaham Harbour. Industrial entrepreneurship is usually associated with middle-class businessmen or factory owners, but in County Durham aristocratic landowners were not always content to simply take the mineral royalties for the coal that lay under their land. The third Marquis of Londonderry was a major owner of coal mines and an aristocrat in business. He built Seaham Harbour (1828–35), a considerable undertaking, to facilitate and gain from the shipment of coal from his mines.

Harbour (Fig. 5.22), which was built by the Marquis of Londonderry to import silver sand and timber, represented a shrewd investment to increase wealth via transport access.[11] The wood went into Londonderry's extensive coalfield concerns and the sand into the manufacture, in the 1890s, of more than 10 million bottles per year. The harbour frontage dramatically changed the seaside landscape in the area and provided connections to the outside world, not least for the shipment of Londonderry's coal. A railway linked the growing port town to nearby Sunderland in 1855. In Blyth, from the mid-1880s, large sums of money were invested to make the treacherous, low-capacity port larger and more modern. By the end of the century, the coastal shipping trade clearly was not expanding at the same rate as other forms of transport; and the coastal trade declined more rapidly thereafter.[12]

Nineteenth-century industrialisation saw shipyards and heavy industry transform the lower reaches of the main rivers. The Tyne had long presented problems for mariners, with a low-water clearance over a sand bar at the mouth of the river which could be as low as 2m, its dangerous rocks at the Black Middens just inside the bar and the long stretch below Newcastle perpetually silting up. From 1850 the Tyne Improvement Commission transformed the river with piers at North and South Shields and dredging for a channel to a depth of 6m between river mouth and Newcastle. Docks, cranes, quaysides and other developments came rapidly to Newcastle and Gateshead, Wallsend, North and South Shields, Hebburn and Jarrow during the second half of the century. Dredging was extended up-river from Newcastle and in 1876 a swing bridge replaced the earlier fixed bridge between Newcastle and Gateshead, to maintain a river crossing while allowing passage of ships up to the Armstrong's shipbuilding and armaments concern at Elswick. While Newcastle, for long the second port of the region, had increasingly to share its maritime position with the lower Tyne as a whole, Hull, the largest port on the north-east coast, was able to maintain its position on the mouth of a great river by the development of new docks in the late 18th and early 19th century (Fig. 5.23).[13]

A commission had been appointed for the River Wear as early as 1717 and a hundred years later the mouth of the river had been improved to the extent that there was some 5m of water over the bar at high water on the spring tides. Piers were built on the south and north sides of the river in 1832 and 1842, respectively. In all, some 85ha of dock had been created by the early 20th century.

Middlesbrough, the classic Victorian new town, developed water-frontage and dug out a new dock in 1842 and expanded it three times thereafter during its growth as an iron and steel town. It provides a spectacular instance of 20th-century industry with the growth of the chemical industry. Billingham-on-Tees possesses one of the most dramatic but disturbing of industrial vistas and was supposedly the inspiration for north-east-born film director Ridley Scott's *Bladerunner*. Heavy industry, save in areas where it was highly concentrated as in the West Riding or the banks of major rivers, had a less marked effect upon the landscape as a whole, though mills, smaller iron works and coal mines peppered the rural landscape. It was only in the south of the region that manufacturing and major towns penetrated far inland, for the uplands running down the centre of northern Britain were unattractive for such developments, though in the north of the region Consett, a one-industry, one-company town, is a rare exception.

It was not just trade and work that favoured the growth of coastal towns. The interest of polite society in the 18th century in health, recreation and sociability saw the growth of spa towns such as Harrogate, which provided curative waters, hotels and social events; but, as doctors waxed eloquent as to the restorative powers of coastal air and sea bathing, the seaside resort became fashionable. With Scarborough (Fig. 5.24) as the flagship, fishing villages and estuary towns began to cater for holidaymakers and day trippers, as from the middle of the 19th century rising living standards enabled wider sections of society to flock to the seaside. Whitby, Robin Hood's Bay and Staithes acquired additional summertime economies and had their charms recorded on camera. Those seaside villages near to commercial centres began to develop as prosperous suburbs, as with Tynemouth and Cullercoats, which were close to Newcastle.

Towns needed water and, as understanding of the causes of disease improved, they demanded clean water. The impact upon the landscape of the work of water companies and local councils has been considerable as, from the mid-19th century onwards, they have created reservoirs and conduits to provide for the water needs

Fig. 5.23 Kingston-upon-Hull. *For centuries the North East coast's most important port, Hull has seen the decline of its harbour and docks. This aerial photograph shows the magnificent docks, diminished since their mid-20th-century peak but still covering an expanse of waterfront.*

ABOVE: ***Fig. 5.24 Scarborough.*** *The town developed for leisure and pleasure is as much a feature of the modern period as the town based on industry. Scarborough is one of the oldest holiday resorts, having become a spa in the 17th century, and it rivalled Harrogate as sea-bathing became as fashionable as 'taking the waters' for reasons of health. The castle set on the headland and divided from the town by a deep ravine provides a spectacular backdrop*

LEFT: ***Fig. 5.25 Kielder Reservoir.*** *Northumbrian Water's Kielder Reservoir is western Europe's largest man-made lake. Its construction involved the controversial flooding of many kilometres of the upper-North Tyne, an area of farmland much prized for its scenic beauty. Completed in 1982 it not only provides a secure water supply for the North East but proffers leisure facilities in the form of yachting and lakeside camping. Surrounded by the 20th-century forests of conifers planted by the Forestry Commission, Kielder and its environs can be considered a landscape sculpted by the modern state.*

of an expanding economy and society. Reservoirs at first were created fairly close to the main centres of population and then, as demand increased, were built in the higher reaches of rivers, notably on the high land of the Pennines and the lower slopes of the Cheviots. Thus in Northumberland, the Newcastle and Gateshead Water Company added such lakes to the county's landscape as the reservoirs at Whittle Dean, Hallington, Colt Crag and Catcleugh while Tynemouth Corporation created Fontburn.[14] In Durham reservoirs were made at Burnhope and later at the top of the Derwent valley and at Cow Green. Upper Teesdale provided a cluster of reservoirs at Selset, Balderhead and Grassholme. Yorkshire examples include Ladybower, Howden and Derwent reservoirs in the Peak District and a further cluster on the upper reaches of the River Nidd. By far the most ambitious scheme is Kielder Reservoir, opened in 1982. It covers more than 595sq km, has a little under 48km of shoreline and is western Europe's largest man-made lake.[15] It not only provides water for Northumberland, Tyne and Wear and Durham but a tunnel to Redcar, originally designed to provide water for British Steel, makes it a potential resource for a much wider area.

Kielder Lake and the 62,000ha forest which surrounds it[16] together illustrate the ability of 20th-century planners and engineers to alter the landscape on a massive scale, even in a remote upland region (Fig. 5.25). Throughout the North East as elsewhere in Britain, road-building programmes were drawing lines on the landscape, with motorway development from the 1960s making the most spectacular changes. Unlike earlier roads they did not go from town to town but proceeded in straight lines or sweeping curves with complex junctions near major conurbations, such as where the M1 meets the A1 at Leeds (Fig. 5.26). The Humber Bridge is not only an engineering feat and a prominent landmark but it has

Fig. 5.26 Motorways. The A1–M1 interchange near Leeds. The railways, once so controversial that landowners and village worthies kept them away from country houses and villages, became an accepted and even admired part of the landscape. Will we ever regard motorways in the same way? Essential conduits for trade and manufacturing, they have a considerable impact upon the landscape, taking up more space than canals, railways or older road systems.

ABOVE: *Fig. 5.27 The Humber Bridge.*
The scale of the enterprise combined with
opposition from other interests and towns
meant that a bridge across the lower Humber
was long in coming. Its absence effectively cut
off Hull from Lincolnshire and the south. The
longest single-span suspension bridge in the
world was finally built between 1973 and 1981.
It is nearly 3.2km long and has twin towers
142m high, with linking cables that are
660mm thick.

LEFT: *Fig. 5.28 Eggborough power*
station. This power station near Selby can
stand for the many unloved but necessary
power stations that produce the electricity upon
which modern society relies. The neighbourhood
of the south Yorkshire coalfield inevitably
produced a number of coal-fired power stations
which, as at Eggborough or Ferry Bridge,
dominate the surrounding landscape.

RIGHT: *Fig. 5.29 Pylons. Pylons dot this landscape of scattered villages and dispersed farmsteads*
with their redbrick buildings in the Vale of York. Disliked by both conservationists and residents,
pylons are preferred to underground lines by the electricity industry on the grounds of cost.

Fig. 5.30 Wind turbines. *Wind turbines and reservoirs are prominent features on Warley Moor in the south Pennines between Oxenhope and Queensbury. The introduction of highly visible wind turbines into areas of scenic beauty is highly controversial, involving as it does conflict between the conservation of rural scenery and claims that wind-power may mitigate climate change.*

in a sense altered geography by bringing Hull and Holderness closer to Lincolnshire and the coast to the south (Fig. 5.27). The coming of the electric grid also had a dynamic economic impact, not least in obviating the need for proximity between coalfields and manufacturing, but also through the visual effects of power stations, as at Eggborough near Selby (Fig. 5.28) and the long lines of pylons parading across fertile fields, which have been held to be intrusions (Fig. 5.29). Nor have efforts to find a sustainable energy resource by harnessing wind power been universally approved of for their effect upon upland landscapes. The North East pioneered offshore wind farms at Blyth, thus altering a seascape off a coastline that had already been dominated by a power station for 40 years (it was demolished in 2003). Even Brontë country at Ovenden Moor, Haworth, has its wind farms (Fig. 5.30).

PRESERVATION AND CONSUMPTION: THE NORTHERN LANDSCAPE AND MODERN CULTURE

Despite the developments outlined so far, the major change to the landscape during the 20th century was the expansion and spread of towns and industry. Motor transport facilitated the growth of the suburbs and then the conurbations while industry, freed from its twin dependence upon coalfields and water and rail transport, expanded along highways or clustered close to motorway or airport. The housing needs of an expanding population (which moved in the late 20th century toward more houses for smaller households) were not simply satisfied by the expansion of housing estates around existing towns, but required the building of new towns such as Peterlee and Cramlington. The cumulative impact of new housing is best appreciated by considering the changes to the landscape at night; whereas in the middle of the last century, areas of concentrated habitation showed up as islands of light amid a sea of darkness, thinly inhabited areas are increasingly becoming islands of darkness in a sea of light.

The modern eye views the landscape through prisms of expectation and learned ways of seeing. We evaluate landscapes through aesthetic sensibilities, which are themselves attached to moral and social values. The landscapes we value most are those which, as we have seen, were created by a conjunction of the agricultural economy of the 18th century and the aesthetic sensibilities of the elite of the period, and those that reflect the later sensibilities of Romanticism with its delight in the wild, the mountainous and the sublime. Historical and literary associations are also vibrant as tourist boards and local authorities realise, with their signs and logos promoting the 'Land of the Prince Bishops', 'Brontë Country' and 'England's Border County'. Modern popular novelists and television programmes imprint associations; South Tyneside brands itself 'Catherine Cookson Country', while tourists come to the Yorkshire Dales inspired by the televised drama based on the recollections of the celebrated Yorkshire veterinary surgeon, James Herriot.

The problem is, of course, that aesthetic and moral sensibilities have been in direct contradiction to the development of the economy in the late modern period. The landscape of industrial Britain has never appealed to more than a minority taste, though its aficionados increase as it becomes past rather than present. Motor transport enabled housing to become more dispersed, thus altering landscapes and, from the 1920s, cars and motorcycles enabled their owners to explore the countryside armed with Shell Guides depicting unspoiled rural idylls while cafés and road houses, of which the Scotch Corner Hotel is a splendid example, sprang up to cater for them.

Tourism can be traced back to the 18th century when, as an addition to the Grand Tour or as a substitute for it, polite society took to exploring the countryside and the country houses of their native land. The cult of walking for pleasure rather than need was largely the invention of Victorian intellectuals but, by the early 20th century, had become widely popular, while from the 1880s the cycle enabled a mass exodus to take place from industrial towns at weekends. Such developments led to the twin drives, not always easily reconciled, to conserve and protect the most valued countryside and its landmarks, while at the same time promoting access to it. By the end of the 20th century there were a multitude of agencies dedicated to the protection of the rural environment and landscape, its castles, mansions, farms and villages and also its flora and fauna.

The aims of conservation have not always been easily reconcilable with the promotion of access, which can bring pressure on vulnerable wild-life habitats, lead to the erosion of footpaths along Hadrian's Wall and bring with it the need for car parks, which can modify the very landscape those who park in them come to see. Similarly, government initiatives aimed at sustaining the rural economy have not always run parallel with the preservation of traditional landscapes. The transformation of west Northumberland by the planting of innumerable fir trees on hitherto moorland and upland pasture was not universally welcomed. While farming remained prosperous, the new farm buildings and silos of the modern farmer could be contentious, while the house- and road-builders' need for stone has increased the demands on Britain's oldest extractive industry, quarrying, with implications for the landscape and for rural roads (Fig. 5.31).

The needs of national defence are also sometimes at odds with access to the countryside and RAF exercises often necessitate low flying across scenic landscapes. A large area in Northumberland is given over to the Otterburn Training Area, but though public access to military areas may be limited the army is a good custodian of traditional landscape and of flora and fauna, content to preserve traditional farming practices and historic sites and bastle houses, while the otter and the blackcock seem impervious to military exercises.

The landscape changes but so does our view of it. Just as tastes in architecture alter over time with, for instance, a revaluation of the Victorian and even a pat on the head for the working-class housing of yesterday, so we begin to imbue industrial landscapes with nostalgic value. The chimneys of lead-smelting mills are consolidated and even rebuilt in areas in the North Pennines Area of Outstanding Natural Beauty where any intrusion on the landscape by a contemporary industry would be rejected. When it comes to landscape, our economic urges jar with our historicist aesthetic views.

Increasingly, however, there is a renewal of interest in the urban landscape. The brutal modernism of the urban landscape, half-realised as in the 'New Brasilia' of the planned Newcastle of the 1960s and '70s, is replaced by the post-modernist city, ever referential to its past, while it re-invents its present in the interests of leisure as much as commerce. Riverside housing and marinas replace the decayed landscape of shipyard and heavy industry, while walkways and cycle tracks attempt to attract the urban dweller in search of exercise with new vistas of old landscapes. Central to new urban development has been an attempt to reverse the tendency of towns to move away from rivers and to emphasise the river as unifier rather than divider. Since the earliest times, spanning rivers has been central to meeting the challenges of landscape. In meeting these challenges, engineers have created some of our most spectacular landscape features, the Tyne Bridge, built in the 1920s, being but one.[17] A new bridge was built across the Tyne between Newcastle and Gateshead in 1976 ready for the Metro, the new urban transport system, and subsequently the Gateshead Millennium Bridge (Fig. 5.32) for pedestrians and cyclists has enabled the riverside to become a cross-river entertainment and cultural centre, its landscape dramatically outlined by two centuries of bridges and industrial buildings transformed into arts centres and hotels and a new purpose-built music venue. New to the urban landscape are the Coliseums of today, the football stadiums which, as with St James's Park in Newcastle and the Stadium of Light in Sunderland (Fig. 5.33), dominate the skyline and point to the importance of sport and its rivalries

OPPOSITE PAGE:

TOP: *Fig. 5.31 Cement works in Weardale. This cement works in Weardale above Stanhope has a certain grandeur. Active until recently, it used limestone from nearby quarries. With its scattered farms, their fields enclosed by stone walls, its lead-mining past and the higher land providing heather grazing for sheep and fine grouse-shooting, Weardale resembles its fellow Pennine valley, Allendale, to the north.*

BOTTOM: *Fig. 5.32 Gateshead Millennium Bridge.
This footbridge is a fine addition to the bridges that cross the Tyne between Newcastle and Gateshead. The name reflects the resurgent pride of the south bank of the river which has been extensively refashioned and has the Baltic Arts Centre, converted from an imposing flour mill, and the spectacular Sage Music Centre, seen here under construction. It also symbolises the return of both towns to their riverside roots and the booming service and leisure culture which now fuels much of the local economy. The bridge is framed by the Tyne Bridge.*

BELOW: *Fig. 5.33 Sunderland. This aerial view of Sunderland taken in 1999 shows a city in transition. Shipbuilding and the export of coal formed the basis of the town's 19th-century prosperity. The Stadium of Light (on the left), the home of Sunderland Football Club, new university buildings and service industries are taking the place of shipyards, docks and coal staithes along the riverside.*

in contemporary society. The *Angel of the North* (Fig. 5.34) has demonstrated that public sculpture can emulate the eye catchers of the 18th century.

CONCLUSION

The changes to the landscape of the North East in the modern period have been on a massive scale, but the main lines of development have been predicated by the same constants in the shape of the rivers, the passes, the coves and inlets, and the contrast between lowlands and uplands that have determined development since the beginning of human settlement. Despite the large-scale impact of modern consumer culture and the conceptualisation of the northern landscape as a playground for day-trippers, excursionists and holiday-makers, the land continues to sustain life and livelihoods as always it did. Farming, hunting, fishing and other rural pursuits – both profitable and pleasurable – still sustain a rural population. At the same time, the flight from the towns has created a new and growing population of commuters living in ever-burgeoning villages. As new communication systems cut through the land, as the armed forces make use of its open spaces, and as government agencies seek to harness, protect and present its contents in National Parks and Areas of Outstanding Natural Beauty, the real rural world is pressed by change.

***Fig. 5.34* The Angel of the North.**
Perhaps the most successful piece of public sculpture of recent years, Antony Gormley's The Angel of the North *has stood on the site of a former pit-head baths overlooking the A1 at Gateshead since 1998. It can be seen for many kilometres and greets motorists travelling towards Tyneside. It complements rather than rivals the Penshaw Monument.*

NOTES

1 The terms 'modern', 'early modern' and 'late modern' are imprecise, but it is conventional to see the modern period as divided into early modern, 1500–1650, and late modern, 1650 onwards.
2 Watts 1975.
3 Lomas 1982.
4 McDonnell 1992.
5 Muir 1997, 215.
6 Thompson 1963.
7 For a detailed account of the development of communications in the North East *see* Chapter 8.

8 Black & MacRaild 2003, 40–1.
9 Rogers 1961, 25.
10 Black & MacRaild 2003, 41–3.
11 Daunton 1995, 290.
12 Aldcroft 1963.
13 For a fuller account of the development of Hull and other towns and cities *see* Chapter 7.
14 Rennison 1979.
15 www.kielder.org.
16 Forestry Commission www.forestry.gov.uk.
17 Linsley 1998.

6

Landscape Components

F H A AALEN and RICHARD MUIR

The landscapes of any region are – unless utterly transformed by modern changes – composed of assemblages of features and facets inherited from many stages of the past. Sometimes the inheritance is preserved almost intact, as with some of the more noble buildings, but very frequently we see the features in conditions of preservation that reflect their long retirement from the working countryside. They all contribute to the aesthetic personality of their localities and at the same time serve as clues to the historical evolution of the setting. Their dereliction reflects profound economic, technological and social changes, which have rendered communal farming, traditional woodmanship, small enclosures and activities such as hedging unviable, while aristocratic recreation on the scales represented by the forest, chase and deer park has vanished. In these ways, rural landscapes comprise legacies of features inherited from many stages of the past and encountered in many different states of dereliction.

A few of the landscapes that are seen today are dominated by a single era of landscape formation; examples include 18th-century countrysides produced by parliamentary enclosure in the Yorkshire Dales and some western parts of County Durham, with their field walls, local roads and farmsteads all built within a few years of each other. Most, however, are accretions of features that were very gradually assimilated into the landscape, with, say, ancient road and lane patterns, medieval woods, 18th-century farmsteads, turnpikes and parks, 19th-century plantations and so on all contributing to the blend. In places not transformed by revolutionary changes, such as the open-field farming revolution of the Anglo/Scandinavian era, the parliamentary enclosures in the 18th or 19th centuries or the post-1945 'prairie farming' movement, the countryside has developed organically for many centuries, gradually acquiring new components while others slowly vanished from the scene. The legacy of features that survive within the visible landscape – though often as economically redundant but scenically and historically invaluable features – can be evaluated under a series of headings: buildings, settlements, fieldscapes, moorlands, woodlands, hunting reserves and deer parks.

BUILDINGS

The countryside contains buildings of diverse ages and functions, including castles and gentry houses, farmhouses, barns and byres, religious, commercial and industrial buildings. Only those buildings numerous and widespread enough to lend a particular character to the landscape will be considered here: foremost are those associated with farming, a massive legacy of structures shaped by local environment, historical circumstances and evolving farming practices, which provides important insights into the development of the historic landscape as a whole.

Fig. 6.1 Examples of the adaptation of the longhouse tradition, North York Moors: BELOW: *Spout House, Bilsdale, is a 17th-century, thatched longhouse with its byre end later converted for domestic use: in the 18th century, mullioned windows were inserted and the roof space converted into rooms.* BOTTOM: *Rose Marie Lodge, Appleton-le-Moors, is an early 18th-century, two-storey farmhouse retaining traditional longhouse features such as the cross passage behind the fireplace and the narrow window alongside the hearth.*

Vernacular building forms

Despite the widespread adoption of 'polite' building styles in the 18th and 19th centuries and the impress in many areas of modern mining, industry and urbanisation, northern landscapes retain a considerable legacy of vernacular, or traditional, buildings in local styles and building materials. Our understanding of their origins and relationships is incomplete but some of the main built forms clearly have medieval roots, which include peasant longhouses, gentry hall-houses and a variety of fortified and defensible residences. In the modern era, however, agricultural improvement, land reclamation, rural mining and manufacturing have also generated a range of local building types, some echoing older traditions, others *sui generis*. In the Pennines, for example, they include the laithe house, the hall house

of the 'yeoman clothier', lead-miners' houses and field barns. In the lowland areas are the substantial courtyard farms of the agricultural improvement and the dwellings of coal miners.

The main ancestral dwelling form in northern England was the longhouse or byre dwelling, an elongated, single-storey building with human occupation at one end and a cow byre at the other; the compartments were separated by a cross passage between two opposite doors and entry to the living area was usually through the byre. Archaeological excavations, documentary sources and the analysis of old houses indicate that longhouses were widely used in the medieval period and many, usually altered and improved, survived well into the post-medieval period (Fig. 6.1).[1] This was the main building type on the plots of land in the medieval villages of Wharram Percy in Yorkshire and West Whelpington in Northumberland. The longhouse was first developed by converting the byre quarter into domestic space; at a later stage a storey was often added to a part or the whole of the house, while still retaining traditional features such as the cross passage. This elongated house form was eventually replaced as fully centralised, double-pile layouts became fashionable in the 18th century. Any lingering influence exerted by the longhouse tradition was confined to the design of small houses and cottages, which as late as the 19th century might be built with a cross passage and an off-centre door (Fig. 6.2).

Although many farms, especially in villages, occupy sites that have been settled since the medieval period, few farm buildings pre-date the large-scale building of formalised, regular steadings in the 18th and 19th centuries and our understanding of earlier stages of farmyard development is thus limited. The formation of yards was linked to the exclusion of cattle from the longhouses and the ensuing need to provide a convenient arrangement for the separate byres, barns and other functionally specialised buildings. There was no evident tendency to form scattered, amorphous layouts; a sense of ordered relationship between buildings generally prevails, and two types of farmstead emerge. The first contains separate buildings grouped, with varying degrees of formality, around one or more

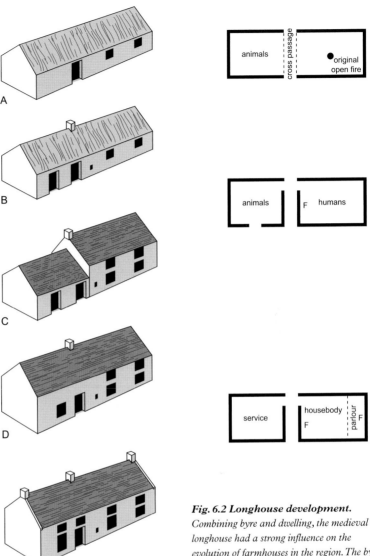

Fig. 6.2 Longhouse development.
Combining byre and dwelling, the medieval longhouse had a strong influence on the evolution of farmhouses in the region. The byre part was first given a separate entrance but later put to domestic use and the cattle moved to a separate building. In the 17th and 18th centuries the house part was raised as eventually was the rest of the dwelling. Old houses often show evidence of this evolution in the layout of their rooms, hearth and doors, the retention of a cross passage and perhaps a small fire window alongside the main hearth (based on Royal Commission on the Historical Monuments of England 1987).

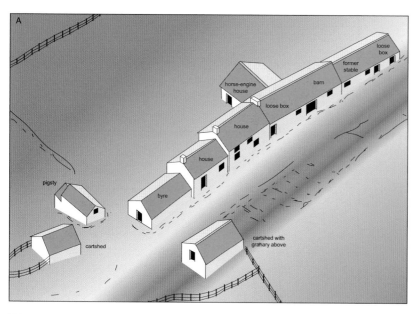

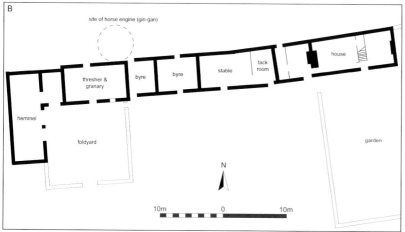

Fig. 6.3 a. Aumery Park, Fadmoor,
North Yorkshire Moors *is a striking, long
range of buildings with house and barn in the
middle. The buildings are of different width
and height and not exactly in the same
alignment, strongly suggesting that the
farmstead developed gradually (based on
Royal Commission on the Historical
Monuments of England 1987, 155).*
b. Southwitton Farm,
Northumberland. *The farm buildings,
constructed from local sandstone probably in
the late 18th century, form a long range to the
west of the house. This farmstead stands on the
site of the deserted village of Longwitton and is
listed among the farms of Hartburn Parish in
1662, but there are no traces of the earlier
buildings (based on Bolter 1993).*

irregular yards. In the second, and probably more common type, the house and various farm buildings are attached and lie in one line; the different width and height of the units sometimes suggesting piecemeal extension rather than any planned, complete rebuilding. From the mid-18th century onwards these two farmyard types, though persisting on smaller farms and in upland areas, were generally replaced in favour of regular and carefully designed courtyard arrangements with more substantial farmhouses usually built in polite style and sometimes aloof from the other farm buildings (Fig. 6.3).

The characteristic dwelling of the medieval gentry was the hall house, comprising a central, open hall flanked by two-storey ends or cross wings; one end or wing contained service rooms, the other domestic family rooms. The main entrance led into a cross passage adjoining the service wing and backing onto the hall fireplace. Thus, in their layout, halls echo the longhouse format but have larger spaces and a services area in place of a byre. Whether they had evolved from the longhouse, or *vice versa*, remains uncertain. In the late 16th century the hall-house style was adopted by wealthy yeoman farmers, especially in the Pennines south-west of our region where substantial hall houses or derived forms remain a considerable presence in the landscape (Fig. 6.4).

The Anglo-Saxon precursors of the hall house have survived only as archaeological remains and they do not seem to have had long-lasting influence on architectural forms or structural techniques. Examples have been identified and excavated at West Heslerton in Yorkshire and at Thirlings, near Wooler in the north of Northumberland. Buildings were rectangular, the length about twice the width, with doors mid-way along the long sides. Inside, most of the area was kept as a single open space, with sometimes one or both ends partitioned off to make small private chambers. There was no accommodation for animals in these buildings.

As security problems grew in northern border areas during the late medieval period, a range of strong, storeyed residences came into use, including various types of tower dwellings for gentry and clergy and small, defensible farmsteads built by tenant farmers and commonly referred to as bastles. In the border uplands, the bastle became one of the most distinctive building types with a stone-vaulted ground-floor byre entered by a doorway in one gable end and a living room above entered by an external ladder or stairs. The buildings had thick stone walls and were generally roofed with stone flags or slates (Fig. 6.5).

Bastles are found in many hamlets and villages and in the open countryside too where they sometimes stand alone or loosely grouped so as to be intervisible or within earshot of each other. Haltwhistle, along the Tyne in Northumberland,

seems at one time to have been composed largely of bastles. Such buildings were not designed to withstand military attack but could provide protection against the small bands of mobile border-raiders habitually involved in the thieving of livestock. Many bastles were built in the 16th century but, significantly, they continued to be built in the early decades of the 17th century after the union of the English and Scottish crowns. This suggests a continued unease about the depredations of lawless neighbours.

Although comparable dwellings accommodating humans above animals developed in periods of chronic unrest in other rural parts of Europe, the bastle is an almost unique vernacular form in the British Isles. A surprising number have survived, either as romantic ruins or incorporated into later buildings, and a small minority are still inhabited or used as barns. Surviving bastles, however, are only a fraction of the original number, which must have run into several hundreds.

Mainly in Allendale and Weardale, on the southern edge of the core bastle concentration, there is an interesting scatter of later houses in which the tradition of living above the animals persisted long after there was a serious security problem. The byre basement has an independent entry and the first-floor living area is reached by an external stair on the gable end: the walls of the houses are thinner than in bastles and the windows larger.

Fig. 6.4 Hopton Hall, Upper Hopton, near Mirfield, West Yorkshire. Hall houses, ranging in size from modest to large residences and built on the common medieval H-plan (hall-and-cross wings), were widely used by the lesser gentry and successful farmer-clothiers throughout the textile area of the Pennines, from Airedale to the south. The central hall block was originally open to the roof and flanked by two-storey cross wings at each end – one for service rooms, the other for domestic family rooms. Medieval timber-frame construction was widely replaced from the 15th century onwards as many houses were increasingly being rebuilt, at least partly, in stone or brick.

Improvement

The great era of agrarian improvement in England and Scotland, from the early 18th century to the mid-19th century, deeply affected the North East. The region possessed lowlands with considerable agricultural potential, though still backward,

Fig. 6.5 Pele towers and bastles:

LEFT: *The vicar's pele (tower-house) in Corbridge, Northumberland, was built in the early 14th century using stones from a nearby Roman site and provided a secure residence for the clergyman in an unwalled town. The tower was restored and re-roofed in the early 20th century.*

BELOW: *Elsdon tower-house in central Northumberland, dominating the village green and medieval church, probably dates from the mid- or late 16th century and long served as the residence of the village clergyman. The windows of the tower have been enlarged and the interior considerably changed.*

TOP RIGHT: *Bastles (defensible farmhouses) remained a standard vernacular form in Northumberland for over a century (c.1550–1650). Black Middens stands on the side of the Tarset valley, near Gatehouse in North Tynedale. External measurements are 10.4 × 7.2m and the rubble walls are 1.5m thick. The ground floor entrance is a later feature. The building is now roofless, but the stumps of crucks have survived.*

BOTTOM RIGHT: *This well-preserved and still inhabited bastle house on the main street of Thropton village, Northumberland, has a barrel-vaulted basement, one full upper storey and also an attic floor, which is an unusual feature in bastles.*

and there were also extensive areas of upland moor and wold awaiting reclamation and enclosure. Moreover, new money to finance rural improvements was available to the many landowners who profited from the expansion of mining, industry and commerce within the region and the growth of its population. Rural houses were increasingly influenced by 'polite' styles, which emphasised symmetry and what was considered good taste, and by the availability of a greater variety of building materials. There was also a strong interest in the improvement of farm buildings and the design of efficient farmsteads. Some of the most impressive 'planned farms' are found in the north of England, established on the estates of major landowners to set exemplary standards in progressive farming: the key objectives were to facilitate the application of scientific and technical principles to farm production and, simultaneously, enhance the aesthetic quality of the landscape as a whole.[2]

There was considerable spatial variation in the nature and timing of change. The North York Moors, for example, experienced a gradual, lengthy transition from medieval longhouses to symmetrical Georgian-type houses, which is still traceable in the structure and layout of many farmhouses. And this tendency for polite forms to progressively incorporate and encase older structures is evident in many other areas, such as Holderness and the Vale of York. The rural lowlands of north Northumberland, in contrast, experienced a delayed but intense wave of improvements in the first half of the 19th century, which transformed the backward conditions. Old farmsteads were completely rebuilt and reorganised, and new, two-storey farmhouses, solid, symmetrical and plain, were widely introduced along with uniform rows of single-storey cottages for the farm labourers. Only the widespread use of local sandstone as a walling material allowed the new built environment to retain an indigenous flavour.

By the early 19th century a standardised type of farmstead design had been widely adopted in lowland areas. The buildings, which are of a substantial nature, lie neatly around open courtyards, occasionally in a square but more typically on three sides of a square and often there are two yards forming an E-pattern. These substantial steadings, originally designed as integrated arable/livestock units, survived largely intact until the second half of the 20th century, despite growing mechanisation and the fundamental shift in land-use from wheat to livestock grazing, which commenced in the second half of the 19th century and continued through the first half of the 20th century (Fig. 6.6).[3]

Mechanisation of farming got underway in the 19th century, most markedly in Northumberland with its exceptional number of great estates and large tenant farms. The introduction of horse-, water- or steam-driven machinery on farms was partly a spin-off from technological developments in the expanding mining industry of the region and was designed to offset the drain of rural labour to the industrial towns. Especially influential was the successful threshing machine developed by Andrew Meikle in Edinburgh in the 1780s. Widely used in southern Scotland, this machine was rapidly adopted in the cattle-keeping and grain-producing lowlands of north-eastern England as far south as the Humber. Beyond that, its application was limited, probably owing to the low level of industrialisation and the availability of plentiful cheap labour. Initially, a rotary horse-powered engine (or horse-gin, gin being short for engine) similar to those already used in northern mines was adapted to drive the threshing machine, and the engine was generally accommodated in a specially designed shed (variously called a gin-gan, gin house or engine house) which was attached to an existing barn where the thresher was installed and the grain stored. Water power was common, with threshers driven by water damned uphill from the buildings, but wind power was rare.

By the mid-19th century, steam engines with chimneys had supplemented the traditional sources of power, especially in Durham with its plentiful coal, and from the end of the 19th century mobile threshing machines generally replaced stationary ones. Now obsolete and an impediment to movement in the farmyard, engine sheds are rapidly disappearing. In recent decades, however, some have been converted for residential and commercial purposes.

Fig. 6.6 'Improved' and industrialised farmsteads.

BELOW: *Enholmes Farm in Holderness was built in 1849 to the south-west of Patrington village, on flat land partly reclaimed from Humberside. The Patrington estate on which it lies was owned by a prominent Leeds flax and linen manufacturer with interests in farming. An outstanding farmstead of the 'high farming' period, from the late 1840s to the 1870s, Enholmes demonstrates the application of factory production to agriculture and was built on the latest scientific principles; highly mechanised, with machinery logically arranged in large, compact rows of brick buildings connected by railway. The basic function was to fatten cattle and produce manure to fertilise the surrounding farmland.* BOTTOM: *Beal Farm, Northumberland. Large isolated farms, often of more than 400ha, are a feature of the northern portion of the coastal plain of Northumberland, an area favoured with loamy soils and the best grass feeding in the county. The farmsteads, which rarely pre-date the 19th century, are characterised by substantial ranges of stone buildings with terraces of farm cottages nearby. A single farm often employed the entire population and formed the only settlement in a parish or township. The buildings are recent, but the sites have often been long settled and the farms may be the lineal descendants of medieval communities that used less substantial structures. Massive sheds have been added to the steadings in recent decades.*

Fig. 6.7 Laithe houses are closely associated with the Pennine dales, *but related structures were built in many parts of the North East from the 17th century onwards.* TOP: *New House (a listed building) in Bishopdale, North Yorkshire, dates from 1653 and was one of the first rebuilt stone houses in the dale. A storey and a laithe were added later in the century and the granary block was built c.1800 (Moor 2001).* BELOW: *Woodhouse, near Morpeth in Northumberland, is a modest farmstead of the laithe type, comprising a two-storey house and a range of stone outbuildings all under the same roofline and probably dating to the 18th century. In the 19th century a gin-gan was attached to the threshing barn.*

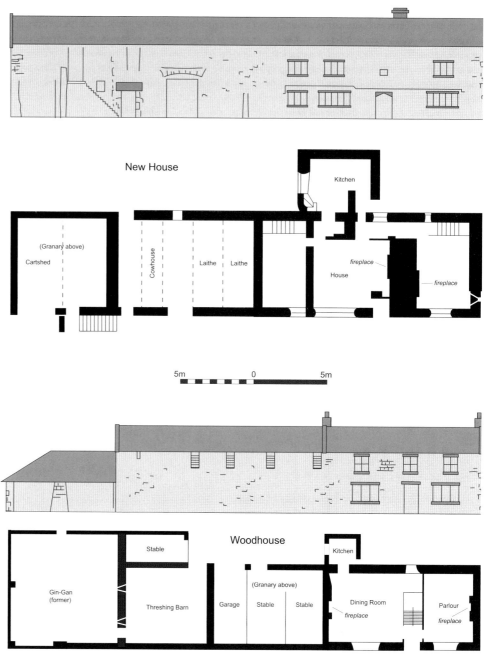

A characteristic building of the Pennine parts of Yorkshire is the laithehouse, an elongated, stone building, usually of one build, containing a dwelling, cowhouse (known in Yorkshire dialect as a laithe) and barn under a single roof of full two-storey height; each unit has a separate entry and there is no direct access between them. Laithehouses vary in size but are generally modest in proportions, their compact, standardised plan suited to the needs of small hill-farms (Fig. 6.7). The oldest surviving laithes date from the 17th century but the majority were built in association with the extensive parliamentary enclosure of moorland and commons between approximately 1750 and 1850. Many laithes are now derelict owing to the recession of settlement from these marginal areas.

Farms in the style of laithehouses, that is with byre and house attached but not interconnecting, are sprinkled along the dales and upland edges of Durham and Northumberland; but they are usually mixed with other types of dwelling, are nowhere so dominant as in the Yorkshire Pennines and generally lack characteristic Yorkshire features such as mullioned windows. They appear, for example, in Weardale and the upper reaches of Teesdale. In lower Teesdale, however, on the extensive Raby estate, the farmhouses tend to be square rather than elongated with separate farm buildings generally clustered around a yard rather than under the same roof, an arrangement introduced in the late 18th and early 19th centuries. The whited walls here are also distinctive, a traditional feature of Cumbrian farmhouses but unfamiliar in the North East. In upper Weardale, the small houses on the lead miners' isolated smallholdings had distinctive features: they were two-storey, incorporating house, byre and hay loft (Fig 6.8).

Fig. 6.8 ABOVE: *Leazes House, near Alston in the South Tyne Valley, is a long steading of laithe-house type with dwelling and barns under the same roofline and whitewashed walls in the tradition of nearby Cumberland.* BELOW: *Whited farmhouses and field barns in Teesdale, County Durham.*

Farm buildings are not always tied to a single steading. In the higher, narrow reaches of the Yorkshire Dales, notably in Swaledale for example, the fields on the floors and lower slopes are strewn with hundreds of stone barns, at a distance from the farmsteads.[4] These field barns, which seem to have multiplied on the newly enclosed meadowlands in the 18th century, served as hay sheds, winter

Fig. 6.9 The enclosed meadows on the lower valley sides in upper Swaledale *have a high density of field barns for housing cattle. Some of the barns against the moorland are hogg houses (sheep barns) where sheep could derive their main sustenance from the adjoining moor and so reduce grazing pressure on the enclosed pasture. Hogg house and field barn are sometimes combined.*

cattle stalls and manure depots. With the recent movement to more intensive farming systems and the use of large sheds to over-winter stock, many of the old field barns are now redundant and left to decay. In the Yorkshire Dales National Park, representative examples are being preserved, along with their setting of flower-rich meadows and walled fields, while others have been converted for low-cost visitor accommodation, light industrial use and other purposes (Fig. 6.9). The equivalent of Dale barns are the large, isolated redbrick barns built on the Yorkshire Wolds after enclosure of the area between 1770 and 1830 to serve as manure stores on the outlying fields of the extensive new farms.

Traditional methods and materials of building

Until modern communications and transport developed in the region, the mass of rural buildings were constructed with materials of local origin, timber, mud, turves, straw and stone. Later there was a growing emphasis on durable materials, with local stone and brick used for walling and flagstones and tiles for roofing, and permanent buildings in local styles became a major ingredient of the landscape.

Use of local materials should not imply that buildings need be in any way ephemeral or of poor quality. The early medieval timber tradition was capable of producing, at the kingly centres of Yeavering and Milfield in Northumberland, buildings with floor areas of 280sq m. Their massive walling was formed from oak baulks of square cross-section, some 130mm wide, placed upright side by side to form a continuous load-bearing wall 28m long. Structural integrity was achieved by setting the uprights in foundation trenches, a technique which was superseded in the medieval period by that of framing in which the uprights were mortised into a horizontal beam, usually set on a low brick or stone foundation.

Such buildings may not have had direct and lasting effects on the form or building methods of the medieval period but they were spaces within which the presence and functions of lordship could be displayed and enacted in some style. In this sense at least, the great hall-type buildings at Yeavering, or their more modest neighbours at Thirlings (with just one quarter of the floor space), were not so very different from the halls of great or lesser lords of the medieval times.

The normal peasants' house of the medieval period was thought to have been flimsy and short-lived, but excavations of houses in Wharram Percy and West Whelpington has led to a re-assessment. The outer walls can indeed appear flimsy, but the cruck blades which supported the roof and gave the building its core structural integrity could last hundreds of years. So these houses began with a capital investment (probably made by the lord of the manor) of a durable structure. The walls were not load-bearing but acted simply as cladding to provide shelter. If a length of side wall collapsed one winter because it was made of poor-quality materials it could be patched up again: a low-cost, high-maintenance feature.

Towards the end of the medieval period, houses of more permanence were being built in some parts of the Pennines and the North Yorkshire Moors. For example, minor gentry and yeomen in the Upper Calder valley west of Halifax, an area notable for its precocity in house design as well as commerce, were building more permanent and spacious houses in the late 15th century; the old hall-house plan persisted, but timber for wall construction was generally superseded by the local and highly durable Carboniferous stone, while old cruck timbers were sometimes reused in the roofs of the new buildings.[5] Durable stone houses and barns subsequently spread widely in the Pennines, the date and pattern of rebuilding varying from dale to dale in response to the particular natural conditions and social circumstances. Many buildings have thus survived in the Pennines from the 17th century onwards, while the legacy of medieval buildings at vernacular level rests in the main on the archaeological evidence of now-ruined buildings on abandoned medieval settlements. Upon excavation, such apparently unprepossessing features have been shown to yield detailed evidence of form, structure and function.

Timber-framed buildings were formerly widespread on the low-lying rural areas to the east of the Pennines, on the Coal Measures and in the city of York. They survived well into the post-medieval period but were subsequently either widely disguised by complete encasing in stone or brick or destroyed in the expansion of industrial towns and villages. The rural areas of Durham and Northumberland did not have such a tradition but the towns did, though here again buildings may later be encased in stone. Good examples can be seen in Silver Street and Saddler Street in Durham, while in Newcastle, the Cooperage, facing the river, is timber framed and probably of 15th-century date. A group of 17th-century merchants' houses also in the waterfront area, Bessie Surtees' House and its neighbours, is outstanding for the proportion of the front walls in between the frames given over to window glass. There was a ready supply available from glassworks a kilometre down-river. Perhaps not until the 20th century did window glass again feature so prominently in urban building.

Bricks and wavy roof tiles, or pantiles, long used on a small scale in the region, became fashionable in the 17th century and from the mid-18th century were widely produced and used in lowland areas where plentiful glacial-clay deposits and the shales and mudstones of the Coal Measures provided the essential raw materials. Indeed, the production of brick and roof-tile production became a considerable regional industry and derelict brickworks and flooded clay pits still dot the countryside. Houses constructed with locally-made bricks and pantiles of varying colour and texture became a feature of lowland landscapes, strikingly dominant in the Vale of York and on the neighbouring Wolds and in evidence as far north as the coastal lowlands of south-east Northumberland. Pantiles were

Fig. 6.10 Vernacular building materials in Northern England. This is a generalised picture of the distribution of vernacular, or traditional, walling and roof materials: it is not a geological map and has limited relevance to buildings of the industrial era. The complementary distribution of stone and brick walling is an outstanding feature. Sandstone or limestone walls, usually combined with slated roofs, dominate the uplands, while locally-made bricks and roof tiles are characteristic of lowland areas. This pattern developed towards the end of the medieval period, replacing earlier traditions of building in mud with crucks or timber frames. Since the Industrial Revolution in the 19th century, vernacular building materials have been comprehensively replaced by mass-produced brick, concrete and other materials (based on Penoyre & Penoyre 1978).

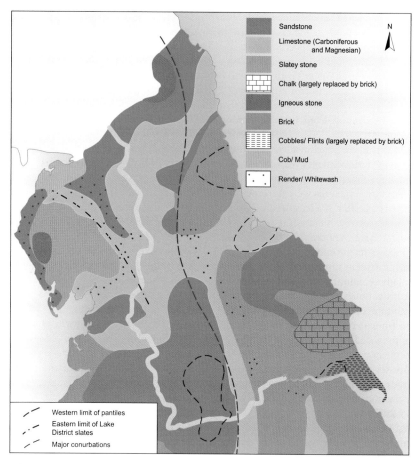

widely adopted on the coastlands of north Northumberland but walls continued to be built in local stone. Buildings in local stone remained a strong unifying influence in upland landscapes such as the North York Moors (Jurassic sandstone) and the Howardian Hills, and on the narrow, elevated strip of magnesian limestone along the western flank of the Vale of York, which provides an excellent and much-quarried white building stone occasionally combined with brick in house walls and with roof pantiles of red clay. In the villages of the Yorkshire Wolds, the local white chalk ('clunch') along with mud and thatch provided the almost universal building materials at vernacular level (indeed chalk was used in substantial buildings such as the old lighthouse at Flamborough Head) until the 18th and 19th centuries when they were gradually but almost completely replaced by brick and red pantiles (Fig. 6.10).

Traditional thatching materials included thick layers of heather and peaty sods, known generally as 'black thatch', in the uplands and straw and reeds in the coastal lowlands and along the Tweed valley. It is still possible to see black thatch on the restored Causeway House near Vindolanda in Northumberland. Thatched roofs were widely replaced in the 17th and 18th centuries, surviving into the 19th century only in remote places or in association with low-status buildings such as miners' cottages. In upland areas, black thatch was initially replaced by local stone flags and often entailed raising eaves to flatten the roof pitch, an adjustment traceable in the gable ends of many old houses. In lowland areas, pantiles were generally substituted for thatch, tending to spread more widely than brick and often being combined with walls of local stone.

Thus by 1800 the walls of rural buildings were predominantly of stone throughout Durham and most of Northumberland, while in Yorkshire a broad contrast existed between stone houses in uplands and brick houses in lowlands. Roofing materials also displayed considerable contrasts: thatch by this time was everywhere much reduced, with pantiles widely used in the eastern lowlands, giving way inland to heavy stone slates.

Developments in the 19th and 20th centuries

As industrialisation in the 19th century brought improved transport facilities and reduced transport costs, it became easier to order cheap materials, such as Welsh and Westmorland roof slates, in large quantity from a distance and local building materials and methods were often abandoned. Long-standing differences in building styles thus became increasingly blurred. Differences were not, however, wholly erased: away from the coalfields and the conurbations, extensive areas of countryside and their built fabric remained remarkably unsullied and today there is still a recognisable patterning of rural building materials that reflects the geological and physical background of the region. Several factors were conducive to this continuity. First, rural housing on many of the great landed estates had been much improved in the 18th and early 19th centuries, using mainly local building materials and simple styles that often melded vernacular and polite features, and in the second half of the 19th century, while industrial towns grew substantially, rural populations remained relatively stable or declined and housing demand in the countryside was therefore subdued. Furthermore, much of the first half of the 20th century was a period of agricultural depression and decline of the great estates. Rural services also diminished, hastened by the development of bus services, which made the towns more accessible. In the inter-war period the only additions to many villages were small council-house estates built in order to maintain a viable level of population during the depression. The 1932 Town and Country Planning Act checked urban sprawl and sporadic rural housing, while planning controls since the Second World War have restricted rural housing and regulated building styles, particularly emphasising traditional materials and design. In the North East a considerable contribution has been made by the three National Parks, with their recognition that the homogeneity of buildings, either grouped or dispersed, is a defining characteristic of the landscape, which must be sensitively conserved.

In recent decades, the decline of agriculture has put traditional farm buildings at serious risk either through their dereliction or conversion to alternative uses, mainly into permanent dwellings but also for new industrial and tourist businesses. Pressure for conversion results mainly from a shift of activities from urban to rural areas, which has been encouraged by government policies in order to stimulate economic development in rural areas and off-set the decline in farming.

SETTLEMENTS

Throughout the North East there is a long-standing contrast of rural settlement patterns between the lowlands and the uplands, which reflects the combined and inter-related influences of physical milieu and agrarian organisation. In the lowlands, where successful cereal and livestock farming was possible, nucleated villages are the basic elements and the isolated farms between the villages are a product of secondary dispersal, while in the uplands, oriented more towards pastoral farming, isolated farmsteads and hamlets dominate. The division is not clear cut and in some areas, such as the lower reaches of the major dales, the settlement patterns are transitional in character. Moreover, there has been considerable fluidity of settlement patterns and forms which cannot always be fully explained. Differences in the physical environment are clearly persuasive but no crude determinism is involved.

Villages

An outstanding feature of the rural settlement pattern is the wide belt of old villages stretching through the Vale of York and the coastal lowlands of Durham and Northumberland, with extensions along the major east–west corridors of the Tyne and Aire and into the lower reaches of many flanking upland valleys and dales (Fig. 6.11). These areas constitute the northern sector of the great tract of 'champion' land running roughly south-west to north-east across central England, territory long characterised by strongly nucleated settlements, communally cultivated open-fields (townfields) and scattered strip holdings. The origin of village and open-field organisation in England remains obscure and seems to have occurred at different times in different regions. In the North East it appears several centuries later than in some areas further south, and may have been imposed in the aftermath of the Norman Conquest, when a new aristocracy undertook a planned concentration of the native farmsteads and hamlets scattered over their estates. The formal layout of many northern villages around greens is consistent with a strong element of settlement planning, and archaeological excavations on deserted medieval village sites in Northumberland, Durham and Yorkshire indicate that the settlements were built on previously unoccupied sites. Pre-Conquest farm sites, absorbed into the new open-field areas, are sometimes marked by diagnostic place-names and productive patches of land enriched by a legacy of concentrated manuring and settlement refuse.

How far indigenous institutions lie beneath Norman manorial and village organisation is uncertain. Pre-Conquest England had a system of extensive estates, known as shires, divided into vills or townships. The names Richmondshire, Hexhamshire, Norhamshire and others have survived to recent times in the North East. The arrangements of tenure and service which pertained in the shires did not

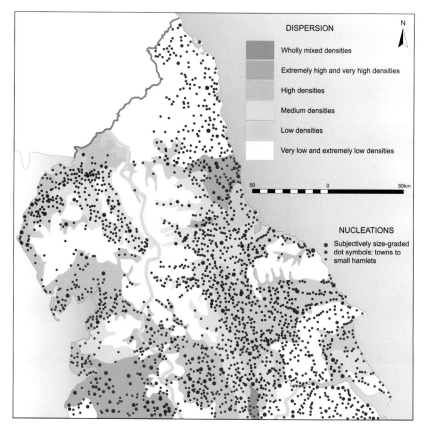

Fig. 6.11 Rural settlement in northern England, mid-19th century. The map shows the distribution of size-graded nucleated settlements and variations in the density of dispersed settlement before the deepening of industrialisation and urbanisation. A feature of the North East is the wide extent of lowland areas with numerous nucleations and a very low to medium density of dispersed settlement (based on Roberts & Wrathmell 2000).

directly determine the form of settlements in the vills, neither is the presence of an Anglo-Saxon church a sure indicator of the existence of a village, since many early churches served wide surrounding areas of dispersed settlement. But there is evidence for clustering at the king's estate centre in Yeavering and at the minor estate centre of Thirlings, though both of these had become abandoned before the end of the 7th century. A strengthening of nucleation may have been underway before the Norman takeover as part of a complex process that involved the beginnings of manorialisation and the shared farming spaces of open fields, but it is difficult to put a date on this because the archaeological methods of dating from pottery are not precise enough.[6] In Northumberland and Durham some aspects of the more archaic arrangements survived into the 12th century, recorded, for example in the Boldon Book of 1183 when the Bishop of Durham conducted a survey of his lands and in the old shire of Bamburgh where the king retained interests. Similarly, the formation of villages in the north may have begun later, given impulse by the bishopric and priory of Durham in the 12th century.

By the 14th century the level of nucleation in the region had probably peaked and the proportion of rural population living in villages was greater than today. Subsequently, as in many parts of England, widespread depopulation and desertion of villages have occurred in many periods and for various reasons. In the North East, village desertion in late medieval and early modern times has sometimes been attributed to border conflict. However, even in Northumberland and close to the Scottish borders the level of desertion at that time was seemingly no greater than in many other parts of England. In fact, the need for manpower for civil defence was an incentive to prevent desertions. Neither was desertion concentrated on 'marginal' upland soils. Indeed, desertion seems to be greatest where the density of villages is high: both the surviving and deserted villages are concentrated in the eastern lowlands of the region (Fig. 6.12).

Some shrinking and desertion of villages is apparent from the 14th to the 16th centuries accompanied by gradual consolidation and enclosure of open-field strip holdings. However, most of the desertion, especially in Northumberland and Durham, occurred in the 17th and 18th centuries as a by-product of wider agrarian improvements centred on the conversion of open-field settlements into severalty farmholds. The process at work here was not depopulation but dispersal of population from the village nucleus. Enclosure, either by private agreements or manorial decree, was thus well underway before the period of parliamentary enclosure in the 18th and 19th centuries, which transformed the rural landscapes of so many open-field areas farther south in England. Parliamentary enclosures had considerable impact on Yorkshire, much less so in Northumberland, but dealt in both cases more with enclosure of moors and wasteland than with enclosure of arable land.

Despite numerous desertions, plenty of medieval villages in the region do survive and their open fields, which have long been comprehensively reorganised and enclosed, have left a strong legacy in the landscape, including former strips fossilised in present-day field boundaries and well preserved ridge-and-furrow corrugations on wetter claylands. However, surviving ridges are not always associated with surviving villages and in some places medieval rigs have been modified and re-aligned by ploughing in recent centuries on a greater scale than previously thought.

Depopulation of old villages continued in the 18th and 19th centuries during the process of emparking around great houses, and was sometimes accompanied by the creation of new, model estate villages. Rebuilding old villages and creating new, planned villages has been a continuing process with many forms: in the 19th century it included hamlets to accommodate labourers on large Northumbrian farms (many now converted for holiday use) and colliery villages in semi-rural settings (many recently demolished as coal mining ended) and, in the 20th century, various small-scale rural resettlement projects and the Forestry Commission's villages in Northumberland designed by Thomas Sharp, such as Stonehaugh and Byreness.

Fig. 6.12 Enclosure of open fields and common pastures, and the distribution of deserted settlements in northern England. Surviving and deserted villages formerly supported by communally organised open fields are widespread on the lowlands of northern England. West of the Pennines the nucleation level is lighter and desertion slight. On the eastern lowlands, desertion levels are high and in some areas deserted sites are comparable in number with surviving ones and may even exceed them. High desertion levels generally correspond with initially high village densities. Extending over many centuries from the Norman period or earlier, desertion had varied causes which include depopulation and retreat from marginal land in the 14th and 15th centuries, Tudor conversions of arable fields to grazing land, Border conflict, and depopulation of villages during the agrarian improvements of the 17th and 18th centuries. Nucleation and desertion levels are generally highest on the Vale of York and the Yorkshire Wolds. Desertion has been slight on the scarp-and-vale topography of South Yorkshire, while the Humberhead Levels and the Vale of Pickering were uncongenial to village settlement in the first place. Many Northumbrian villages disintegrated early due to enclosure by private agreements and landlord initiatives, while conservative ecclesiastical control may partly account for the retention of villages in Durham. Enclosure by agreement had early and widespread effects in Northumberland and Durham where open fields often occupied a small proportion of the townships, large extents of waste facilitated agrarian reorganisation and Border lords and prelates had power to introduce change. Before the end of the medieval period, piecemeal enclosure by agreement was underway in Yorkshire and many villages had lost their open fields and common grazing. Parliamentary Acts were required to complete the process of enclosure and had considerable impact on moor and waste in the Wolds, Holderness, the Vale of York and Pennine dales (based on Roberts & Wrathmell 2002, 11 & 61).

Parliamentary Enclosures	Enclosed before 1801	●	Deserted village site as recorded by DMVRG
	Enclosed 1802 - 1845	□	Enclosures and conversions 1485 - 1607
	Enclosed after 1845	▲	Durham enclosures and conversions 1551 - 1740

Dispersed settlement

In the extensive uplands of the region, with their pastoral leanings, nucleated settlements tend to be small, widely separated and of varied nature and origin. Single dispersed farms, where each family lives at a distance from its neighbours, are the dominant settlement units; a pattern produced at different periods by piecemeal clearance of waste and retained owing to its convenience for livestock farming. Upland dispersal seems to be a long-standing attribute and scattered, fragmentary remnants of earlier habitation, which include hut sites, field systems,

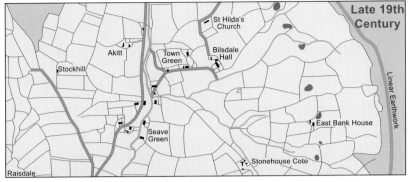

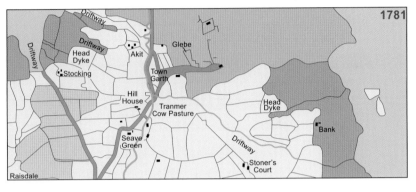

Fig. 6.13 Seave Green and Bilsdale, Cleveland Hills, North York Moors.
Numerous scattered hamlets with patches of town-field and outlying farms are an interesting feature of the settlement in this area. Some of the hamlets may be decayed villages or represent a settlement type ancestral to villages proper. Bilsdale contains a chapel and manor house and the place-name 'Town Green' suggests an earlier small village. Seave Green is merely a loose collection of farms around a green (based on Spratt & Harrison 1996, 99).

linear earthworks, cairns and burial sites, are widespread and sometimes impressive. Their extent, chronology and functions, however, are difficult to interpret coherently owing to poor documentation and the limitations of conventional archaeological approaches.

There is a range of transitional forms between wholly nucleated and wholly dispersed, and evidence of considerable fluidity in the form and pattern of settlements over time. Numerous villages have changed their form quite radically, shifted position, totally disappeared or shrunk to a single farm. In many locations, the single farms may be the only remains of planned dispersal from a village that is now scarcely identifiable. Moreover, old farm clusters may sometimes have been simply consolidated into one large holding, without any dispersal occurring.

While villages are closely associated with champion farming, hamlets have diverse origins and particularly fluid forms, reflecting, for example, agrarian reorganisation, developments in transport and communication systems, or the rise and fall of local mining and industrial enterprises. In the 18th and 19th centuries, for example, the West Riding valleys experienced a marked phase of 'late nucleation' associated with the rise of rural textile manufacturing and population growth. Much of the medieval rural settlement in this area consisted of scatters of single farms on the periphery of cultivated ground reclaimed from the vast moorlands and loosely focused on a local church and a hall. However, as industry and population grew, more compact, village-like settlements were formed by infilling between the existing steadings.

This raises the intriguing and never satisfactorily answered question of whether the hamlets and isolated farms in some areas are relics of a dispersed settlement pattern that preceded the development of nucleated villages and open field farming, and that where nucleation and dispersal occur together the dispersal may be older than the nuclei. On the North Yorkshire Moors, for example, some hamlets seem to have resulted from the decay of former nucleations while others may be traces of a settlement type pre-dating the villages where a manor hall provided the focus for later growth (Fig. 6.13).

Fig. 6.14 Dispersed farms in Weardale.
Farming in Weardale is essentially pastoral. The open moorland is grazed as stinted pastures for cattle and sheep, while on the floor and sides of the dale hay is much the major crop and drystone walls of late 18th and early 19th-century origin outline the patchwork of grass fields. Woodland is largely confined to the courses of valley streams and daleside gills. The dominant pattern of dispersed settlement is partly of medieval origin but has been intensified and extended by lead mining, which until the late 19th century was a widespread supplement to farming. Hamlets and villages are strung out along the floor of the dale.

In the late medieval period, the pattern of settlement became generally more dispersed as early enclosure of open fields led to secondary dispersion in the lowlands and piecemeal encroachment intensified on the edges of upland moors. In Northumberland and Durham, where transhumance was deeply established, the seasonal sites or shielings on the extensive inland moors were often converted into permanent farms. In the upper reaches of the Yorkshire dales the granges and vaccaries (cattle-raising farms) owned by great lay and ecclesiastical landowners were gradually subdivided and leased out, and reclamation of the moorland edges for new holdings was also underway. By the 16th century the present pattern of small scattered farms had been established in the Yorkshire dales, and by the middle of the 17th century the farms were largely occupied by freehold farmers. From the end of the 17th century, lead mining grew to become a major activity in the north Pennines. A combination of mining with subsistence farming was encouraged by the mine owners who provided their employees with smallholdings. Thus, lead mining sustained a semi-rural pattern of living and, unlike coal mining in the lowlands, intensified and extended dispersed settlement units. In the late 18th and early 19th centuries, pastoralism reasserted itself in upland areas with an emphasis on extensive sheep farming. This regime has since retained the settlement pattern and general character of the moorlands and, along with grouse shooting, has been a deterrent to afforestation (Fig. 6.14).

Settlement morphology

While there is considerable diversity in the form and layout of nucleated settlements in the North East, many villages have a distinctive morphology, with the houses located in rows around elongated, square or polygonal greens. Comparable 'green villages' are found in many parts of England, indeed over wide expanses of the North European Plain: it is the high proportion of green villages within the North East that requires emphasis and explanation. Are these village shapes stable and of long standing, perhaps the product of wide-scale rural reorganisation and settlement planning after the Norman Conquest?

Fig. 6.15 Green villages.

ABOVE: *The green at Elsdon, Northumberland, is a large informal space, distinct from the more regular plan of village greens in Durham and Yorkshire, which are mainly of Norman origin. The geographer M R Conzen considered Elsdon to be characteristic of an early type of Anglian settlement in the north, alongside which the fine Norman motte-and-bailey earthwork was built in the 12th century.*

ABOVE RIGHT: *Piercebridge, County Durham, with its spacious rectangular green, is on the site of a Roman fort to the west of a Roman bridge that carries Watling Street across the River Tees. The walls of the fort are clearly traceable (especially bottom left and top centre). There is, however, no clear evidence of continuity of settlement. The village buildings, most of which are connected, include old farmsteads, a church and graveyard.*

RIGHT: *The layout of Hutton-le-Hole (North York Moors) around a green is possibly the result of a re-ordering of an earlier settlement devastated during the Norman Conquest. The open fields here were enclosed by local agreement in 1671, but the settlement has retained much of its medieval form.*

Or have the settlements been shaped by progressive alteration of earlier, less differentiated forms? That a substantial measure of planning was involved at the outset does seem likely and there is little to suggest the replanning of medieval villages to accommodate greens. Individual villages have sometimes extended their green and, in some cases, encroached on it, but it seems that most green villages adhere essentially to their earliest plan, and any changes have generally tended to regularise and formalise their layout (Figs 6.15 and 6.16).

As the forces of agricultural improvement transformed the countryside in the 18th and 19th centuries, industrial enterprise also quickened, the two trends mutually reinforcing and creating growing demands for new housing. Before the 19th century, the main industrial activities, based on coal, iron, lead and textiles, were small-scale and scattered in the countryside rather than the towns; coal miners' cottages, which were often in the form of a single or small number of terraced rows close to the pits, were superimposed on the older pattern of green villages and dispersed farms and only in limited areas were they numerous enough to appreciably modify the landscape. However, with the rapid advance of coal mining technology in the 19th and early 20th centuries, new and bigger mining settlements appeared, some of them virtually small, carefully planned towns, either joined to older agricultural villages or built in the open countryside. A distinctive semi-industrial/semi-rustic type of coalfield landscape emerged in which farmland, industrial installations, old villages and new industrial settlements were indiscriminately mixed. Such landscapes were recurrent features in the region and are still identifiable despite substantial and determined policies of environmental regeneration and settlement modernisation in the post-industrial era.

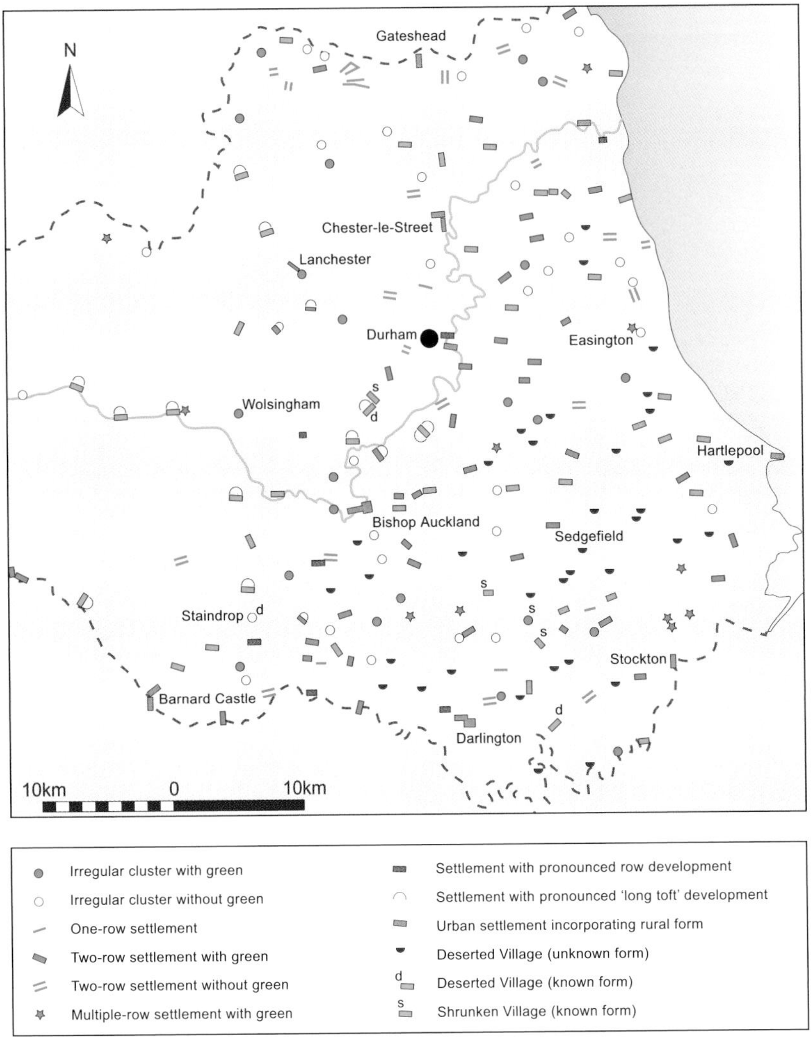

WOODLANDS

By the close of the prehistoric era, if not well before, woodland in many places had been reduced to the minimum area needed to sustain communities that required large quantities of locally-produced timber for fuel, building, fencing and various tools and utensils. Similar demands ensured the endurance of managed native woodland until the 19th century, when cheap, imported softwood became available and estate owners looked for more rapid returns on investment and less labour-intensive land management. On the broad scale, the woods seen in the region today reflect the abandonment of traditional woodland practices, the partial change of use to shooting, public recreation and nature conservation and the preference for fast-maturing, mainly alien, softwood timber (Fig. 6.17).

Fig. 6.16 Village forms, Co. Durham.
A high proportion of the traditional rural settlements in Durham are green villages in which homesteads cluster around open grassy spaces. Long, narrow two-row villages with elongated greens are most characteristic but there are numerous one-row villages and irregular clusters, as well as larger four-row villages, some of which developed into market centres (based on Roberts 1970).

● Irregular cluster with green	▬ Settlement with pronounced row development
○ Irregular cluster without green	⌒ Settlement with pronounced 'long toft' development
— One-row settlement	▭ Urban settlement incorporating rural form
Two-row settlement with green	▼ Deserted Village (unknown form)
= Two-row settlement without green	d Deserted Village (known form)
✴ Multiple-row settlement with green	s Shrunken Village (known form)

A form of timber production that was extremely widespread in the earlier part of the medieval period was wood pasture, though this former facet of the day-to-day rural scene has virtually vanished. Often existing on the less windswept northern commons, wood pasture consisted of pollarded trees that were sufficiently widely spaced as to allow sunlight to reach the sward between the trees. Pollarding at a height of around 2.4m allowed the new shoots to develop above the reach of browsing animals. In this way, the raising of timber and of leafy fodder – in the form of poles and 'green hews' cut from the tops of the pollarded trunks – could be combined with grazing. Frequently, medieval landlords, like the great monasteries, would allow their tenants to lop green hews but would forbid the felling of trees. The ecological balance was, however, a delicate one and with increasing pressure on the land, the delightful park-like landscapes of wood pasture were displaced. In the lower sections of the Dales, documentary evidence suggests that the last enclosures of wood pasture, with excessively old and gnarled trees, were being removed in the 17th and 18th centuries (Fig. 6.18).

The visual legacy is far more prominent and extensive in the case of the woods managed as coppices or

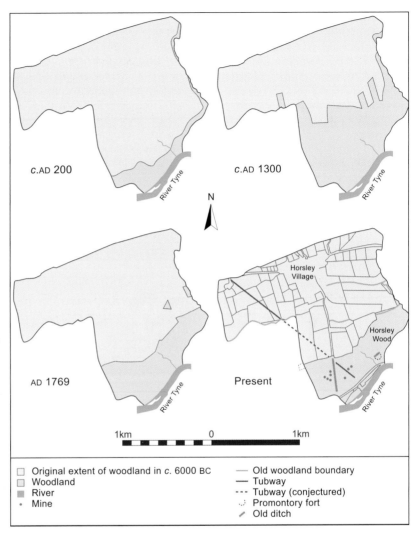

'coppice with standards'. These woods were divided into compartments, with the trees and shrubs in each compartment being felled on a rota to produce a constant stream of light timber. The trees were cut at ground level, with the coppice 'stool' then producing a crop of poles suitable for fuel, wattle, light construction, charcoal and many other uses. Because the soft growth springing from the stools was very vulnerable to grazing, special protection from cattle and deer was necessary, in the form of hedges grown on woodbanks or dead hedging, though in the north of England drystone walls were very commonly used to enclose woods. Frequently, the underwood was coppiced, while above them woodland trees, normally oak, elm or ash in the north, were grown as standards on a much longer felling cycle to provide heavy timber for houses, bridges and boat-building. In the typical northern wood, coppicing (and the pollarding of any mature trees growing around the margins) has been neglected for one or two centuries. Consequently, the coppice stools are no longer seen to be crowned in a fuzz of leafy growth swaying on slender wands or poles. Rather, they have the appearance of giant squid buried in the ground, with tentacles, formed of uncut poles as thick as thighs, reaching skywards. Working coppice stools never looked like this, but the typical northern wood displays the consequence of abandoning the management of native hardwoods. In mining areas there was a demand for rods for corves (baskets for carrying coal out of mines) (Fig. 6.19).

Fig. 6.17 Horsley Wood. This wood lies on the north bank of the Tyne in the ancient township of Horsley close to Hadrian's Wall; an area of enclosed fields, small villages and dispersed farmsteads. The Romano-British landscape here was well developed agriculturally and largely devoid of woodland. Woodland regenerated after the Roman occupation but by the mid-13th century was again much reduced and the medieval open fields incorporated prehistoric and Romano-British antecedent features. Medieval Horsley Wood was contained by large woodland banks and until the 18th century its uses included coppicing, pig- and cattle-grazing and game. The open fields were enclosed in the early 18th century and half of the woodland removed, its boundaries left as ghost features in the new field pattern. In the 20th century the wood was felled and replanted with conifers (based on Tolan-Smith 1997, 50–3).

Fig. 6.18 Wood pasture with stunted oak pollards above Leighton Reservoir, *between Nidderdale and Wensleydale. Part of the estates of Fountains Abbey and subsequently of a deer park, this is a relic of a much more extensive area of wood pasture. Pollards in wood pasture were well spaced to allow grass growth and grazing between them.*

Fig. 6.19 Changing structure of woods on the Coal Measures in the Sheffield area*, 1650, 1890 and 1980. Until the 19th century, the woods of South Yorkshire were largely confined to native trees growing mainly on valley sides where their composition varied in response to soil and drainage conditions. Rowan and oak grew on the poorer, high slopes; ash, elm and taller oaks on lower slopes; and willows and alders in the waterlogged valley bottoms. Woods formed an integral part of the rural economy, traditionally managed as coppice (small, multi-stemmed trees for periodic cutting) and standards (tall, single-stemmed trees for timber). Mines, quarries and prehistoric earthworks indicate that many woods had long, eventful histories of human usage. By the 19th century, coppicing was in decline and mixed plantations appeared including conifers and other introduced species. By the late 20th century, woods were no longer worked commercially and became dominated by a dense canopy of mature trees of similar age, which allowed only a sparse shrub layer with decaying trees. Some surviving woods are now being managed for recreational and educational activities, and coppicing has been revived (based on Jones 2000).*

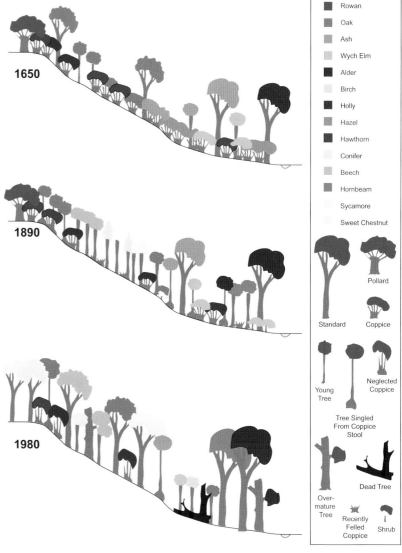

The presence of the former woodlands is very evident in the heritage of place-names. In the north-eastern part of England 'spring' names are very common and the great majority do not refer to the season or to water but to coppiced woods. 'Fall' is a similar name that is quite commonly found, while 'hag' or 'hagg' are often encountered and they refer to the divisions within medieval coppiced woods. The medieval woodland economy was often bolstered by grazing swine (or cattle) amongst the trees, though these were normally removed when vulnerable fawns were present. Place-names including 'den' denote woodland swine pastures (though this element can also mean a valley). Common wood-related names in the north deriving from the Old English, Old Danish and Old Norse languages include 'frith', 'lund', 'shaw', 'skew', 'with' and 'wood'. A very special class of medieval wood that has left a numerous legacy of place-names across the northern countryside was the holly grove or 'hollins'. With the onset of autumn, the branches with thornless leaves that grow at the top of holly trees were lopped and stored in 'helms' or barns, being fed to hungry beasts as the reserves of hay declined. One of many examples of ancient woods is Hareshaw Dene near Bellingham, Northumberland, a steep valley lined with oak and ash, while the Strid Woods in Wharfedale contain both ancient woodland vegetation and an extensive legacy of landscaping and planting.

Despite the efforts of many estate owners, the woodland resources of the north contracted and deteriorated during the medieval period and at the end of the era, in 1546, Leland bemoaned the condition of hunting reserves and saw many that were like Knaresborough, where: 'The principal wood of the Forest is much decayed'. He found the great wood of Cheviot to be spoiled, with but crooked trees and scrub remaining. The demands by estate joiners for large supplies of softwood timber, as fencing replaced hedgerows, and the reluctance of their employers to have investment tied up in a hardwood crop that took up to a century to mature, all led to the coniferisation of many northern woods. In some places, two thirds or more of the old medieval woods were cleared and replanted with conifers: Scots pine and European larch at first and later Norway and Sitka spruce and Douglas fir or other fashionable imports. Beech was sometimes combined with the larch, producing a dense canopy that suppressed the growth of an underwood, while pheasants were introduced into the sheltered environment. Coniferised ancient woods can often be distinguished from softwood plantations (which can simply be likened to fields growing crops of softwoods) by their curving boundaries, sometimes marked by medieval walls or wood banks and punctuated by surviving pollards that are hundreds of years old. Bluebells, herb Paris and ramsons may still burst from the woodland floor, while glacial erratic boulders may reveal land never cleared for cultivation. The landscape of the coniferised wood is thus a strange juxtaposition of ancient and recent features.

MEDIEVAL HUNTING RESERVES AND DEER PARKS

Today's countrysides contain many reminders of the medieval aristocratic obsession with hunting deer, although the remarkable importance of hunting in northern England is not reflected in a mass of very obviously enduring features. After the Norman Conquest, vast areas had been subjected to Forest Law that was imposed to conserve the game. Several of the royal forests were established in the North East: Galtres in the Vale of York; Pickering in the North York Moors; Wensleydale in the Dales; and, in Northumberland, the forests of Redesdale, Rothbury and Cheviot with, just north of the Roman wall, Lowes. While King John displarked the forest of Wharfedale in 1204, most of the northern forests endured well into the medieval era and three Yorkshire examples, Pickering, Galtres and the immense Forest of Knaresborough, running right up the south-western side of Nidderdale, still existed at the start of the 17th century. In 1608, about 17 other forests survived in regions of England lying to the south, but all those that had existed further north than Yorkshire had gone. Some of the hunting rights in royal forests were later assigned to nobles, as when, in 1199, King John passed his rights in Redesdale to Roger de Umfraville or six years later when his rights of hunting and pasture in Rothbury were granted to Robert Fitz-Roger. Meanwhile, the greater nobles and churchmen were acquiring their own chases, like the great Langstrothdale Chase in the wilds of the Dales or the Clifford's Barden Chase in Wharfedale, with its nine different lodges.

Extensive hunting reserves had existed before the Norman Conquest, but the new dynasty standardised the regulations and made them more rigorous. Under Henry II the kingdom was divided into two jurisdictions, to the north and south of the Trent, and within each division was established a circuit of four judges termed an 'Eyre of the Forest'. Forests, rather than being the vast and continuous woods of popular imagination, were areas subjected to the special laws for the protection of game. The word did not refer to trees but to outlying, usually marginal, land: '*foras*'. The fact that so much land in the north-east of England could so easily be designated as hunting territory must in some part have been related to the terrible Harrying of the North by the Norman armies in 1069–71, which left many estates still partly or wholly barren at the time of Domesday Book in 1086. Within each forest and chase there was an uneasy co-existence between bloodsports and feudal cultivation. The peasantry were disadvantaged by the regulations preventing the disturbance of the deer, while their obligations to their lord would often include special responsibilities such as the care of hunting dogs. Substantial herds of red deer roamed the northern fells and surviving woodlands and roe deer and boar were also found in the woods. Even at the end of the medieval period Leland had mentioned a 'great plenty of Redd Dere and Roo Bukk' in Northumberland. On the whole, however, boar were effectively exterminated and deer were very greatly reduced in the northern forests during the medieval period. The creators of new deer parks began to rely upon largesse in the form of grants of animals from established reserves, while only gifts and calculated restocking policies retained a presence for the boar.

Gradually, over-hunting and the expansion of the farmed area reduced and finally eliminated the red deer. In the 16th century both the wolf and the deer seem to have disappeared from Redesdale. Then, in the first two decades of the 17th century, the armed followers of Sir John Yorke, who was obsessively pursuing a feud with the Cliffords, the great hunting lords of the Dales, systematically exterminated red deer across the Dales from Langstrothdale to Washburndale. It was in that century that the red deer disappeared from the open country of dales and fells, but much more recently wild deer have made a vigorous return. This may reflect the lower levels of human disturbance associated with the mechanisation of many formerly labour-demanding tasks but, at least in Northumberland, is due to excessive 20th-century afforestation providing a congenial habitat for roe deer. Roe, in fact, are probably more numerous in the northern woods than they were in late medieval times, while small wild herds of fallow deer result from escapes from deer parks and a few red deer are present again in Ribblesdale. Today, with the north-east countrysides being cultivated and having less indigenous woodland than most regions of Europe, it is difficult to credit that in the medieval period a horn was blown at the foresters' village of Bainbridge, in the Forest of Wensleydale, at 10 pm each evening from September 27 to Shrovetide to guide travellers who might be lost in the forest.

As the population of the northern counties expanded quite rapidly in the centuries following the Harrying, incursions into the great forests and chases increased and the kings and nobles explored more economic ways of running their estates. Increasingly, recreation became focused on deer parks.[7] These differed from the forests and chases in being much more compact and in having deer-proof boundaries protected by earthworks, palings, hedges or walls that were constructed in manners that allowed wandering deer to enter the reserve, but prevented their escape. By the second half of the medieval period, it was conventional for a castle or substantial manor to have a deer park close at hand, and in some cases, like that of the royal castle at Middleham, in Wensleydale, a small constellation of deer parks was available. The fallow deer, introduced by the Normans from southern Europe, was the species suited to the park enclosures and they could be hunted inside the park, either on horseback or by firing arrows from a hunting tower, or they might be released and pursued across the adjacent working countryside. Associated with the parks were the towers, often positioned on the highest ground within the park, a lodge for the parker, kennels for hunting dogs and the perimeter defences. The parks became so fashionable that they were a major feature of the north-eastern countryside, particularly in places where the land was less valuable in agricultural terms. In Wharfedale and Wensleydale they punctuated the valley flanks at frequent intervals, while in Northumberland the castles at Alnwick and Warkworth had their associated parks. Harrogate is embraced by another small constellation of parks, which were associated with the royal castle and Forest of Knaresborough: Bilton, Haya and Haverah (Fig. 6.20). In Weardale, the Bishop of Durham's park lay between present-day Eastgate and Westgate. Arrangements for the annual great chase in the 12th century were complex and involved the participation of people from across the county. The people of Auckland and Stanhope were required to build a great hall, chapel, chamber, dog kennel and other buildings in the forest and drengs (minor landed gentry) from as far afield as the coastal townships attended with greyhounds.

In some parks, like those around Knaresborough, secondary uses, such as the pasturing of domestic livestock, were part of the park economy from the outset. In many cases, land within the park would be let-out to agricultural tenants, while over the years the hunting and game conservation aspects tended to be overtaken by commercial uses. Most typically, these were the introduction of vaccaries or cattle farms and horse studs, particularly those connected with high-quality animals. For example, Edward III established what became a celebrated stud in his park at Haverah. While most deer parks were created in the 12th and 13th centuries, a few late creations are found, such as Scale Park in the Yorkshire Dales above Kettlewell, which was enclosed for the Earl of Westmorland in 1409. The deer parks were seldom continuously wooded and many, like Ripley in Nidderdale, would have been created by ejecting people from parts of their farmland. Most deer parks, however, included areas of woodland and wood pasture as well as open lawns where the deer could graze. Pollarded trees will have existed, some perhaps originating as hedgerow trees and surviving after the

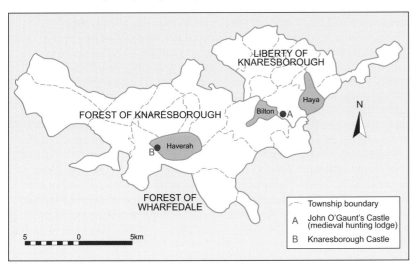

Fig. 6.20 The Forest of Knaresborough and its associated deer parks lay to the south of the River Nidd. *Forests were associated with royal estates, castles and palaces more than with woodland. Deer parks were strongly enclosed to contain deer and exclude poachers. Haverah Park, near Harrogate, was unusually large and covered 900ha.*

135

emparking of the countryside. Such trees would produce leaf fodder, the loppings sometimes being left for the deer. In parks such as Ripley, ancient pollards originating from before the medieval emparking may still be seen.

The creation of a deer park required a special royal licence to empark, and when this was obtained the construction of the encircling deer-proof boundary could commence. Sometimes these boundaries were banks crowned with hedges, palings or palisades, but in the north, stone walls were also common. Scores of lodges crumbled away when forests, chases and parks were abandoned, but the Barden tower in Wharfedale is an impressive late-medieval survival, while the ruined 'John-o'-Gaunt's castle' in Haverah park, with its great moat, was really a fortified lodge visited by several Plantagenet kings. Boundaries of all kinds frequently survive, though today most function solely as field or wood boundaries. Often a section of river would be incorporated into the perimeter. A surviving drystone wall to the north of Lordenshaws, near Rothbury in mid-Northumberland, was the boundary of Robert Fitz-Roger's deer park. A generous heritage of place-names provides clues to the former deer parks. 'Park' names are themselves plentiful, though sometimes they seem to refer to enclosed pastures

Fig. 6.21 Deer herd, Ripley.

rather than true parks. The farm names East-, Middle- and West Park by the A1 in Northumberland derive from the Earl of Northumberland's Callie or Cawledge park. Names including 'dob' appear to indicate places where hunting dogs were kennelled or walked, as with Dob Park, near Harrogate and Dob Lane, Ripley.

One of the most significant legacies of the medieval deer park was its contribution to the design of the landscape parks of the 17th, 18th and 19th centuries. The contrived landscapes of lawns, woods, pollards and spinneys created by Repton and his kind were heavily influenced by the aristocratic hunting countrysides that had existed centuries earlier. Parks have also proved to be of historic landscape value because, so long as they served as reserves or pastures, they protected the land from ploughing. In this way they not only protected the landscapes derived from hunting, but they also preserved monuments from the era preceding emparking. So, in a park like Ripley one can find the holloways of roads and tracks abandoned after the creation of the park, earthworks of medieval farmsteads, hamlets and villages, ridge-and-furrow ploughland, quarrying remains and ancient trees, as well as traces of boundary earthworks and the lodge that were part of the park. Very few parks still contain deer. Ripley still accommodates a herd of fallow, and a fallow herd of a lighter hue can be seen as Studley Royal, near Ripon, while Chillingham, near Wooler, was enclosed by the 13th century and achieved fame for its herd of white park cattle (Fig. 6.21).

MOORLAND

While much moorland in the region consists of acidic grassland, bracken or various types of bog, the upland heather heaths are a special feature. The greater part of the moorland, including the heather heaths, has resulted from the destruction of the natural woodland by humans from the Mesolithic period onwards. For many centuries the moors were regarded as being among the most unrewarding and marginal of environments and, apart from scattered and sporadic coal and lead-mining activities, were used primarily for rough grazing. However, the development of organised shooting of red grouse in the 19th century brought celebrity, celebrities and considerable profits to the upland estates of northern England, especially in Yorkshire. Previously, heather and other moors had formed components of hunting forests and chases like Knaresborough and Cheviot, while sheep had been grazed on moors that were burned to stimulate the growth of young shoots providing a 'soft bite'. This practice of 'swaling' still continues, for grouse also feed on the young heather growth (Fig. 6.22). (Black grouse, a bird rather of the moorland fringe, was also a shooting quarry.)

Fig. 6.22 Heather burning, or 'swaling', is a fundamental feature of the management of Pennine grouse moors. Burning provides a patchwork of heather of varying ages, a necessity for a large grouse population. Normally the heather burn is controlled, but due to a high wind this burn on Reeth High Moor in Swaledale is almost out of control.

The rise of grouse shooting depended on a variety of developments, some were social and concerned the development of ideas about fitting activities for gentlemen, while some were technological and related both to the evolution of firearms and to that of transportation. Before the emergence of an organised 'sport', the fast flying birds may have been pursued in a casual manner by local people, though they were elusive targets and their remote moorland setting could only be enjoyed by those of a hardy constitution. More systematic hunting seems to have developed by the late 18th century when John Byng, who became the 5th Viscount Torrington, recorded that 'hawks' residing in quarries were being destroyed because they preyed upon grouse. By the end of that century the pursuit of 'moor game' was still restricted to those prepared for arduous treks to and across the moors. This, however, was a time when shooting prowess was regarded as socially significant and only the red grouse could match the challenges to marksmanship posed by the woodcock and snipe. At first the shooting was of the 'walked up' variety, with pointer dogs being employed, but subsequently changes to the weaponry transformed the activity.

When organised grouse shooting developed in the northern counties, the region had seen its poorer communities further impoverished by the parliamentary enclosure of the commons, falling sheep prices and later the collapse of lead mining and packhorse trading. The development of grouse shooting offered hopes of revival to the depressed upland economy, though public amenity was lost as the once accessible commons became exclusive private reserves. Such losses were made socially more acceptable as the newly fashionable pursuit of the aristocracy and the rich, rapidly expanding in its popularity, became associated with royalty and the culture of Empire. The sizes of the bags were broadcast in the newspapers as though they were indicators of the manly virtues of the leading guns and the status of the owners of the moors. The activity arrived in an area in which the ability to travel had already been markedly improved by turnpikes, and then the development of railways – reaching Richmond in 1864, Pateley Bridge in 1862, Ilkley in 1865 and Masham in 1875 – allowed participants from southern England to reach a favoured moor within a day's travel. With that the moors were opened to the privileged members of the nation no matter how unfit or aged they might be. George V could take the royal train to the very doorstep of the moors when he made his annual visit to shoot on the Bolton Abbey Estate in Wharfedale, while the railways also allowed the rapid export of birds to London restaurants. In one week in 1901 a game dealer from Richmond sent 17,352 of them southwards.

Changes in the design of firearms played a crucial role in broadening the appeal of the activity and enabled the dramatic expansion in grouse shooting. In the 17th century the birds had been shot over pointing dogs, sometimes by marksmen who could shoot grouse on the wing with flintlocks. Breech-loading shotguns firing self-contained cartridges were displayed at the Great Exhibition in 1851 and they opened the 'sport' to participants of far more modest abilities. By the 1870s hammerless guns and smokeless powder were available, which gave the shooter a clear view of the game when firing the second barrel.

These innovations resulted in the development of characteristic landscapes of grouse shooting.[8] Because of the changes the birds were too easily massacred and so the element of difficulty was increased by having them driven towards, rather than away from, the shooters. The clientele, which tended to be mature in years, over-indulgent in habits and not wedded to strenuous lifestyles, preferred to have the social aspects of shooting maximised and those of a physically demanding nature kept to a minimum. An answer to all these problems was found in the 'battue' form of shooting, from the French *battre*, to beat. A line of beaters flushed the grouse from the heather and drove them to the line of shooters waiting in butts. The shooting was more challenging, though in seconds scores of birds could be dead: in 1888 Lord Walsingham employed two loaders and used four breech-loading guns to slaughter 1,070 birds in 20 drives (Fig. 6.23).

The impact on the setting was immense. Inns, which had hovered on the margins of profitability, now flourished and expanded, new shooting lodges appeared as distant successors to those of the old Forests to accommodate the shooting parties and also to serve as the places where economic and political deals of profound importance were sealed. Less imposing shelters, in the forms of shooting houses and lunch huts, also appeared on the moors, some of them served by new carriage tracks enabling the ladies to join the shooting party for lunch. Perhaps the most characteristic structure to appear in the landscape was the shooting butts, behind which the shooters were concealed. These were built in a variety of forms: round, semi-circular, square, sunken, H-shaped or built from wooden sleepers. All were carefully positioned according to terrain, drainage, visibility and prevailing wind direction. Occasionally, convenient enclosure walls were made to double as butts. The shooting, which provided employment for keepers and additional income for the tenants who served as beaters, and its spin-offs in the area of transport, poaching and catering, all contributed significantly to the otherwise marginal environments associated with grouse moors.

Changing social and employment conditions following the Great War resulted in a retreat from the golden age of grouse shooting, while in the 1970s a parasitic worm began to undermine bird populations. Labour to maintain the moors, including by regular burning, is harder to find or afford and bracken is invading some heather moors. However, the activity is still far from dead and will continue both to encourage the traditional swaling and maintenance of the upland environments and to antagonise interests concerned with access and animal welfare. Whatever one may think of the activity, its claims concerning landscape conservation are stronger than many: between the Tyne and the Teviot vast coniferous plantations have colonised the once open moorland and the moorland habitat is one that most would prefer to conserve.

FIELDSCAPES

Below the unenclosed moors and conifer plantations are fieldscapes of varied forms.
Some are composed of fields of types that are seen throughout England, while
others display relics of those that were more particular to the region. Prehistoric
fields can be seen in numerous upland locations and several very fine examples are
included within the region. They can be very loosely divided into the localised
clusters of irregular fields and little paddocks that served a local community, hamlet
or farmstead and the far more extensive and organised systems of co-axial fields that
represented the wholesale reorganisation of enclosure and land-holding patterns
across extensive areas. Field patterns of the former type include the small paddocks

of different sizes seen at many places that have escaped destruction by later ploughing, such as Burton Moor on the southern flanks of Wensleydale and in the Cheviots around the Breamish and College valleys. Low, parallel banks survive as visible relics of extensive prehistoric partitioning of the landscape and can be seen in many places, like the Nappa Hall region of Wensleydale. The co-axial patterns are best represented on the moors on the northern side of Swaledale, where a wholesale reorganisation of fields and property seems to have taken place in the centuries around 1000 BC, with the associated fields being abandoned when a second co-axial system was introduced. Co-axial systems were not used in the Cheviots but areas of ploughing with narrow riggs (known as cord rigg) are associated with hillforts and other prehistoric settlements (Fig. 6.24).

Fig. 6.24 Wharfedale is rich in fossil and functioning field systems. On the marginal land above Grassington (left of centre, background) there are extensive tumbled walls, lynchets and cairns, the remnants of a late prehistoric/Romano-British co-axial field system partly subdivided by transverse walling between the axial boundaries. Around the village, plough ridges associated with medieval open-field cultivation are discernible within the present-day fields. The edges of Grass Wood, a former deer park, are visible top left. Today's wide network of walled fields is partly the product of enclosure of the village's arable open fields by agreement begun in the 17th century. Parliamentary Enclosure at the end of the 18th century created the large, mainly rectilinear divisions on the open grazing land, which cut across the long-deserted prehistoric field systems. The conspicuous convergence of enclosure walls on the edge of the settlement indicates the importance in limestone country of giving livestock access to a stream.

Piles of stone grouped together in prehistoric cairnfields survive in many upland areas of northern England and the Scottish borders where they are frequently associated with early field boundaries and probably result from the clearing of stones to form or improve fields. Good examples are found on Bollihope Common in Weardale, at Chatton on the Northumberland sandstones and on the North York Moors, where Bronze Age fields, in places like Near Moor and Snilesworth, have been masked by subsequent extension of heather moors into areas that had previously existed largely as green pastures.

Ancient field systems are apparent on the flanks of many fells in Northumberland and there, in the Yorkshire Dales and particularly on the North York Moors and Yorkshire Wolds, can be seen the traces of linear earthworks that partitioned the farming territories. The Wolds, with light, well-drained soils, will have had the most intense settlement and cultivation in the prehistoric era, though later cultivation has erased earlier evidence (as well as much of the topsoil). Here, the linear earthworks, the 'dykes' or 'entrenchments', like the Great Wold Dyke, are the best surviving evidence of ancient land-holdings and they suggest that communities defined and guarded the boundaries of their landholdings with great care.

Indigenous farmers were left to pursue their traditional methods of farming during the Roman occupation, though during this period or the one that followed, rectilinear fieldscapes appear to have been set-out from some of the Roman roads. The imperial homeland and the numerous garrisons will have provided eager markets for northern farm production, while the stability imposed by the occupying forces encouraged commerce. Agriculture is likely to have become more intensive and some land appears to have fallen out of use after the Roman departure, and as it was later re-colonised a revolution affected many northern townships. The transformations had begun around the 8th and 9th centuries in the English Midlands with the appearance of open-field farming, changes in the organisation of worship and the establishment of new villages.

In some lowland locations, from the Vale of York to the coastal lowlands of Northumberland, patterns of open-field farming not too different from the '3-field systems' of the school textbooks were introduced. However, north-eastern England adopted its own intriguing variations, notably the 'long-strips', which were introduced at a very early stage in the development of medieval communal farming. The reasons for adopting field strips that were up to a mile long (often showing the same reversed-S plans seen in conventional strips) is uncertain. In some eastern parts of Yorkshire their dimensions have been preserved through the early enclosure of communal ploughland and around Middleton, just west of Pickering, hedgerows mark the sides of many former long strips. In other locations, variations on the 'infield–outfield' systems of northern Britain were found, with nutrients being lavished on the ploughlands of the infield, which were kept constantly in production, while outfield land was periodically broken-in, briefly tilled and abandoned. Such systems were favoured in places where good land for the infield was found in limited and localised pockets.

Sheep were prominent in farming economies of the north and sometimes farming communities, such as that of Cayton near Fountains Abbey, were dislodged to make way for the monastic farms or 'granges' of the Cistercians, staffed by a priest and small contingent of lay brothers. Sometimes the traditional peasant mixed economy would be replaced by specialised shepherding or the breeding of cattle. An expansion of sheep farming that was far more destructive took place in Tudor times and accounted for the desertion of scores of northern villages, particularly in the Wolds, though with sheep already prominent in their medieval economies, the Dales and parts of Northumberland were less affected. Outchester and West Chirton in Northumberland were among the villages destroyed. Nearest the Scottish border, the ancient system of herdsmen who

moved with their stock in the summer to huts or shielings set amongst the upland grazings survived into the 17th century, longer than elsewhere in England. Today, the stones from the former thatched huts litter the slopes near rivers and streams and throughout the uplands '-shiel' and '-scale' names denoting the old summer settlements are very common.

In this region the corrugations of the arable land surface seldom reached the heights of the plough ridges seen in the Midlands. Much faintly-ridged ploughland, particularly in the Dales and uplands, seems to have resulted from the phase of population growth preceding the Black Death, with ploughing not continuing for long enough to corrugate the surface to a degree that is plainly visible under normal weather conditions. Following light snow or a snow melt, however, the extent of ridged ploughland is seen to be remarkable (Fig. 6.25). Some particularly interesting examples of very late ridge and furrow can be seen from the road or the train when approaching York from Harrogate. These ridges are straight, fit into the grid of parliamentary enclosure fields and result from ploughing by steam engines during the 19th century. There is a marked contrast in the small township of Fenton, just north of Morpeth in Northumberland, where the broad ridges of medieval ploughing can be seen in the long fields with sinuous boundaries around the village nucleus. The higher land in the western edge of the township, however, was not enclosed and cultivated before the 18th century and here the fields were laid out with straight boundaries in rectangular blocks and the ridges are narrow and straight. The remarkable strip lynchets of the Dales, perhaps best seen in the vicinity of Linton in Wharfedale, are hillside terraces that are produced by ploughing and are known locally as 'raines'. They, too, may largely result from attempts to plough very marginal sloping land during the population increase of the 13th century, though some examples could be much older. Other resources of communal land existed as upland commons and as meadowland

The privately-held land of the medieval period was concentrated in enclosed pastures and house plots or 'tofts', though, as the period advanced, so more and more land was extracted from the furlongs or 'cultures' of the open ploughland and enclosed by hedges or walls. The hedges were probably at this time composed of seedlings and saplings of various types gathered in the woods – and

Fig. 6.25 Snow cover gives a sharpness to this impressive flight of strip lynchets or cultivation terraces (known as 'raines' in the Yorkshire dales) in Wharfedale, formed by medieval ploughing of valley slopes.

Fig. 6.26 Contrasting field patterns:

TOP LEFT: *The remarkably long and narrow fields around Pickering and Middleton in the Vale of Pickering reflect the length and curvature of medieval plough strips in the narrow village territories, stretching from the upland moors to the lowland carrs. Many of these strips were fossilised by hedges after the Enclosure Act of 1765.*

BOTTOM LEFT: *There is a contrast in the pattern of fields on either side of the long village of Flaxton in the Vale of York. On one side are long, narrow curvilinear tofts formed by gradual consolidation and enclosure of medieval cultivation ridges, and on the other a formal layout of large rectilinear fields and dispersed farmsteads. This contrast is repeated in a number of villages in the Vale.*

TOP RIGHT: *North Northumberland, for a long time backward and unenclosed, was deeply influenced by improvement projects in the late 18th and 19th centuries. Ewart Park estate in Glendale was transformed around the end of the 18th century by the landlord Horace St Paul who introduced ornamental parkland around his new residence, substantial isolated farmsteads, and large rectilinear fields defined by hedges and sheltered by scattered copses. Despite 20th-century changes, the improved area (foreground and middle of photo) still conveys the sense of a 'landowner's landscape', one where progressive farming was combined with aesthetic considerations.*

BOTTOM RIGHT: *Lying above Keighley and the well-populated valley of the River Worth, the plateau surface of Keighley Moor has traditionally been used for sheep grazing and quarrying of Millstone Grit. Parliamentary Enclosure on the lower plateau slopes produced the extensive regular layout of small- to medium-sized fields defined by drystone walls, which stretches to the open moorland on higher ground.*

through the inclusion of standard timber and fruit trees they also seem to have compensated for woodland resources lost during the clearance of woods and wood pasture. Even by Victorian times, the panoramas of ancient hedgerows regularly punctuated with massive old pollarded oaks and ashes was still spectacular. The old hedges with their remaining pollards follow curving courses and generally include stretches of holly, oak, elm, hazel and crab apple, with field maple appearing as one moves towards the Vale of York. In the uplands, where the hedging shrubs grew less readily, excesses of stone and boulder litter were available and walls were employed. The medieval examples often have quite large boulders or 'orthostats' incorporated into their bases, the stones sometimes being derived from the clearance of ground for cultivation. Some walls can be dated by their styles of construction, though sections of wall are frequently blown down by the gales that sweep the north and original walling can become patched out of existence. The most impressive walls were built here during the years 1750–1850 under Acts concerning the parliamentary enclosure of remaining common land in the parishes and normally strict specifications concerning height – often 6 ft (1.8 m) – and methods of construction (including topstones and the frequency of through-stones) were prescribed. These walls were built as double walls packed with stone chippings, and they inclined inwards until close enough to be spanned by a single row of topstones (Fig. 6.26).

Many upland districts in the region derive their character more from enclosure in the decades around 1800 than from any older period, for the terms of the survey provided not only a new, enclosed fieldscape of angular, straight-sided units, but also a local system of similarly straight enclosure roads. Then, as the beneficiaries of the arrangement took up occupancy on their compact new holdings, farmsteads and out-buildings, also in the style of the period, would appear. Of the many fine examples of this type of scenery, some of the best can be seen in Nidderdale, between and around Darley and Dacre. Also associated with the agricultural landscape in this and earlier periods were the lime kilns, producing the lime needed to sweeten sour, upland soils, and the field barns. Hay from the surrounding meadow swept into these barns could be forked down from the hay loft to feed sheltering cattle in winter, while the manure accumulated in the barn then fertilised the hay meadow. One of the most remarkable galaxies of field barns is seen in Swaledale, on the slopes around Muker. Now both the kilns and the barns pose problems of archaeological conservation. A good example of a kiln is at Crindledykes, near Vindolanda on Hadrian's Wall, while another, recently opened to the public, is above Pateley Bridge, beside the road to Grassington. The surviving traditionally-managed dale meadows, from the Yorkshire Dales to the Cheviots are famously rich in flora.

NOTES

1	Wrathmell 1989.	5	RCHME 1986.
2	Martins 2002.	6	Austin 1989.
3	Barnwell & Giles 1997, 66–93.	7	Muir 2000, 15–22.
4	White 1997.	8	Done & Muir 2001.

7

Townscapes and Cityscapes

THOMAS FAULKNER and LINDA POLLEY

INTRODUCTION

The North East region of England includes some of the largest and most
important cities and towns in the country, such as Bradford, Leeds, Newcastle,
Sheffield and Hull, as well as some of the most historic, Durham and York for
example. There are ports, large and small; industrial, railway and former mining
towns; spas, such as Harrogate; and resorts, such as Scarborough. Some smaller
ports, such as Whitby, are also noted for their planned 19th-century resort
development. In the region we also find Victorian planned developments,
including Middlesbrough and Saltaire, and modern settlements such as Newton
Aycliffe and Peterlee.

Yet much of the North East is comparatively sparsely populated, with few
large inland towns. Probably because of its vulnerability to incessant conflict with
the Scots, the county of Northumberland had in the 16th century only eight
market towns, compared to, for example, 45 in Devon at this time.[1] Even today,
widely scattered pre-industrial towns, in many cases with a function and relative
status that has changed little over the centuries, form what is probably the
region's largest single urban category.

In spite of the scattered nature and exceptional diversity of the North East's
cities and towns, the extent of their interdependence through communication
links cannot be over-emphasised (*see* Chapter 8). The importance of roads and,
later, railways is obvious, while, from the medieval period to at least the 19th
century, waterborne transport was also crucial. This was particularly the case in
Yorkshire where, for example, the River Ouse was a major route for the carriage
of goods between Hull, Selby and York. Further north, where the rivers were
navigable for shorter distances, inland waterborne transport was much less
significant.

COMPARATIVE ANALYSIS

Of the towns and cities in the North East, Leeds, Sheffield and Bradford are now
ranked by population, 3rd, 4th and 5th respectively in England. They are
followed in order by Wakefield (9th), Sunderland (11th), Newcastle (14th) and
Hull (16th), although it should be noted that the figures for Wakefield, which
never really industrialised and does not have a genuine large-city character, are
distorted by the inclusion of outlying villages and areas. Hull has hardly changed
its position in the ranking over the centuries but Newcastle, despite its status as
the unofficial sub-regional capital of County Durham and Northumberland, has
dropped down the league table to be out-ranked even by its younger rival
Sunderland, which was accorded city status as late as 1992.

By contrast, up until at least the later 18th century Newcastle was second only to York within the North East. Durham, Hull and Beverley – today a relatively small town – followed behind, although up to about 1600 Beverley, only 13km from its neighbour, was almost certainly larger than Hull. Linked by an early canal to the nearby River Hull, Beverley was an important communication centre and a junction of at least six main roads. It derived further importance from the wool trade and from the presence of major religious institutions, and for a time became east Yorkshire's principal market, trading and manufacturing town.

For the antiquary William Camden, writing in 1586, York was 'the second city in England' and Newcastle 'the glory of all the towns in this country'. He found Beverley 'large and very populous' and Hull 'a town very considerable for merchandise'. Leeds, however, was only 'a royal village', albeit one 'now enriched by the woollen manufacture'[2] (it received a charter only in 1626).

The numerous smaller ports along the North East's lengthy coastline have seen some especially dramatic fluctuations of relative status. The planned medieval settlement of Alnmouth in Northumberland, now a quiet resort, was once a thriving port for the export of grain – until landslips shifted the course of the River Aln in 1806. In east Yorkshire, the silting up of the Humber estuary during the later medieval period resulted in the demise of the flourishing seaport of Hedon, once a rival to Hull and, like its larger neighbour, another planned medieval settlement. By the late 18th century Hedon, despite repeated attempts to dredge and canalise its haven, had metamorphosed into a quiet market town with no harbour facilities at all. Conversely, the erosion of the coastline further north towards Flamborough Head has caused numerous former small towns to completely disappear.[3]

In addition, rivalry between towns could cause one or other to become subservient or even seriously decline. Again, this applied particularly to the North East's ports. An early example occurred in 1560 when Newcastle saw Hartlepool – the only port in County Durham free to trade outside its boundaries – as a threat to its virtual monopoly of the export of wool from the far northern counties. Therefore, it successfully petitioned for its smaller rival to be constituted as a member of the port of Newcastle, a situation which prevailed until the 19th century.

The reasons for the origin of many of the towns and cities of the North East are extremely diverse. A common factor has often been close proximity either to rivers or to the natural meeting or fording places of overland routes. But other reasons also apply. As we shall see, some of the region's settlements were consciously planned, although medieval towns, while sometimes planned or 'planted', more often grew pragmatically around an established meeting-point, market place, road junction, or even a road wide enough to accommodate a market. Often, therefore, their street patterns were extremely irregular, as in the case of Newcastle (*see* below).[4]

Whether planned or not, many towns and cities developed around natural harbours, while others owe their existence to the presence of religious foundations. Others still have yet more localised reasons for their development. Harrogate's occurred following the discovery of mineral springs, and Bishop Auckland's because the Bishops of Durham resided there. Beverley is said to have originated where it did, rather than in a more obvious position closer to the River Hull, because of the presence of an exceptionally plentiful water supply.[5] Malton, a market town in North Yorkshire, is unusual in having evolved from two independent settlements, one based around the former priory, the other along the east–west (Scarborough) road; it is the latter, newer part that now contains the market place.

Some of the region's settlements came into being for military purposes, using the natural defensive capabilities of their sites, particularly during the wave of castle-building following the Norman Conquest, which had a dynamic effect on settlement throughout the North East. For example, Durham, Knaresborough

Fig. 7.1 Knaresborough, aerial view from the north. *Knaresborough was laid out following the initial construction of its castle (upper right) shortly after the Norman Conquest. The spectacular railway viaduct dates from 1851.*

(Fig. 7.1), Newcastle and Richmond all have their castles sited high above a river. By contrast, Scarborough Castle was built (on the site of a Roman signal station) on a plateau-like headland that juts out into the sea, separating what are now known as the North and South bays; the old town spreads down from this, with the harbour to the south (Fig. 7.2).

Richmond ('riche mont') and Knaresborough, both in North Yorkshire, are market towns that came into existence under the Normans, specifically to service their new castles. At Richmond the castle (its well-preserved keep dates from *c.*1150–80) has a commanding position above the River Swale and protected the medieval town behind. The town's semi-circular market place actually developed within what was once the castle bailey, and streets soon spread out from this central location. At Knaresborough, which was laid out on one side of a double

Fig. 7.2 Scarborough: aerial view from the east.

bend of the River Nidd, streets around the market place still follow the original medieval grid plan of *c.*1100. Here the market received its official charter in 1310, having by this time expanded to also service the town's growing agricultural community. Unusually, Knaresborough's fine parish church is set in open ground (well to the north), perhaps because of the density of the town's original grid plan.

Yet religious establishments themselves often encouraged economic development and provided a core to which urban activity could adhere. Thus the old centre of Whitby, with its narrow streets and alleys, lies just below the majestic abbey and the parish church, on the east side of the River Esk (Fig. 7.3), while Selby owed even more of its medieval prosperity to a close relationship between monastic institution, market place and community. Here the wealthy Benedictine abbey, founded by William the Conqueror in 1069, invested in building staithes

on the River Ouse and established a market place, thereby transforming the town's economy (Fig. 7.4).[6]

Needless to say, the common factors of origin and identity described above often co-existed. For instance, nearly all the towns and cities of the North East had markets as well as other functions. Hartlepool and Whitby were monastic as well as harbour towns, while both military and religious factors were crucial in the evolution of Durham (*see* below). Berwick upon Tweed, which evolved on the north side of the lowest possible bridging-point of the Tweed, combined the roles of military stronghold (Fig. 7.5), market town, harbour and port.

The geology of the North East is inevitably reflected in the building materials of its urban settlements. In west Yorkshire many types of building stone were readily available, including limestone (magnesian limestone was used in the east of the county), sandstone and, especially in the more industrial areas, the tough

Fig. 7.3 Aerial view of Whitby. 'There is no other town in England so wholly and happily related to its setting, or the setting of which is so obviously the reason for its existence.' (Girouard 1992, 65)

and durable millstone grit. In North Yorkshire we find both pale grey limestone and brown sandstone, while in the counties of Durham and Northumberland a honey-coloured sandstone is the traditional building material. Non-local stone could sometimes be brought considerable distances for the construction of particularly important buildings – even during the medieval period. For example, St Mary's Church, Beverley, and the Minster and parish churches of York were largely built of a fine-grained, whitish magnesian limestone, quarried near Tadcaster and brought to these sites by water. Ripon and Selby minsters and the later parts of Beverley Minster were also built of this stone, described as the aristocrat of Yorkshire's building stones.[7]

In east Yorkshire the preponderant building material has long been brick. The area around Hull and Beverley was the first in England to develop a local brick-making industry and in the 14th century it supplied bricks for the construction of the town walls of Hull, probably the most substantial use of the material in the country since Roman times. Unusually for its date, Hull's medieval Holy Trinity Church is also largely of brick; another early brick structure is the gateway in Beverley known as the North Bar, dating from 1409. Many older buildings in east Yorkshire are roofed with pantiles and this usage persists all

along the east coast to Berwick upon Tweed and beyond. In the flatter parts of North Yorkshire, from York to Northallerton, brick and tile again predominate, and in Newcastle much early use was made of brick, some of which was imported from the Low Countries.

Even earlier, as elsewhere in the region, there had been a strong tradition of timber-framing in both Newcastle and York. Before a massive fire devastated the area in 1854, Newcastle's quayside was lined with timber-framed merchants' houses dating mainly from the 16th and 17th centuries. Of these, the buildings known as the Cooperage and Bessie Surtees's House are impressive survivals, the latter being of no less than five storeys and having carved vertical posts, formed into Renaissance-style 'pilasters'. The Shambles, York's former butchers' quarter, is an outstanding example of a medieval street. It is full of timber-framed buildings with picturesque overhanging gables, almost touching at second-floor level. To judge from old engravings, many similar buildings survived within the city until at least the early 19th century, for example in North Street.

PRE-INDUSTRIAL TOWNS

Roman towns

Although Newcastle had originated around a Roman fort and river-crossing near the eastern end of Hadrian's Wall, the best illustration of Roman influence can be seen at York, founded in AD 71 as 'Eboracum'. Here, as elsewhere, the Romans superimposed a rigid, grid-like pattern regardless of earlier layout and terrain and Eboracum was initially established as a standard rectangular fortified settlement, or *castrum*, facing the north-east bank of the Ouse. It soon acquired a civilian 'service town', or *colonia*, across the river, which expanded into a substantial administrative and trading centre. The Romans remained in York until the early 5th century. Later, in the 7th and 8th centuries, the town expanded on the north-east bank of the Ouse into areas formerly kept clear.

York's Roman walls remain beneath their medieval counterparts, and the minster sits diagonally across the site of the Roman legionary headquarters, the *Principia*. The two main Roman axes, the *Via Praetoria* and the *Via Principalis* underpin Stonegate and Petergate respectively, although most of the streets around the minster are medieval in origin. Across the river, the original shape of the Roman *colonia* is partially discernible in that of York's medieval city walls and the roads parallel to them (Fig. 7.6).

Rarely, however, did the layout of a Roman town determine that of its medieval successor. For example, Chester-le-Street (still strategically placed, on the Great North Road and on the main north–south railway line), possesses a large medieval church and a substantial market place marking the junction of six roads or lanes, but there is little to indicate its Roman origins. On the other hand, the exceptional length of Bishop Auckland's main street derives from the fact that it is on the line of Roman Dere Street, running from York to Corbridge.

Medieval towns

Whatever its shape, the market place provided the hub of the medieval town, and invariably over the centuries associated buildings were built and rebuilt in and around it. A good example of a later structure of this kind is the market cross of 1790 at Selby. Thirsk's rectangular market place, created in the later medieval period as an improvement on an earlier long-street arrangement, once contained not only a market cross and a tollbooth, but also some open-sided shambles and a row of small shops. Beverley retains to this day two historic market places within its elongated, linear street pattern: the Saturday Market

OPPOSITE PAGE:

TOP: **Fig. 7.4 Selby, aerial view.** *From about the end of the 18th century Selby further developed as an industrial and transport centre because of its position on the River Ouse. In more recent times the town became a major focal point for coal-mining.*

BOTTOM: **Fig. 7.5 The fortifications of Berwick upon Tweed.** *Berwick upon Tweed became permanently English only in 1482 and its unique fortifications were put into effect by Elizabeth I. These were designed on an Italian system involving arrow-shaped bastions giving fire cover to all parts.*

FOLLOWING PAGES:

Fig. 7.6 Maps of York indicating different phases of development. *Roman, medieval, Georgian and modern developments are superimposed. Eboracum shrank after Roman withdrawal but the settlement was renewed under Viking control and old Scandinavian elements in street names indicate that the present-day street pattern is of Viking rather than Roman origin. The Normans renewed the walls, built two castles and strengthened the city's eastern defences by damming the Foss to create a lake and marsh, features subsequently filled in by silt and rubbish. In the 18th century, York developed as a cultural and social centre enhanced with new houses, shops and public buildings. Expansion was modest and the walls survived substantially intact. The arrival of the railway in the 1830s stimulated industrial, commercial and population growth within the city but the suburban expansion was modest until the 20th century.*

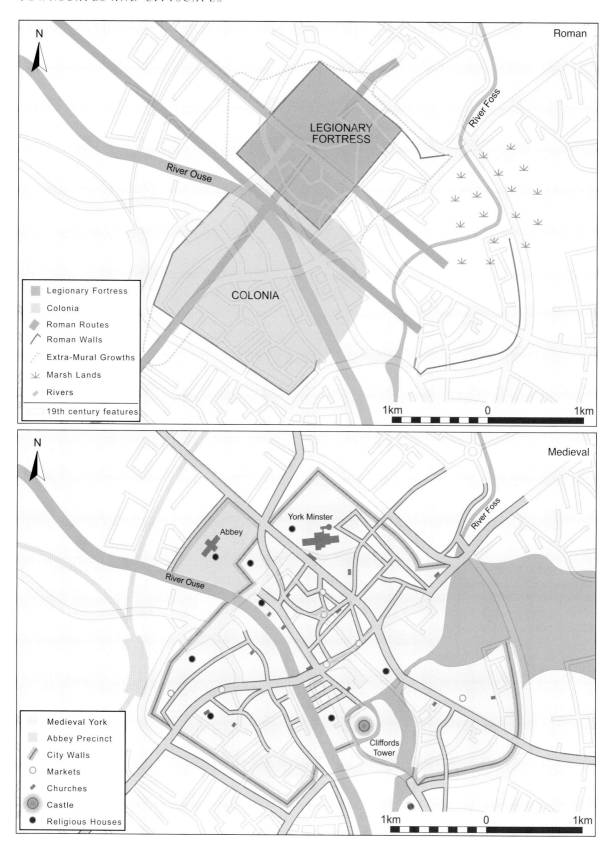

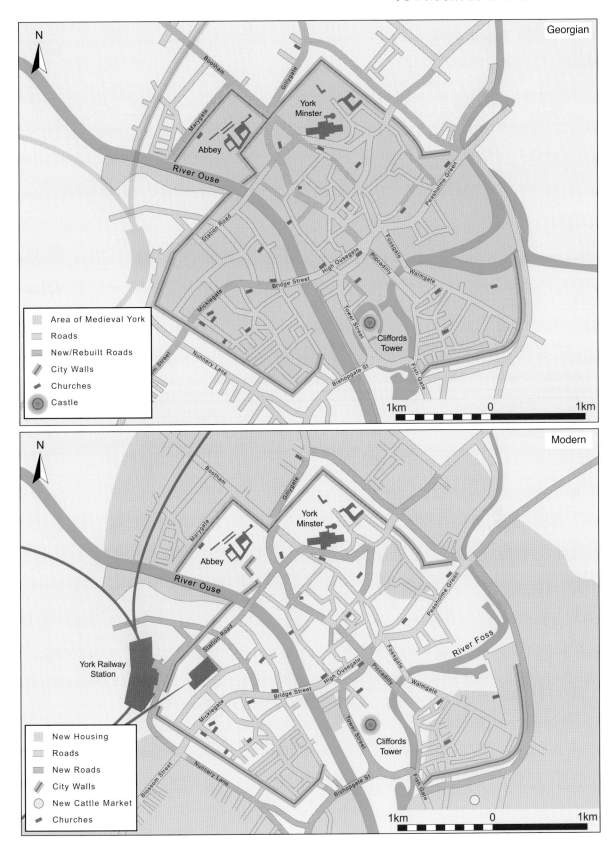

Georgian

N

Bootham

Gillygate

Marygate

York
Minster

Abbey

River Ouse

Station Road

Peasholme Green

Fossgate

High Ousegate

Piccadilly

Walmgate

Micklegate

Bridge Street

... Street

Tower Street

Cliffords
Tower

Nunnery Lane

Bishopgate St

Fish Gate

	Area of Medieval York
	Roads
	New/Rebuilt Roads
	City Walls
	Churches
	Castle

1km   0   1km

Modern

N

Bootham

Gillygate

Marygate

York
Minster

Abbey

River Ouse

York Railway
Station

Station Road

Peasholme Green

River Foss

Fossgate

High Ousegate

Piccadilly

Walmgate

Micklegate

Bridge Street

Tower Street

Cliffords
Tower

Blossom Street

Nunnery Lane

Bishopgate St

Fish Gate

	New Housing
	Roads
	New Roads
	City Walls
	New Cattle Market
	Churches

1km   0   1km

ABOVE: *Fig. 7.7 Beverley's Saturday Market, looking south.* Beverley occupies a flat site and its skyline is still dominated by the Minster and fine guild church of St Mary. From the Saturday Market, Toll Gavel and Cross Street lead to the Wednesday Market, from which Eastgate leads southwards to the Minster.

RIGHT: *Fig. 7.8 Map of medieval Alnwick, after Conzen.* Alnwick's Norman castle was reconstructed during the 18th century and then again in the 19th century. The Hotspur Tower remains from the town's medieval wall (Bondgate, 'B'), as do the deep burgage plots off the streets.

A Alnwick Castle
B Bondgate Tower
C Clayport Tower
G Green Well
Mi St. Michael's Church
N Presumed Narrow Gate Tower
P Pottergate Tower (on Mayson's map, 1622)
Pi Pottergate Tower (rebuilt in 1767)
S Stone Well
SL Salisbury Lands
‑‑‑ Roads & Closes on west side of Bailiffgate as shown on Mayson's map, 1622
Conjectural Anglian route to Eglingham

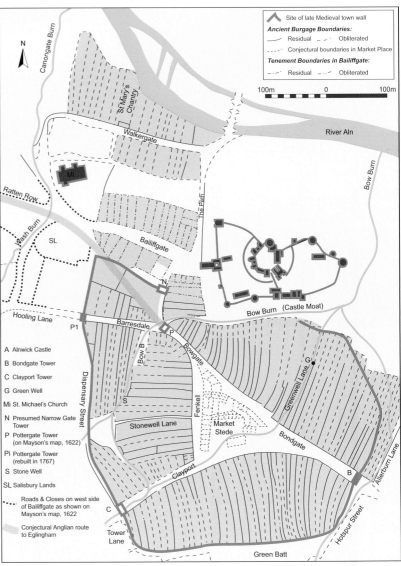

(Fig. 7.7) and the smaller Wednesday Market, which serviced the minster community.

At the same time, burgage tenure, which had evolved during the Saxon period, became another defining feature of the emerging medieval boroughs. Burgage tenure in England could be freehold, or could free the tenant from certain feudal obligations, replacing these with an annual fixed rent paid to the borough overlord. In either case, time and effort spent on tied agricultural production could thereby be diverted to more specialised urban trades and craft activity. Plots held under burgage tenure were usually long and thin. Survivals of such plots, with their narrow elevations fronting on to the street or the market place and with alleyways leading between the buildings to yards, gardens or tenements behind, can often be detected in many of our older towns. Examples are discernible behind Yarm's front market rows, running down towards the river on the eastern side, and behind the frontages of Newgate Street in Morpeth. The burgage plot arrangement is also particularly evident in both Durham and Alnwick (Fig. 7.8)[8].

Generally, medieval features of this kind are less visible in the region's larger cities and towns, because of the enormous transformations that have taken place. However, traces of burgage plot survivals can be found at Briggate in Leeds, with its courts and yards, and even behind the classical façades of Newcastle's Grey Street, in this instance still occupying land largely undeveloped at the time of the area's reconstruction during the 1830s and 1840s (see Fig. 7.16). The characteristic alleyways between buildings acquired different names in different towns: 'chares' in Newcastle, 'vennels' in Durham, 'wynds' and 'peths' elsewhere.

York was the region's foremost medieval city and flourished especially at this time. Its surviving Norman castle, Clifford's Tower, was reconstructed between 1245 and 1265. Later, in the heart of the city's medieval commercial centre, the magnificent timber-framed Merchant Adventurers' Hall was built by the Guild of Mercers and Merchants between 1357 and 1361, while from the middle of the 15th century Stonegate linked the minster directly with the large and impressive Guildhall, located on the north bank of the river. Also from the medieval period date York's visible and well-preserved city walls: along with Chester's, the most substantial in the country. The end of the period 'saw the medieval city in its picturesque and pinnacled splendour', with its guildhalls, alms-houses, monastic foundations, 40 parish churches and recently-completed minster.[9] During the early Tudor period York was the virtual capital of northern England, being the main base for the powerful King's Council of the North.

Newcastle had developed as the site of the most eastward convenient crossing point of the Tyne. After centuries of obscurity its strategic position, guarding eastern England's main north–south route against the Scots, was recognised by the Normans with the building and re-building of its castle keep. The Normans used much the same site as the Romans had employed, a small area enclosed by walls, which was rendered virtually impregnable by the flank protection provided by the deep ravines of small tributaries flowing into the Tyne (now mostly filled in).[10] On the south bank of the river was Gateshead, then and subsequently a much less substantial settlement which evolved, ribbon-like, on each side of the Great North Road.

By the 14th century, thanks to the coal and to a lesser extent the wool trades, Newcastle was ranked third in wealth among English towns.[11] Its walls had been much enlarged, so that the town now presented an irregular, horseshoe-like layout on the north bank of the Tyne; there was one bridge over the river, probably on the earlier Roman alignment.[12] The Town Moor, a large area of inalienable grazing land owned by the Freemen of Newcastle and still present today, lay outside the walls to the north-west. The town's still-existing principal medieval streets, Pilgrim, Newgate and Westgate Streets, ran north, north-west and west respectively. The Nunnery of St Bartholomew and the adjacent Franciscan Friary to the east were situated between Newgate and Pilgrim Streets.

OPPOSITE PAGE:
Fig. 7.9 Durham, aerial view of cathedral and castle.

After the Dissolution this substantial site – so crucial, as we shall see, for the later development of Newcastle – was sold. On part of it a large manor, Anderson Place, was built by the merchant Robert Anderson from about 1580. Before long this was surrounded by large formal gardens. The town's centre of activity was the waterfront. Massive reclamation of land on the foreshore allowed for the construction of a long quay along the River Tyne during the 13th century and, behind this, an infrastructure of long narrow plots and narrow parallel streets leading back to a link road that connected the waterfront with Pilgrim Street. It has been calculated that 11 per cent of the total land area within the town walls was reclaimed riverside used for port infrastructure.

At Berwick upon Tweed, port installations, not unlike those in Newcastle, lined the riverside and their layout can still be detected in the town plan, which shows long narrow plots reaching forward across reclaimed foreshore from Bridge Street. These plots are now separated from the river by the town's defensive wall, beyond which a quay later developed. This intrusion of the wall in the townscape is an eloquent reminder of the abrupt change after 1296, whereby Berwick upon Tweed became a fortress town.

Hartlepool had the benefit of a natural bay, its pool well sheltered by the headland that wraps around it. The street of Southgate now consolidates a spit of land on the south side of the pool, around which ships could come for shelter. Construction of harbour installations of some sort – part of a retaining wall has been identified – began in the 12th century and thereafter docks were set out with their side walls running at right angles to the line of Southgate across the sand and into the water. In time, the land was consolidated in much the same way as happened at other east-coast ports. Calculations made on the tidal range suggest that there could only have been enough depth of water for smaller coastal vessels, and indeed, despite archaeological excavations, types of imported pottery which have appeared at Newcastle and Hull have not been reported at Hartlepool. This port too was affected by the Scottish wars: the town was walled and its harbour protected by a chain stretched across the pool between towers at the wall ends.

Durham has always been a comparatively small settlement, much smaller than Newcastle for example. Yet it has enjoyed great political and religious significance, not least in the medieval period. With its spectacular cathedral, built on the western edge of a towering sandstone promontory in a loop of the River Wear (Fig. 7.9) containing a unique shrine to Saint Cuthbert, Durham is probably more identifiable in terms of its relationship to the Church than any other town or city in the North East. Here too the so-called 'Prince-Bishops' of Durham, created by William the Conqueror, ruled over what was in effect a buffer state against the Scots. The Prince-Bishops represented the king, with regalian powers of tax-raising, justice and prerogative. By 1189 County Durham was consolidated as a 'palatinate' (a border area with a ruler having special powers), which gave the Prince-Bishops political jurisdiction between the Tees and the Tweed.[13] Their domain was Durham Castle, facing the cathedral. It combined fortification with an appropriate level of residential splendour, while the walled and gated Palace Green precinct delineated the source of the Prince-Bishops' power and symbolised Norman authority.

However, the city grew up almost independently around this fortified enclave, comprising six separate but adjacent boroughs. Each had its own church, court house, guild buildings, mills and bake-houses, though there was only one market place (Fig. 7.10), located in the Bishop's borough on the peninsula. Framwellgate Bridge (*c*.1120) and Elvet Bridge (*c*.1180) were built to link this central market place firstly to the main north–south road, and then to the hinterland to the east and west, thus establishing Durham as the crossroads of the county. By the end of the 13th century a street layout had been established along the river banks, which remained more or less unchanged until the city's expansion during the Victorian period.

Further south on the main north–south overland route is the sizeable market town of Darlington, again possessing a strong medieval legacy. Originally, Darlington combined what has been described as the 'four row' type of plan (a square situated around a market place) with the 'two row' type, consisting of two rows of houses on either side of the main street. In this case, the four rows round the market place constituted the chartered borough, while the other two rows were those of the medieval 'villein', or peasant, settlement. The town's medieval core layout is still very much in evidence, as are the names of the original streets or 'gates'.

Among the region's smaller pre-industrial towns, reference has already been made to those, such as Richmond and Knaresborough, that had an essentially military function, especially after the Norman Conquest. Helmsley, which developed around a river crossing and a junction of roads from the east and north, was another settlement of this kind. Its unusually substantial Norman castle – 'slighted' by Cromwell's troops during the Civil War – guarded the Rye valley and was protected by a double ditch. Here, admittedly, the castle reinforced rather than initiated Helmsley's development, for there had been a church and burial ground near the road crossing as early as the 10th century. Later, in about 1190,

Robert 'Fursan' de Roos created a 'borough' to the south of this and eastwards of the river crossing, at which time the castle was also enlarged. The town's large market place is near to both the castle and the church.

Similarly, the importance of both Alnwick and Berwick upon Tweed was always as much military as commercial. However, again there had been a Saxon settlement at Alnwick (*see* Fig. 7.8), where the 'central triangle', now occupied by the Town Hall (Assembly Rooms) and the market place, may once have been a village green. The medieval town developed in the lee of its massive Norman castle, begun in the 12th century, though the town wall was only completed around 1500.

Like Alnwick and Berwick upon Tweed, Morpeth lies on the main north–south overland route. Situated where this highway crosses the River Wansbeck and developing on the north side in a loop of the river, Morpeth was also attached to a small feudal castle of which little now remains. Yet here the market place is not, as one might expect, adjacent to either the castle or even the old church (which, like Knaresborough's, is somewhat removed from the centre), but is situated at the right-angled junction of the town's two main streets: Bridge Street and Newgate Street. It is dominated by an unusual free-standing belfry.

Among the region's small or medium-sized market towns, fluctuations in prosperity could be considerable. The history of Driffield, in east Yorkshire, is by no means untypical. The town flourished in Saxon times and again under the Normans, by which time it had a weekly market and an annual fair, but was almost obliterated by the Black Death (*c.*1350). It languished for centuries, until in 1770 the new Driffield Navigation reinforced its links to the River Hull and it became a minor industrial centre. Like many of the region's towns, Driffield has been repeatedly rebuilt: indeed, except for its church none of its buildings are earlier than 1770.[14]

Rather unusually, Northallerton, in North Yorkshire, grew and prospered more or less continuously, even though it appears to have been so vulnerable to attack that its Norman castle was abandoned as early as *c.*1292. It was a linear settlement, based on one long street incorporating a market place, and to this day the town has retained the narrow plan it established in medieval times. Its favourable location on the main north–south road enabled it to support a relatively resilient mixed economy.

Hull was by far the largest of planned medieval towns in the North East. In the late 12th century the monks of nearby Meaux Abbey founded it as a new trading

OPPOSITE PAGE:

Fig. 7.10 Durham, view of market place. While much of its traffic has now been re-routed, the market place remains very much the centre of Durham. It contains the Market Hall and the Victorian St Nicholas's Church and still houses enough commercial, retail and tourist activity to retain the air of a busy urban nucleus.

town, with an excellent natural haven on the west bank of the River Hull, and Hull (formerly 'Wyke') soon became the sixth-ranked port in England. In 1293 it was acquired by Edward I to serve as a military base ('King's Town on Hull') and plots were immediately appropriated by the king for the construction of a new quay, completed in 1302 and later known as the King's Staithe. At the same time roads leading to the port were improved.

Hull was subsequently walled. Within the walls, the town's planned grid of streets spread westwards from an initial core to centre on Holy Trinity Church and the market place; much later (1541–3), Henry VIII built a massive citadel on the other side of the river (Fig. 7.11), by which time the port's facilities had also been much enlarged. Although Hull's medieval walls no longer exist, their line is marked by the former Prince's and Humber Docks, and by Queen's Gardens to the north. The area within this demarcation is now known as the Old Town. The port of Hull traded with the whole of Western Europe and as far north as Iceland; for even more distant destinations it used the Low Countries as an entrepôt. It now possessed not only the King's Staithe, but also an additional riverside dock at Trippett, just to the north of the town walls. There were also common staithes, maintained by the town council, and a number of private quays, owned by leading merchants and accessible from their High Street[15] dwellings which ran down to the river.

Ripon was another town that was largely a planned medieval creation. Developed from an existing trading settlement by the Archbishop of York during the 12th century, it was 'planted' west of an earlier church and monastery and slightly south of the original market place. Streets soon began to spread out from its new, rectangular market place (Fig. 7.12). Aided by the close proximity of Fountains Abbey, a wealthy wool-producing community, Ripon became one of

Fig. 7.11 Hollar's 'bird's eye view' of Hull, c. 1640, from the west. Virtually no trace of Hull's medieval fortifications now remains.

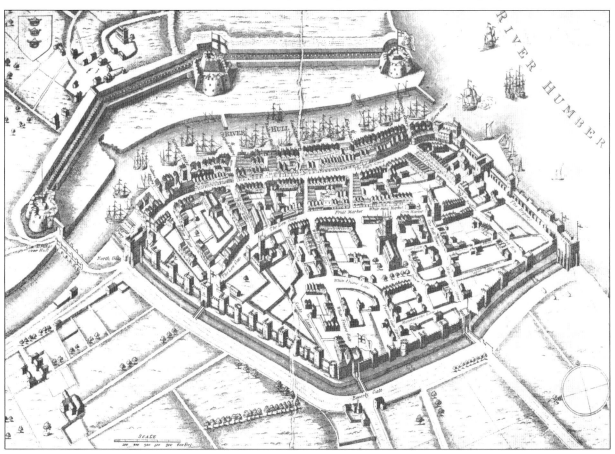

the leading cloth-towns in Yorkshire. Before long, it was responsible for about a third of the county's output, exporting through the pre-eminent wool port of Hull.

TOWNS IN THE EARLY MODERN PERIOD

During the late 16th and 17th centuries there were clear intimations of changes to come in the ranking order of the region's towns. After the Dissolution, Ripon, for example, fell on harder times, as did Durham, which had to come to terms with the loss of its lucrative position as a place of pilgrimage. In York the Dissolution seriously undermined the city's woollen textile-based economy, though during the 17th century the city saw the construction of such buildings as a Royal Mint (1642), a Quakers' Meeting House (1642) and several almshouses. Even so, Thomas Baskerville could still write of the city in 1670, albeit perhaps somewhat erroneously, that 'the whole town is old timber buildings'.[16]

Beverley also began to lose much of its erstwhile status and prosperity. However, because as a consequence it did not greatly expand, it retained the unusual asset, granted during the medieval period, of 'Beverley Pastures': a large area of open, common land that still surrounds the town on three sides. Moreover, Beverley's minster, though no longer an official place of sanctuary, survived the Dissolution to become a parish church (as did Ripon's) and the town at least partially recovered during Georgian times (*see* below).

Fig. 7.12 Ripon, view of market place.
The recent removal of car parking in the market place has helped to restore both meaning and quality to this impressive space.

Meanwhile, changes in the patterns of industrial and mercantile enterprise began to have a direct impact on the North East's urban development. For example, in Hallamshire (the district in and around Sheffield), the manufacture of iron, and later steel, tools from medieval times onwards, led to the development of an industry that was both rural and, increasingly, urban. Fast-flowing streams joined the River Don from the eastern slopes of the Pennines and these tributaries and the main river provided power for the grinding wheels and forges essential to producing staple products such as cutlery and edge tools. The valleys were well wooded – providing the charcoal essential for the smelting of iron – and were filled with small industrial sites. Complementing these early powered sites were hundreds of small workshops for the forging of small goods and the assembly of cutlery; these were usually attached to or beside houses.

Similarly, though there was now a huge expansion in weaving activity, this occurred not in the larger, established towns but as a cottage industry, mainly in and around the Pennines. The expanding woollen towns of Halifax and Leeds were particular beneficiaries of this development. Halifax, set amid moors rising to nearly 460m, had originated as a village around the confluence of four roads at a hermitage dedicated to St John the Baptist – the four 'Holyways'. By 1580 it had grown rapidly to a population of about 12,000. Its splendid parish church of St John the Baptist is a product of this late 16th-century prosperity. Leeds had developed on the north side of the River Aire, initially as a hamlet based on the manor of Kirkgate, and centring on the one parish church. Kirkgate itself was its first thoroughfare. From 1207 the lord of the manor, Ralph de Paynal, laid out Briggate as a market place with burgage plots on either side, which formed the basis of the town (Fig. 7.13).

During the early modern period, pre-industrial towns throughout the region were beginning to be transformed, as brick, stone and tile gradually replaced timber and thatch. Reconstruction and alteration, often involving the re-facing of older properties, incorporated new and fashionable architectural ideas. Indeed, many of the town houses that we identify as 'Georgian' were the product of a ubiquitous 17th- and 18th-century process of upgrading from traditional local styles to a brick or stucco classicism, particularly for wealthy merchants' houses and for the town houses of the landed gentry.

There was also much new building during the period. In Hull's narrow High Street, running parallel to the riverside, some splendid 17th-century merchants' houses were constructed, including Wilberforce House which is now a museum. Later in the century the traveller Celia Fiennes famously commented of Newcastle, then the fourth largest English town, that it 'most resembles London of any place in England, its buildings lofty and large of brick mostly or stone'.[17]

Fig. 7.13 Map of Leeds in 1612, after Ward. The street pattern indicated here largely survives.

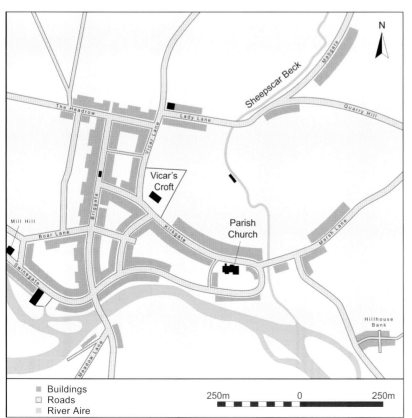

During the 1720s Newcastle was further described as 'a spacious, extended, infinitely populous place',[18] and the town now boasted recently-built merchants' houses in fashionable classical styles, as well as new public buildings such as the (now-demolished) Mansion House.[19] Built near the riverside in 1691, and set within a spacious terraced garden, this was one of the earliest provincial structures of its type. In about 1720 work also began on Hanover Square, Newcastle's first formal square, centring on a Dissenting chapel built by voluntary subscription, though only a few houses were actually completed.

GEORGIAN TRANSFORMATION

The 18th century was especially crucial for urban expansion throughout England, nowhere more so than in the North East. In fact, this embryonic industrialised region helped to provide the driving forces for this transformation in the shape of both raw materials and technology. The further development of existing manufacturing centres created an increasingly diversified industrial base, substantially assisted, as discussed in Chapter 8, by the growth of the canal network and by considerable improvements in the region's roads. Similarly, bigger and more specialised ports, servicing ever-larger ships, were required to meet the demands of naval warfare and of international trade.

At the same time, social and cultural changes encouraged the emergence or re-emergence of towns and cities increasingly devoted to leisure and to the pursuits of 'polite' society. Thus, the decline of its trade and manufacturing actually encouraged York's renaissance as a social and cultural centre. When Daniel Defoe visited in the 1720s, he found it 'a pleasant and beautiful city', a focus for 'the confluence of the gentry'.[20] The city hosted the Assizes Court and all its trappings twice a year, and from 1709 organised horse-racing, the increasingly fashionable and accessible 'sport of kings'. York's prestigious new Assembly Rooms, designed in the Palladian style by Lord Burlington in 1732, not only provided a location for winter entertainment and a platform for leisure activities such as dancing, card playing and tea-drinking, but also placed the city at the forefront of architectural as well as social fashion.

More than any other town or city in the North East, York was architecturally transformed during the 18th century. Large new town houses were constructed, mostly of brick,[21] and many to the designs of the highly successful local architect John Carr, and numerous street façades of shops and houses were rebuilt in similar classical style. Notable public buildings of the period include the Mansion House of 1725–7, possibly by Francis Bickerton, and the Assize Courts (1772–6), the former County Lunatic Asylum, now Bootham Park Hospital (1774), and the Female Prison (1779), all by Carr.

The Corporation was not slow in recognising the benefits to be gained by urban 'improvement'. Upgrading the city's fabric and amenities facilitated 'polite' social interaction and encouraged visitors, leisure pursuits and retail activity. In 1732 the Corporation laid out the New Walk promenade, planted with an avenue of trees along the north bank of the Ouse (Fig. 7.14). It then enclosed Pikeing Well, a medicinal spring in the vicinity. John Carr was responsible for Pikeing Well as well as other improvements to pavements, bridges and street furniture on the Corporation's behalf. In 1755 he built the classical Knavesmire Grandstand (now demolished) at the new racecourse to the south of the city.

Fig. 7.14 **The 'New Walk', York** *by* *Nathaniel Drake, c. 1755.*

Other, but less important, Georgian centres in Yorkshire were Richmond and Beverley. Beverley's renewed importance during this period is reflected in its wealth of 18th-century domestic architecture, both terraced and detached. Good examples of the latter type are Lairgate Hall (*c.*1700, altered in the 1760s) and Norwood House, built around 1765. The former, once set in landscaped grounds, now serves as council offices; the latter is now a school. The elegant market cross in the 'Saturday Market' was rebuilt in 1714 (*see* Fig. 7.7), while the town's finest public building is the Guildhall, re-fronted in 1832 but with a court room dating from the 1760s, which has stucco decoration of exceptional quality.

Richmond held Quarter Sessions and housed the North York Militia

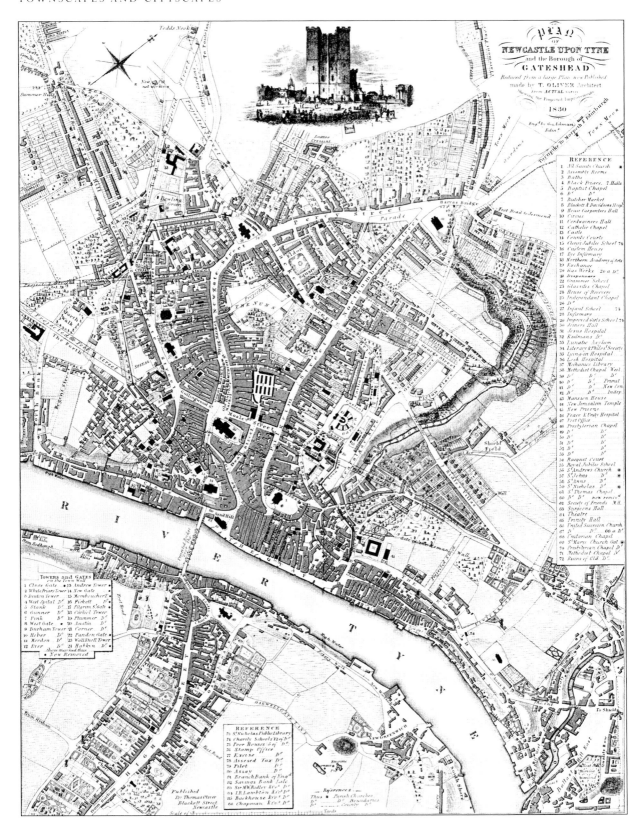

depot. During the 18th century the Castle Walk was laid out. This planned promenade winds around the side of the castle hill, giving superb views of the river as well as of two characteristically Georgian adornments to the town, the 'Gothick' Culloden Tower of 1746 and John Carr's three-arched river bridge of 1789. Richmond also retains some good 18th-century houses and streets, while the Town Hall (containing an elegant assembly room on the first floor) dates largely from 1756. The delightfully intimate Theatre Royal was built in 1789 and the (now derelict) grandstand of the former racecourse about ten years before.

Within the North East as a whole, Newcastle remained second only to York during the 18th century. The coal trade to London and the south mitigated the town's geographical distance from the capital, and there was a movement towards increasing sophistication, both culturally and architecturally. Elegant new structures included the town's first completed Georgian square, Charlotte Square (begun 1770) and the Assembly Rooms (1774–6), both by the local architect William Newton. The church of All Saints, dramatically sited high above the quayside and with an unusual, oval-shaped nave, was designed in 1786 by David Stephenson, another local man. Meanwhile, from the 1770s good quality residential streets began to be built outside the old town walls. These typically Georgian terraces were invariably of brick.[22]

During this period, too, Newcastle possessed not only the unique amenity of the Town Moor, now used for horse-racing, but also a remarkable number of gardens and public open spaces (mostly no longer in existence). For example, the Blackfriars, one of the few surviving structures from what had once been the town's many religious foundations, was still surrounded by orchards and gardens. People could stroll in the Carliol Croft, an area between the rear gardens of the houses on the east side of Pilgrim Street and the town wall, or in the attractive Forth Walk, on the west side of town. The banks of the Pandon Dean also provided scope for pleasurable perambulation and even the new Infirmary, designed by Daniel Garrett in 1751, had impressive, landscaped grounds. The evangelist John Wesley said of Newcastle that he knew of 'no other place in Great Britain comparable to it for pleasantness'.[23]

These typically Georgian trends towards classicism and fashionability were further reinforced in Newcastle during the late 18th and early 19th centuries by a number of municipal 'improvements'. These included the construction of Dean, Mosley and Collingwood streets, giving better access from the quayside. However, the town was still constricted, with its expansion inhibited by its medieval street pattern and encircling walls – admittedly now beginning to be demolished (Fig. 7.15). It was only from the mid-1830s that a coherently-planned, classical city centre, unique in Britain for its date, was created thanks largely to the efforts of the builder and entrepreneur Richard Grainger and a number of talented local architects.

In 1834 Grainger purchased the still-surviving site comprising the 'Nuns' Field' (from the Nunnery of St Bartholomew) and Anderson Place; this lay centrally within what remained of the town's medieval walls. Around it, he had already constructed Blackett Street (1824), on the site of a northern section of the old town wall; the monumental Eldon Square (1825–8), just to the north of this; and the Royal Arcade (1830–31), at the junction of Pilgrim and Mosley Streets. All these developments were designed for Grainger by the prominent local architect John Dobson.

Now Grainger's major innovation was a new commercial street, Grey Street (Fig. 7.16), running northwards from Dean Street to the eastern end of Blackett Street. It linked eastwards to the existing thoroughfare of Pilgrim Street and westwards to the newly-constructed upper Grainger Street, the latter being one of a quadrilateral of streets surrounding the new 'Grainger Market', again designed by Dobson. The most northerly of these streets became Clayton Street, originally connecting with Eldon Square. For his operations, Grainger had to

OPPOSITE PAGE:

Fig. 7.15 Plan of Newcastle upon Tyne by Thomas Oliver, 1830.

Fig. 7.16 Grey Street, Newcastle, the lower east side. *The portion of Grey Street illustrated here was designed by John Dobson.*

level a considerable extent of ground and fill in the valley of the stream known as the Lort Burn, the line of which Grey Street largely followed. Most of Newcastle's remaining denes and ravines were also filled in during subsequent 19th-century building works, and much of its hilly terrain smoothed out.

Leeds, meanwhile, continued to benefit from its strategic location, just east of the Pennines, as an intersection of north–south and east–west overland routes.[24] It was also conveniently situated on the River Aire, which, joining the Ouse a little north of Goole, provided an all-important link to the Humber. Now Leeds had its already favourable trading position further reinforced by the construction of the Leeds and Liverpool Canal. This was opened in 1774 (although not finally completed until 1816), in effect linking England's east and west coasts.

Leeds was now firmly established as the West Riding of Yorkshire's largest town and by the 1820s was 'a rising alternative metropolis on the eastern side of the Pennines',[25] threatening the historic status of York. New public buildings in Leeds included a second, more impressive White Cloth Hall, constructed in 1775,[26] although this was demolished in the 19th century. Georgian residential development also occurred, mostly in the west end. However, this was rather limited because industrialisation soon caused the better-off to move out to the higher suburbs. Park Square (1788–1810) does contain attractive, if modest, two-storey houses built of brick, but similar developments were largely abortive.

Hull, by contrast, once possessed a much more impressive Georgian heritage. In 1770 the town was still 'exceeding close built'[27] and largely confined within its medieval walls. Improvements to its increasingly congested harbour, even though this had been for more than a century under the control of Trinity House, remained long overdue. Now, however, large sections of the walls were replaced with new docks. Queen's Dock (1774–8) lay on the northern side, while Humber Dock (1803–9) and Junction (now Prince's) Dock, opened in 1829, were situated to the west. Fashionable middle-class housing, in the shape of a grid of streets and squares, was laid out to the north of Queen's Dock. Unfortunately, little of this development remains. Indeed, this is the case with most of Hull's 18th-century architecture. One noteworthy survival, however, is the administratively important Trinity House (1753), near the old market area close to Holy Trinity Church.

Elsewhere in Yorkshire, the many impressive Georgian buildings in Knaresborough reflect the town's linen-based prosperity at this time, while its riverside Long Walk was planted in about 1739, affording fine views of the crags. For the Picturesque tourist, this beautiful wooded walk's other attractions included the 'Petrifying Well', as well as 'Old Mother Shipton's Cave', the legendary birthplace of a 15th-century witch. Halifax, too, saw considerable 18th- and early 19th-century 'improvement'. Here a Cloth Hall was built in 1708, followed by a number of expensive clothiers' town houses. The magnificent Piece Hall, containing more than 300 merchants' rooms, was constructed in 1779, while by 1822 the town possessed 'Chapels for almost every class of Dissenters; two National Schools ... Public Baths, Assembly Rooms, Theatre, Benevolent Society ... and Dispensary'.[28] Similarly, 18th-century 'improvements' in Ripon included the market place obelisk, designed by no less an architect than Nicholas Hawksmoor in 1702 and remodelled in 1781 (see Fig. 7.12). This structure – like the similar one at Richmond – creates an air of architectural sophistication perhaps unexpected in a town of this size.

In the mid-18th century Sheffield was an expanding, but much more workaday, industrial town. It had become a national centre for steel-making, and distinctive building types within its landscape included the bottle-shaped furnace, where iron was turned into blister steel, and later the crucible furnace. Here too were large numbers of small forges and workshops, as also in the rural areas surrounding the town. However, some kind of recognisable town centre was now emerging, with decent brick terraces being built around the 15th-century parish church (now the cathedral). Paradise Square, Sheffield's most complete Georgian ensemble, lies just to the north; it dates from the 1770s.

SPAS, PORTS AND RESORTS

As the citizens of York – and of much of the rest of Yorkshire – began to enjoy the amenities of the city's new Assembly Rooms, alternative pursuits, both pleasurable and recuperative, could by this time be found at Scarborough. As we have seen, this town once had a considerable military role. Having achieved fame as a spa late in the 17th century, it now became the region's first seaside resort. The sea-bathing machine appeared and by the 1750s parading on the sands was a well-established practice in polite society. A Long Room had been constructed where, we are told, there were balls every evening with a 'great number of noble personages present'.[29] All this helped to offset the fact that Scarborough's ancient natural harbour was rapidly becoming too small to accommodate the larger ships now in use.

Even nearby Whitby, although rather more isolated geographically, had become a minor spa, while sea-bathing here is mentioned in the 1770s. However, Whitby's growth during the 18th century was much more commercially based. The town was then at its zenith as a port, thanks especially to the export of alum and coal, and to the recently-established whaling trade. A new market place was laid out, forming a square in front of the Town Hall, or 'Tollbooth'; this building in turn was reconstructed in classical style in 1788 with an open trading area on the ground floor. Nearby are some fine Palladian merchants' houses; especially noteworthy is Airy Hill, built on the edge of town for a wealthy ship-owner in 1790. The Georgians (and the Victorians) built mainly on the west side of the river.

By the mid-19th century Whitby was declining as a port and attempts to convert the town into a substantial resort never really met with much success. However, its Royal Crescent and associated terraces on the West Cliff, laid out during the 1850s by Dobson of Newcastle for the railway entrepreneur George Hudson, form an impressive if incomplete development (*see* Fig. 7.3, top right). Down the slope to the west lies the earlier, and even more elegantly classical St Hilda's Terrace (*c*.1800), while between the two developments are several attractive Victorian streets, some, unusually, in the neo-Gothic style.

The North East's largest spa town, Harrogate, is more a product of 19th- and early 20th-century development. The town had been promoted as the first 'English Spaw' as early as 1596, but it remained largely undeveloped before the passing of an Improvement Act in 1841. Until then, the two small villages of High and Low Harrogate, each with their own wells, springs, hotels and inns, were separated by 200 acres (81ha) of open land. The Stray, as this area is still known, had been enclosed and protected by an Act of Parliament of 1778 and provided Harrogate with an axis around which future development could occur. Meanwhile, the growing medical popularity of Low Harrogate's sulphur spring encouraged a number of associated public buildings in its vicinity: the Promenade Room, 1802; Montpelier Baths, 1834; the Royal Promenade and Cheltenham Pump Room, 1835. These gradually established that area as the amalgamated town's new centre.

After 1844 the railways ensured a steady growth in visitor and resident populations and from the 1860s the in-filling of Harrogate's centre began, creating the graceful crescents, circles, avenues and streets that still characterise the town. These are punctuated by an unusually high quantity of green open spaces, such as the Valley Gardens, which, originally not much more than a footpath, became a new focal point as early as the 1880s. Further Victorian extensions and generous municipal planting ensured the increasing popularity of these gardens for exercise and promenading.

Typical forms of 19th-century development can also be found at Scarborough, which, again thanks to railway links, grew apace both as a spa and especially as a resort, with hotels, public buildings and domestic architecture to match. Much of the town's Victorian (and Georgian) development – such as the terraces of the South Cliff – lies above the spa complex, overlooking the South Bay. This latter is penetrated by the wooded 'Valley', near to which is the splendid, stone-built Crescent (*c*.1830–2) and the enormous Grand Hotel of 1863–7, the latter designed by Yorkshire architect Cuthbert Brodrick.

For centuries Hull and Newcastle had been the North East's major ports. As mentioned earlier, Newcastle's prosperity in this regard was founded largely on the coal trade. In 1400 the town was given separate county status by Henry IV, while a subsequent charter granted by Elizabeth I further reinforced its position by according it a monopoly of local trading in coal – an activity that greatly expanded during her reign. Newcastle lost this monopoly during the Civil War but, even so, it is estimated that its exports of coal rose from an already substantial 616,000 tons per annum in 1685 to almost 2 million tons by 1800, meeting almost half of the country's rapidly increasing demands. However, during the late 19th century Newcastle gradually lost business to Sunderland, Middlesbrough and even Hartlepool (*see* below) and, unlike Hull, no longer has the status of an international port.

It was in the early 18th century that Sunderland at last become prominent in the roll-call of north-eastern cities and towns. It had originated in three older communities: Monkwearmouth on the north bank of the river, and Bishopwearmouth and 'old' Sunderland on the south. All three made little progress until Newcastle's monopolistic hold on coal trading was broken. There then emerged ship building and other industries on the banks of the Wear, along with a dramatic increase in coal exports. Old Sunderland was the growing point, ultimately at the expense of its neighbours.

With major improvements to the harbour already under way, Sunderland achieved parish status in 1719. The town's growing prosperity was reflected in the richness of the interior of its new parish church (Holy Trinity), probably designed by William Etty of York. The church was soon surrounded by fashionable new residential developments, the most desirable of which was Church Street itself. Bishopwearmouth expanded too, although less rapidly. As industry and commerce spread up along the river banks and the two settlements grew towards each other, Bishopwearmouth managed to retain its lower density, though by the early 19th century Sunderland became increasingly crowded and industrial.

So too did Hartlepool, which, after centuries of subservience to Newcastle, had declined during the 18th century almost to the status of a fishing village. Now, mainly because of the growth of the coal trade and, crucially, that of the railway system, the town was revived and redeveloped and was re-designated as a separate port in 1845. Up to this point Hartlepool still showed traces of its medieval origins, but it was soon substantially rebuilt, albeit with rather basic terraced streets. Then, in 1847, the new coal port of West Hartlepool was established. It was not built on quite such a grand scale as had been intended but, even so, its population rose to an astonishing 73,000 within 20 years. By 1880 its docks were joined with the earlier ones in Hartlepool itself to create one of the largest systems in the country.

More minor ports in the region also important for the coal trade at this time were Seaham and Blyth. Seaham was developed by the coal-owner Lord Londonderry from 1828 onwards as a venture to avoid the harbour dues at Sunderland. His architect was John Dobson of Newcastle (whose sophisticated classical layout for the new town was soon largely abandoned in favour of comparatively haphazard development). Blyth, originally a fishing and salt-manufacturing village known as 'Blythe's Nook' or 'Blyth-snook', had by the mid-18th century become a thriving local coal port, drawing most of its ouput, via an early waggonway, from collieries at Plessey and Hartford. The present town, of which the eastern portion is the original settlement, evolved after 1815 through the amalgamation of two smaller ports: Cowpen and South Blyth. It then further expanded following the abolition of coal export duties in 1845 and 1850, and the construction of the Blyth and Tyne Railway from 1847. In 1852 its harbour was greatly enlarged. Here we can still find a considerable number of 19th-century coal staithes.

By contrast, Yarm and Stockton are interesting as examples of small inland ports. Both lie on the River Tees, one of the few even partially navigable rivers in the northern part of our region. Although again of medieval origin, these towns were at their most prosperous during the 18th century. Yarm's Market Hall in the middle of the High Street dates from 1710, as do most of the buildings along either side. Stockton, meanwhile, achieved parochial status in 1711. Land opposite its new parish church was planted and enclosed to form The Square, which became the fashionable social centre of the town, surrounded by two- and three-storey houses. In the early 19th century even larger houses were erected to the north, adjacent to the main north–south axis, and to the west along Yarm Lane.

Stockton, hitherto overshadowed by Yarm, was now superseding its neighbour. However, after about 1830 both ports began to lose custom and influence to the new town of Middlesbrough (see below), founded closer to the river mouth. Stockton was included in the new railway network and did retain some industrial production, but The Square became a cattle market; only two of its original 18th-century houses remain, and those are much modified.

An example of a much later – and larger – inland port is Goole. From the late 17th century the rivers Aire and Calder had been used as the basis for canalised transport in West Yorkshire. Following an Act of Parliament of 1689, the Aire and Calder Navigation was created, connecting Leeds and Wakefield with the Humber. In 1774 the Aire and Calder Navigation Company created a new link from the Aire to the Ouse at Selby (thereby greatly enhancing the commercial and industrial importance of this town). In 1826 the company built a more southerly canal from Knottingley to Goole which, strategically situated on the Ouse a little upstream from where this river joins the Trent to form the Humber, rapidly developed as a new, 'company' port. It was laid out according to a typical 19th-century industrial grid plan.

VICTORIAN AND INDUSTRIAL TOWNSCAPES

The 19th century saw an immense and rapid increase in population. This partly explains the commensurate growth of Victorian towns and cities, but at the same time industrialisation also encouraged the migration and concentration of that population, creating a much more complex urban environment and experience. The impact of technology, new systems of municipal organisation and increasingly complex social hierarchies all helped to create this new, urbanised way of living. This was fully expressed in the fabric and direction of town development, which

changed radically, in scale, texture and materials. Up to this time, as we have seen, local or near-local materials were employed for the vast bulk of ordinary building. During the 19th century, however, improved transport resulted in the near-universal use of more standardised and mass-produced materials such as brick, tile and slate, even where local building materials were still available. The vast areas of 19th-century terraced housing that still survive in cities such as Newcastle, Sunderland, Sheffield, Hull and Leeds testify to this development.

At the same time, industrialised society required new or enlarged types of buildings and thus the expanding towns and cities were provided with churches,

chapels, town halls, railway stations, factories, hospitals, schools, mechanics' institutes, exchange buildings, theatres, banks, warehouses, retail shops, covered markets and arcades, museums, libraries, hotels, public houses and music halls. Despite much subsequent demolition, examples of this impressive legacy can still be found throughout the North East.

Leeds Town Hall, for instance, dates from 1852–8 and must be regarded as the definitive expression of burgeoning civic pride and prestige (Fig. 7.17). It was designed by Cuthbert Brodrick. North of the Town Hall lie other Victorian public buildings, including the Civic Theatre (1865–8, formerly the Mechanics' Institute) and the Infirmary (1863–8), by Brodrick and Sir George Gilbert Scott respectively. By the late 19th century Leeds had become the fifth largest municipality in England; it was designated as a city in 1893. Three years later one of its most monumental civic spaces, City Square, was laid out to commemorate this achievement. By now the city was also successfully diversifying from its original textile base.

Newcastle's Central Station, a massive classical design by John Dobson of 1846–50 (the portico was added in 1862–3), seems to epitomise the confidence of north-east England at that time, while even Darlington, a much smaller municipality, has a 'Market Hall and Public Offices' built (1861–4) by Alfred Waterhouse, one of the leading architects of his day. Darlington had developed steadily as a result of the coal, leather, textile, and later the iron industries. In addition, it benefited from its convenient location on the main north–south overland route, being also an important early railway centre.

Fig. 7.17 Leeds, view of the Town Hall.
An innovative public space, 'Millennium Square', has recently been created north of the Town Hall.

Fine Victorian buildings in Halifax include Sir Charles Barry's Town Hall of 1859, while Bradford's St George's Hall (1851), Wool Exchange (1864) and Town Hall (1873), all by local architects Lockwood and Mawson, form one of the finest ensembles of Victorian public buildings anywhere in the country and are tangible evidence of the town's 19th-century success. So too are its many impressive mills and other commercial buildings, such as the palatial warehouses of the district known as 'Little Germany'. Bradford, in fact, had been a late urban developer. Until the mid-18th century it remained a small market town serving the needs of nearby Pennine farming and weaving villages. It received a boost with the opening of the Leeds and Liverpool Canal in 1774 and in 1800 some local manufacturing moved out of the cottages and into the first Bradford factory. By 1850 the town had expanded to become second only to Leeds in the West Riding and the eighth largest in Britain, serving as 'the global centre of worsted production and exchange'.[30] It was accorded city status in 1897. However, only by the third quarter of the 20th century had it managed to diversify from its almost total reliance on the textile industry.

Sheffield, in the far south of our region, has a not dissimilar character and history, although it is a more diffuse and less centralised city, reflecting both the rugged terrain of the area where it developed and its origins in a series of separate industrial villages. Here the 19th century brought a considerable change of scale and a broadening of the area's industrial product base. After 1850 Sheffield, like Bradford, served a global market, especially in cutlery, and became filled with small, brick-built workshops, sometimes tucked away behind houses. More substantial, three- or four-storeyed courtyard complexes were also now common, with some larger, integrated firms building additional, classical-style office blocks facing the street (Fig. 7.18). The more rural industrial sites that still surrounded the town specialised in the manufacture of agricultural implements.

Before long, however, the widespread adoption of steam power, and the development of new products such as armaments and railway lines, resulted in the appearance in and around Sheffield of massive new factories. The lower Don valley developed into a vast industrial suburb, dominated by huge forges, foundries and assembly shops and covered, we are told, by 'a thick pulverous haze';[31] crucially, the area was now served by the railway. Most of the great names of the steel industry – Browns, Cammells, Firths, Naylor and Vickers – were located here, in factories with names such as Atlas and Cyclops, suggesting their titanic scale. Within inner Sheffield, however, an equivalent monumentality was missing. The exception is the

Fig. 7.18 Sheaf Works, Maltravers Street, Sheffield, 1823. This works manufactured steel and finished goods. Note the classically-styled office block, workshops and furnaces, and smoking chimneys.

Town Hall, by E W Mountford, but even this was not built until 1890–7. Incorporated as a borough in 1843, Sheffield became a city in 1893.

Overall, the best example of 19th-century urban development in the North East is surely provided by Middlesbrough. Population growth alone would identify it as such; after the town's establishment in 1830 the original small rural community had grown to 5,463 by 1841 and to nearly 40,000 by 1871. But one has only to walk its streets to appreciate the importance of this period in the town's relatively short history. There are still enough rows of identical terraced houses left to show how the majority of Middlesbrough's working population lived; still enough streets laid out with uniform regularity to indicate the utilitarian grid that passed for town planning even towards the end of the century; and still enough large public buildings left standing as indices of the town's past wealth and civic pride.

In contrast to the accumulative 'organic' growth of most of its medieval counterparts, Middlesbrough started life as a speculative development, created virtually from new in 1830 by the Darlington banker Joseph Pease and his Quaker associates. Their original plan consisted of a straightforward, symmetrical grid

Fig. 7.19 Middlesbrough: detail from OS Map, 1882.

with church and market in a central square. The 123 building plots were spacious and the 12 streets were wide, with every attempt being made to maintain 'respectability', but the uniform environment intended was almost immediately compromised by the choice of a convenient but low-lying riverside site. Damp was always one of the great problems of the town, followed by smoke and noise: 'None would have chosen the site if their first consideration had been people rather than coal'.[32] By the early 1850s Middlesbrough was still a compact, albeit increasingly dense, settlement which extended only slightly beyond its original layout, surrounded by undeveloped countryside.

However, the discovery of iron ore in the Cleveland Hills in 1850 initiated a second, more intense, phase of growth, which soon led to severe overcrowding and a growing need for further expansion. The earlier period of house building had been controlled by the owners of the Middlesbrough estate, who were in sole possession of the available land, but during the 1860s Thomas Hustler sold land for development lying beyond the north-eastern boundary of the estate. This is physically manifested in the rather awkward coming together of the Middlesbrough Owners' east–west pattern of roads and streets, and the diagonal grid of Newport and Cannon Wards (Fig. 7.19).

Much of the town's still-existing row or terraced housing was constructed

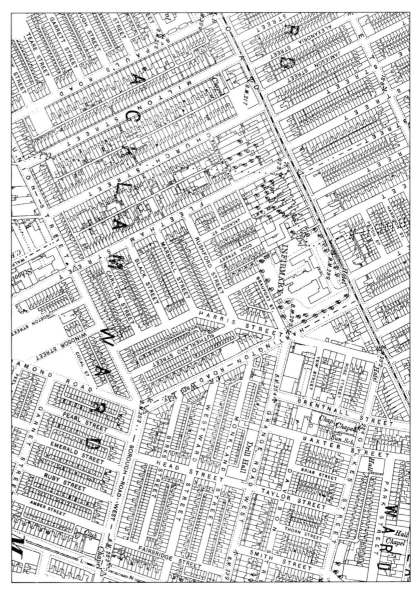

under local byelaws during the 1880s and '90s and exhibits the solid uniformity of the type, much more impressive when viewed collectively than when considered alone. Withdrawal of the middle classes to the outskirts of town after about 1850 meant that by the end of the century Middlesbrough also boasted four increasingly grandiose residential suburbs: Southfield Villas, North Park Road, Grove Hill and Linthorpe.

Needless to say, Middlesbrough's expansion had been much more rapid than that of some of the older north-eastern towns and cities at this time. Nevertheless, the population of Newcastle rose during the 19th century from about 28,000 to 215,000. Once-rural villages encircling the still compact city, such as Benton, Benwell, Elswick, Fenham, Gosforth and Jesmond, were swallowed up and most of the gardens and public open spaces that were such a feature of Newcastle during Georgian times were built over. Even so, much of Newcastle's growth during this period came comparatively late; it also tended to be peripheral, mainly along the river, especially to the east. Meanwhile, the other once pre-eminent city of the North East, York, largely failed to industrialise. Although it did become a major railway centre, it was overtaken principally by Leeds and for York this period was one of relative decline.

Mention has already been made of the immense quantity of working-class terraced housing built throughout the region during the 19th and early 20th centuries. Standardised though this housing was in the North East, a number of interesting localised variants of the type did emerge. In west Yorkshire, especially in Leeds and Sheffield, the notorious 'back-to-back' system, whereby two terraces shared a single rear internal wall, was prevalent. In Sheffield numerous streets of 'back-to-backs' clustered round the factories and works. Hull possessed the even more compact 'courts'. These were separated by walls and had two short rows of houses facing one another behind an even shorter row that fronted the main street. In and around Newcastle, the distinctive Tyneside Flat is an ingenious two-storey arrangement whereby one household lives above another, each having its own individual front (and back) door. Even more unusual is the Sunderland Cottage, a single-storey terraced type not unlike some of the row housing once prevalent in Durham and Northumberland mining villages.

Also noteworthy are some of the model industrial townships built by philanthropic manufacturers for their workers in more rural locations in the North East during the later 19th century. Of these, Saltaire, now enclosed by the suburbs of Bradford, was both the most ambitious and the most architecturally unified. It was the creation of Bradford's largest employer, Sir Titus Salt. The style adopted was Italianate, the architects again being Lockwood and Mawson. When completed in 1871, the township supported a population of about 4,500 in 824 model dwellings. The gigantic, six-storey mill was built first and the houses were added later. Saltaire is quite cramped by modern standards, its houses packed close together in a geometric grid of narrow streets. Many are quite small but they were still a great improvement on the earlier working-class terraces in Bradford, and also provided varying degrees of accommodation related to tenants' status within the workforce hierarchy. Salt also provided a variety of communal facilities ranging from a town hall to a laundry.

Saltaire can be compared to Akroydon, near Halifax, the second of two 'industrial villages' built from 1861 onwards by Edward Akroyd, a local mill owner. Akroydon was designed in the Gothic Revival style by Sir George Gilbert Scott, who created a large rectangle of houses around a central garden area, giving a strong sense of an enclosed, medieval village community. Another, later example of philanthropic manufacturers' housing can be found at New Earswick, just outside York. This early garden suburb was built by the chocolate-manufacturer Joseph Rowntree at the turn of the century to house his employees. Designed by Barry Parker and Raymond Unwin, New Earswick demonstrates the benefits that thoughtful, rational vernacular-style design can bring to even the most minimal of dwellings.

THE 20th CENTURY AND LATER

As elsewhere, the period between the First and Second World Wars saw a great expansion of municipal housing in the North East. This almost invariably comprised estates of conventional semi-detached houses, in and around what were then peripheral areas of the region's larger cities and towns. Examples include the Cowgate, Heaton, Kenton and Pendower (West Road) estates in Newcastle; the East, North and Orchard Park estates in Hull (Hull especially also has much classic, ribbon-type, private housing development dating from the inter-war period); and the huge Gipton, Meanwood and Middleton estates in Leeds. The layouts of such estates were frequently rigid and unimaginative, often blandly flanking the new suburban and arterial roads. However, at their best they successfully broke away from the grid-like arrangements of earlier, speculatively-built working-class housing, particularly through the use of diagonals, crescents and cul-de-sacs. Their existence, of course, depended heavily on the growth of motor bus transport at this time.

During the inter-war period numerous monumental public buildings were constructed in the region, usually designed in the then-fashionable 'stripped classical' style and built of Portland stone on a steel frame. The period was also notable for a number of large-scale civic planning schemes, not least in Newcastle. Here the new Tyne Bridge, built 1924–8 by engineers Mott, Hay and Anderson, consolidated Pilgrim Street as the main north–south route, prior to the construction of the inner-city motorway during the 1960s. It also encouraged the city's increasing shift of emphasis northwards. In the area of Pilgrim Street were built Carliol House, the new headquarters of the North East Electricity Supply Company (1924–8, by Burnet, Tait and Lorne with Couves and Partners) and the Magistrates' Courts, Police and Fire Stations (1931–2). The latter complex was designed by Robert Burns Dick, a talented local practitioner who had also been responsible for the architectural treatment of the Tyne Bridge itself. In similar 'stripped classical' style was Sheffield's new City Hall (opened in 1932), designed by Vincent Harris as part of a scheme for the siting of public buildings devised by the planner Sir Patrick Abercrombie.

At this time there was also a great deal of building in Leeds. Much of the design work for this was placed in the hands of London-based architects, perhaps befitting the metropolitan effect desired and achieved. The enormous Queen's Hotel in City Square, by William Hamlyn and W Curtis Green, was opened in 1937, while north of the Town Hall arose the impressively-sited Civic Hall (again by Vincent Harris, 1930–3). Still further north, on rising ground along Woodhouse Lane, came a complex of university development including the Brotherton Library, opened in 1936, and the towering Parkinson Building, both designed by Lanchester, Lucas and Lodge; the latter structure was begun at this time though not completed until 1951.

The Leeds inner ring-road was begun in 1921 and soon afterwards, in 1924–32, the city centre saw the reconstruction of the Headrow (by Sir Reginald Blomfield), one of the national landmarks of inter-war architecture. This monumental exercise in the neo-Georgian style provides an axial route from the Town Hall down towards Quarry Hill. This latter was the site of a pioneering municipal housing scheme of the period, the Quarry Hill Flats, designed in 1935, in contrasting avant-garde modernist style by the city housing architect, R A H Livett. The flats were officially opened in 1938 but were still incomplete at the outbreak of war. They have now been replaced by a substantial group of buildings including massive government offices and the new West Yorkshire Playhouse.

Hull, by contrast, was unusual in that its main earlier programme of redevelopment had come not in the mid-Victorian period but only in the very late 19th and early 20th centuries. This had created a belated monumentalism via a new system of intersecting routes, centring on the new Queen Victoria Square, with public buildings such as the City Hall (1903–10, by J H Hirst) and the

Guildhall and Law Courts (1903–16, by Sir Edwin Cooper) nearby. The inter-war period did, however, see the construction of Ferensway (1931), a boulevard leading into the western city centre, and of Queen's Gardens, created out of the old Queen's Dock and opened in 1935 (Fig. 7.20).

After the Second World War came the era of large-scale planning and 'comprehensive' redevelopment policies nationwide, their results only too evident in all the larger cities of the North East. Steel and concrete construction became the norm for most major urban building projects, such as the high-rise office developments increasingly popular at this time and the 'tower block' housing estates favoured by numerous major local authorities until at least the 1970s. Indeed, such structures are prominent on the skylines of most of the region's cities.

During this period Newcastle underwent a programme of comprehensive redevelopment, albeit ultimately unfinished, involving the removal of large areas of Georgian and Victorian townscape, while the centre of Hull was also largely redeveloped after extensive wartime bomb damage. In Hull, for example, the Queen's Gardens precinct formed the central point of another major, if uncompleted, post-war civic planning exercise, at which time it was remodelled (1959–61). One of the most imposing post-war 'monuments' in Sheffield was built by the university, in the form of its main library (designed in 1953) and adjacent arts tower (1960–65), both by Gollins, Melvin, Ward and Partners. The high-rise, steel and glass tower is visually offset against the lower 'plinth' of the earlier library, which has a fully-glazed reading room overlooking a lake.

Wholesale demolition of Victorian terraced housing was now standard. Replacement housing was usually provided in the form of outlying 'tower blocks', such as Seacroft on the north-eastern outskirts of Leeds (Fig. 7.21). This gigantic development, created during the 1960s, comprises high-rise flats and an industrial estate, and has its own 'town centre' adjacent to an old village green, which has been preserved. A very different answer to the problem of post-war re-housing was provided by Sheffield's City Architect of the period, J L Womersley, with his design for the enormous Park Hill Estate, completed in 1961. This 'megastructure', housing up to 3,500 people, sits on a hillside just to the east of the city centre and comprises a series of huge slab blocks, built of brick and (mainly) exposed concrete. These curve round in groups to form a sequence of semi-enclosed communal spaces. Innovatively, the blocks are all linked by 'streets-in-the-sky' decks, intended to provide safe pedestrian access from the ground and also, as they run right through each building, to replicate the effect of the back lanes of traditional, working-class terraced streets.

Among the more interesting of the North East's innumerable mid-20th-century developments are the planned New Towns of County Durham and Northumberland, created as part of the post-war policy of decentralisation. Successfully or otherwise, they incorporated the new, 'scientific' ideas regarding housing, employment and communication routes (especially those involving the motor car), which underpinned official thinking at the time.

Newton Aycliffe, designated in 1947, had its beginnings in the location there of a wartime munitions factory and subsequent industrial estate. Designed as a cluster of six neighbourhoods around a series of 'village greens' encircling a small central pedestrian precinct, the town has traditional-style houses set on a relatively flat site. Essentially, it remains a suburban environment, but with a central commercial and administrative core. At nearby Peterlee there was initially a more adventurous approach, thanks to the appointment of the cosmopolitan modernist Berthold Lubetkin as Chief Architect-Planner in 1948. His vision was of 'an ordered geometric arrangement of housing'[33] for the town's mainly mining population, sited around a monumental urban centre. But conflicting official interests caused serious delays and Lubetkin resigned in 1950. Much later, an altered and reduced version of his proposed centre was built (Fig. 7.22), successfully incorporating a number of ideas tested earlier at Stevenage

OPPOSITE PAGE:

TOP: *Fig. 7.20 Queen's Gardens, Hull.* *The building visible at the far end of this precinct is the former College of Technology (1962), now part of the University of Lincolnshire and Humberside. In front of this is the Wilberforce Monument (1834).*

BOTTOM: *Fig. 7.21 Leeds, aerial view of Seacroft estate.*

and Coventry. Meanwhile, conventional semi-detached housing was constructed piecemeal in various outlying neighbourhoods of Peterlee. The arrival of the artist Victor Pasmore in 1955, to oversee aesthetic aspects of the development, produced the well-known flat-roofed houses of the south-west neighbourhood and the controversial 'Apollo Pavilion' (c.1963–70). The latter is a public sculpture-*cum*-footbridge of reinforced concrete, now in a sorry state of disrepair.

Killingworth 'Township' was constructed in the 1960s for a population mostly relocated from nearby Newcastle. Here an uncompromisingly modernist vision was implemented, involving concrete deck housing and a shopping precinct raised above an artificial lake. However, these socially disastrous structures have now been largely replaced with more conventional developments. The original Township was once likened to 'a set for Fritz Lang's *Metropolis*'[34] though in fact, however improbably, its imagery was intended to suggest that of a Northumbrian castle.

By contrast, Washington New Town, designated in 1964, was intended as a visually pleasant 'garden city' environment, which would cater for increasing car ownership and attract commuters as well as overspill population from Tyneside and Wearside. Its buildings are for the most

Fig. 7.22 Peterlee, view of town centre.
A pedestrian way broadens to form the main town centre square, within which is located a two-tier shopping precinct accessed by ramp and escalator and arguably well adapted to its hilly site.

part low-rise and the town contains an innovative mix of housing, even including some 'executive' dwellings. Like Newton Aycliffe, Washington is based on a series of villages, though here they operate on a much larger scale and sit within a more regular grid of roughly one-mile squares. Motorway-style roads take traffic around and through the town, with limited access at roundabouts to a network of dual-carriageway routes. These in turn encircle each grid square and feed into a decreasingly accessed hierarchy of roads, while pedestrian walkways link the villages at specific focal points. The town centre incorporates 'The Galleries' shopping mall, a library, a health centre, a police station, a sports centre and a number of office buildings. Arguably however, Washington is too much divided into segments. It has also been suggested that the town remains over-dependent on Sunderland and Newcastle and that, despite their informal planning and purpose-designed centres, 'the villages are really only housing estates writ large'.[35]

Perhaps the most striking feature of the present-day situation in the North East is the way in which many of its larger cities and towns are being transformed as they enter a 'post-industrial' phase. As traditional industries have declined, many of the areas formerly supporting these activities have been redeveloped, usually for entertainment, retail, leisure and cultural purposes (often in combination with housing). With tourism also becoming an increasingly important factor, history and 'heritage' are now marketable commodities and once-expendable structures are being conserved. Indeed, the whole process usually involves a fashionable 'post-modern' mix of innovative new architecture and converted former industrial buildings, often in riverside locations. For example at Leeds, now the commercial and financial capital of the North East, the old waterfront area has been redeveloped with housing, much of it converted from 19th-century commercial buildings; some of these have also become offices, restaurants and hotels. There are new pedestrian bridges and nearby attractions include the Brewery Wharf, the Granary Wharf Shopping Centre and the new Royal Armouries Museum. At Hull, with the centre of shipping activity moving eastwards along the Humber estuary, the old Prince's Dock has become the setting for the Prince's Quay Shopping Centre, opened in 1991, while the adjacent Humber Dock is now a marina. Just to the east of this marina, and linked to it by a pedestrian bridge, is The Deep, an eye-catching 'submarium' designed by Sir Terry Farrell and opened in 2002. In a comparable location is Sunderland's St Peter's Riverside. This complex contains a cycle route, public art, a residential teaching campus for the university and the futuristic National Glass Centre.

At Hartlepool, part of the old dock area has been redeveloped for tourists as the Historic Quay Museum, an 'authentic' reconstruction of an 18th-century seaport. Middlesbrough, too, has recently embarked on a dock reclamation project at Middlehaven, just north of the town centre, where a combination of commercial, residential, educational, leisure and business development is intended to act as a catalyst for social, economic and cultural change. However, among many developments of this kind the most striking have surely been in Newcastle and Gateshead. Here, derelict land on both banks of the Tyne has been redeveloped around the new Gateshead Millennium Bridge (by Wilkinson Eyre, Gifford and Partners, 2001), linking both sides of the river as never before (Fig. 7.23). On the south side, the Baltic Centre for Contemporary Art (opened in 2002) has been imaginatively converted by architect Dominic Williams from a disused flour mill. This new 'art factory' has already assumed an iconic status equivalent to that of Antony Gormley's *Angel of the North* public sculpture south of Gateshead near the A1. So too has Gateshead's spectacular Sage Music Centre (designed by Foster and Partners), just upriver from the Baltic and opened in 2004.

Fig. 7.23 Newcastle with Gateshead, aerial view looking upriver. *Landmarks in Newcastle (right) include All Saints' Church, the castle and the Central Station. From the top, the bridges are the High Level (1846–50), the Swing (1876), the Tyne and the Millennium. To the lower right is the East Quayside development of bars, restaurants, hotels and (off picture) housing. On the Gateshead riverside is the Sage Music Centre (seen here under construction). Just downriver of this is the 'Baltic'.*

The term that probably best characterises the region's current urban landscape is diversity. The towns and cities that make up this landscape provide a varied but also enduring system of settlements. As we have seen, this pattern, though distinctive, has also been in turn modified and refined in response to national and even international influences, from the Roman invasion and the diffusion of Christianity, through the period of medieval mercantilism, to industrialisation and post-industrialisation. These wider forces have continually altered the balance between settlement types, as with the expansion of conurbations under industrialisation and, in many cases, their subsequent contraction. Similarly, the current emphasis on leisure, entertainment and 'culture' (now defined in many new and varied ways) impinges strongly on all these elements, as conurbations de-industrialise, outworn areas subject themselves to redevelopment and towns and cities of all kinds seek to capitalise on tourism. Yet the historic structure of the North East's settlement patterns, in all its diversity, largely persists, even as functions change and evolve.

NOTES

1 Newton 1972, 146. Northumberland's market towns were Alnwick, Bellingham, Berwick upon Tweed, Haltwhistle, Hexham, Morpeth, Newcastle and Wooler.

2 Camden 1695 (1971), 718, 855, 738, 743 and 711 respectively.

3 Examples include Cleton, Dimlington, Hyde, Monkwike, Newsham and Southorpe.

4 In spite of its seemingly pragmatic layout, Newcastle was in fact 'planted' by the Normans, as can be seen from taxation records, etc. It was chartered early in the 12th century (the exact date is unknown). *See* Beresford 1967.

5 Clifton-Taylor 1981, 180.

6 J. Kermode, 'Northern Towns', in Palliser 2000, 674.

7 Clifton-Taylor 1972, 95.

8 For more detail on Alnwick *see* Conzen 1969.

9 A G Dickens, 'Tudor York', in Tillott 1961, 117.

10 Smailes 1960, 113.

11 Musgrove 1990, 147.

12 For more on the possible alignment of Newcastle's Roman and medieval bridges, *see* Bidwell and Holbrook 1989, 99–103.

13 Thus, for example, Bishop Cuthbert Tunstall was frequently used by Henry VIII to negotiate with the Scots and to defend the border or invade across it. In 1544 he was stationed in Newcastle to support a proposed invasion of Scotland.

14 For more detail *see* Harrison 2002.

15 In the Middle Ages this street was known as Hull Street.

16 Quoted in M Reed, 'The Urban Landscape', in Clark 2000, 295.

17 Morris 1949, 209–11.

18 Defoe 1724–6 (1927), vol. ii, 659.

19 Around the margin of James Corbridge's map of the town of 1723 are numerous illustrations of such buildings. This map is reproduced in Graham 1984.

20 Defoe, *op cit*, vol. ii, 636 and 642.

21 Centuries earlier, York had quickly followed Hull and Beverley in developing a brick-manufacturing capacity and it is no surprise to find that most of its many fine Georgian houses are of brick.

22 It was not until the early 19th-century central redevelopment of Newcastle by the entrepreneur Richard Grainger, discussed later in this chapter, that stone became the norm for the city's public buildings and major commercial streets.

23 Curnock 1909, vol. iv, 323 (from Wesley's Journal, 4 June 1759).

24 This position is still reflected in the city's present-day proximity to the M1, M62 and A1 and is one of the reasons for its enormous growth during the last 200 years.

25 J K Walton, 'North', in Clark, *op cit*, 117.

26 For more detail see Grady 1989.

27 Defoe, *op cit*, vol. ii, 653.

28 Langdale 1822.

29 Quoted in Page 1914–23, vol. ii, 540.

30 Koditschek 1990, 79.

31 From a report in *The Builder*, 1861; quoted in Hey 1986, 266.

32 Bell and Bell 1969, 137.

33 Allan 1992, 458.

34 Pevsner *et al*. 1992, 361–2.

35 Pevsner *et al*. 2002, 489.

8

Communications
and Routeways

RICHARD MUIR

In the north of England, as elsewhere, communications provide a framework upon which many other elements of the cultural landscape are arranged. The roads and waterways do not constitute a rigid skeleton, but rather the transport network evolves in response to the rise and fall in importance of settlements, changing political and military factors or changes in commercial activity. At the broadest level, the north can be seen as a zone traversed by major north–south national/international routeways linking the English political heartland and Scotland. At the regional level it emerges as an area of contrasts. In the low-lying south-east, movement is relatively easy and conditioned mainly by bridging points on the rivers, while elsewhere, contacts are strongly influenced by the high watersheds of the Pennine and Border fells and the numerous dales that compartmentalise the land into valley units. Then at the local level there are the webs of winding lanes and pathways that were developed by villagers trekking to their plough strips and markets, by cowherds, shepherds and miners bound for the common and by fish sellers moving a few kilometres inland from the coast.

The system of communications is forever in a state of change, with roads sinking back into the pasture when the villages they served withered and decayed, while elsewhere communities might drift towards a bustling highway linking two expanding towns or gather at a new bridging point. Change also reflected trends in technology, with the rivers and streams that had been crucial in the medieval economy gradually losing importance as long-needed improvements transformed the capabilities of land transport in the 18th century.

PREHISTORIC ROUTEWAYS

We know that routeways, by land and by water, must have existed in abundance in prehistoric times, even though our knowledge of specific examples is modest. The reasonably dense agricultural populations of the Iron and Bronze ages must have traded to obtain essential commodities, such as metal ores and salt, that were not generally available, and from the earliest stages of human settlement stones suitable for tool making were essential. It follows, therefore, that in addition to the farm and field tracks serving the village, hamlet and farmstead communities, and as well as the routes leading to tribal power centres and ritual sites, there must have been branching networks of long-distance routeways used in the dissemination of trade goods. For stone tools, two sources were particularly significant: the volcanic tuff from the Langdale Pikes in the Lake District, which was an excellent axe-making material, and the flint from the seams of nodules found in the chalk cliffs near Flamborough Head. Flint axes were roughed-out on the cliff tops and then traded inland, but the Lakeland volcanic material could have been traded to this region by itinerant Cumbrian axe-makers; it might have been brought back by herdsmen returning from the summer grazings of the high Pennine fells, or it might have been shipped right around the English coast by seafaring traders. Dolerite from the Whin Sill outcrop that carries Hadrian's Wall was used for making the Early-to-Middle Bronze Age tools known as 'axe-hammers', probably used as wedges for splitting trees or as the cutting tips of simple 'ard' ploughs. Some examples could have been brought to Yorkshire from Northumberland and upper Teesdale, but it is equally likely that the rocks were carried south by glaciers and deposited in the glacial tills around the Yorkshire coast.

Ancient routeways are very hard to identify. If, as was traditionally believed, the long-distance trackways followed ridges and watersheds then some will have vanished beneath heather, peat and blanket bog, while others will now be tramped and scarred by the boots of modern ramblers. On the lower farmland, however, there can be no doubt that much of the legacy of roads, twisting lanes and winding footpaths follows lines of movement first established in prehistoric times. Countless ancient tracks have been abandoned, often existing only as faint hollows in the pasture. On Calverside in Swaledale little field tracks were found in association with an Iron Age system of co-axial fields that was dated to around 300 BC. Normally, when a routeway continues in use within a network of local roads and tracks it almost certainly becomes undatable. At Heslerton in the Yorkshire Wolds, a broad, ditched Bronze Age track, rutted by the passage of narrow wheels, was excavated and dated to about the end of the Bronze Age.

ROMAN ROADS

The prehistoric system of routeways must have been largely organic, developing in a piecemeal manner as new destinations were incorporated into the net. Roman roads imposed a much more coherent vision of the organisation of territory. The basic pattern of land routes in northern England was established in Roman times. It involved strategic routeways concerned with imperial military and political objectives and roads to link developing towns, garrisons and administrative centres within the region. Efforts were also made to improve the provision and condition of local roads, many of these doubtless created by indigenous communities before the occupation. Though most highways developed important commercial functions, they began as roads of imperial conquest. In the years immediately following the invasion of AD 43, much of the north existed as a puppet state under the client queen, Cartimandua. In AD 69, however, a palace revolution and nationalist uprising in Brigantia precipitated a Roman invasion, with the 9th Legion moving north from Lincoln to cross the Humber and establish a camp near the confluence of the rivers Ouse and Fosse. Here, at what is now the city of York, there developed one of the greatest fortresses of the Empire and one of only four civilian centres of *colonia* rank in Britain. It became the centre of the military command for the northern area and a nodal point on the road systems that supported the frontier. But, well to the north of here, the fort at South Shields on the Tyne estuary was furnished with massive grain storage capacity and at Benwell, some 20km upriver, the British Fleet (*Classis Britannica*) was commemorated in a monumental inscription. And so we are reminded that the foot soldier slogging his way along the Roman road had support also from ships at sea and in the navigable rivers.

The pattern of communications reflected the strategic priorities. A great military highway left the fortress of York along a line represented by Bootham (the A19) and headed northwards, reaching the small town of Aldborough and the camp at Catterick. (Other roads radiating outwards from Roman York include the precursors of the A166 towards Driffield, the A1079 to the Humber, the A64 towards Leeds and the Pennines and the A59 to Harrogate and Wharfedale, so that all the most important roads serving modern York were established in the Roman period.) Dere Street, marked south of Bishop Auckland by the B6275 and A1 (A1M) was the main supply and invasion road leading to the frontier and beyond. At Scotch Corner, just north of Catterick, a road branched off Dere Street on a north-westerly course, linking Pennine garrisons of Bowes and Brough and continuing to the military base at Carlisle, near the Solway estuary. Its course is marked by the A66, which crosses the Pennines over Stainmore, and the A6. Dere Street continued northwards, crossing the Tees at Piercebridge and the Tyne at Corbridge, after which it struck off north-west and across the Cheviot watershed in difficult terrain at some 500m above sea level (Fig. 8.1). A little north of Corbridge another road, the Devil's Causeway, branched north-east and then north throughout the length of Northumberland, heading for the Tweed estuary. East and west sides between Corbridge and Carlisle were linked cross-country by the Stanegate, with its intermediate forts at

Vindolanda (Chesterholme), Carvoran and elsewhere. This line, which used the valleys of the Tyne-Solway gap, was superseded by the building of Hadrian's Wall in the AD 120s on the higher ridges north of the valleys. The wall was furnished with its own road, the Military Way, which can be seen as an earthwork in places along the central sector of the wall. The present-day Military Road, the B6318, is not the Roman road, but was built by General Wade after the 1745 rising.

Fig. 8.1 The A1 route over the Tees lowlands follows the straight course of the Roman Dere Street, which linked York to Corbridge on the Roman wall. The medieval village of Piercebridge (bottom right) lies on the site of a Roman fort located at a bridging point of the Tees.

The Roman roads provided the region with the main alignments in its road network for more than a thousand years, and almost two millennia after the roads were set out they still guide the courses of many of the 'A' routes. In the north of England the old roads appear in many guises. They can take the form of bustling city streets, like High Petergate inside the former fortress at York. They are frequently encountered as major roads that proceed across the countryside in a series of straight stretches, these perhaps having been originally set out by Roman surveyors working from hill-top vantage points. Often too, the original route has become 'hyphenated', with the straight alignments being linked by curved or winding sections. This could happen when part a of neglected Roman road became waterlogged, rutted and churned, obliging travellers to break into the neighbouring fields and establish a new length of road to link the still-passable sections, as seems to have happened at various places on the A59 west of York. While some sections of Roman road have probably been used continuously since the early years of the

ABOVE: *Fig. 8.2 The Pennines were crossed by a network of Roman roads, stretches of which were used as lines of communication long after Roman withdrawal. One of these routes, probably connecting a fort at Ilkley with the Dere Street, is traceable on Blubberhouses Moor (running straight down the centre of the photograph and accentuated under light snow).*

BELOW: *Fig. 8.3 The foundations of the Roman road known as Wade's Causeway are preserved at Wheeldale on the North York Moors between Whitby and Pickering. This is one of the few exposed Roman roads and generally regarded as the most impressive piece of original Roman highway in Britain. The large boulders or cobbles, however, are the foundations of the road, not the finished surface. Wade is a legendary local giant alleged to have constructed the road for the passage of his cattle to the moors.*

occupation, others have declined, decayed and almost vanished. A new bridge built across the River Ure at Boroughbridge in the 12th century pulled the Great North Road 800m west of the line of Dere Street and the Roman site of Aldborough. In Northumberland, the first 30km of the Devil's Causeway is now all but lost as a routeway, with no modern road taking that north-west alignment. From its River Coquet crossing, the A697 picks up its course, though only for short distances do the two share exactly the same line. At the Breamish crossing the two diverge, with the modern road keeping close to the edge of the Cheviots, through Wooler and into Scotland at the Coldstream crossing of the Tweed. The Roman road strikes off almost due north, mostly as a now-disused line. But the 8km near-straight run in to Lowick retains the old alignment, after which the B6525 wanders through Ancroft towards Scremerston, in place of the direct line of the final stretch of the Devil's Causeway to Tweedmouth. To the west of Harrogate an old road survives as the A59 but is abandoned by the modern route at Fewston and is then scarcely visible in the rough grazings and moorland further to the west. Similarly, the Roman route briefly represented by the A688 is abandoned by the modern road about 5km to the east of Barnard Castle, and the Roman and modern roads pursue different courses towards Bishop Auckland, the former being the more direct (Fig. 8.2).

In addition to the major routeways of the British outpost of the Roman Empire there were other, less imposing roads and tracks. On Wade's Causeway on Wheeldale Moor, near Pickering, can be seen the foundations of a small road which probably joined the Roman base at Malton and the signalling stations on the east coast that gave warning of approaching barbarians. Here, the conventional surface of rammed gravel has been washed away and only the bottomings of stone remain. The Cam High Road to the south-west of Bainbridge in Wensleydale appears like a rather nondescript farm track, but it was a road serving the remote garrison occupying the crown of a glacial hummock beside the (later) village of Bainbridge. Beyond Ribblehead it assumes the guise of the B6255. Some of the minor, narrower and curving Roman routes probably adopted the courses of tracks used by the indigenous people of Britain. This could be true of the road that is seen today heading north-eastwards towards Aldborough from a crossing of the Nidd at Hampsthwaite. By the deer park near Ripley some sections are exposed, with massive kerbstones retaining the core of a road little more than 2m (6ft) in width (Fig. 8.3).

There were other structures associated with the Roman roads of the north. They included the fortlets built to guard travellers, such as Chew Green in Northumberland, with its parking area for wagons bound to cross the Cheviots. Bridges were essential. At Chesters, the stone piers that carried a timber superstructure are visible at low water on the North Tyne. The south-bank pier of the bridge bringing Dere Steet into the fort at Corbridge has recently been identified and investigated. This is some half a kilometre west of the present bridge, which leads directly into the village. Pons Aelius (now Newcastle) was (and is still) the lowest bridging point on the Tyne, with the road approaching the fort from the south through the fort of Chester-le-Street on the line that later became part of the Great North Road. No fabric of the bridge can be seen now but a pair of handsome stone altars dedicated to Neptune and Ocianus (spelt thus), found in the bed of the Tyne during bridge works in 1876, could well have stood as a pair at the bridgehead or at its mid point. At Piercebridge, the Roman bridge was abandoned when the Tees migrated, and the buried south abutment of the bridge has been excavated. Conditions in the wetlands posed a special challenge for road makers. Near Scaftworth on the South Yorkshire–Nottinghamshire border the road was build as a raft that floated on sodden peat. Where it crossed the River Idle parallel rows of oak posts were driven through the water and peat into the clays beneath the river bed to support a bridge that might have been more than 150m in length. The Roman roads have had immense influence on patterns of travel and trade, and their influence seems to have extended into other, less obvious areas. To the south and west of Aldborough a minor Roman road seems to have provided the alignment from which a network of co-axial fields covering dozens of square kilometres was laid-out. Rectilinear patterns in the landscape in the vicinity of Dere Street south of Catterick hint that similar planning was associated with the major route. The roads also influenced the later positioning of both Christian churches and feudal villages,

Fig. 8.4 The Border uplands, like the Pennines, were traditionally traversed by a network of routeways that served the area's small, scattered settlements and pastoral economy and were long used in cross-border trade, especially the droving of Scottish-reared cattle to southern markets, which peaked in the 18th century. Some tracks may even have linked Iron Age hillforts and some are marked with the remnants of medieval crosses. Though exposed, the hill routes were probably easier to traverse than the waterlogged routeways on the lowlands and only in the 18th and 19th centuries were they superseded by the new communication systems of the industrial age restricted to lower, easier routes. Many former upland routes have either disappeared or remain fossilised as footpaths. The modern road (A68) to Jedburgh via Carter Bar, however, follows in the main a medieval track through Redesdale (based on Newton 1972, 220).

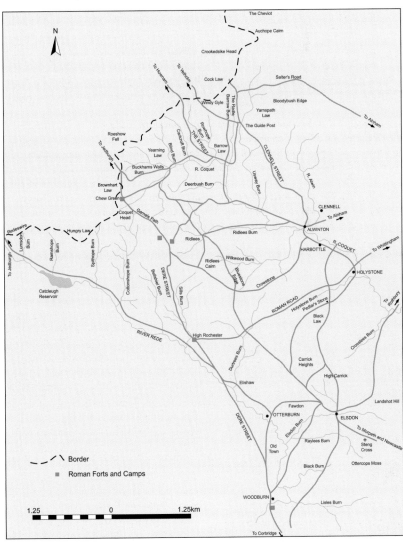

these often developing beside or close to the old routeways. The successive churches at Hampsthwaite, Ripley (the original church here) and Nidd along the road to Aldborough and the villages of Eglingham, Whittingham and Edlingham close to the old Devil's Causeway near Alnwick are good examples (Fig. 8.4).

AFTER THE ROMANS: ROADS, WATER AND TRAVEL

After the collapse of Roman rule, the Romanised aristocracy failed to preserve the integrity of Roman Britain, and the organisation needed to develop or even maintain the Roman routeways was lost. The roads remained in use, but the lack of central authority ensured their neglect and partial decay. Road building on any scale was unusual, and the patching of damaged sections by reluctant conscripts from the local estates was the best that might be expected. But the demands of commerce and war resulted in some new routes being developed. At the local level the additions to the transport network in the north often existed as causeways paved with hard sandstone slabs. Such roads, some of which lie intact but masked in turf, are very difficult to identify. They not only resemble some of the minor roads built in Roman times, but they are also similar to 'causeys' created in the three centuries following the end of the medieval period. Occasionally, their destinations will suggest a date, as when one is seen to serve a deserted medieval settlement with a roughly known date of desertion. An example is the narrow, paved track in Ripley deer park to the north of Harrogate, which is apparently heading for Owlcotes, a village that was abandoned around the 14th century.

The old highways provided the framework for long-distance movement. Catterick, Binchester, Ebchester and Corbridge along Dere Street all have traces of use by the first English speakers, who gave '-chester' and '-burh' names to places along Dere Street. In AD 627 the Deiran king Edwin accepted conversion to Christianity and began building a church within the old fortress in York and we see his bishop Paulinus engaged in missionary work at Catterick, which suggests journey along a Roman road. Later in the 7th century, a string of monasteries emerged on coastal headlands and river estuaries: Whitby, Hartlepool, Wearmouth, Jarrow, possibly Donmouth, Tynemouth, Coquet Island, Twyford (forerunner of Alnmouth), Lindisfarne and, beyond the Tweed, Coldingham. Here the sea was a highway for church and state business, as on the occasion when the Archbishop of Canterbury and the King and Bishop of Northumbria came to Twyford (possibly Alnmouth, as it became known) to cajole the reluctant Cuthbert to take the bishopric.

Once Viking raiders began to appear the sea was no longer a safe highway and the now-exposed monasteries were all abandoned or destroyed. The Lindisfarne community sought refuge inland. As they accumulated estates, so they needed to travel to administer these lands. The Durham historians tell us that in the 9th century St Cuthbert took a house at Crayke 'so that he might have a *mansio* there whenever he should go to the City of York or return from it'. Of course, it was not St Cuthbert in person who was making these journeys – he had died in AD 687 – but his people developed a set of staging posts which mapped out a routeway: Bamburgh, Warkworth, Bedlington, Chester-le-Street, Sedgefield, Northallerton, Crayke, York. This is not Dere Street, nor is it quite the Great North Road, but it is an axial route for long-distance traffic through the region.

If clerics needed to travel, so too did armies and the sites of battlefields pick out the routeways of road and river. King Edwin began his reign in AD 616 and ended it in AD 633 in battles, on both occasions on the marshy lands south of the Humber near the Roman road between Doncaster and Newark. The river system also enabled seafaring invaders to penetrate deeply into the Yorkshire lowlands. When the host of the Norwegian king, Hardrada, invaded in 1066, the English fleet sheltered near Tadcaster on the Wharfe while the Scandinavians sailed their ships up the Ouse for 19km before anchoring at Riccall. (Meanwhile, the speed of Harold's march north, largely along ancient roads, suggests that the Roman system of main arteries was still in reasonable shape.) The Vale of York saw the movement and clashing of armies from time to time throughout the medieval period: in the reign of Edward II; in the Wars of the Roses when there were battles at Hedworth Moor, Stamford Bridge and Towton; and in the Civil War with battles at Hambledon, Marston Moor, York, Tadcaster and Selby

MEDIEVAL PORTS, RIVERS AND TRADE

The movement overland of heavy cargoes presented great challenges for any goods too bulky to travel in the panniers of a pack pony. Rivers too played their part in the movement of goods both inland and to the coastal ports. In 1363 a shipment of 168 pigs of lead was sent from Nidderdale to Hull via the Ouse transport network, for shipment on to Windsor. Two years later, a slightly heavier shipment was sent to Boroughbridge on the Ure and then via York to the Humber; next down the coast to London and onwards via the Thames to Windsor. The initial stage of the journey by land involved two wagons and ten oxen. It must have had a traumatic effect upon those concerned, for the chroniclers told of muddy roads, which are very credible, but also high and rocky mountains, which are not. Groceries that the Durham Priory bought at the fair in Boston (Lincolnshire) in the 14th century were carried up the River Witham by boat to Lincoln. Here they were unloaded and put on carts for a short overland journey to Torksey at the mouth of the River Trent. A second boat journey then took them across the Humber estuary and up the River Ouse beyond York to Aldwark where, for the second time, they were loaded on to carts for the final part of the journey to Durham. When the bursar bought wine imported into Hull, he shipped it to Newcastle or Hartlepool, as close to Durham as he could. It is conceivable that in Roman times small ships could penetrate inland as far as Middleham on the Ure, while in the medieval period goods were transferred from boats to packhorses at Nun Monkton, lying by the confluence of the Ouse and Nidd and 11km to the north-west of York. The head of navigation on the Wharfe was at Tadcaster and on the Derwent it was at Stamford Bridge. York Minster was built from stones hewn in nearby quarries on the magnesian limestone, such as the celebrated quarries at Huddleston. Without water transport the building materials might never have been assembled at the site and, even so, the transport costs were probably double those of quarrying.

York had port facilities in Roman times and by the 8th century it had developed a trading centre at the confluence of the Ouse and the Fosse, outside the old Roman fort and colonia. Its river-banks were strengthened and Viking York, connected to the sea via the Ouse and the great gateway of the Humber, became part of a north European trading network that exported the craft goods of northern England and imported luxuries from the continent. During the medieval period, jetties or moorings, known as 'staiths', are known to have existed here and at the river/estuary ports of Howden, Selby and Hull. The port at Brough (the place where travellers on Ermine Street were ferried across the Humber) may, however, have been abandoned due to rising water levels during the Roman occupation. On the coast the landings took various forms. At the Spurn Head ports of Ravenser and Ravenser Odd (which were both lost in the great sea surges of the 14th century), ships were simply beached on the shore on a falling tide. Some of the medieval seaports are ports still, like Bridlington or Newcastle, but in other cases archaeological evidence reveals the past. At Flamborough the first record of a port dates from 1323. At the start of the next century a quay is mentioned. The medieval harbour was destroyed by the sea, rebuilt in the second half of the 16th century but almost immediately destroyed again. Lines of boulders running out to sea trace the former quays.

OPPOSITE PAGE:

TOP: *Fig. 8.5 The long-established tracks on the border moorlands*, *although relatively easy to cross, were generally superseded by new roads in the 18th and 19th centuries and are now traceable only as 'green roads'. One of these, the Salters' Road (north-west of Alnham, Northumberland) was an established route for conveying sea-salt from the coastal salt pans at Blyth across the Cheviots; it survives today as a hiking trail.*

BOTTOM: *Fig. 8.6 A reconstruction of the different ages and origin of routeways in medieval Ripley, North Yorkshire.*

Waterfront infrastructures of the larger sea and estuary ports of the medieval centuries are described elsewhere in this volume. Through these, by the 13th century, the North East was participating in a trading network around the North Sea, into the Baltic and down the French Atlantic seaboard to Gascony. The pottery produced in Scarborough, apparently a desirable commodity, is a good indicator of this. These wares have been found on east-coast ports from East Anglia to Aberdeen and on the European seaboard in the Low Countries and in Bergen in Norway, while the fine wares of Saintonge in south-west France appear in Newcastle and other North Sea ports.

Newcastle and its riverside neighbour of Pandon had prosperous merchant communities with connections to the Low Countries and the finance houses of Italy. Wool and hides were its principal exports in the 13th century but difficulties in its rural hinterland arising from the onset of wars with Scotland in 1296 and the collapse of the price of fleeces from the northern hills contributed to Newcastle's decline as a wool port. Coal, however, was the commodity that turned Newcastle into a great port, and during the 14th century the coal trade developed and Newcastle was exporting to Baltic ports as far east as Gdansk, ports of the Low Countries and along to Normandy, as well as to English east-coast ports.

Berwick, on the north bank of the Tweed, was a Scottish port until it was taken by the English in 1296, and a spectacularly successful one it was, shipping wool from the great abbeys in its Borders hinterland. In 1286 it returned revenue to the Scottish king six times greater than that raised in Newcastle for the English king. Berwick maintained a merchant community for some time into the 14th century but, in the longer term, war damage and the loss of its Scottish hinterland undermined its trading position.

Hull was the North East's great wool port in the 13th century and, in the mid-1400s the Low Countries' ports of Veere, Westenschouwen and Zierickzee were Hull's principal European contacts, and Edam, then as now, exported cheese. A trickle of ships came from Calais, Normandy and Brittany, and occasionally a Spanish vessel. Among Hull's own seafarers, Robert Stephenson would sail for Iceland in May or June, having first made a round trip to Bordeaux, presumably for a cargo of wine.

MEDIEVAL SALTWAYS, DROVERS AND PACKHORSES

In the absence of any capability for freezing meat or fish, salt was an essential commodity and saltways developed to move the product from coastal saltings and inland workings. Some must have been prehistoric and many Roman, with others of medieval date. In the 12th century the monks of Newminster in Northumberland managed salt pans at Blyth and the route known as the Salters' Road conveyed the salt over the Border fells and into southern Scotland. Some of the routes employed, such as the section of the A59 west of Harrogate that crosses Saltergate Hill, incorporated sections of Roman routeway. Like most of the other saltways, it was a very old road, with a first recorded mention in 1175. Running from this route towards Otley is a country road known as 'Psaltergate', the spelling of which plainly evolved from a misunderstanding after the track's function had been forgotten (Fig. 8.5).

The saltways had a deep but unspecified antiquity and over the centuries they developed various other uses. All this was also true of the fell tracks of the northern Border zone known as 'streets', an Old English word more usually applied to Roman roads. They led upwards to 'swires' or passes on what became the Anglo-Scottish border and many of them were probably created in prehistoric times to serve hillforts and summer camps used by herdsmen. In the medieval period, they were still used by herdsmen and shepherds bound to exploit the high

summer grazings but the hostilities between the Northumbrians and Scottish border dynasties disrupted their broader function as drove roads. Following the Union of the Crowns in 1603 and the arrival of more stable conditions for trading, the old streets rose in importance as routes for the export of Scottish cattle (Fig. 8.6).

The development of local markets established by royal charter quickened the economic activity of the country and caused some roads and tracks to rise in importance as market roads. Some centres, such as Ripon, Beverley, Leeds or Knaresborough, attracted significant trade, though in districts like Wensleydale the over-provision of market centres caused debilitating competition. A barony or other great landed estate could expect to derive economic benefit from having a market on its land and so, by 1300, Northumberland, with its clutch of baronies, had as many as 19 markets.

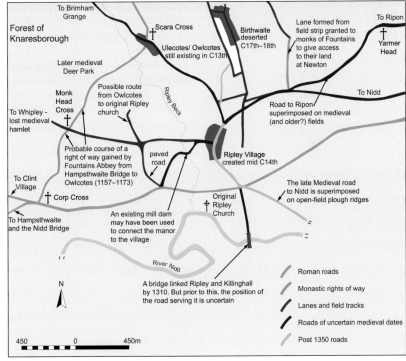

Corbridge, in the Tyne valley, was one of the most prominent and was the main centre for iron tools and goods. In County Durham the Bishop was the dominant force. He established markets at Durham and Darlington but there were none on lands held by the Durham Priory. Only two lay lords had markets, the Balliols at Barnard Castle and the Bruces at Hartlepool. Long-distance trading was associated with the great annual fairs, often granted to a market settlement on the day of the patron saint of its church. Such fairs introduced the products of international trade to the English backwaters and must have revealed the severe limitation of the kingdom's roads.

Countless roads and trackways across the ancient commons had for long been used for local movements of livestock, with broad verges, greens and watering places being provided to sustain the animals. Large-scale movements of animals took place under the monastic economy as animals and their by-products were moved between lodges, granges, markets and the controlling abbey. Fountains had estates extending into the Lake District, while networks of tracks linked it to its numerous granges. Many of the routes involved were rights of way granted to Cistercian communities willingly or under pressure by lay lords – people who were also frequently concerned about their prospects in the afterlife. At Ripley, for example, at some time between 1157 and 1173 the lords of each of the two manors granted rights of way to the monks of Fountains, resulting in the construction of a road (now abandoned) that was 12m wide and which linked Fountains Abbey, via its grange at Cayton, to the bridge on the River Nidd at Hampsthwaite. Meanwhile, the monks of Byland, who shared upper Nidderdale with Fountains, had to negotiate special concessions with their Cistercian colleagues to gain two access ways to their own holdings there.

However, large-scale trading in livestock imposed problems of finding forage en route and of trespass and damage caused to the farmers and householders bordering the droveways. The Scottish drovers, known to have operated in the mid-14th century but probably for long before, sought out tracks through the thinly inhabited fells that stood above the fields and settlements of the lowlands. In such lofty settings, grazing for hungry cattle could be found by the track, while the animals could pass the night in the pastures attached to the special droving inns that developed in association with the traffic. Black cattle from the Scottish highlands and islands, many of them the booty from inter-clan raiding, were driven southwards from the upland grazings to faraway markets or 'trysts' in the lowland towns, such as Falkirk. In the decades following the Act of Union of 1707, as many as 100,000 Scottish cattle, their feet shod with iron shoes, might make the journey to England in any year. Then they were driven along the droving tracks that traversed the Southern Uplands and onwards across the high fells of the Pennines. There, their southward progress was not assisted by the north-west to south-east grain of the terrain in the Dales, which made it more difficult to hold to the high plateaux. Eventually, a herd of around 200 cattle or a flock of perhaps 2,000 sheep would descend with its attendant plaid-garbed and Gaelic-speaking drovers and their dogs to one of the northern English market centres. At a place such as Malham and Hawes the beasts would be sold on to English dealers. They would be fattened and then driven to meet their fates at markets in the English Midlands, to great fairs, like the October fair at Horsham St Faith, near Norwich, or to Smithfield market in London.

The droving trade survived the first few decades of the railway age, but in the last quarter of the 19th century the drovers, just like their fellow travellers, the packhorse traders, passed away into history. They left a legacy that can still be recognised in the upland landscape. Some of their higher tracks have been abandoned and vegetation will slowly colonise the rocky tracks with their stones worn smooth by the hoofs of the cattle. Other sections have been incorporated into the network of metalled roads, like the Muker to Askrigg road that links the dales of the Swale and the Ure or the roads crossing Carter Bar. Variable prospects were also faced by the numerous hostelries – most of them isolated and remote – that had sustained the drovers during their travels. If the old drove road survived within the road network then such places could survive as inns, particularly if the decline of droving was accompanied or followed by the arrival of tourists in carriages, charabancs or cars, all attracted by the bleak vistas of stone-walled pastures and moorland. The Tan Hill Inn, at the southern end of the Stainmore Pass in the Pennines, is probably the most celebrated of the drovers' inns. It is at

the convergence of several ancient roads, some of them still green and some metalled. It was also used by miners working the local coal seam and by shepherds. It is the venue for a very old sheep fair and lay upon a road running eastwards from Kirkby Stephen that was much used by packhorse traders (Fig. 8.7).

Like droving, packhorse trading was an activity with roots that were probably deeply buried in prehistory. The high profile of this form of transport in the region until little more than a century ago was testimony to the severe inadequacies of the land transport network. Packhorse roads were not a specially designated category of routeways. The ponies followed tracks that were generally impassable to wagons or wains, but which were shared with horsemen, local farmers and pedestrians. The attraction of this form of transport was its ability to move varied cargoes, even including ironwork, salt, coal and woollen goods, for

*Fig. 8.7. **The Pennines moorlands are threaded by a network of rough tracks, footpaths and roads** of varied age and origin, mainly used by shepherds, miners and traders. Tan Hill Inn (centre), one of the most isolated of English inns, lies on moorland between Stainmore Forest and upper Swaledale at a convergence of old roads and on the old droving route from Scotland down the Pennine ridge to southern markets. Numerous old coal workings are visible in the foreground. This area is now crossed by the Pennine Way.*

long distances across ground that was impassable to wheeled traffic. The northern market towns existed as hubs in the packhorse trading network and in each of them one would find contractors who would undertake to move goods at a given rate. When the system was flourishing on the eve of the railway age, this was around one shilling (5p) per ton per mile. Each pony – often a Scottish Galloway or a German 'Jaeger' – could carry about 220 pounds (100kg) in panniers slung on both of its sides. In this way, a fairly typical team of 20 packhorses, walking in line behind a lead horse with jingling bells swinging on its harness, could move a cargo of 2 tons (c. 2,000kg) over 20 miles in around 8–10 hours for a charge of about £2. The man who guided the lead horse was often known as a 'Jagger' after the German ponies and the contractors or operators were often people with other trades too, ranging from innkeepers and farmers to less obvious ones, like besom-making. Teams of packhorses were also operated by the 'badgers', dealers who began as traders in grain, but who became involved in passing from farm to farm to buy many forms of produce. Some country roads with the name 'Badger Gate' commemorate this practice, like the one from Skipton to Bolton Bridge which continues as Penny Pot Lane from Fewston to Harrogate. Packhorses were also employed to bring down and distribute coal from the thin seams in the fells, such as those of the Garsdale collieries near Dent, down tracks described by the locals in the latter part of the 18th century as being as rough as the stones in the bed of a beck.

The packhorse trade, with its long and varied history, had allowed manufacturing and commerce to take place in remote uplands and backwaters that were inaccessible to wheeled vehicles. It surrendered to road improvements and competition from canals and railways in the closing decades of the Victorian era. It left behind a legacy of routeways, some now metalled and negotiable, some enduring as green lanes, but others just hollows in the pasture and for the aficionado of rural landscape it also left a multitude of particularly attractive bridges. An example of a packhorse track of proven medieval antiquity is the celebrated Mastiles Lane, a green lane on Malham Moor which runs from the former grange of Fountains Abbey at Kilnsey in Wharfedale to Helwith Bridge and beyond. The remains of wayside crosses punctuate the route, while in Nidderdale the monks of Fountains seem sometimes to have erected crosses wherever a road or lane entered their estates. One sign-posted example, erected by the green of the lost hamlet of Whipley, survives in a conifer plantation.

The landscapes of the north are noted for the multitude of packhorse bridges. Many of these must have served shepherds, farmers and other members of the local community more than actual jaggers, but they all display a diagnostic feature: the adoption of parapets so low as not to rub against the panniers slung from pack ponies. Another feature of these bridges reflects the volatility of becks and rivers that were not constrained by reservoirs or drainage works (in 1771 floods swept away all the bridges over the Tyne except the one at Corbridge, which still stands). In order to avoid damage to piers by floodwater armed with tree trunks and other debris, the stone bridges were designed so as to avoid placing any pier on the stream bed and in the path of violent waters. Instead, the watercourses were spanned by single, graceful arches of stone, with the abutments being placed on either bank.

Occasionally, the ephemeral timber structures preceding the arched stone bridges are described in place-names, with Fellbeck in Nidderdale being a contraction of 'Felebriggabec', meaning 'the plank bridge over the beck'. Normally, a succession of timber bridges was obliged to perish before investment would be raised to fund an alternative. The fact that bridges were recognised as being crucial to the economic, social and religious lives of communities is evidenced by the frequency with which benefactors would leave donations for the upkeep or replacement of a local bridge. The use of medieval bridges was not always freely given. Some were toll bridges, while many of those that were not were so weak and narrow that they were barred to wheeled traffic and beside the bridge there would be a ford that was used by the horse and ox-drawn traffic. Most of these bridges were replacements for preceding wooden structures that had failed, with the early 19th-century example crossing the Nidd at Birstwith being called 'New Bridge' and standing on a packhorse route that had probably served the grange of Fountains Abbey at Brimham. Stone bridges became numerous in the period between about 1650 and 1800, some being built by private bequests and many by local or regional levies. In most cases they were more impressive than the actual routeways that they served. Sometimes these routes are sinking back into the fieldscapes or have degenerated into footpaths, and both the Nidderdale bridge at Birstwith and the one at Thornthwaite, a few kilometres up the dale, served pack horse roads that have decayed.

Corpse ways reflected both the difficult nature of movement and the thinness of the provision of churches in the rural north before the 19th century. Parishes in the Dales were vast, so that Grinton church served the whole of upper Swaledale. Bodies of people from places like Muker or Keld destined for burial at Grinton had to be carried to church by neighbours, with the corpse being placed in a wicker coffin. Such journeys in winter, when the snow was deep and the rivers in spate, testified to the strength of neighbourly sentiments in former times. Eventually, the problem was alleviated by the construction of chapels of ease, which were provided with burial rights. Muker gained such a chapel in 1850, but the chapel of ease at Hubberholme in Langstrothdale did not acquire a right of burial until long after a corpse was lost during an attempt to convey it across the flooded River Wharfe to the parish church over at Arncliffe. On another occasion a party of bearers bound for Arncliffe almost perished in snowdrifts. Any road or rocky track that led to a churchyard could serve as a corpse road, but some were especially associated with this grim function, like the Corpse Way running down Swaledale to Grinton.

Medieval societies that were capable of constructing impressive and durable stone bridges, like the one over the Till at Twizel or that spanning the Nidd at Killinghall or the fortified bridge crossing the River Coquet at Warkworth where the bridge tower still survives, were incapable of operating an effective system for building and maintaining roads. Royal power was generally too remote to have lasting effects, while the manor was too local and restricted a unit for the task. In 1555 a national system of statute labour was introduced and it brought some improvements in the (non) achievements of quasi-feudal authorities. Such earlier attempts are exemplified by the efforts of the Honour court of Knaresborough, which decreed in 1528 that all inhabitants should appear on two specified days of the year to make and mend local lanes and highways. A fine of 1s (5p) was levied for failure to provide a horse and cart and one of a quarter of this amount for every absentee man. The decree is unlikely to have been enforced with much effect. When the neglect of the road system finally ended it was caused in part by changes in administration and partly by technological advances.

THE GREAT NORTH ROAD

Three days of hard riding with overnight stops at Doncaster and Widdrington brought Sir John Carey from London to Edinburgh with Elizabeth I's ring. Such was the speed of hot news in 1603: it was not a normal journey time. An argument that had broken out in Durham in 1360 gives some insight into travel in the north in the medieval period. Summoned to answer a claim in a church court in York, Bishop Hatfield protested that he could not possibly be expected to reach York in a single day from the boundaries of his diocese at the River Tees, especially in winter. This led to an enquiry which heard much evidence. Thirty miles per day would be good going in winter; 36 or even 40 in summer, depending of course on the quality of both horse and rider. But, said others, a bishop's entourage in its full pomp could not be expected to make such haste as that. All were agreed that the place to cross the Tees was Newsham, close to Darlington. The normal route from Durham to York was via Darlington, Northallerton, Thirsk, Helperly and Tollerton. It was a two-day journey with an overnight stop at Northallerton or Darlington. Except that Crayke is not on this route, it is St Cuthbert's route of old, still in use.

There is no single definition of what constitutes the Great North Road through Yorkshire. The route, which became designated the A1, came north from Doncaster, through Ferrybridge, Wetherby, Boroughbridge and Catterick to Darlington: in the main, the Roman road. This bypasses York, keeping along the west side of the Vale of York. York, though, was a destination for coach traffic in the 17th and 18th centuries, which cut eastwards after Ferrybridge, through Tadcaster. North from York another route towards Darlington held close to the North York Moors through Thirsk and Northallerton, along the east edge of the Vale of York: the Durham churchmen's route. King Edward I, much-travelled, had used just about all variants of the route through Yorkshire, but both he and Edward II were most likely to use the eastern route through Northallerton.

A hundred years and more after Carey's ride, the long-distance coach traveller between London and Edinburgh could expect a journey of 13 days; London to York in four days; two days on to Newcastle where, on the seventh day, the traveller rested; then six days to Edinburgh. But travel conditions on the Great North Road were about to change.

TURNPIKES AND ENCLOSURE ROADS

A seemingly minor Act of 1663, which allowed the Justices of Peace in three counties straddling a section of the Great North Road lying well to the south of our region to levy tolls to finance improvements to the road, proved immensely influential. It metaphorically paved the way for the establishment of scores of turnpike trusts, which used the tolls collected at toll-houses beside the highway to recover their investment in road building. The resulting turnpike network gradually expanded, until a reasonably effective national road system had come back into being. When the last turnpike was dis-turnpiked in 1895 the country could at last boast a road system that was better than that of Roman Britain. Between the battle of Culloden in 1746 and the close of the main era of turnpike building after the first third of the 19th century, more than 800km of highway had been improved in Northumberland alone. The work mainly involved the widening, straightening and surfacing of established roads, with the provision of toll-houses at intervals and the barring of lanes that might be used to evade them. Bridges too could have their tolls. When Morpeth was provided in 1831 with a handsome new bridge built by Thomas Telford and John Dobson, people still used the medieval bridge to avoid the toll on the new one. The authorities put a stop to this by dynamiting the old bridge. But later, in 1869, they placed an iron footbridge across the ruins. In some places, however, new stretches of road were built to provide lower, less challenging or more appropriate itineries, like the new stretch built to link-up youthful centres of water-powered industry on the sides of the Nidd between Burnt Yates and Pateley Bridge.

On the Great North Road, turnpikes were introduced between Doncaster and Boroughbridge and also on the road from near Ferrybridge to Tadcaster in 1741. Following this, turnpiking proceded rapidly throughout the network of routes, with Boroughbridge–Northallerton–Darlington–Durham connected up in 1745. The York–Thirsk–Northallerton route followed in 1753. By 1747 turnpikes were available north through Northumberland as far as Belford and, after some delay, the roads extended into Scotland in 1753.

For a measure of the effects of turnpiking we can turn again to the long-suffering coach passengers whose lot was now much improved. In 1764, a coach left London for York daily at 10.00 pm. A night–day ride reached Grantham for an overnight stop and then onward on the second day to York. On Mondays and Thursdays the Edinburgh-bound traveller could then pick up a Newcastle coach from York. This was now a one-day journey via the Boroughbridge route. The weekly coach to Edinburgh left Newcastle on Monday morning with an overnight stop at Kelso, reaching Edinburgh at the end of the second day. So, with optimal connections, London to Edinburgh was an eight-day journey, of which five days and a night were spent on the road.

The turnpikes intensified the effects of the accompanying Industrial Revolution, for they increased the abilities of both buyers and sellers to get to markets and effectively lengthened the distances that they were prepared to travel. Towns, such as Sedbergh and Skipton, that were blessed with turnpikes experienced surges in commerce, while those that lacked them were likely to decline. In addition, the turnpikes marked a stage in the decline of packhorse trading, for the improvement in roads that made markets more accessible meant that fewer horses were needed by hauliers who were now employing wagons to move goods. Roads improvement was associated with a vigorous phase of bridge building and increased coach traffic led to the development of many famous roadside inns.

Proceeding at more or less the same time, though at generally more local levels, enclosure roads were built in great numbers between about 1750 and 1850. They were products of the redesigning of fieldscapes and the privatisation of common land associated with Parliamentary Enclosure. Generally around 30 to 40 feet in width (9.14 to 12.19m) and normally arrow-straight like the new hedgerows and field walls set out to either side, the roads could rationalise the links between a few little townships or hamlets within a parish. However, since Parliamentary Enclosure was enacted piecemeal, on a parish-by-parish basis, they generally terminated at, or before, the parish boundary.

This era was also a time of improvement in the technology of road building. The most remarkable of the innovators, John Metcalf (d 1810), came from Knaresborough. He was blinded by smallpox at the age of six in 1723, yet became a celebrated fiddler and forest guide. Before launching a haulage business between Knaresborough and York he encountered military roads being constructed in Scotland by General Wade's men as part of the pacification of the Highlands. Like the Romans, 'Blind Jack' appreciated that the key to successful road building involved the creation of well-drained foundations, and he drove a causeway across the mire between Knaresborough and Harrogate using countless bundles of heather in the footings. He also made the Pateley Bridge to Grassington road, using his staff both to test the footings and establish the levels, as well as building more than 240km of roads outside the Dales. In the early years of the 19th century, John Macadam's roads, surfaced in small stones that were bonded together, provided the next stage in improvement.

CANALS, RAILWAYS AND MODERN ROADS

By the time of Macadam, however, two new systems of transport were emerging to challenge and supplement the roads. The enthusiasm in England for canal building in the last three decades of the 18th century had slight influence on the North East, save in the south of Yorkshire with its endowment of rivers, the Humber, Aire, Calder, Ouse and Don, which were navigable or could be made so by building canals to bypass difficult stretches. Thus the West Riding became connected, via the Humber, to the North Sea, and canals, albeit with numerous locks and limited traffic, were built through the wide transverse valleys and low Pennine passes to connect Yorkshire and Lancashire.

The first railways, like the first canals, were mainly constructed to transport coal which, as early as the 17th century, was being conveyed in horse-drawn wagons along wooden rails, or wagonways, from the pitheads to navigable

OVERLEAF:
Fig. 8.8 Print after a painting by John Dobbin, showing crowds at the opening of the Stockton & Darlington Railway. The S&DR was built under the guidance of the company's chief engineer George Stephenson (1781–1848) to link collieries in West Durham and Darlington with the docks on the River Tees at Stockton in Durham. The line was opened on 27 September 1825 from the Witton Park Collieries near West Auckland. It was the world's first passenger railway. Published by T Wood & Sons, Darlington.

OPPOSITE PAGE:

Fig. 8.9

TOP: ***The exceptionally dense network of rails*** *on the south-east Northumberland coalfield was mainly constructed to transport coal to the Tyne and coastal ports of Blyth and Amble. There were, however, many extractive enterprises (small coal-pits, ironstone, limestone, lead, sand and gravel quarries, and timber) scattered in remote rural areas, which relied on temporary light railways and tramways. All the railways that opened up rural Northumberland have long been closed. Only the major east-coast and Tyne Valley links survive (based on Warn 1978).*

BOTTOM: ***In 1925 the railway system on the North York Moors was at its fullest extent****, serving major towns, the industrial areas to the north and the needs of many communities on the moors. The system has been much reduced since the 1960s and some lines converted to footpaths. However, the distinctive buildings and engineering works developed by early local railway companies have often survived (based on Spratt & Harrison 1989).*

stretches of the Tyne and Wear. Iron rails replaced wooden ones in the 18th century; by the early 19th century, wagons and passenger carriages were being pulled up inclines by chains and fixed steam haulage engines, and soon the draught horse was replaced by the steam locomotive. There was thus a direct evolution from wagonways to railways, both of which were designed mainly for the transport of mineral cargoes, and the choice of steam as the motive power required the adoption of the most level course that could be found (Fig. 8.8).

As well as cutting swathes through towns and cities and fundamentally altering streets and streetscapes, the railways and their attendant clutter of stations, crossings and embankments, introduced new linear elements to the countryside whose visibility was heightened by the telegraph wires running alongside the tracks. Throughout the region railways were linked with major achievements in civil engineering, the most spectacular being the arched viaducts that span the valleys of the north: these were necessitated, for example, where the Lancashire/Yorkshire railway crossed the upland tributaries of the Aire and Calder and also to cross the deep, narrow lowland ravines, or denes, of east Durham. However, it was the railway's indirect but complex and far-reaching influences that most changed the character of the surrounding landscape. For example, roads were sometimes adapted to focus on railway stations and, more important, the appearance of many places was transformed as non-local building materials became widely available and affordable for the first time. In the Yorkshire Dales the stone slabs or 'thack-stones' from local quarries were abandoned as roofing material and replaced by purple slates transported by rail from huge Welsh quarries, or green slates from Cumbria. In the towns, the products of huge brickworks, like those around Peterborough, often, though not always, evicted local materials such as magnesian limestone and Millstone Grit from the townscape. Railways also quickened the development of mass tourism, growth and rebuilding in a string of coastal centres from Alnmouth to Bridlington as well as upland settlements such as Rothbury and Alston (Fig. 8.9).

By the mid-19th century railways had made a deep impression on the landscape and though there was a multitude of unsuccessful schemes, branch railways, mineral and quarry lines continued to multiply. Expansion was finally checked in the early 20th century by the competition of motor car, lorry and bus. The retreat began in earnest in the 1960s with Dr Beeching's proposals for the closure of more than 2,000 stations. Had the north's tourism and recreation industries existed at today's level then branch lines in the Yorkshire Dales and some other picturesque rural settings might not have been lost. Parts of the abandoned rail systems have been reused in recent decades as footpaths, roads or plantations and, most recently, within a national network of cycle trails. Moreover, various lines have been taken over by enthusiasts and operate successful steam services, such as the Wharfedale line running from Embsay, across the North York Moors from Pickering, and the Worth Valley service from Skipton, the South Tynedale Railway from Alston and the Tanfield Railway in County Durham. Extensions or revivals may add to the track length devoted to sentimental journeying. Meanwhile the canals that influenced industrial development on the southern margins of the region have become venues for recreation. The Leeds Liverpool canal is particularly popular and the boating and canal traffic are greatly helping to raise Skipton's recreational profile.

The development of the modern motorway and trunk road service has created none of the mystique, awe and

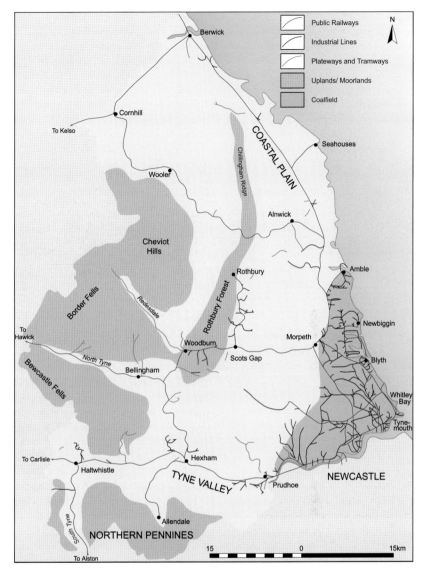

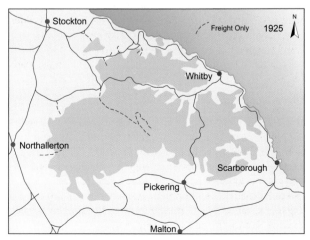

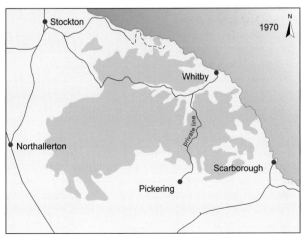

Fig. 8.10 Bridges.

BELOW: *Berwick-upon Tweed lies along an estuary crossed by three bridges. Old Bridge, in the foreground, is built of local red sandstone and dates from the early 17th century; beyond it is the Royal Tweed Bridge, a concrete structure of the 1920s and, in the distance, the Royal Border Bridge, brick and stone faced and built in 1847–50.* BOTTOM LEFT: *Kingsgate Bridge, Durham city, is an impressive narrow footbridge of granite aggregate built in the early 1960s, spanning the high banks of the River Wear and providing a new link between the cathedral/university precinct and the surrounding town.* BOTTOM RIGHT: *The Humber suspension bridge, built in the 1970s, crosses one of the largest river estuaries in England, transforms pre-existing spatial relationships on Humberside and is a significant modern addition to the surrounding, low-lying landscape.*

affection associated with the railway; though the Humber road bridge, which became the world's longest single-span suspension bridge when completed in 1981, is a structure of considerable grace and style (Fig. 8.10). Perhaps the most striking characteristic of the transport network in the north-east of England is the enduring influence of the anonymous Roman route-makers. The nature and location of industry have been transformed and the urban hierarchy is very different; only as the private and commercial use of cars and lorries increased hugely in the 20th century were roads built to avoid towns. Even so, the spine formed by the A1–A1(M), the radial pattern of routes converging on York and a good proportion of the routes that serve the uplands derive from the military roads initially provided to police and subjugate an outpost of empire that not every Roman thought worthy of the investment in military manpower. Throughout the region, however, the road systems consist of elements inherited from many different ages of road building. Often, much research is needed before dates can be attributed to the different components, while a residue of undated lanes and minor roads will almost invariably remain. Of these, a fair proportion is likely to pre-date the Roman occupation.

9

Mosaic of Landscapes

F H A AALEN and RICHARD MUIR

In order to illustrate the rich variety of the landscapes in the North East region, a number of areas are described here, each of which has a distinctive physical structure and an accumulation of human features which are adapted to it. The selected areas include a cluster of contiguous but contrasting landscape areas in Yorkshire (the North York Moors, the Yorkshire Wolds, the Vales of York and Pickering, Holderness and Wensleydale), the east Durham plateau, and the north-west of Northumberland with its scarplands arranged around the Cheviot massif. Understanding of landscape variation and identification of landscape character areas can have important practical implications, such as the adaptation of agri-environmental schemes to suit specific places, or encouraging the sensitive siting of new landscape features such as housing, woodland and water bodies, as well as generally helping local communities to understand their immediate environment and to nurture local landscape character (Fig. 9.1).

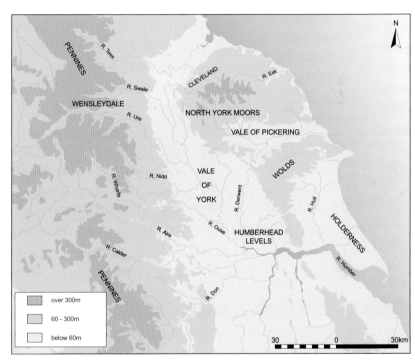

Fig. 9.1 Yorkshire landscape units, relief and drainage.

THE NORTH YORK MOORS

Like the Yorkshire Dales to the west, this region is divided between expanses of limestone and sandstone scenery. Virtually the entire area of upland and the adjacent coast, with the exception of Whitby and its immediate surroundings, forms part of a North York Moors National Park some 1,400sq km in area. In the south are the calcareous Tabular and Hambleton Hills of limestones, clays and grits, rising up from the Vales of Pickering and Mowbray. As one moves northwards towards the high sandstone plateaux the soils become more acidic and the heather, which is so much an emblem of the region, carpets the ground. In places the moorland rivers, such as the Esk, have cut through the sandstones to reach the shale beds. The uplands rise to a height of *c.* 460m on Urra Moor, while

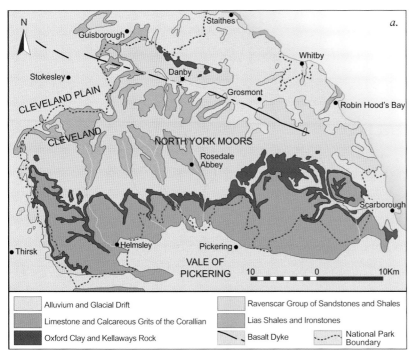

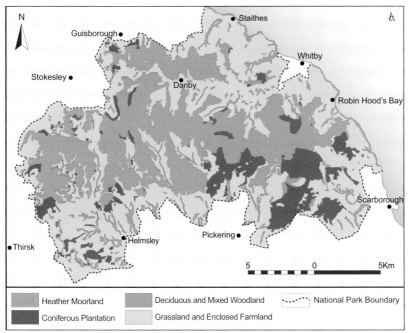

Fig. 9.2 North York Moors. a. This compact upland is formed by resistant Jurassic sandstones, which are bounded to the north by a massive scarp overlooking the Tees valley and dip gently southwards towards the Vale of Pickering. Southward-flowing streams have cut steep valleys and exposed strips of older rocks. On the east the uplands reach the sea in spectacular cliffs, while on the west there is an abrupt descent to the Vale of York. Glacial drift and alluvium cover the surrounding lowlands and coastal stretches. b. Vegetation cover and land use are related closely to geology: the moorlands and recent coniferous plantations correlate with sandy rocks; grassland and enclosed farmland with clays and limestone. Thin strips of deciduous woodland lie in narrow ravines cut by post-glacial streams (based on Spratt & Harrison 1996).

on the coast at Boulby Head the highest cliffs on the east coast of England tower to 200m above the beach. Tilted and truncated layers of fossil-packed Liassic rocks are seen on the coasts around Robin Hood's Bay (Fig. 9.2).

During the glaciations, streams of ice from many sources merged and swept around the margins of the uplands. In the glacial deposits that carpet the coast can be found pebbles from Scottish and Scandinavian mountains and fragments of Baltic amber. During the most recent glaciation the snow-clad moortops were free of ice, but as the surrounding ice sheet receded, torrents of water flowing under and at its margins carved meltwater channels, such as Scarth Nick, deep into solid rock, while the spectacular trench of Newtondale (Fig. 9.3) was cut by overflow from ice-dammed Lake Eskdale, feeding into ice-dammed Lake Pickering. Gormire lake, below Sutton Bank, was formed of waters trapped in a blocked spillway and survives to this day.

The landscape that most visitors probably regard as 'natural' is, to a very great extent, the creation of hundreds of generations of humans. The tousled heather, now managed as grouse moor and for hill sheep, conceals different landscapes of occupation, of which the most comprehensive is associated with the Bronze Age, when today's barren moors were well-populated farmlands, divided into fields and traversed by droves and trackways. Land was cleared for farming, with the litter of boulders and pebbles being deposited in cairns. Round barrows, some of the smaller examples looking much like the domed clearance cairns, were often placed to be seen silhouetted on the skyline, while some marked out the courses of territorial boundaries along the watersheds. As the upland populations swelled, hunting on the moortops declined in importance and massive linear earthworks were dug to emphasise the partitioning of the landscapes. As the period progressed, a landscape of woodland clearings had, by around 1500 BC, become a landscape of thinned and scattered woodland islands in an agricultural setting. Today, the heather both protects and conceals the exceptional Bronze Age legacy, with only the larger round barrows from the millennium before 1600 BC standing above the mauve carpet. Danby Beacon above the Esk valley and Lilla Howe on Fylingdales Moor are examples.

Impoverishment of soils by over-farming probably combined with climate changes to make intensive land use unsustainable in the upland, and the later stages of Bronze Age occupation were marked by further efforts to clear land of stones and mark and enforce territorial boundaries. Life in the Iron Age seems to have been less secure; some upland sites had become deserted and in other places fortifications appeared. After the Romans entered the region in AD 70, the moors were surrounded by a crescent of pacified lowlands. The occupiers built a few forts such as Cawthorn Camps and Lease Riggs, while the foundations of one of their minor roads, Wade's Causeway on Wheeldale Moor, survive as one of the best known examples of a Roman road in Britain. The declining stages of the Empire in north-eastern England were marked by the construction of five fortified signalling stations between Filey and Saltburn to warn of barbarian raiders.

Very gradually, the links with the Roman world and the British kingdoms to the north and west were replaced by contacts with the Germanic North Sea arena and domination by Anglo-Saxon monarchs. As the new identity developed a Christian dimension, the North York Moors acquired a religious identity. This is preserved in numerous stone crosses, the oldest being Lilla's Cross on Lilla Howe, which commemorates the minister who was killed protecting King Edwin against an assassin in 626. Many other crosses served as way-marks, while narrow causeways known as monks' trods traversed the moors after the establishment of some 25 monastic houses in the North York Moors, including the enormous Cistercian institution at Rievaulx, founded in 1131. After the traumatic depopulation of many places in the Conqueror's Harrying of the North, the semi-wilderness of the North York Moors appealed to the continental orders seeking isolated bases in the Norman kingdom. Mount Grace Priory, a Carthusian foundation of 1398, was the last monastic house to be established. A remarkable endowment of religious houses exists, including the Benedictine foundation of 1074 at Whitby thought to have been founded among the ruins of the 7th-century monastery of St Hilda. St Gregory's minster at Kirkdale, on the southern flanks of the moors, displays the best surviving Saxon sundial, though it stands, incongruously, in the shadows of a later porch. Hog-back tombstones, which represent houses for the dead and signify the conversion of those of Scandinavian culture, are seen at Lastingham and Osmotherley.

Fig. 9.3 The deep narrow gorge of Newtondale is the most spectacular of numerous glacial meltwater channels, now dry or occupied only by modest streams, which cross the Tabular Hills between the upland moors and the Vale of Pickering. In recent decades, much of the semi-natural woodland in the dale has been replaced by coniferous plantations.

Industry played an important role in determining the post-medieval character of the North York Moors. Jet from the shales of the cliffs near Whitby was worked and exported in Roman times; ironworking has an even longer pedigree, while alum shale has been mined as a colour-fixing agent since the end of the medieval period. Ironworking petered out in the region in the mid-17th century, though the development of coke-fired furnaces allowed iron to be collected or mined on the shores and exported to furnaces by the River Wear. Then, in the mid-19th century, a multitude of iron mines, mainly on the northern fringe of the moors, were opened to serve the blast furnaces at Teeside. The remains of ore-drying kilns, abandoned workings and trackways joined the relics of monasticism and Bronze Age farming on the moors.

THE YORKSHIRE WOLDS

The name of this region of rolling chalk hills signifies woodland, although this is seldom apparent in the open agricultural countrysides. Inland, the landscapes are un-dramatic and sometimes scoured of all detail by prairie-style farming. The coastline, however, north of Flamborough Head is outstanding (Fig. 9.4). White, wave-cut arches form bridges to the sea and scores of caves pock-mark the bases of chalk cliffs seamed with flint and capped with glacial drift. Seabird colonies abound, with different species occupying different levels, the puffins burrowing at the top of the cliff, while at Bempton the chalk face below is home to the only gannet colony on the British mainland. The Wolds form part of a great crescentic band of chalk which runs from Wessex through the southern Midlands and East Anglia before disappearing beneath the North Sea and then emerging to form the Lincolnshire and Yorkshire Wolds. In Yorkshire, the chalk forms a crescent which begins just to the west of Hull, runs to the southern outskirts of Malton and then curves eastwards to meet the sea between Bridlington and Filey, presenting a marked escarpment to the north and north-west. The dry periglacial valleys (formed in a frost-dominated climate) known as 'slacks' or 'dales' are a distinctive feature of the rolling chalk landscape, as are the crater-like marl pits at places where the limey rock and subsoil

were dug for use in sweetening the land. The Gypsey Race in the Great Wold Valley is the only permanently-flowing stream in the interior of the region (Figs 9.5 and 9.6).

The light, well-drained, calcareous soils of the area appealed to prehistoric farmers and, as in the North York Moors to the north, Bronze Age population growth resulted in competition for territory with the establishment of defended enclosures and the marking of boundaries with chains of pits and massive linear earthworks.[2] Already, the region of the Wolds had acquired its most spectacular prehistoric relic, the Rudston monolith. This, Britain's tallest standing stone, is a pillar of gritstone that was hauled across country for 16km from Cayton Bay and erected as a component in a ritual landscape of three cursuses (linear prehistoric monuments so called because they resemble race tracks). The complex may have superseded an earlier religious focus centred on the great Neolithic tomb, Duggleby Howe. Many centuries after the monolith was erected, the founders of a Christian church attempted to appropriate its sanctity by building their church beside

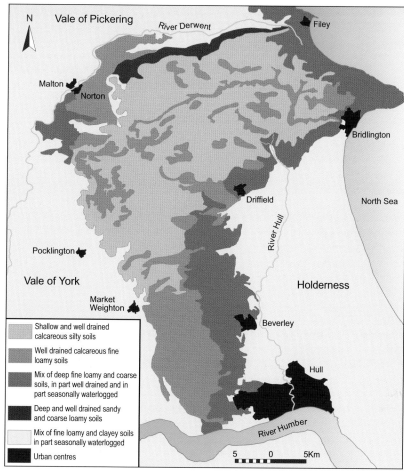

Legend:
- Shallow and well drained calcareous silty soils
- Well drained calcareous fine loamy soils
- Mix of deep fine loamy and coarse soils, in part well drained and in part seasonally waterlogged
- Deep and well drained sandy and coarse loamy soils
- Mix of fine loamy and clayey soils in part seasonally waterlogged
- Urban centres

it. The late Bronze Age decline that affected the Moors was not experienced in the richer country of the Wolds, and the marking of boundaries continued into the Iron Age. As the period continued, rich chariot burials under square barrows signified the cultural distinctiveness of this, the territory of the Parisi. In the Roman era, however, an over-working of land, perhaps to supply grain for the garrisons at Malton and York, seems to have caused widespread soil erosion.

The medieval population of the Wolds was devastated by the Black Death, which struck in 1349. Landowners took advantage of the weakened communities by extending their sheepwalks across village lands. Rabbits soon joined the sheep in what had become a largely treeless expanse of closely-grazed downland. The substitution of a pastoral for an arable economy and the enforced depopulation of villages have left strong marks on landscapes where the gaps are often more numerous than the surviving settlements. Following painstaking excavations spanning four decades, the deserted village of Wharram Percy, sprawling down to its ruined church on the flanks of a slack, is by far the best-known example of its kind.

The next stage in the evolution of the landscape was enacted in the 18th and 19th centuries by the great estate-owners who established parks, shifting roads and occasionally villages that intruded on their plans, and then set out to convert the grasslands back to lucrative husbandry and woodland.[3] At Sledmere a somewhat slanted inscription of 1840 to Sir Christopher Sykes describes how he transformed the landscape in the space of 30 years, turning : '… a bleak and barren tract of country to become now one of the most productive and best cultivated districts in the county of York'. By this time, around 100,000 ha in the Wolds had been enclosed, the high pastures had almost vanished and the hedgerows deriving from numerous Parliamentary Enclosures criss-crossed the landscape. Improved rotations were introduced, growing turnips for sheep fodder, and these survived into the latter part of the 20th century. Now, countless kilometres of the hedgerows have gone as has much of the topsoil – victims of over-confident farming. Today's landscape varies according to ownership. Some expanses express the sterility of unbridled agribusiness, while in estate landscapes woods or neat beech plantations managed as pheasant cover diversify the stream-less, rolling scene (Fig. 9.7).

Fig. 9.7 Sledmere. The comprehensive transformation of the countryside and its strong linkage with wealth derived from outside of agriculture is well illustrated at Sledmere in the centre of the Wolds. Here, the formation of a great house in ornamental parkland and large-scale improvement of the surrounding wolds were undertaken in the final quarter of the 18th century by the Sykes family, wealthy merchants operating in the Baltic trade out of Hull. Roads were re-routed, a village moved to enable emparkment, and large new farmsteads built away from the village as the extensive open sheepwalks on the surrounding downs were enclosed into large rectangular fields bounded by low hawthorn hedges.

THE VALES OF YORK AND PICKERING

The landscapes in these lowlands of north-eastern England are more easterly than northerly in character. They echo the vales of the East Midlands and East Anglia rather than the harsher landscapes to the north and west. Being neither devoid of charm nor particularly beautiful, the Vale of York (*see* Figs 2.14 and 5.29) may perhaps be best-known nationally as a place that regularly features in the weather forecasts: '… and fog will linger in the Vale of York'. The Vale is fringed by higher ground where hard-rock geology plays a large part in determining the character of scenery. On the low ground, however, weak rocks are partly covered by glacial and riverine deposits.[4] Prehistoric occupation is also less apparent, with many sites being obscured by deep accumulations of recent river sediments. The Vale of Pickering, lying between the North York Moors and the Yorkshire Wolds and containing the River Derwent and its tributaries – the Seven, Dove, Riccal and Rye – probably contained a great lake, dammed by ice at either end, during the last glaciation. Upon ice retreat there may have survived a complex pattern of minor water bodies. At Star Carr, in the region of sodden peatlands and former alder swamps known as The Carrs, this vale certainly did contain one of Europe's most noted excavated Mesolithic sites, though the exact nature and the seasonal aspect of the usage of this camp of hunters, fishers and gatherers are much debated (Fig. 9.8).

Between the vales of Pickering and York are the Howardian Hills, whose name was only coined as recently as 1788. They are formed where the limestone rises above the plains to form a narrow ridge and their presence is marked in the cultural landscape by the appearance of buff stone cottages with pantile roofs whose walls contrast with the russet brick of the vale below. Unlike other eastern regions of England, the Vales are rather lacking in medieval dwellings in the timber-framing traditions. This relative deficiency in older buildings partly reflects the late persistence over much of the region of woodland and waterlogged alder carr, wet commons and lowland heaths. As in other parts of Yorkshire, however, the hunting potential was great and the devastation caused by the Harrying of the North must have increased the potential for forest creation. Wooded land to the north of York became the royal Forest of Galtres, while Pickering, at the junction of the Vale and the southern flanks of the North York Moors, was a castle centre administering the royal Forest of Pickering.

The Vale of York has been a military corridor and a place of battlefields since AD 71, when Roman troops engaged in the invasion of the north established a marching camp at the junction of the rivers Ouse and Foss at what is now York. In 1066, after the defeat of the northern earls at Fulford near York, by the Norse host, the English king Harold marched his army north to win a victory at Stamford Bridge on the Derwent just to the north-east of the city. This English victory was followed by the disaster of Hastings, while successive insurrections against Norman rule in York triggered the Harrying of the North. This programme of

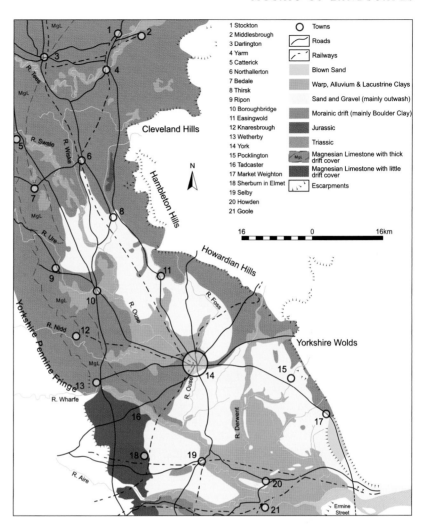

Fig. 9.8 Vale of York. The generally low-lying, level landscape of the Vale contains a variety of soils formed from glacial outwash sands, lacustrine clays and alluvium deposits including riverside warp. Especially in its southern areas, which are crossed by sluggish rivers in wide shallow valleys, efficient land drainage is needed to counter seasonal waterlogging. Arable crops are dominant and the flat farmland of medium- to large-sized fields bounded by low, gappy hedges is dotted with numerous villages and isolated brick farmsteads (based on de Boer 1964).

calculated devastation probably provided the circumstances for the establishment of scores of planned villages as the north repopulated. Most of the villages in the Vales display signs of medieval planning in their disciplined layouts of street-facing dwellings, elongated house plots terminating at back lanes, and triangular or long, rectangular greens. In some cases, such as Middleton near Pickering, pre-existing churches seem to have provided the nuclei for planned Norman settlements. Middleton also stands among a system of long field strips, which radiate from the village across a great swathe of land. The settlement pattern of the Vales is not as dense as in other counties of the eastern lowlands, with gaps in the village pattern reflecting both the persistence of poorly-drained, 'moorish' country and the desertion of settlements. The Carrs forms a large void in the map of villages and most nucleated settlement is found around the margins of the Vale of Pickering, on drier sites at the foot of the Wolds and Tabular Hills.

The attraction of the Vales to great religious houses was less than that of the uplands, with Rievaulx Abbey exploiting a perch in the lee of the Hambleton Hills and Byland Abbey standing at the foot of these hills and the junction of the two Vales. Having depopulated a village to clear a site for their new abbey, the founders of Byland caused confusion as their bells conflicted with those of Rievaulx, just 3km away, so in 1147 they moved to their final destination, clearing woodland and digging great ditches to drain the site. Fountains and Jervaulx, other great Cistercian houses, exploited sites on the western marches of the Vale; Kirkham Priory was on the western margins of the Wolds and, York foundations such as the Benedictine abbey of St Mary apart, only minor foundations such as Allerton Mauleverer or Healaugh actually stood in the lowlands.

Where the earthworks have survived levelling by modern ploughing, the ridges in the Vale are seen to be more strongly developed from longer usage than those of the flanking uplands. There the faint traces of plough ridges often reflect only a brief episode of arable cultivation in the face of the pressures of population in the decades preceding the Black Death. The characteristic countrysides of the Vales today are geometrically partitioned by hawthorn hedges dating from the Parliamentary Enclosure, which divide the common ploughlands and meadows, as well as the extensive moorish wastes with their marsh and heaths. Standard oak trees planted at intervals among the thorns give a vertical dimension to the landscapes, though modern farming has greatly reduced the hedgerows and few are well tended. In nooks and corners that have escaped the steam engine- and tractor-drawn ploughs, earthworks from earlier eras, such as medieval moats, fishponds and former settlements, can be detected. The characteristic rural dwellings are of locally produced brick and pantile and mainly date from the 18th and 19th centuries, their predecessors in timber, wattle, daub and thatch having largely perished. It is to the city of York and bordering towns such as Knaresborough that one must go to see successions of ancient buildings. Today, the Vale of York exists as a reasonably prosperous area of mixed farming, with cereals, root crops, maize and cattle pastures all featuring in the scene. Perhaps the most characteristic crop is the sugar beet, destined for the huge sugar works at York, whose chimney, belching steam in autumn and winter, rivals the towers of the minster as a landmark while bestowing a distinctive cabbage-like aroma on downwind sections of the city.

HOLDERNESS

Holderness is a triangular lowland, which has its base defined by the Humber and its apex pointing towards the chalk cliffs of Flamborough Head. Though it is certainly not devoid of attractions – Beverley Minster and the medieval seaport of Kingston upon Hull figuring high on the list – in most minds Holderness is associated with catastrophic inundations. It has waters to the east and to the south, and on both sides significant settlements and areas of farmland have been lost to the sea. The River Hull drains southwards down the centre of the region across a plain that is patterned with moraine ridges formed at the western margins of the oscillating North Sea ice sheet, and covered in glacial tills and meltwater gravels with lakes and, later, peat, filling the hollows after the ice withdrew. Subsequently, the low mounds of higher ground formed by the moraines were exploited as the sites for villages, while the exotic boulders or 'erratics' dumped by the waning ice were used as building materials in this stone-deprived region (Fig. 9.9).

During the medieval period, the frequently sodden character of the land deterred development, and effective land drainage schemes were not introduced until the second half of the 17th century. The land remained heavy, but Holderness did then become a significant region for the production of wheat and legumes (Fig. 9.10). However, the land area has been contracting since prehistoric times and no region in the United Kingdom is so strongly associated with coastal erosion. Some 200sq km of territory have been lost from the eastern shores of Holderness since Roman times, while since the Norman Conquest more than 20 villages and hamlets have been undermined and overrun by the sea. The buttery glacial clays are easily eroded by North Sea storms and the coast is retreating at a rate of around 1.85m per year. During a phase of accelerated erosion in the early 1950s, the coast to the south of Bridlington retreated some 20.3m in just five years. Coastal erosion has also affected the southern shores of Holderness. Ravenser, on Spurn Head, was the probable port of departure for survivors of Hardrada's defeated Norse army;

nearby, in 1241, the Count of Aumale built the town of Odd, which became known as Ravenserodd, on an island of sand and stones that was linked to the mainland by a narrow, sandy track. The town flourished as a port with three markets and a fair lasting 30 days and it supported many traders in herrings. But a sea storm in 1256 signalled the end for the two raven towns and Ravenserodd's causeway was breached. By the middle of the next century, the sea was sweeping away buildings and carrying bodies from the graveyard, those that remained being exhumed and reburied at Easington. The towns lay somewhere to the west of the great spit, which has shifted its position since medieval times. A beneficiary of these disasters was the competing port of Kingston upon Hull, which appeared in the second half of the 12th century as Wyke, a planned foundation of the monks of Meaux Abbey. A modest exporter of Holderness wool, Wyke encountered a new patron in 1293 in the shape of Edward I who improved the quay and the roads from Beverley and York that served it, extended the market and established a mint. During the 14th century it became a town walled in brick – a material virtually unused since the departure of the Romans – and one of England's foremost seaports.

Fig. 9.9 East Yorkshire lost villages.
The low-lying, subdued terrain of Holderness is mainly formed by glacial deposits and, especially along the Hull valley, younger deposits of river alluvium and peat accumulation. Since medieval times poorly drained locations have been improved by enlarging and diverting watercourses and cutting new channels, and the area made congenial to arable and livestock farming. A striking feature is the rapidly eroding clay coast and the inundation of farmland and over two dozen settlements during and since the medieval period. North Sea encroachment, however, has been offset by reclamation of valuable land along the Humber shore (based on Harris 1961 and Muir 2000).

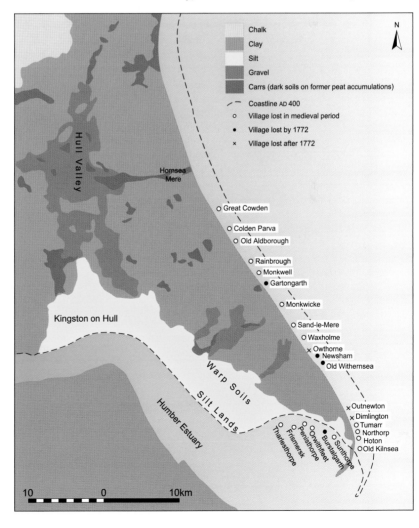

The great Cistercian abbey of Meaux, which had estates beside the Humber, was also afflicted. Low pastures on estuarine silt, traversed by winding creeks, were grazed by great flocks of the abbey's sheep in the area surrounding the villages of Sunthorp and Orwithfleet. During the 1320s, however, seas driven by the gales of a rapidly deteriorating climate washed across the pastures and destroyed the two villages. The land known as 'Sunk Island' that bulges into the estuary today was inundated during the Tudor era and three villages vanished. Struck firstly by the floods of the 1320s and shortly afterwards by the arrival of the Black Death, the monks of Meaux spent the remaining years of the abbey's existence battling to repair and maintain their sea walls and floodbanks, losing their grange at Tharlesthorp at the beginning of the 15th century.

Holderness still takes its identity from the continuing retreat of its vulnerable cliffs of glacial clay. Given a climate that appears to be shifting in the direction of warmer, moister and more cyclonic conditions, rising sea-level and the fashion for laissez-faire environmental protection policies, the future for the region seems mirrored by its past. There is, however, much more to the region than a retreating shoreline. The spectacular minster at Beverley has been noted, but there are also the beautiful churches at Patrington, Lockington and Ottringham as well as Hull's fine churches, such as Holy Trinity and St Mary.

Fig. 9.10 Farmland in Holderness.
Conversion of the medieval open fields of Holderness into the present pastoral landscape of hedged fields was spread over several centuries and produced considerable contrasts in local field patterns. Early enclosure by agreement, largely completed by the end of the 17th century, produced large fields of varied shapes around the old villages, in contrast to the rectilinear fields and dispersed farms formed later by Parliamentary Enclosures. Along the Humber there is a distinctive, productive belt of flat, fen-like country, reclaimed in recent centuries from former salt marsh by drainage and 'warping', with large fields divided by wide drainage ditches rather than hedges.

WENSLEYDALE

With an association with a mild, white cheese that has made its name known worldwide, Wensleydale also offers much of historical interest. In the realms of rural settlement and fortification it would be difficult, if not impossible, to think of another area of such diverse and concentrated interest. Within the Yorkshire Dales in the centuries around the Norman Conquest, the speakers of several different languages – Old Welsh, Old English, Old Danish and Old Norse – met, mingled and married, with a simplified version of English perhaps resulting as a lingua franca from these cultural interactions. The region of the Yorkshire Dales is particularly rich in names of Scandinavian derivation and 'dale' comes from a Danish word signifying a valley. Of the major valleys of the region, the Swale, Ure, Nidd, Wharfe and Aire, that of the Ure is the broadest and most spacious; though it is flanked by high ground, as Penhill (550m) and Dodd Fell (675m), it does not seem as confined as the other Dales. It is the only one that does not take its name from its river, the now declined market centre of Wensley giving its name to replace 'Yoredale', the valley of the Ure (Fig. 9.11).

Like the rest of the Dales, Wensleydale's geology is essentially Carboniferous. Limestones, deposited on the bed of a warm sea, impart distinctive qualities to its

scenery. Although precipitation in the
Dales is quite high, little lingers on the
surface in puddles, ponds, becks or
gills. Instead, the trickles soon find
paths through the networks of fissures
in the limestones to subterranean
watercourses that have carved tunnels
and huge caverns in the rock.
Consequently, the surface of the land
is surprisingly dry and generally
carpeted in bright green springy turf.
More still needs to be learned about
the natural environments of the Dales,
but it seems that were it not for human
interference the limestone areas would
be clothed in ash-dominated
woodland. On some of the flanking
upland benches are areas of limestone
pavement, the bare rock patterns of
'clints' and 'grikes' partly created by

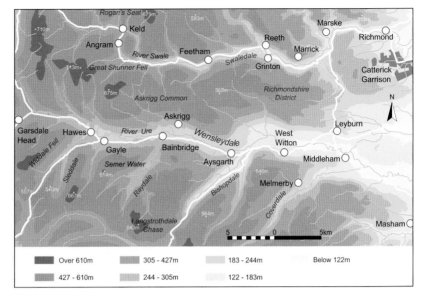

the stripping-away of overlying weaker rocks by glaciers, and partly by over-
grazing, which has encouraged the flushing away of loose soil through the
fissures. No less prominent in the countrysides of Wensleydale are the staircase
forms on the sides of the dales, while differences in their chemistry produce
subtle but rapidly alternating variations in the hillside vegetation. Glacial erosion
varied enormously in its intensity according to position and terrain; in the
tributary valley of Bishopdale, glaciers diverted by the mass of Buckden Fell
scoured deeply into the valley floor, though elsewhere their effect could be much
more modest.

Fig. 9.11 Wensleydale is the widest and most varied of the Pennine dales, with a series of narrow north-east/south-west trending dales on its south side. The scenery is dominated by the stepped flanks of the Yoredales, with limestone scars, narrow, horizontal tree belts and terraces of quality pasture running along the dale sides. Settlement features include well developed lynchets, a scatter of small villages and numerous field barns in the walled fields.

   Whether with its indigenous woodland or its fieldscapes, Wensleydale has
always been a beautiful area, though never an affluent one; it did develop small
water-powered textile and hand-knitting industries, but lacked the resources of
lead that brought measures of prosperity to the adjacent dales of Swaledale and
Nidderdale. There are a few small prehistoric tombs and monuments, but thinly-
spread pastoral populations could not sustain great ritual monuments. These
were built in a spectacular ritual landscape that developed where the Ure met the
richer territories of the Vale of York, in the form of the three remarkable
Thornborough henges, the nearby Hutton Moor henge trio, so sadly damaged by
agriculture, the Devil's Arrows monoliths at Boroughbridge and the swarms of
round barrows that congregated around the Neolithic temples. All seem
associated with the River Ure, causing one to wonder if the river itself was the
subject of veneration. The dale itself was rather a backwater in prehistoric times
and was peripheral to Roman concerns, with a fort being built upon a drumlin
on the margins of the valley at Bainbridge, to guard routeways and police the
surrounding tribal lands of the Brigantian federation.

   The rather desolate condition of the valley was recognised and exploited by the
designation by Henry II of a great royal hunting reserve, the Forest of Wensleydale,
covering the whole dale above the junction of the River Bain. There were 11
vaccaries (farms specialising in cattle breeding) in the forest around Bainbridge.
This village is quite unusual in that its origins are clearly known. In 1227 it was
recorded that the village had been created to provide a house and 3.6ha of land for
each of 12 foresters employed in the surrounding hunting territory. Another village
with a certain past is East Witton, lower down the dale. After a Cistercian
monastery was established at Jervaulx in 1156 (the name is a corruption of
Yoredale), the abbey acquired extensive estates in the dale. The Cistercians sought
solitary, rigorous existences and lay settlements were unwelcome. Around 1300 a

211

village was removed from the vicinity of the abbey and its community was re-established as a planned settlement organised around an elongated green and provided, in 1307, with charters for a Monday market and a cattle fair. This village, East Witton, still preserves the many property divisions of its medieval plan, though the houses were all rebuilt by the Earl of Aylesbury in 1809 to commemorate the jubilee of George III.

Just across the Ure is Wensley, once sufficiently important to lend its name to the dale, but now a shrunken village that never recovered from an onslaught by the plague that left it with a large church it could no longer fill. Churches in the dales were few during the medieval period, when the one at Grinton served much of Swaledale and Aysgarth church served the whole of upper Wensleydale. Markets, however, were too numerous and fierce

Fig. 9.12 Near Askrigg in Wensleydale. *Lynchets (man-made cultivation terraces) associated with medieval arable cultivation underlie today's enclosed pastoral landscape. The irregular pattern of walled fields and high density of field barns, often located in the corner of fields or serving two fields, indicate that the process of conversion was gradual and by local agreement.*

competition undermined the trade of most. Middleham was no ordinary village, for its castle was a base of the Nevilles. Its landscape is interesting but challenging; the land between the castle and the River Cover was once one of several deer parks that clustered around the family seat. Now racehorses train on the springy turf. The village itself has encroached upon what must formerly have been an enormous rectangular green or market square, such areas being associated with butchers' stalls and the cattle trade. Middleham seems to have been set-out on a rectilinear grid and this appears to extend into the adjacent fields, suggesting that the settlement failed to expand according to expectations (Fig. 9.12).

An interesting sequence of medieval castle building can be explored at Middleham. The original power centre of the Normans, Ribald, was a ringwork, overlooking the valley on a spring site whose water was used to power a tiny mill set in the moat. Subsequently, thoughts of comfort triumphed over security and there was a move downslope with the building of a commodious hall keep, which gained a curtain wall in the 13th century. On the other side of the valley, Castle Bolton overlooks another planned castle village. It is of a later design, a quadrangular palace castle, with walls and corner towers surrounding a rectangular courtyard. When Sir Richard Scrope obtained a licence to build his castle in 1378, the notion of the impregnable dynastic castle was falling from fashion and the building, with its many chambers and large windows, was more a comfortable venue for entertaining numerous guests than a stronghold. Even so, in 1645, when hopelessly obsolete, it was defended for a while against a Parliamentarian force. Far less imposing, though no less interesting, is the defended house tower known as Nappa Hall. Towers were quite common in areas exposed to border warfare involving English and Scots raiding parties, but they were concentrated in the zone to the north. Nappa Hall is also unusual in having two towers rather than one. It was built during the 1450s by the Agincourt veteran Thomas Metcalfe, whose descendents served as stewards for the abbots of Jervaulx and wardens of the Forest of Wensleydale.

Under the custodianship of the Yorkshire Dales National Park, Wensleydale has preserved much of its traditional character and beauty, though many problems, such as whether to allow distinctive but redundant field barns to decay or to be converted into holiday homes, remain. Comparison with parts of the Dales, such as Nidderdale, that were excluded from the Park when its bounds were far too tightly drawn, will testify to the conservational value of the authority. Being less accessible to the Tyne-, Tees- and Wearside towns than Swaledale and further from Leeds and Bradford than Nidderdale and Wharfdale, pressures for commuter housing are reduced. Tourism presents a threat to the traditional culture, as well as offering hopes of salvation to family farms rendered insolvent by European economic changes. These, globalisation and the foot-and-mouth epidemic that was so rampant in this region at the start of the millennium, have combined in a lethal conspiracy against hill farms and small farms of the Dales. As yet, the annual sheep fair at Masham is still more a farming occasion than a tourist event. However, the farming economy of the Dales, like that of the North York Moors, is fragile and, in the minds of some economists, anachronistic. If countrysides even remotely like those of today are to survive then policies and planning must look beyond financial balance sheets and take account of the social, conservational and ecological aspects of the case.

EAST DURHAM PLATEAU

In east Durham the outcropping magnesian limestone conceals the underlying Coal Measures and forms a low, undulating coastal plateau with an average height of 90–120m. The plateau is a distinct physical unit, roughly triangular in shape and bounded on the east by the sea and on the west by a near-continuous escarpment, some 180m high at Quarrington and Coxhoe, which stretches south-westwards from South Shields almost to Bishop Auckland. From the escarpment, the plateau surface dips eastwards to the sea and in the south slopes gradually towards the Tees lowlands (Fig. 9.13).

Save for exposures along the western scarp and in the coastal cliffs, the limestone is almost entirely obscured by a mantle of glacial drift. This superficial deposit has buried earlier river valleys and given the plateau its undulating surface and sometimes difficult drainage. Moreover, the constitution of the drift is a major determinant of soil character; till deposits are usually heavy clays, and glacial sands and gravels have lighter brown soils. Pollen records from the area indicate extensive forest clearance during the Bronze Age and the simultaneous appearance of cereal pollen and clearance weeds as agriculture began to make an impact. Long traditions of mixed farming, artificial drainage, fertilising and liming of the drift soils have nurtured and sustained the generally good to medium quality of the land.

The most dramatic natural features in this generally subdued plateau

Fig. 9.13 The East Durham Plateau contains a range of contrasting settlement types: agricultural villages, colliery settlements, coastal ports, a conurbation and the New Towns of Peterlee and Newton Aycliffe. The north of the region is dominated by urban and industrial development centred on Sunderland, while the south retains some attractive rural stretches with old agricultural villages together with more recent mining settlements, which are larger and more numerous towards the coast and on the approaches to the Durham coalfield in the south-west.

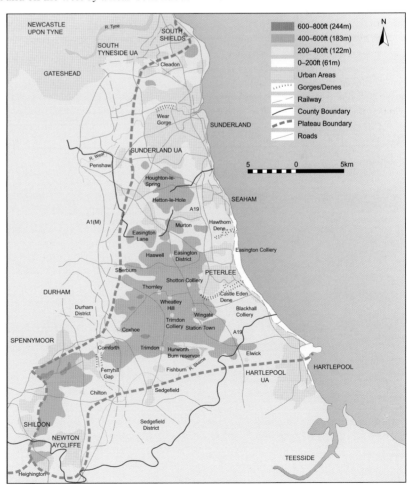

landscape are the coastal cliffs and the gorges cut through the limestone, by the River Wear as it approaches Sunderland or by glacial meltwaters at Ferryhill (the main east-coast railway line makes use of this) and Tunstall Hope. Along with these are the deep, secluded, post-glacial ravines, or denes, along the coast, which are incised through the drift and into the underlying solid rock. The larger denes, especially Castle Eden Dene (a National Nature Reserve) and Hawthorn Dene, provide some shelter from the cold winds of spring and harbour attractive woodland stretches of native and imported trees (Fig. 9.14).

Broad landscape differences can be recognised.[5] On the higher areas of the escarpment scattered outcrops of limestone support remnants of an unique grassland flora, and the scarp has been dissected in places by streams into small, attractive embayments where woodland and scrub survive on the steeper slopes and limestone exposures. Large quarries, active and abandoned, are also numerous. The northern end of the escarpment is fragmented into isolated knolls, such as Penshaw (around which the legendary Lambton worm coiled in post-prandial sleep) and Carr Hill. To the east of the escarpment, where drift blankets the limestone plateau, heavy and seasonally-waterlogged clay soils support a mixture of pasture and arable land. On the lower, coastal stretches of the plateau, the terrain, although incised by the deep narrow denes, is generally open and gently rolling with wide sea vistas. Arable farming predominates, settlement is dense and includes new towns of 19th- and 20th-century origin.

Fig. 9.14 Durham's coastland is deeply incised by numerous narrow, steep-sided and wooded denes of which the most spectacular is Castle Eden Dene (foreground) spanned by a graceful brick viaduct used by the coastal railway. The spacious, planned New Town of Peterlee, with its dense new housing, industrial estates, open spaces and allotments, lies to the north of the dene and was developed as a modern alternative to the old declining pattern of small, scattered mining settlements. Hawthorne Dene crosses the landscape to the north of Peterlee, with Easington lying beyond it.

The landscape of the plateau epitomises a major theme of landscape history in the industrial north, namely the abrupt, large-scale imposition of 19th-century coal-mining settlement on an older, tenacious agrarian order, with the two elements, even where contiguous, often remaining distinct. Dominated by Sunderland, Seaham Harbour and numerous old mining settlements, the northern part of the plateau now has a strongly urban character. Hutton-le-Hole, Houghton-le-Spring, New Hayton and Murton together form an almost-continuous urban belt running south-east from Washington towards Easington. However, despite widespread mining, most of the land in the centre and south of the plateau is still farmed. Planned medieval villages are still conspicuous in the texture of the rural settlement – Easington, around its rectangular green, Elwick, Hart, Bishop Middleham, Hutton Henry to name a few – along with a secondary pattern of dispersed farmsteads and roughly rectangular fields, which developed as the old open fields were consolidated and enclosed by agreement among freeholders between 1550 and 1700. The village commons, enclosed in the main at a later date and in a more systematic way with straight field boundaries, form distinctive localities often associated with the place-name 'moor' and most numerous on the clayey soils of the central plateau. Whitton Moor, Mordon Moor, South Moor and Butterwick Moor are all within a few kilometres of Sedgefield. Throughout east Durham, the fields are bounded mainly by fences and hawthorn hedges, which are generally low and gappy with only a few hedgerow trees, mainly ash, oak and sycamore. Thus, though enclosure is near-ubiquitous, the countryside appears open, with wide if uneventful vistas. Woodland cover is slight and the significant stretches are confined to valleys and the deep denes and hence have limited scenic impact. In many places the field patterns have been modified by industrial development and settlement growths in the 19th and 20th centuries and, especially in recent decades, by agricultural mechanisation and intensification and the enlargement of fields.

Until the 19th century, coal mining had only a limited and indirect influence on the plateau landscape. Indeed, before it was recognised that coal lay concealed beneath the limestone, the plateau was seen as an obstacle, between the exposed coalfield inland and coastal shipping points.[6] Throughout the 18th century, wagonways focused on the Wear Gorge at Penshaw, the nearest navigable location on the lower Wear. Coal was brought there by wagons to the wooden staithes (jetties) on the river banks and emptied into keels (flat-bottomed vessels), that transferred it to sea-going ships at Sunderland. In the early 19th century, direct wagonways were built across the plateau to the coast and the coal wagons were wound up the escarpment by stationary engines and then conveyed to the ports on wagonways by horse-power or early locomotives. From around 1830, however, coal was increasingly mined from beneath the limestone, a development which in the following two decades was to have far-reaching implications for communications, settlement and the wider landscape. This was indeed the period when mining colonisation in north-east England reached its peak and over wide areas farming ceased to be the mainstay of the population.[7]

The new mines were linked by rail to the coastal staithes at Bishopwearmouth (near Sunderland) and to the new port of Seaham Harbour built between 1828 and 1831 by the Marquis of Londonderry. Situated on the very edge of the coalfield, the planned new town of West Hartlepool equipped with new port facilities developed rapidly in the 1840s and 1850s as an additional outlet for the produce of the new deep mines. Its rapid expansion engulfed the old green village of Stranton. Rail links along the coast of Durham were retarded by the deep denes until brick viaducts were built at the turn of the century, which allowed a direct rail line from Seaham Harbour to the Hartlepools. The new collieries and colliery settlements at Horden, Blackhall Colliery and Easington Colliery were facilitated by, designed around, and built at the same time as the railway.

The character of buildings and settlements was deeply transformed. Some of the old agricultural villages on the plateau retain, around their greens, houses and churches built with the pale yellow magnesian limestone or imported sandstone from the west of the county and roofed with red pantiles. Early pit cottages were, it seems, built in the same materials and squeezed within or grafted onto the old villages, sometimes colonising the greens. However, from the 1830s larger pits and mining settlements were introduced to exploit fully the concealed coalfield, and these were developed by colliery companies on new sites and with little regard to pre-existing settlement. In contrast to older mining settlement on the exposed coalfield areas of west Durham, where a sprawling pattern of small detached groups of houses was characteristic, the new settlements were specialised, compact and ordered entities, more like towns than villages. Each was dominated by a pit and, in time, a massive pit heap which grew within or on the edge of the settlement; housing for the miners was provided nearby in blocks of parallel terraces built with mass-produced bricks and roofed with slates. The heterogeneous composition of the immigrant population as well as the diverse religious movements of the period resulted in a variety of places of worship even in quite small mining developments. Methodist chapels, Wesleyan or Primitive, were the most common non-residential buildings but there were chapels used by other Nonconformist groups such as Baptists, as well as churches for the sizeable Church of England and Catholic populations, the latter mostly of Irish descent, though their churches were sometimes supported by 'old money' from the local Catholic gentry. Among other noteworthy buildings might be a substantial Cooperative store, a Miners' Institute or Miners' Welfare Hall, colliery offices and even a modest Station Hotel. The surroundings of the settlements were highly distinctive; unplanned fringe-lands containing allotments, paddocks, sheds and pigeon crees; they were scraggy, intensively used yet serene precincts which are now, sadly, disappearing (Figs 9.15 and 9.16).

As on other coalfields, much of the housing for miners was provided on a speculative basis by private developers and this typically fronted the existing roads and formed long tentacles of growth between the nucleated settlements. Tracts of farmland were thus almost concealed from the main roads giving in many places an exaggerated impression of urbanisation.

In the inter-war and post-war periods, local-authority housing estates were attached to both the mining settlements and old villages, but certain villages were allowed to slip into decline as an act of deliberate planning policy because they were judged to have no long-term future. With the rapid increase in car use over the past generation commuter dwellings have spread in the less industrial localities. With the decline of mining, there have been concerted efforts to remove industrial clutter and to reorganise the settlement structure. Areas of dereliction remain, but much of the legacy of coal-mining has been reduced by, for example, removing pit heaps and restoring the sites to forestry or agriculture. Perhaps the most spectacular changes are those brought about by the Turning the Tides Project under which beaches, ravaged by colliery waste which had been tipped for many years into the sea, have been cleaned and the limestone cliffs can again be appreciated for their scenic and ecological qualities. This coastline was possibly the most polluted in the whole of Britain. The building of new towns, exemplified in the 19th century by Seaham Harbour and West Hartlepool, was renewed after the Second World War with the creation of three government-sponsored New Towns (Peterlee on the plateau and Washington and Newton Aycliffe close to it) to solve problems of poor housing and replace the scattered collieries with larger, planned centres able to attract new industrial development. The landscape of east Durham in modern times has thus experienced a succession of marked changes: agrarian reorganisation in the 17th and 18th centuries; laissez-faire industrialisation in the 19th century; and regional physical planning combining environmental rehabilitation and 'social engineering' in the second half of the 20th century.

OPPOSITE PAGE:

TOP: *Fig. 9.15 Ferryhill, County Durham*, like many mining settlements, contains a mixture of 19th-century terraced housing of brick or stone and slate, considerable 20th-century inter-war housing influenced by garden city layouts, and post-war housing. Almost overwhelmed by modern developments, the medieval village with its elongated green running east/west is still identifiable on the northern edge of the town.

BOTTOM: *Fig. 9.16 Elwick in south-east Durham* has Saxon roots but the lay-out of the village is typical of the Norman period, with two gently curving lines of homesteads fronting onto a green which is divided by a through road. Patches of well preserved medieval ridge-and-furrow survive in the surrounding fields. The ancient church (St Peter's) lies apart to the south-west of the village, and the hall to the west of the village may be on the site of a medieval manor house to which the nearby fishponds with wildfowl islands would have been connected. Most of the village growth to the north of the green is relatively recent.

217

THE UPLANDS OF NORTH-WEST NORTHUMBERLAND

This is essentially a vast moorland and forest environment where climate and physical configuration have ensured the importance of animal husbandry and settlement is dispersed and sparse. Old villages are few and lead mining, which once promoted relatively dense settlement in the Pennine parts of south Northumberland and Durham, has here been insignificant. These uplands rank among England's most secluded, empty regions but are not, as is often implied, a natural wilderness: the present solitude and wide moorland vistas belie a long history of settlement vicissitudes and environmental change, now being elicited by the research of landscape archaeologists and palaeobotanists.[8] Far from being natural, the landscapes carry the imprint of millennia of human management by burning, grazing and mowing, activities which have developed resources particularly for sheep, cattle, grouse and the honey bee.

Natural forces have strongly moulded the distinctive physique of the region, which consists essentially of the Cheviot massif and an enveloping system of concentric ridge and vale. Thus, the upland here is not a single entity but consists

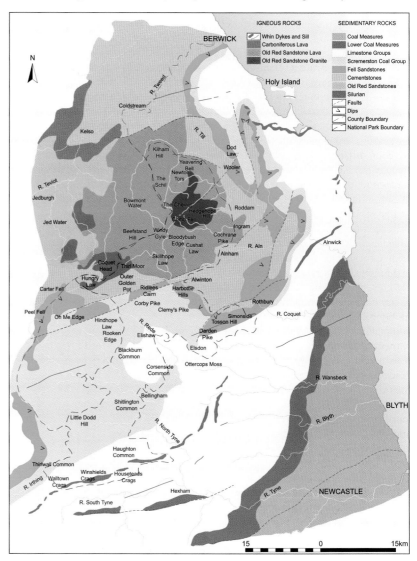

Fig. 9.17 The geology of the uplands of Northumberland correlates closely with the pattern of relief. Lava and granite underlie the Cheviot massif, which is surrounded by concentric ridges formed on resistant sandstones, while vales developed on softer rocks.

of distinctive units, differing in their geological and topographical character, vegetation cover and patterns of human usage, and in places separated by lower areas of well-settled farmland. Over millennia, as humans have worked on this varied landscape, the economic bases of the various sections have become complementary and the visual contrasts accentuated (Fig. 9.17).

Apart from the vast tracts of commercial conifer forest planted since the 1920s, the moors are generally unenclosed, uncultivated and treeless, a landscape dominated by acidic grassland, heather heath and peat bog. Shepherding, involving hardier stocks of hill sheep, is much the dominant activity. Cattle are also grazed but mainly on the lower moors, and wide tracts of heather are managed as grouse moor and periodically burnt to encourage fresh heather growth. Although modified and managed, the vegetation cover remains semi-natural, since it is spontaneous rather than planted and its species composition continues to be determined by local physical conditions.[9]

The igneous massif of the Cheviot Hills is the highest component; a compact area of broad, rounded hills of which the highest is The Cheviot (815m). Rock exposure is sparse as most of the area is covered by spreads of glacial drift, mantles of frost-loosened debris and peat and, in the valleys, alluvial deposits. Granite underlies the central and highest part of the area where the gently sloping tops of the hills are covered by blanket bog. In contrast, lava underlies extensive rolling foothills, supporting mainly acidic grassland and bracken; the grassland, some with a light-green hue, is known to local countrymen as 'white country': it provides reasonable grazing and is the homeland of the big white-faced Cheviot sheep and elusive herds of feral goats. The original forest cover of the hills, dominated by oak and alder, has long disappeared; its removal was instigated in prehistoric times by human actions, climatic changes or a combination of both. The present vegetation developed as the forest was gradually cleared, and was subsequently maintained by the grazing of sheep and cattle. Today, natural woodland is slight and the fragments are confined mainly to deeply incised cleughs (ravines) where deforestation was neither practical nor profitable and livestock grazing is inhibited.

The massif is divided by a radial pattern of steep-sided valleys that broaden where the rivers leave the granite and cut deep into the lava. They include the valleys of the Bowmont Water, College Burn, Harthope Burn, Breamish and Coquet, all of which harbour a wealth of archaeological sites and palaeoecological evidence bearing witness to the landscape's evolution over at least 4,000 years. Sites such as Houseledge in the north Cheviots and Stendrop Rigg, well into the interior above the Breamish valley, with their loose groupings of house-foundations and small cultivation plots testify to an episode of dispersed settlement in the second millennium BC on terrain and at altitudes which have never since been cultivated. After this episode, people clustered together into enclosed settlements protected by timber palisades, such as the two at High Knowes above Alnham where the

Fig. 9.18 Distribution of hillforts in northern England and southern Scotland. There is a striking concentration of around 150 hillforts, dating mainly to the Late Bronze Age and Iron Age, on the steep hills and spurs of the Cheviots and the eastern end of the Southern Uplands. The bulk are of modest proportions but a small number of large, widely dispersed forts were probably tribal centres (Yeavering Bell, 6.5km west of Wooler, is the largest, enclosing 5ha and 60 house sites). Elsewhere in northern England the distribution of hillforts is generally sparse (based on Higham 1993).

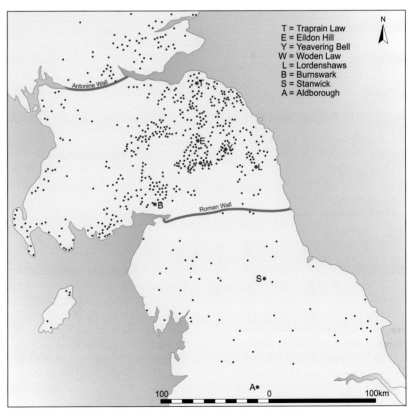

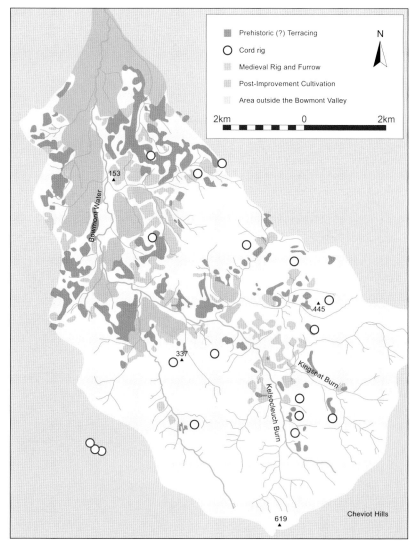

Legend:
- Prehistoric (?) Terracing
- Cord rig
- Medieval Rig and Furrow
- Post-Improvement Cultivation
- Area outside the Bowmont Valley

N

2km   0   2km

Bowmont Water
153
Kingseat Burn
445
Kelsocleuch Burn
337
619
Cheviot Hills

Fig. 9.19 Upper Bowmont valley. *The drainage basin of the Bowmont Water on the northern edge of the Cheviots has been undisturbed by cultivation but intensively grazed by sheep for a millennium and a half. Like many parts of the hill mass, however, it displays impressive traces of earlier, advanced native farming and organised landscape, especially from the Middle Bronze Age and Late Iron Age. Phases of prehistoric erosion and movement of soil from hillslopes to valley floors seem to have followed deforestation and settlement expansion, and terracing of slopes was probably a soil conservation measure (based on Mercer & Tipping 1994).*

outlines of the palisades' foundation trenches can still be traced on the ground surface. In some cases, these sites evolved into the ditch-and-bank fortifications of the late prehistoric era which are so numerous in these hills. Most are small, with no more than a handful of circular buildings within the defences; but at the other end of the scale, the wall encircling the twin peaks of Yeavering Bell shelters more than a hundred buildings (Fig. 9.18).

The idea that this was 'cowboy country' in late prehistoric times has been firmly refuted by discoveries during the 1980s of extensive areas of cultivation marks. Narrower than the ridges formed by medieval and post-medieval ploughing, this cord rigg (so called by analogy with corduroy) is visible evidence of intensive working of the land around hillforts and other settlements (*see* Fig. 3.14). On Hartside Hill, the near-complete skeleton of a Romano-British-period landscape survives, with settlement clusters and trackways between fields whose boundary banks criss-cross the whole of the hillside. To walk up the valley of the River Breamish is to have an almost complete record of human habitation unfold in front of one. The hamlet of Ingram – hardly a village – with medieval beginnings, marks the upward limit of settlement clusters; beyond here are only single farms, Hartside and, at the end of the metalled road, Linhope. In between Ingram and Linhope are, among many other features to be seen, the stone-walled hillfort of Brough Law on the steep scree-slope of a hill which forces the river to curve around it. From this viewpoint, settlements across the valley on Ewe Hill are clearly visible. Further upstream is Hartside and the complex remains of the fort and Romano-British settlement of Greaves Ash (Figs 9.19 and 9.20).

How the hills were used after the Roman period is not so well understood, but the 7th-century monastery of Lindisfarne had an estate at the top end of the Breamish which, we might suppose, was worked in conjunction with coastal estates. Transhumance was a widespread practice in the medieval period and conducted at different scales. In the 12th century, the Cistercian monks of Newminster, near Morpeth, a daughter foundation of Fountains Abbey and prominent in wool production, organised vast tracts of summer hill grazing from their granges between the Coquet and the Border. But seasonal movements of livestock to hill pastures were also organised on a smaller scale by herders who lived over the summer months with their families in temporary huts, termed shielings or shields, usually located in groups alongside the upland streams. No doubt Alnham Shiels began in this way, as summer pasture for the village of Alnham. But in the 13th century, a new population of farmers built a cluster of

houses on the shieling ground and began to cultivate the hills, forming the broad riggs, which are typical of the ploughing of this era. For whatever reason – it may have been some combination of climate change and population decline – this intensive use of the hillside was not long-lasting. The settlement failed; its houses were abandoned and, later, across the lines of the by then grassed-over ridges, boundary banks were set out for large paddocks and trackways for the management of livestock.

These fossilised landscapes are a distinctive feature of the Cheviot Hills and are as extensive and well-preserved as any area of prehistoric and early historic landscapes anywhere in England. Their preservation has been favoured by the Cheviot turf, closely cropped by sheep and generally undisturbed by cultivation or damaging tree roots for a millennium or more. The riggs, boundary banks and settlement clusters, stranded on the hillsides like so many tidelines, are graphic evidence of episodes when some favourable combination of climate, population and economics made it both possible and desirable for people to break in new

Fig. 9.20 Valley of the College Burn, looking southwards to the 815m high Cheviot, gashed by Brizzle Crags and Bellyside Burn. The collapsed stone ramparts of Great Heatha hillfort (343m) lie on the summit in the foreground, with traces of prehistoric settlement visible below to the right. Another hillfort is identifiable on the summit of afforested Sinkerside Hill (334m), behind Great Heatha.

Fig. 9.21 Sheep stell in Harthope Valley.
Stells (circular drystone sheepfolds) are a familiar feature of the Cheviot moors and valleys, used to collect hill flocks at shearing or dipping times and shelter them during snow storms; driven snow piles up against straight walls but swirls around circular constructions leaving the walls clear. The walls are about 1.5m to 1.8m high and approximately 11m in diameter. In the 18th and 19th centuries there was considerable experimentation with forms of sheep shelter, including stells, cross walls and other constructions.

lands to the plough. Their abandonment, and their survival as fossil landscapes, are likewise evidence of times of retrenchment in the long-running and constantly moving interface between intensive and extensive land use.

In some isolated localities, such as the Bewcastle and Gilsland Fells and the moors surrounding the North Tyne and Redesdale, transhumance lingered into the 17th century and perhaps even later, but generally it seems to have been replaced by a modern commercialised form of pastoralism that matured in the Border regions in the 17th century and involved large, specialised stock farms, lying on the estates of major gentry landowners and managed by wealthy graziers. By the end of the 18th century, most of the moorland had been consolidated into extensive sheep farms, many of several thousand hectares, with their shepherds' cottages often located on the patches of nutrient-enriched soil associated with former shieling sites. Enclosure in the uplands seems to have begun as early as the 17th century, quickened through the 18th and continued up to the mid-19th century. Increasingly, the cattle, sheep and horses, instead of being herded on open moorland, were able, on lower ground, to graze unattended in enclosed pastures defined by substantial, permanent boundaries. On deeper soils the new fields were bounded by quick-set hedges planted on earthen banks, but elsewhere drystone walls were generally built, while areas of high moorland remained entirely open. In the Cheviots, the requirements of sheep and the wide scale of grazing organization are reflected in large moorland grazing units marked out by impressive stretches of stone walling; the steadings of sheep farms on in-bye land (patches of improved, enclosed and sheltered ground); isolated herdsmens' dwellings deep in the uplands, now mainly deserted; and a profusion of sheep pens and distinctive, circular sheepfolds or 'stells' skilfully built in local stone and mainly used to gather flocks prior to shearing or dipping (Fig. 9.21).

This is a landscape of few farms, and such villages as there are – Alnham, Powburn and Kirknewton for example – are around the edges of the massif and not in its interior. Consequently, the use of the Cheviot igneous rocks as a building material has been limited, but they are employed in the substantial rubble walls of older structures such as churches and fortified buildings. Sandstone and roof slates were often imported for the solid stone houses and farm buildings of recent centuries. Local stone from small quarries or salvaged from prehistoric cairns and other structures has been widely used in the drystone field walls or dykes, which are often over 1.5m high and serve as boundaries and windbreaks. These are built in a style used widely in the Northumbrian hills, with two walls leaning inwards towards each other and the centre filled with rubble (fillers or chatter) and through-stones (thrufts) used to bind the construction. The walls are crossed by stiles and also possess low, ground-level openings (smoots) to allow sheep but not cattle to pass through.

Northwards, towards Scotland, the Cheviot massif is flanked by isolated and lower hill masses and, beyond them, by the broad fertile valley of the Tweed. To the east and south the massif is girded by a wide zone of various sedimentary rocks, which dip gently outwards towards the coast and Tyne to produce a succession of marked ridges and intervening vales, each with distinctive landscapes. Thus, immediately surrounding the Cheviot to the east is an elongated, well-cultivated lowland developed in the more easily eroded cementstones (mainly soft shales) and opening northwards into the Tweed valley. Local people have no traditional name for this Cheviot fringe zone as a whole. That parts of it are named, such as Whittingham Vale, Glendale and the Milfield Basin, reflects the division of the lowland by low watersheds and by the Coquet, Aln and Breamish rivers, which flow across it, as well as local variations of topography, soils and drainage conditions. The well-drained delta surface of the Milfield Basin, for example, drew Mesolithic, Neolithic and Bronze Age settlement including a group of henge monuments. Indeed, Neolithic settlement seems to have been attracted to the lowlands and valleys and evident settlement in the Cheviot Hills themselves was delayed until the early second millennium BC. Modern farming on the Till lowlands is still based on livestock but the large farmsteads which enjoy light, gravelly soils and the shelter and rain shadow of the Cheviots also grow cereals.

Encircling this lowland belt in turn are the coarse sandstones which characteristically form high, barren ground, described by locals as 'black country' after the darkness of the heather, with long, gently-tilted surfaces covered only by a thin layer of acidic soil, which is bracken- or heather-clad. From Berwick to the Redesdale, these sandstones form an almost continuous scarp facing towards the Cheviots, marked in places by prehistoric fortifications, at Old Bewick and Ross Castle spectacularly so. Flat outcrops of rock, and occasionally rounded boulders, around the scarp have been inscribed with the geometric designs known as cup-and-ring marks. At Broomridge, Roughting Linn, Dod Law, Weetwood and Fowberry these overlook the Milfield Basin from dominating high points in ways that suggest that the high and low ground were intimately linked in human perception and use of the landscape. The Aln and Coquet cut deep gorges through this scarp but, further north, it acts as a drainage barrier separating the Cheviots from the coast and deflecting local rivers, such as the Till, northwards.

West of Redesdale, towards the Cumbrian county boundary, the Fell sandstones form bulky hills, much afforested, to be replaced southwards, on lower ground, by the classic cuesta ridge country on either side of Hadrian's Wall. The ridges here are of younger sandstones or limestones, but the Wall itself was built on the rim of the much-photographed Whin Sill. The Sill possesses a distinctive flora, and here and elsewhere provided major defensible sites in various historical periods. In modern times it has been extensively quarried for road metal, to the detriment of the Wall before measures were introduced for its protection.

The population of this fell and forest country south-west of the Cheviots is sparse and scattered, and the hamlets, small villages and most of the farms are restricted to the improved land (hay meadows and pastures) in the narrow valleys of the North Tyne and its tributary the Rede, which run through wide tracts of almost deserted moors and coniferous forests. The older farms and cottages are mainly constructed of local sandstones with slated roofs, and there are numerous, ruinous bastles which were the vernacular housing form of the troubled times up to and beyond the 16th century. The rough grassland on the moors is grazed by hardy Scottish Blackface and Swaledale sheep but there are areas dominated by heather and managed as grouse moors. In recent centuries the thin coal seams in the area were exploited on a small-scale at numerous places by adit mines and shallow bell-pits, some lasting into the 1970s. Plashetts colliery was a larger concern and was active until the 1920s. Small-scale iron- and lead-working has also taken place here.

The 20th century saw three major land-use changes. Much the most fundamental has been large-scale conifer afforestation, initiated by the Forestry Commission in the 1920s and supplemented in recent decades by private forestry companies. The impact of forestry here has been huge: the great Kielder Forest in particular, in upper North Tynedale, upper Redesdale and the area west of the lower North Tyne, is much the largest afforested area in Britain and has dramatically changed the landscape and ecology of the area. Reservoirs, large and small, have also become a significant landscape feature since the late 19th century. Catcleugh in upper Redesdale is the oldest large reservoir, completed in 1905. Kielder Water (1982) is much the largest, and the largest entirely man-made lake in Britain; formed by damming the North Tyne to provide water for the industrial areas of the North East, it has created a new, unfamiliar but impressive landscape of water and coniferous surrounds that is perhaps more reminiscent of the Baltic Shield than any part of England. The final 20th-century feature is the Ministry of Defence's Otterburn Training Area in upper Coquetdale and upper Redesdale, which provides 'realistic training facilities for the Armed Forces'. The military first came to Otterburn in 1911 and the training area now covers over 23,000ha of moorland partly pre-dating the new forests, and occupying around a fifth of the Northumberland National Park designated in 1956.

CONCLUSION – EXPERIENCING THE MOSAIC

England is not a country of extreme land forms, of wide plains and lakes or high mountain ridges. Its qualities are in the constantly changing textures of its landscapes and in the patterning of the mosaic which we have here described. The joy of a journey through north-east England is to observe the mosaic unfolding, for it is hardly possible to travel even a score of kilometres without becoming aware of gradually changing textures: the patterns of fields, vegetation cover or relief. Sometimes change comes abruptly: the climb from Stokesley out of the valley of the Tees to the top of the scarp of the North York Moors before the long unfolding descent into Helmsley; the suddenly-appearing backdrop of the Cheviots as, travelling north, one crosses the bridge at Powburn. The Pennine dales of Yorkshire and Durham unfold more slowly; but reaching a watershed can be a breathtaking moment. A set of medieval plough ridges in lowland pasture, their corrugations suddenly glimpsed in low sunlight, carries one deep into time; while a line of trees, standing now without the hedge within which they grew to maturity, in the midst of wide arable hectares, is a reminder that the textures are constantly being reworked. Words can describe the mosaic but it is there to be experienced.

NOTES

1 Spratt & Harrison 1996.
2 Fenton-Thomas 2003; Stoertz 1997.
3 Harris 1969, 61–96.
4 de Boer 1964.
5 Durham County Council 2003, 3A6; Countryside Commission 1998, 71–6.
6 Creigh 1966, 220–21.
7 Smailes 1960, 161–73.
8 Frodsham 2004.
9 Swan 1993.

10

Art and the Landscape of the North East

ANDREW GREG

A love of landscape painting has long been a particularly British phenomenon. The reasons for this surely lie in two features of British life: the key role that landed property plays in Britain's dynastic, economic and political systems and a love of travel, both at home and abroad.

Certainly landscape painting first became important in the recording and proud display of property ownership and in the more private recording of travels. Early northern landscapes are prominent in the backgrounds of paintings of castles, houses and country estates. These landscape elements emphasise the value of agriculture and the status of hunting parks. The country estate is an island of culture in an untamed wilderness. The very earliest such paintings, such as Alexander Kierincx's *Richmond Castle*, 1639–40 and the anonymous *Pontefract Castle, c.*1633 are both from series of depictions of royal castles, and are therefore explicit records of ownership and power across the nation. Many later 17th-century northern house paintings, an anonymous *Brancepeth Castle* of 1680–90 and Peter Hartover's paintings of Capheaton, Alnwick and Harraton, for example, conscientiously depict the surrounding countryside and the activities of humbler classes of servants and cottagers. But in the 17th century 'Landskip' was '... all that which in a picture is not of the body or argument thereof ...'. It was 'bywork'.[1] Landscape plays this subordinate role also in the otherwise informative prints of the country's great houses and their grounds by Leonard Knyff and Johannes Kip in their *Nouveau Théâtre de la Grande Bretagne* (1708 and later), which included many northern subjects.

ANTIQUARIANISM AND THE PICTURESQUE

A sense of the discoveries awaiting the 17th-century traveller in the north is provided by the lines once attributed to John Cleveland:

England's a perfect World, hath Indies too;
Correct your Maps, Newcastle is Peru[2]

But to travel in the 17th and 18th century was an adventure, even in England. The roads were so poor that Thomas Kirk in 1677 could get lost between Ripon and Dinsdale and end up riding through meadows. He welcomed the sight of well-kept gardens and orchards among the moorland and ruined castles and noted approvingly the earliest industrial technologies, such as the waterwheels or

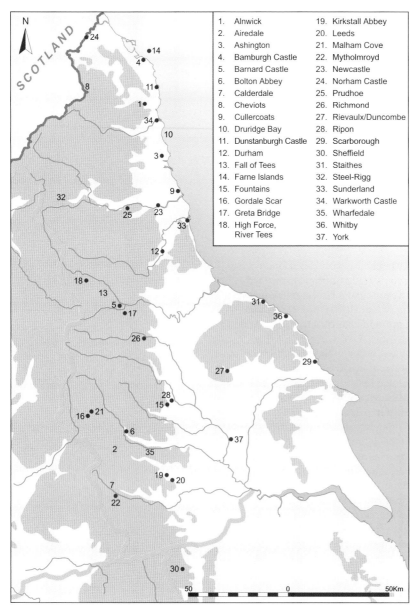

1. Alnwick	19. Kirkstall Abbey
2. Airedale	20. Leeds
3. Ashington	21. Malham Cove
4. Bamburgh Castle	22. Mytholmroyd
5. Barnard Castle	23. Newcastle
6. Bolton Abbey	24. Norham Castle
7. Calderdale	25. Prudhoe
8. Cheviots	26. Richmond
9. Cullercoats	27. Rievaulx/Duncombe
10. Druridge Bay	28. Ripon
11. Dunstanburgh Castle	29. Scarborough
12. Durham	30. Sheffield
13. Fall of Tees	31. Staithes
14. Farne Islands	32. Steel-Rigg
15. Fountains	33. Sunderland
16. Gordale Scar	34. Warkworth Castle
17. Greta Bridge	35. Wharfedale
18. High Force, River Tees	36. Whitby
	37. York

Fig. 10.1 Map of towns, cities and other features in the North East that are referred to in the text.

horse-mills for draining coal mines. Fifty years later Daniel Defoe still found the roads almost impassable. Despite deliberately avoiding ruins as much as possible ('Antiquity not being the Business of this Work'), he could not help noting in his *A Tour thro' the Whole Island of Great Britain* that:

> *Here is abundant Business for an Antiquary; every place shews you ruin'd Castles, Roman altars, Inscriptions, Monuments of Battles of Heroes killed and Armies routed …*[3]

Defoe was dismissive of natural wonders, Hell's Kitchen near Darlington being 'nothing but old Coal Pits filled with water by the River Tees'. It was commerce and industry that interested him more. Even so, 'the prodigious heaps, I might say Mountains of Coals' at Lumley and the distant view of smoke from the saltpans at South Shields clearly had aesthetic as well as economic appeal for him.

As interest in the country's history developed among a wider audience than scholars and the clergy during the course of the 18th century, a growing number of books were published that specialised in the visible remains of English history. One of the earliest and most comprehensive, Samuel and Nathaniel Buck's *Antiquities …* of 1726 and 1742 (and reissued in 1774) was extensively illustrated with ancient ruins, modern mansions and panoramas of major towns and gave prominent coverage to the north. These books were most prolific from the 1770s. Francis Grose's *Antiquities of England and Wales* began publication in 1773, its mostly undistinguished engraved views being widely plagiarised during the rest of the century. Thomas Hearne's artistically more sophisticated *Antiquities of Great Britain* was published from 1778 and contained many fine views of the North East. Although these books concentrated on cathedrals, castles and monasteries, they also featured notable industrial sites such as Coalbrookdale, whose cast-iron bridge, together with that at Sunderland, were proudly illustrated. The tradition of the history book illustrated with engravings of antiquities continued into the 19th century but, as we shall see through the example of Turner, by the 1820s the engravings themselves achieved an artistic and technical independence that transcended their role as mere illustrations of antiquities.

James Thomson's poems *The Seasons* (1726–30) greatly encouraged a purely aesthetic appreciation of the English landscape. Thereafter, travellers, writers and artists had a literary foundation on which to build their responses to landscape.

Turner appended quotations from Thomson to many of his works. The landscapes of the north, less cultivated, more varied and more historically resonant than the south, were particularly valuable to the formulation of artistic responses. Thomson was followed by Thomas Gray, whose journal through Cravendale and the Lakes (1775) became a model for future literary tourists. The most popular northern tours of the period were Arthur Young's *Six Month Tour through the North of England* (1770) and Thomas Pennant's *Tour* of 1774.

Thus, in the spirit of the Enlightenment, a philosophical framework arose to define these aesthetic responses, and the depiction of landscape was an important means by which the terms 'beauty', 'picturesque' and 'sublime' were analysed and defined.

The philosopher Edmund Burke distinguished between the Beautiful – smooth and gentle – and the Sublime – vast and terrifying – in his *Philosophical Enquiry into the Origin of our Ideas of the Sublime and the Beautiful* (1757). In the 1760s and 1770s William Gilpin toured the country analysing the landscape for its painterly potential as he went. He defined 'Picturesque' as 'a term expressive of that peculiar kind of beauty, which is agreeable in a picture',[4] and defined its qualities: roughness, irregularity and variety being the most important. On his tours he would note when he felt monastic ruins could be improved by the judicious use of the mallet to remove their 'regularity and ... vulgarity' and when nature itself should be corrected of its deformities.

One of the early topographers and one of the most charming draughtsmen of this period was the delightfully named Samuel Hieronymous Grimm. Under the patronage of Richard Kaye, prebend of Southwell and Durham, Grimm made tours of the north, including a visit to Northumberland, Cumberland and the Isle of Man in 1778. Grimm's depictions of the picnics on the Farne Islands, one for the gentlemen and their families and one for the servants, provide a delightful picture of the necessarily informal nature of these tours (Fig. 10.2). The Farnes, then and now famous for their bird and sea life, are rocky outposts of the Whin Sill in the North Sea, in the past inhabited by monks and hermits, to Grimm the source of picturesque views and exotic experiences. The natives could see travellers from the south as exotic too. In Newcastle, Grimm records, '... I was dogged and on the point of being arrested for a Spy had not Broadie the Landlord turned the constables out.'[5]

By 1795 the typical tourist such as Henry Skrine of Somerset still preferred well managed agriculture to wild moorland but could also admire the verdant and romantic setting of Durham alongside the 'opulence, improvements and luxury' of Newcastle. Notably, however, he could shiver with delight at Weathercote's Cave, near Ingleborough, which 'though confin'd is strikingly

Fig. 10.2 S H Grimm (1733–94), **Dinner on Pinnacle Island**, *pen and wash. In the 18th century, artists accompanied their patrons on their travels. Here the family of Dr Richard Kaye, prebend of Durham, are on a tour of the antiquities of Northumberland. They picnic on the Farne Islands, attended by their servants and recorded by their artist.*

horrid'. Turner was to paint the waterfall and cave twice in the 1810s. In contrast to Skrine, Richard Warner, in his *Tour of the Northern Counties ...* of 1802, regretted the neatness and uniformity of Studley Royal and the lack of ivy on the ruins of the abbey, a criticism made of many historic sites to this day.

The Picturesque also shaped the emergence of the landscape garden. Its most famous exponent, Lancelot 'Capability' Brown, was born in Kirkharle, Northumberland in 1715/16. His youthful experiences in Northumberland and at the great garden at Stowe in the 1740s, led to his employment by many of the greatest landowners of the land. Few 18th-century parks do not reveal the work or pervasive influence of 'Capability' Brown in their clumps of trees, the ha-ha, and the serpentine lake over which a Palladian bridge carries the drive. He tried to work, as he wrote about Roche Abbey in 1774, 'With Poet's feeling and with Painter's Eye'. His first great ducal commission, at Alnwick in 1760 for the Duke of Northumberland, gave him the opportunity for many visits, plans and commissions for lesser gentry in Yorkshire, Durham and Northumberland en route from the south: at Wallington and Rothley for Sir Walter Blackett in 1765; at Sandbeck, Harewood and Temple Newsam in Yorkshire for example. Here the artist is inspired by the possibilities of the natural landscape to create a new kind of work of art in which architecture, gardening and landscape are united.

THE ROMANTIC ERA

The turn of the century saw romanticism expressed in English painting. The features of romanticism are essentially: a personalised and spontaneous response to experience; an appreciation of originality; and the quest for authenticity. These were in contrast and opposition to the classical aspiration towards an unattainable ideal, endorsed by historical precedent. Watercolour was the perfect medium for the romantic impulse, well suited to recording immediate impressions. In the search for the authenticity of direct experience, watercolours were often spattered with rain or the spray of waterfalls.

The three earliest full-blooded proponents of the romantic landscape were John Mallord William Turner, Thomas Girtin, and the slightly younger John Sell Cotman. As an architectural draughtsman, Turner knew of the north and its antiquities from the work of Girtin, Dayes and Hearne that he copied either for his patron Munro or as hack work for publishers. Turner's first northern tour of 1797 marked both the origin of his public success and his change of direction from architectural to landscape painter. It was appropriate then that the tour was motivated by a commission from Edward Lascelles, the son of the first Earl of Harewood, to make views of the family house and estate, a programme of patronage that was to last for ten years.

The 1797 tour encompassed Derbyshire, Yorkshire, Durham, Northumberland, the Scottish borders and a return through the Lakes, Lancashire, Yorkshire, Harewood again, and Lincolnshire. At the time, Kirkstall Abbey, Ripon Cathedral, Fountains Abbey, Durham, Melrose Abbey, York and Harewood itself made the deepest impression on him but other sites, such as Dunstanburgh and Norham Castle, were to become iconic images of his long career. The 1797 sketchbook was to remain a source for many later works, developed far beyond their meticulous topographical beginnings into some of the most dramatic images to emerge from Turner's brush. Subsequent tours were made in 1801 and 1808, the latter under the patronage of his greatest friend and patron Walter Fawkes, of Farnley Hall, which overlooked the junction of the Wharfe and the Washburn near Otley. Turner visited Farnley Hall almost annually from 1810 until Fawkes's death in 1827.

Turner travelled north again in 1816, 1824 and 1831 for three of the numerous, onerous but productive commissions that inspired his finest finished watercolours. It may surprise us now to realise that these watercolours were commissioned by publishers to be engraved as illustrations to books of local history and poetry. But Turner's imagery was by now a major selling point for publishers and the finished watercolours themselves were highly valuable. The work of the engravers, in their almost miraculous transformation of Turner's highly coloured, atmospheric and almost abstract watercolours into linear black and white, was also highly valued. While Turner was paid 25 guineas for each watercolour, the engravers were paid an astonishing £100 per plate.

Turner's work is never pure landscape. He was as interested in the human aspect of landscape as in its topographical and aesthetic qualities. Human activity is omnipresent, walking in the wildest upland scenery, fishing in front of abbey ruins, farming in productive countryside or travelling to market in the newly burgeoning industrial cities. W B Cooke's *Rivers of England* project of 1823–5 resulted in a powerful watercolour *Shields on the River Tyne*, depicting keelmen transferring coals onto colliers in the moonlight. The subject was also the basis for a related oil painting in 1835, a companion piece for a picture of Venice and thus a deliberate contrast of new industrial wealth and decaying imperial splendour.

Fig. 10.3 Thomas Girtin (1775–1802), Kirkstall Abbey, Yorkshire, from Kirkstall Hill, 1800, watercolour. The ruins of Kirkstall Abbey had long been a favourite picturesque subject but to Girtin, one of the great artists of the Romantic period, they are but one element in a wider landscape. Girtin, with his contemporary Turner, transformed topography and antiquarianism into a personal response to the totality of the landscape, in which light, colour and tone express the artist's experience.

Thomas Girtin was Turner's exact contemporary but died tragically at the age of 27, just as he reached a peak of accomplishment that arguably exceeded Turner's achievements at the time. He had made his first tour of the north in 1796 visiting Ripon, Fountains Abbey, York, Richmond, Durham, Newcastle and the castles of Northumberland's east coast. He exhibited views of Jedburgh and Lindisfarne Priory at the Royal Academy the following year. Like Turner, Girtin relied on patrons and antiquarian publishers for his commissions. From the home of his patron Edward Lascelles at Harewood House he explored the Yorkshire moors and made at least one further trip to Northumberland and Durham. Among antiquarian patrons James Moore stands out; his two important works on monastic remains and castles were illustrated with plates from Girtin's and other artists' drawings. While ruins had more commercial value, Girtin's talent, even more than Turner's, lay in pure landscape. Harewood House gave him easy access to Kirkstall Abbey, Wharfedale and Bolton Abbey, the site of some of his finest works (Fig. 10.3).

The third in our triumvirate of romantic watercolourists, John Sell Cotman, is an artist whose most famous and finest work was made in our region. Like Turner and Girtin, Cotman had benefited from the encouragement of Dr Munro around 1799 and had first discovered conventionally picturesque and romantic landscape on tours to Wales around 1800–2. Cotman's exploration of Yorkshire was also dependent on an enlightened family of patrons and friends. The Cholmeleys of Brandsby, north of York, were hosts to the young artist for summer tours in three consecutive years from 1803. Through them he also met and found patrons in the Worsleys at Hovingham Hall, the Smyths at Heath Hall, Wakefield, the Ballasis family at Newbrough Priory and, most grandly, the Marquis of Stafford at Trentham Hall. Cotman visited and drew the usual sites – Rievaulx, York, Fountains and Kirkham – and in 1805 he visited the Cholmeleys' friends the Morrits at Rokeby Park. The Morrits introduced Cotman to the intimate pleasures of their park and the neighbouring Greta Woods and River

Greta. Here Cotman made the most exceptionally beautiful and original of his works. Based on pencil drawings made on the spot, these exquisite works were consciously created and coloured later in the studio, as exemplified by the famous *Greta Bridge*, which exists in two versions made in 1807 and 1810 (Fig. 10.4). Other wooded valleys in the region, such as Duncombe Park and Castle Eden Dean, also provided suitable material for this aspect of Cotman's genius.

THE SUBLIME

Like other aesthetic categories of the Enlightenment, the appreciation and eventual enjoyment of the Sublime in landscape, first investigated by Burke in 1757, originates in literature. John Langhorne remembered:

Ye rocks on precipices pil'd;
Ye ragged deserts waste and wild!
Delightful horrors hail!

in his *Lines left with the Minister of Riponden, a Romantic Village in Yorkshire* of 1758. What had distressed earlier 18th-century travellers now evoked an attractive frisson of horror, even fear. As crossing the Alps had been transformed for the Grand Tourist from a dangerous necessity to an essential part of the experience, so the wild wastes of the dales and moors joined castles and abbeys as 'lions' to be witnessed by the intrepid traveller. The sublime also encompassed the wide open spaces and skies of the moors, which could elevate the viewer's mind to the infinities of space and time.

There can be few more powerful expressions of the Sublime in landscape painting in our region than James Ward's *Gordale Scar* (1812–14) (Fig. 10.5). This remarkable limestone cliff, through which the Gordale Beck tumbles, had been an attraction for Picturesque tourists for 50 years, together with the herd of wild white cattle owned, like the landscape itself, by Lord Ribblesdale, who commissioned Ward's painting in 1811. Gordale Scar was said to be unpaintable but Ward, the country's most famous animal painter, had no qualms about dramatising its topography still further to create his spectacular masterpiece, over 4m wide.

Turner, on the other hand, did not rely on scale of execution. The extent

to which illustrated books were to become the impetus and vehicles for the development of Turner's conception of the Sublime in landscape can be seen in his commissions for Whitaker's *History of Richmondshire* (1822) and *Picturesque Views in England and Wales* (1825–38). Turner had already worked more conventionally for Whitaker in around 1800 on the latter's *History of Whalley* and *History of Craven*. The *Fall of the Tees*, for example, was first treated in conventional Sublime fashion: small figures look up towards the double falls, deep in shadow, with a narrow strip of sky above. In the later version (and the related *Chain Bridge over the River Tees* (Fig. 10.6) a tiny figure still studies the falls but the artist stands back and we, like him, look down to blend the water, trees, rocks, moorland, sky and distant hills in a sunlit haze.

A masterpiece of Turner's *Picturesque Views* series, and one that harks back to the 17th-century 'classical landscapes' of Claude and Poussin, is *Prudhoe Castle*, a rare Tyne valley view of 1825 based on sketches of 1817 (Fig. 10.7). The somewhat formal composition is imbued with the heat of a summer afternoon; the distant castle rising blue above the haze forming the focus of the work. This

TOP: *Fig. 10.6 J M W Turner (1775–1851),* **Chain bridge over the River Tees,** *1838,* **engraving.** *Turner achieved sublime effects on a modest scale. The watercolour is in a private collection but this engraving, made for* Picturesque views in England and Wales I, *shows the enormous skill of the engravers in successfully preserving Turner's vision in black and white lines.*

ABOVE: *Fig. 10.7 J M W Turner (1775–1851),* **Prudhoe Castle, Northumberland,** *1825,* **watercolour.**

Fig. 10.8 J MW Turner (1775–1851)
Leeds, *1816, watercolour.*

was a treatment he was to bring to the verge of abstraction in the oil of Norham Castle on the Tweed of *c.*1845, at the end of his career.

Industry could provide sublime experiences too. Coalbrookdale in Shropshire, the fiery heart of the Industrial Revolution, had long been a subject for artists, most notably de Loutherbourg, but the Iron Bridge over the Wear at Sunderland attracted almost as much attention as that at Coalbrookdale. Unsurprisingly Turner was attracted both to the essentially dramatic nature of the iron-making process (his 1797 tour began in Rotherham, where he sketched Walker's famous ironworks), but also to the burgeoning growth of the region's industrial cities. Leeds, for example, is bathed in optimistic light in his 1816 drawing for *Picturesque Views* (Fig. 10.8). Industry, dependent at first on waterpower, then on coal and on access to other raw materials, was as much a rural as an urban activity, and it was the contrast between the rural and the industrial that provided much of the frisson of the 'Industrial Sublime'.

THE 19th CENTURY: CELEBRATION AND ESCAPE

During the 19th century, as industrialisation took over many of the valleys, lowlands and estuaries of the North East, the artistic and popular perception of the north gradually changed from one of unspoilt wilderness to one of smoky cities, coal tips and industrial grime.

At the same time the pattern of artistic patronage also changed. A new class of industrial magnates began to rival the old aristocracy in wealth and artistic pretensions. Industrial growth also led to an expansion of a wealthy middle class. The professional classes, merchants and manufacturers began to patronise artists, usually local ones. Art institutions were founded throughout the country in the early 19th century and promoted local talent to local patrons. Less comfortable with the values of the old masters or intellectual theorists, these patrons became supporters of modern art, the Pre-Raphaelites in particular, whose greatest collectors were to be found in the industrial midlands, North East and North West. The Pre-Raphaelite landscape, with its search for photographic exactitude and its scientific approach to botany, geology and meteorology, is exemplified by John William Inchbold and the early work of Atkinson Grimshaw in Yorkshire and by Alfred William Hunt in the North East.

If much Victorian landscape is 'either the result of intense looking or myopic nostalgia',[6] there was also a strand of celebration of industry apparent in the production and consumption of northern landscapes. Coal owners commissioned paintings of their coal pits, as country house owners had of their houses and estates. The spectacular achievements of railway and harbour engineers, transforming the landscape with their monumental structures of brick and steel, were also popular subjects, both as celebratory oil paintings and as series of popular prints. John Wilson Carmichael, better known as a marine artist, painted coal mines, railway structures and the opening of docks, all to commission, in the 1830s and '40s. Thomas Hair's delicate *Sketches of the Coal Mines in Northumberland and Durham* (1838–49) were published as popular etchings. In the same period, industrial genre paintings by artists such as George Walker in Yorkshire and Henry Perlee Parker in Newcastle depicted the lives of pitmen and glassmakers, as previous artists had those of shepherds and gipsies.

William Bell Scott, a Pre-Raphaelite follower, painted a great series of eight murals of Northumbrian history for Wallington Hall, Northumberland, between 1857 and 1861. The series included *Building of Hadrian's Wall*, *Descent of the Danes* and *Grace Darling*. It culminated in a spectacular celebration of Tyneside's industrial might, *Iron and Coal*. Blacksmiths hammer iron in Robert Stephenson's railway works, in the foreground lies the barrel of one of Armstrong's 100-pound guns, in the background an Armstrong hydraulic crane works on the quayside in front of Stephenson's recently completed High Level Bridge.

Science is also apparent in the sequence of landscape watercolours of Hadrian's Wall commissioned in 1848 by the antiquarian John Collingwood Bruce from Henry Burdon Richardson, of the Newcastle artistic dynasty. Richardson's watercolours seem to be an objective record of the current state of the Roman Wall, then undergoing its first serious excavations. They are unusually undemonstrative Victorian landscapes, with few concessions to conventional Picturesque composition (Fig. 10.9).

The strand of social concern that originated in a Pre-Raphaelite interest in modern-life subjects transferred later to a previously ignored workforce, the fishing communities of the north-east coast. The creation of the artists' colonies of Cullercoats in Northumberland and Staithes in the North Riding reflected in part the social concerns of a younger generation of artists but also their self-conscious search for 'undiscovered' places. In the working lives and environments of North Sea fishermen and women they became aware of traditional communities that had been bypassed by modern life. These people lived dangerous and uncomfortable lives, the women's overshadowed by the constant fear of widowhood.

Staithes, first 'discovered' by Gilbert Foster in the 1880s, soon became the summer home for 20 or 30 artists. Laura Knight, the best-known member of the colony, who lived there almost continuously from 1896 to 1910, found its appeal in

> *... the freedom, the austerity, the savagery, the wildness ... I loved the cold and the northerly storms when no covering could protect you. I loved the strange race of people who lived there, whose stern almost forbidding exterior formed such contrast to the warmth and richness of their natures.*[7]

*Fig. 10.9 H B Richardson (1826–74), **The wall sinking into the hollow at Steel-Rigg...**, c. 1848, watercolour.*

Staithes was attractively difficult to get to, so it escaped the summer crowds found at resorts such as Whitby. The group held its first exhibition in 1901 but was broken up by the First World War.

It is a little harder to appreciate the appeal of Cullercoats in Northumberland and how in 1895 it could have come to be called 'a little Bohemia-by-the-Sea'.[8] It had been a fashionable bathing spot since the 18th century and was now readily reached by train from nearby affluent Newcastle. But like Staithes, it had an ancient, hardworking and picturesque race of fishing folk, with traditional working dress and a heroic closeness to nature. It had become well-known through John Dawson Watson's illustrations in the *Graphic*, the home of English social realism, and in 1881–2 was famously visited by the great American artist Winslow Homer. The experience of Cullercoats can be credited with changing the direction of Homer's art from a pretty bourgeois lyricism to a tougher and more dramatic intensity. However, the most interesting local artists working in Cullercoats, such as Arthur Hardwick Marsh and H H Emmerson, were more interested in the people than the landscape.

Contemporary with the artistic focus on the fishing communities of Cullercoats and Staithes was the photography of Frank Meadow Sutcliffe in Whitby. The son of a Leeds artist, he took up the new technology and set up a studio in the popular fishing port and resort to sell local views. His work is notable for its posed and picturesque depictions of local characters and harbour scenes, most famously *Water Rats* of 1886. His work is relatively unsentimental and Sutcliffe took his profession seriously, being prominent in the early debates about the status of photography as an art and a member of the prestigious Linked Ring.

The railway rapidly opened up areas of the country that had previously been inaccessible. Increased wealth and leisure generated by industrial growth created the opportunity for working people to get fresh air and a break from everyday life by visiting country and seaside resorts. The photographic potential of these places for the amateur was promoted as early as the 1860s in the railway guides that became indispensable to the 19th-century traveller and tourist. To promote railway travel in the 20th century a genre of commercial art developed, the railway poster, large scale for display on stations and smaller for inside carriages. In the North East the LNER became the dominant company after the 1922 grouping of the railway companies. These posters portrayed the countryside, its market towns and cathedral cities as leisure destinations for the city dweller. They helped to redefine the countryside in its distinctness from the city: traditional, picturesque, historic, relaxing, yet easily accessible (Fig. 10.10).

Fig. 10.10 Austin Cooper (1890–1964), **Old World market places, Barnard Castle,** *c. 1930s, lithograph. By the turn of the century the north was becoming synonymous with industrialisation, as increased leisure time and wages allowed the railway to become a means of escape for the modern urban worker, and the countryside came to represent a quieter, gentler, mythical past.*

THE 20th CENTURY: CRISES AND CHANGES

In the 20th century it was rural Yorkshire that became an archetypal subject for traditional 20th-century artists. Wensleydale has boasted its own artists' colony and its appealing combination of distinctive geology, sparse population and ease of access has allowed it be presented as an ideal English landscape by generations of Royal Academy exhibitors. Henry Epworth Allen, Rowland Hill, Fred Lawson, Bertram Priestman, Henry Royle and others did much to promote the traditional beauties of the dales in the first half of the century.[9]

In contrast to the predictable subjects of most amateur artists, a Workers' Educational Association art appreciation class in the 1930s encouraged the pitmen artists of the Ashington Group to seek their subject matter, not in the pretty villages or rocky shores of Northumberland, but among the familiar streets of their own pit villages around Ashington. Their loving depictions of their homes, terraced streets, pigeons, pubs and whippets are refreshingly honest and allowed them, and us, to value the unrecognised and undervalued aesthetic character of their everyday surroundings (Fig. 10.11).

Avant-garde artists have mostly ignored the region. Although three of the century's greatest British artists, Henry Moore, Barbara Hepworth and David Hockney, were born in Yorkshire, their subject matter does not obviously reflect their native landscape. However, Moore has recognised the impact of the Yorkshire Moors on his art: 'Perhaps what influenced me most over wanting to do sculpture in the open air and to relate my sculpture to landscape comes from my youth in Yorkshire'.[10] While the origins of his forms lie ultimately in the human body and animal bones, the success of his works when carefully placed in the open landscape confirms the depth of the relationship between the two. Hepworth, too, acknowledged the influence of her native landscape: 'All my early memories are of forms and shapes and textures. Moving through and over the West Riding landscape with my father in his car, the hills were sculptures, the roads defined the form ... [The] sensation has never left me. I, the sculptor, *am* the landscape.'[11] A late public work *The Family of Man* (1970) was designed to be set in the Yorkshire landscape.

Moore and Hepworth both studied in the early 1920s at Leeds School of Art, which had two periods of artistic adventurousness and achievement. In the second decade of the century the critic Herbert Reed, himself a Yorkshireman

Fig. 10.11 Harry Wilson, Ashington Colliery, *1936, oil on paper.*

whose personal identity was tied closely to nature and to Yorkshire, made the Leeds Art Club a focus for interest in German culture and the avant-garde, in reaction to Roger Fry and the Bloomsbury Group's promotion of French Post-Impressionism. In the 1950s and '60s Harry Thubron brought artists such as Victor Pasmore, Terry Frost, Patrick Heron and Richard Hamilton to teach at the art schools at Newcastle, and later Leeds, from where they influenced a whole generation of British abstract artists. During Terry Frost's period as Gregory Fellow at Leeds in the mid-1950s he made work inspired by his experience of the Yorkshire Dales – 'I was minute and the dales were huge.' Pasmore was Professor of Fine Art at Newcastle University from 1954 and 1961 and became heavily involved in architectural and urban planning projects, including murals for Newcastle's Civic Centre and the planning and design of part of Peterlee, a new town in County Durham (*see* Chapter 7).

The Vorticist artist Edward Wadsworth is an exception to the relative neglect of the urban and industrial character of the region by imaginative artists in the 20th century.

Fig. 10.12 Edward Wadsworth (1889–1949), **Mytholmroyd, c. 1914,** *woodcut. The mill towns of West Yorkshire, originally dependent on waterpower, tumble down their valleys and provide a geometric jumble of roofs and factory chimneys for Wadsworth's celebratory vision of the modern industrial landscape.*

He was born in Cleckheaton in 1896, the son of a successful worsted spinner and some of his finest work consists of the woodcuts of industrial and urban scenes he made between 1913 and 1920 (Fig. 10.12). Newcastle upon Tyne, Yorkshire mill towns and Black Country slagheaps are treated to a harsh geometric process of abstraction ultimately derived from Cubism. The subject matter however reflects the Vorticists' and Futurists' worship of mechanisation. Wadsworth and Jacob Kramer were among the artists commissioned for a series of murals for Leeds town hall in the 1920s, an imaginative project which was, sadly, abandoned.

The Depression was to draw Britain's greatest documentary photographers to the industrial north: Edwin Smith was in Ashington and Newcastle in 1936, while Bill Brandt contributed several photo stories to *Picture Post* and *Lilliput* in the 1940s, celebrating the idiosyncrasies of the English countryside and urging its protection in *The Threat to the Great Roman Wall* (1943), *The Craven Fault (Malham Cove)* and *Hail, Hell and Halifax* (both 1948).

Lowry's most characteristic industrial subjects could be situated in many a Yorkshire mill town, if we did not know of his Salford and Manchester roots. He did, however, make journeys to the east of the country and had important support from the Stone Gallery in Newcastle. Many views of the empty north-east coast and a flat, featureless North Sea evoke an unexpected sense of solitude, even of loneliness. The *River Wear at Sunderland*, 1961 (Fig. 10.13), however, is among the finest of his later works, the busy river mouth full of ships, and the deep gorge dramatically winding inland.

Fig. 10.13 L S Lowry (1887–1976),
River Wear at Sunderland, *1961,*
oil on board.

As traditional industries, rural and urban, suffered their crises during the course of the 20th century the attitudes of artists responded. Before and during the Second World War, rural Britain became a symbol of British identity that could be evoked to help create a necessary patriotic mood. The neo-Romanticism prevalent on the 1920s and '30s, in the work of Graham Sutherland and John Piper for example, sometimes self-consciously recreated the sense of discovery felt by 18th-century Picturesque tourists. Piper, editor of the Shell Guides, reinterpreted natural wonders such as Gordale Scar and Malham Cove, and ruins such as Seaton Delaval. Unfortunately he found that tourists often detracted from his full appreciation of the Sublime.

Changes in the landscape, such as the replacement of traditional heavy industries by shopping centres and of traditional farming by intensive agriculture and the pursuit of leisure, have continued to be noticed by contemporary artists. The greatest contemporary British landscape photographer, Fay Godwin, has explored several distinct landscapes around Britain, notably the Calder valley in *Remains of Elmet* (1979). Ted Hughes, who wrote the book's poems, explained in its introduction the appeal that the valley and its neighbouring moors had for them both:

> *The Calder Valley, west of Halifax, was the last ditch of Elmet, the last British Celtic kingdom to fall to the Angles. For centuries it was considered more or less uninhabitable wilderness, a notorious refuge for criminals, a hide-out for refugees. Then in the early 1800s it became the cradle for the Industrial Revolution in textiles, and the upper Calder became the hardest-worked river in England…Throughout my lifetime, since 1930, I have watched the mills of the region and their attendant chapels die… the population of the valley and the hillsides, so rooted for so long, is changing rapidly.*[12]

Godwin considers her photographs documentary rather than Romantic. However, here her work seeks to reconcile the moorland, with its sheep, curlews and drystone walls, with the ivy-clad mill chimneys and blackened chapels, wet streets and canals of the towns. They are all weathered and ruined by the same skies. Godwin's *Our*

Fig. 10.14 John Kippin (b.1950), Hidden, 1995, photograph.

Forbidden Land (1990) is angrier, a diatribe against the institutional landowners who control the appearance of the landscape, public access to it, and the very ways we appreciate it. The Forestry Commission, the National Trust, English Heritage, and the Ministries of Defence and Agriculture are all grist to her mill.

These changes and intrusions are also the concern of photographer John Davies, whose major series *Druridge Bay* (1983) coincided with the threat to build a nuclear power station on this stretch of Northumberland coastal dunes. John Kippin's work has included ironic juxtapositions that, too, are a critique of our use of, and attitude to, the natural and built heritage: the heritage 'fayres' in the landscaped park beneath the ramparts of Alnwick Castle; a panorama of car parking next to the Metrocentre in ex-industrial Tyneside; the ruins of a fighter plane used for target practice on a firing range high on the Cheviots (Fig. 10.14). Sirkka-Liisa Konttinen's photographic masterpiece, *Byker* (1983), records in words and images the loss and destruction of a different landscape and community, the tightly knit urban and human fabric of the strikingly situated Newcastle industrial suburb. Her recent project *The Coal Coast* (2000–02) shows how the industrial debris of the Durham coalfield is now being reabsorbed into nature through processes of corrosion and erosion.

If art records the history of our region, it provides a true enough picture.

NOTES

1 Blount 1665, quoted in Godwin 1985.
2 Anon 1651.
3 Defoe 1724–7.
4 Gilpin 1768, x.
5 Hedley 1982.
6 Arts Council of Great Britain 1983.
7 Knight 1935, 69.
8 quoted in Cooper 1986, 85.
9 for local artists in the region *see* Turnbull 1976 and Hall 1982.
10 James 1966.
11 Hepworth 1970.
12 Hughes 1979.

11

Landscape Change, Conservation and Management

F H A AALEN

Thousands of years of interacting natural and human processes are responsible for the wide range of scenic contrasts in the North East. The main landscape types in the region include wide upland moors, seemingly natural but in fact much humanised; rural lowlands moulded over long periods by a succession of farming communities; industrial areas which have a strong individuality imparted to them by the intermingling of farming and mining; and massively urbanised areas. As well as these broad categories, there is a mosaic of distinctive local landscapes produced by the adjustment of local communities to the physique and resources of their close environment. Protection of this rich landscape heritage requires land-use policies that promote the diversity, beauty and accessibility of the countryside and the careful management of urban growth.

Concern for the character and quality of the wider landscape (as distinct from mere sites and precincts) is not entirely new. A reformed countryside, combining the production of vital products such as food and timber with an attractive landscape, was the objective of many landowners and farmers involved in agricultural improvement of the 18th and early 19th centuries and their activities have certainly left a considerable legacy in the farmed landscapes of the North East. In that same period, a growing awareness of the historical and aesthetic character of the region's landscape finds expression in art and literature and, not least, in antiquarianism with the Roman wall and the numerous ruined castles and monasteries as objects of scholarly interest.

Before improvement had run its course, the landscape of many areas in England was being transformed by industrialisation, urban growth and the development of improved roads and railways, and as these forces gathered momentum in the 19th century there was increasing concern for the protection of nature and the countryside. In northern England, literary figures such as William Wordsworth and John Ruskin, were particularly eloquent spokesmen.[1] Numerous voluntary environmental organisations were formed in England in the second half of the 19th century to protect different aspects of the countryside and also to introduce rural elements, such as trees, parks and gardens, into urban environments. For example, the Commons Preservation Society, founded in 1865, struggled to preserve public rights over the commons and forests around London and other cities. In time, the concern for the countryside spread to rural areas and threats in the Lake District led to the formation of the National Trust in 1895 to protect beautiful landscapes for cultural and amenity reasons and, as the Trust developed, to be custodian for properties given to the nation. The Trust has played a significant role in the

Fig. 11.1 Wallington Hall, near Cambo in Northumberland, *was built at the end of the 17th century by Sir William Blackett, a Newcastle merchant, on the site of a medieval border castle and a Tudor house. The wide moorland wastes on the Wallington estate were transformed by fields, roads and woods. The Trevelyans moved to Wallington at the end of the 18th century. Capability Brown laid out the gardens and Ruskin advised on the development of the Hall. Wallington is now a National Trust Property.*

Fig. 11.2 George Macaulay Trevelyan, 1876–1962, *inherited the Wallington estate. A distinguished historian and lover of Northumberland's landscapes, he gave impetus to the 20th-century movement for countryside conservation through his writings and involvement with the National Trust and youth hostels.*

North East, especially through the acquisition in the 1930s of stretches of the Roman wall and its dramatic landscape setting, acquisition of landed estates such as Wallington (Fig. 11.1) and, most recently, care of the coastline through the Enterprise Neptune scheme.[2]

A broad, diverse movement for the planning and preservation of the English landscape emerged in the 1920s and 1930s,[3] in which the historian George Macaulay Trevelyan, a Northumbrian squire and strong supporter of the National Trust, became an influential voice (Fig. 11.2). His publications *Must England's Beauty Perish* (1926) and *The Calls and Claims of Natural Beauty* (1931) mark him as one of the outstanding champions of countryside preservation of his generation. In 1926 the Council for the Preservation (now Protection) of Rural England was set up to co-ordinate the activities of the growing range of voluntary bodies involved with countryside preservation and to act as a 'watchdog over the landscape as a whole' (Fig. 11.3).

No serious approach to conservation and planning of the wider landscape in England was achieved until after the Second World War when the National Parks and Access to the Countryside Act was passed in 1949. Three National Parks were designated in the North East, all in upland areas: the North York Moors (1952); the Yorkshire Dales (1954); and Northumberland (1956). These territories, each administered by its own National Park Authority, occupy together some 4,220sq km, roughly the area of an average English county. Unlike their counterparts in most parts of the world, English National Parks are not wilderness areas but are defined as 'extensive areas of beautiful and relatively wild country'; the land remains in private ownership and people continue to live and work there. The park authorities have undertaken the delicate balancing act of conserving the upland landscapes while promoting recreation and tourism within them. Conservation and recreation are not mutually exclusive but their interests are not identical. Recreation can generally defer to conservation without undue harm; but were conservation to constantly yield to recreation, then both, ironically, would soon decline. National Parks contribute to the environmental and economic well-being of the North East and have further potential as laboratories for the pioneering of large-scale, sustainable, multi-purpose rural development, which can be of relevance to the broader landscape and the countryside as a whole. The increasingly vulnerable position of upland livestock farming presents a formidable challenge. Extensive pastoralism lends the hills a serenity and assurance, which belie economic and environmental realities. However, another event such as the foot-and-mouth disaster of 2000, could be

fatal to the ailing farm economy, seriously undermining the basic land-use system and leading to deep changes in the ecology and vegetation cover. This in turn would diminish the picturesque qualities of the landscapes on which leisure, tourism and services, the activities which have now replaced farming as the mainstay of local rural economies, depend.

Along with the National Parks there is now an array of additional landscape protection measures. The region is well-endowed with Areas of Outstanding Natural Beauty: the Howardian Hills, the Nidderdale Moors and, much the biggest, the North Pennines. These areas do not have separate administrative arrangements but are given special protection in national and local administrative arrangements. Heritage Coasts, a designation introduced in the 1980s to place emphasis on coastal protection, include North Northumberland, North Yorkshire and Cleveland, Flamborough Head and Spurn (the tip of Holderness). In 1987 the Roman wall and its surrounds was designated a World Heritage Site by UNESCO and is now subject to comprehensive management as an intrinsic part of the Northumbrian landscape.[4] Among recent innovations in the region are the Community Forests, which are being developed around the fringes of towns and cities in industrial areas and include the Great North Forest to the south and west of Newcastle, Cleveland Forest around Teesside, and the South Yorkshire Forest on the southern borders of the region between Rotherham, Barnsley and Sheffield. These multi-purpose projects will create a mosaic of woodland and other land uses, restoring areas scarred by industrial dereliction. They will protect areas of historical and ecological interest and provide opportunities for recreation and employment by developing, for example, timber and other woodland products (Fig. 11.4).

Over the last three or four decades of the 20th century, major landscape change in the North East occurred in two distinct settings, namely areas of mining and industry in decline and farming areas increasingly affected by a revolution in agricultural technology and tight economic circumstances. In the extensive, densely populated areas that have experienced terminal decline of coalmining and other traditional industries, an objective of planning was to erase the old image of widespread industrial clutter and dereliction and replace it with one that would stimulate economic regeneration by attracting inward investors and tourists alike.[5] A visitor to Consett in County Durham would hardly know that a generation ago this was a steel-working town. Massive programmes of clearance and rehabilitation were carried out to transform the devastated landscapes of mining in many parts of the region, including south-east

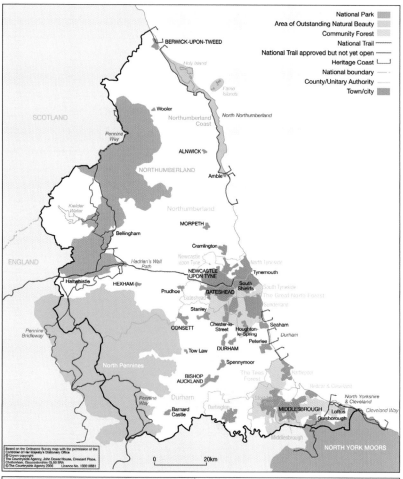

National Park
Area of Outstanding Natural Beauty
Community Forest
National Trail
National Trail approved but not yet open
Heritage Coast
National boundary
County/Unitary Authority
Town/city

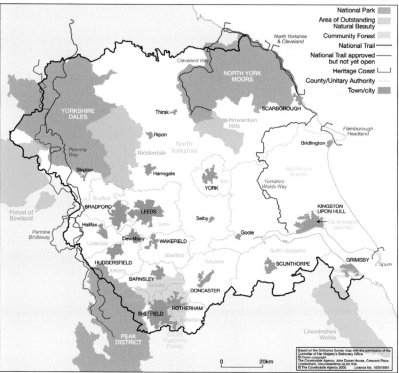

National Park
Area of Outstanding Natural Beauty
Community Forest
National Trail
National Trail approved but not yet open
Heritage Coast
County/Unitary Authority
Town/city

Northumberland, lowland Durham, Cleveland and West Yorkshire. The outcome has been in part an engineered restoration of the earlier pre-industrial countryside with, for example, collieries and mountains of mining refuse levelled and planted with trees or restored to agriculture; however, other introduced elements, such as the extensive new road systems and the numerous housing and industrial estates, are a clear break with the past.

In the rural lowlands, and especially the arable lands, farming techniques have changed substantially since the Second World War, with intensive use of agro-chemicals, powerful machinery and 'prairie farming'. This has led to widespread removal of enclosures and has wreaked havoc on flora and fauna; at the same time, old farmsteads have acquired massive metal sheds and barns of white, grey or vaguely green sheet-metal with little architectural character or individuality, which now often dominate the original buildings. Many of these innovations were first encouraged by an unprecedented level of support from the national exchequer and later by subsidies and other land-use measures introduced by the European Commission in order to increase agricultural production. There is now, however, a growing European emphasis on reducing rather than increasing the levels of agricultural production, and on the development of policies to protect the environment and landscape. There is still a shortage of rural employment and it is only agricultural subsidies that keep many of the farmers on the land and a growing number of them have taken up part-time occupations. Farm activities have diversified and now include tourism and leisure, camping, holiday letting, growth of specialist foods and the conversion of the larger farmsteads into residences, workshops and businesses.

In the countryside, the sheet-metal structures are limited to farms and tend to be spread out, but over a generation or so groups of large buildings of this sort have come to be a

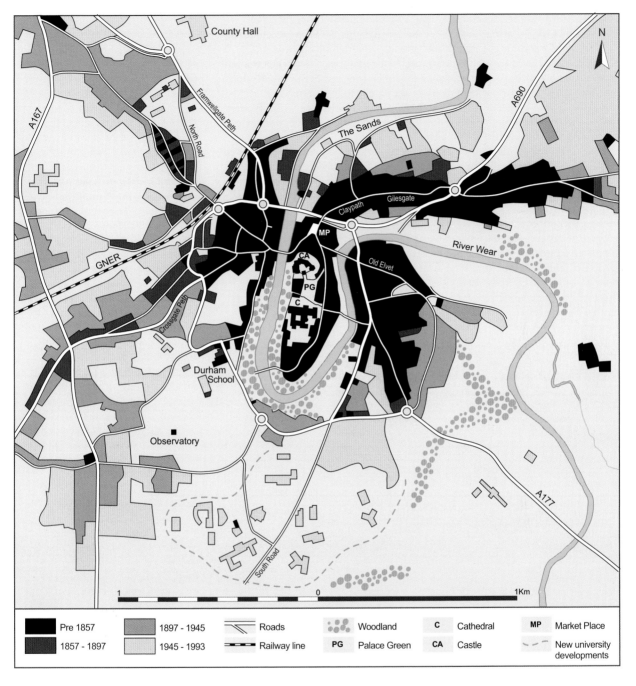

| Pre 1857 | | 1897 - 1945 | | Roads | | Woodland | **C** | Cathedral | **MP** | Market Place |
| 1857 - 1897 | | 1945 - 1993 | | Railway line | **PG** | Palace Green | **CA** | Castle | | New university developments |

OPPOSITE PAGE:

Fig. 11.4 Designated and defined interests, Countryside Agency, 2005.
Landscape protection is strongly biased towards upland areas where the National Parks and Areas of Outstanding Natural Beauty are located. In the lowlands, stretches of dramatic coastal scenery are protected as Heritage Coast and Community Forests are being developed around major urban areas.

Fig. 11.5 Durham. *Landscape concerns generally focus on the countryside but many towns and cities also have outstanding landscape attributes. At Durham, the medieval castle, cathedral and town stand on a rock almost encircled by a deep wooded gorge in a loop of the River Wear, and early suburbs grew along ridge routes converging on the old settlement. Durham thus gives the appearance of having grown up organically, with natural and human elements enhancing each other. At least until the suburbanisation and ribbon development of the 1930s, the city escaped the physical degradation common to towns in industrial parts of England. In his plan for Durham in 1944, Thomas Sharp, like Ruskin before him, saw this historic city as a superb landscape, the most dramatic in England, and emphasised that future developments should be undertaken with serious regard to their context, scale, siting and building materials (based on Roberts 2003).*

distinctive feature of the landscape of motorways and urban fringes: the now-familiar retail and industrial parks. They are conspicuous, for example, along the M62 west of Leeds or at the edge of the Tyneside conurbation on an axis alongside the A19 north of the Tyne Tunnel. Along motorways and trunk roads they create ribbon developments, pulling the urban fringes into the countryside; and, with their extensive car-parking areas, they come to form a new and distinctive type of built landscape without the density of structure which typifies the traditional urban area, yet being in no sense rural, despite the attention which is often given to their landscape architecture.

Landscapes can legitimately be considered as heritage, that is a set of inherited benefits, but they cannot be frozen in their present form, unique and admired though they may be. However, neither can we allow unrestrained forces, private or public, to continue to degrade and standardise our landscapes. The challenge is to protect and enhance landscape quality and character in the course of change, accepting that change is inevitable but insisting on a better kind of progress. Conservation and creation are not antithetical. Landscape conservation cannot be a purist pursuit governed by aesthetic or preservationist values to the neglect of other interests: it must be located within the framework of broader policies for overall economic and social development. The landscape, in short, must be simultaneously used and protected, with socio-economic progress and landscape quality as mutually supportive rather than competitive goals. The primary objectives therefore are the maintenance of valued features and the

Fig. 11.6 Wensleydale is the widest and most varied of the Pennine dales. Its broad, level floor supports productive pastureland with stone-walled fields and considerable woodland, in contrast to the open moor on the surrounding hills. Sustaining this beauty and scenic interest is dependent on a successful rural economy with a sensible balance of farming and recreational activities, and a combination of the cultural lessons of the vernacular with a sustainable view of the future.

accommodation of change. Regular upkeep of the working landscape by informed positive action on the ground is fundamental and this can either be done directly or through public bodies able to influence such work by advice, grants and regulations. Although declining in economic significance, farming is still the major land use and environmentally sensitive farming systems that maintain the distinctive local character of the countryside must be more strongly and consistently encouraged. We must ensure that significant changes made in the landscape are attentive to historical continuity, and that a concern for landscape quality is injected into all new land uses.

The European Landscape Convention, which is supported by the Council of Europe and became effective from March 2004, is the first international treaty specifically concerned with landscape. It is a Europe-wide agreement prompted by concerns that the quality and variety of Europe's landscapes are being diminished by many potent forces, including intensive farming and forestry, expanding tourism and rural suburbanisation, urban and industrial growths and a general standardisation of culture. The Convention emphasises the need to 'identify, evaluate, protect, manage and plan our landscapes', rural and urban.[6] The objective is not to resist the process of landscape change but to guide and manage it. Of course, the full implications of this will take some time to work out. Putting the Convention into practice will require, among other things, increased collaboration between central and local government and local communities to reconcile a wide range of opinion about the future of the landscape and to develop the means of achieving the objective.[7]

Our present countryside has been moulded and managed primarily by farmers and landowners. But countryside and towns are inextricably linked and many of the landscape-consuming pressures in the countryside result from urban requirements (Fig. 11.5). Planning and regeneration within the towns and cities might reduce these pressures but are unlikely to eliminate them. The decline of farming, save perhaps in upland areas, is thus unlikely to result in depopulated landscapes and gradual reversion to woodland. On the contrary, new and essentially urban-generated pressures, residential, recreational and commercial, will multiply in the countryside as farming contracts, and increasingly it will be questioned whether the fabric of the historic landscape created by farmers can realistically be retained. We have to develop a coherent vision for the countryside as traditional farming shrinks (Fig. 11.6). It is not simply a mere patchwork quilt of land-use designations that is required, but positive provision for the wide range of old and new activities that will jostle to use the rural environment – residual farming, forestry, a variety of recreational pursuits, rural housing and amenities, wind farms, mineral extraction, and other infrastructure projects.[8] Some specialisation for agricultural use may well arise on areas of highly productive land but the main challenge for landscape management lies in the wider countryside where the overall aim is surely not to segregate production and conservation but to fuse them, to inject landscape quality into all land uses and encourage sensitive design for new developments so as to enhance the diversity and distinctiveness of the historical landscape. These considerations particularly apply to the North East with its varied landscapes and the complex juxtaposition of deeply rural, farmed lowlands, upland moors, old industrial areas where urban and rural settlement intermingle, and extensive conurbations.

NOTES

1   Bate 1991; Wheeler 1995.
2   Woodside & Crow 1999.
3   Matless 1998.
4   Woodside & Crow 1999.
5   Ward & Lowe 2001.
6   Council of Europe 2000.
7   Jenkins 2002; Sissons 2001.
8   Green & Voss 2001.

Bibliography

Albert, W 1972 *The Turnpike System of England, 1663–1840.* London: Cambridge University Press

Aldcroft, D H 1963 'The eclipse of the coastal shipping trade, 1913–1921'. *Journal of Transport History* **6**, 24–38

Allan, A J 1992 *Lubetkin, Architecture and the Tradition of Progress.* London: RIBA Publications

Allison, K J (ed.) 1961 *The Victoria History of the County of York: East Riding* Vol. I. London: Oxford University Press for the University of London Institute of Historical Research

Allison, K J 1976 *The East Riding of Yorkshire Landscape.* London: Hodder & Stoughton

Anon 1651 *News from Newcastle.* London: William Ellis

Appleton, W 1966 'Transport and the landscape of northern England' *in* House, J W (ed.) *Northern Geographical Essays.* Newcastle: Oriel Press

Arts Council of Great Britain 1983 *Landscape in Britain 1850–1950.* London: ACGB

Austin, D 1989 *The Deserted Medieval Village of Thrislington, County Durham.* Lincoln: Society for Medieval Archaeology **12**

Barnwell, P S and Giles, C 1997 *English Farmsteads, 1750–1914.* Swindon: Royal Commission on the Historical Monuments of England

Bate, J 1991 *Romantic Ecology: Wordsworth and the Environmental Tradition.* London: Routledge

Bateman, E *et al.* (eds) 1893–1940 *A History of Northumberland* (15 vols). Newcastle upon Tyne: Andrew Reid & Co Ltd

Bates, C 1891 'Border holds of Northumberland'. *Archaeologia Aeliana*, 2 ser **14**, 16–25

Bell, C and Bell, R 1969 *City Fathers: the Early History of Town Planning in Britain.* London: Barrie & Rockcliffe

Beresford, M 1967 *New Towns of the Middle Ages: Town Plantation in England, Wales and Gascony.* London: Lutterworth Press

Beresford, M and Hurst, J 1990 *Wharram Percy: Deserted Medieval Village.* London: Batsford

Bidwell, P T and Holbrook, N 1989 *Hadrian's Wall Bridges.* London: English Heritage

Black, J and MacRaild, D M 2003 *Nineteenth-Century Britain.* Basingstoke: Palgrave Macmillan

Blount, T 1656 *Glossographia.* London: Scholar Press

de Boer, G 1964 'The Pennines, wolds, moors and coast of Yorkshire' *in* Steers, J A (ed.) 1964 *op. cit.*

Bridgland, D, Horton, B and Innes, J (eds) 1999 *The Quaternary of North-East England, a Field Guide.* London: Quaternary Research Association

Burgess, C 1984 'The prehistoric settlement of Northumberland: a speculative survey' *in* Miket, R and Burgess, C (eds) *Between and Beyond the Walls.* Edinburgh: J Donald

Butlin, R (ed.) 2003 *Historical Atlas of North Yorkshire.* Otley: Westbury

Camden, W 1586 *Britannia, or a Corographical Description of England, Scotland and Ireland.* Facsimile edition 1971. Newton Abbot: David & Charles

Campey, L 1989, 'Medieval village plans in County Durham'. *Northern History* **25**, 60–87

Cantor, L 1987 *The Changing English Countryside 1400–1700.* London: Routledge & Kegan Paul

Charlton, B 1987 *Upper North Tynedale: a Northumbrian Valley and its People.* Newcastle upon Tyne: Northumbrian Water

Clack, P A G 1980 'The origins and growth of early Darlington' *in* Riden, P (ed.) 1980, 67–84

Clack, P A G 1982 'The Browney Valley'. *Transactions of the Architectural and Archaeological Society of Durham and Northumberland* new ser **6**, 13–17

Clark, P (ed.) 2000 *The Cambridge Urban History of Britain* (Vol. II, 1540–1840). Cambridge: Cambridge University Press

Clifton-Taylor, A 1972 *The Pattern of English Building.* London: Faber & Faber

Clifton-Taylor, A 1981 *Six More English Towns.* London: BBC

Conzen M R G 1949 'Modern settlement' *in Scientific Survey of North-Eastern England*, 75–86. British Association for the Advancement of Science

Conzen, M R G 1960 *Alnwick, Northumberland: a Study in Town-Plan Analysis.* London: Institute of British Geographers Publication no. 27

Cooper, H A 1986 *Winslow Homer Watercolours.* Washington & New Haven: Yale University Press

Council of Europe 2000 *European Landscape Convention.* Strasbourg

Countryside Commission 1998 *Countryside Character, Vol. I: North East.* Cheltenham: Countryside Commission

Craster, H H E 1914 *Northumberland County History* Vol. X: *The Parish of Corbridge.* Newcastle upon Tyne: Andrew Reid

Creigh, J C 1996 'Landscape and people in East Durham' *in* House, J W (ed.) *Northern Geographical Essays.* Newcastle: Oriel Press

Curnock, N (ed.) 1909 *The Journal of the Rev John Wesley*, A M (8 vols). London: Robert Culley [Vol I] and Charles H Kelly [Vols II–VIII]

Dark, P 2000 *The Environment of Britain in the First Millenium AD* London: Duckworth

Daunton, M J 1995 *Poverty and Progress: An Economic and Social History of Britain, 1750–1850.* Oxford: Oxford University Press

Defoe, D 1724–7 *A Tour thro' the Whole Island of Great Britain.* London: G Strahan

Defoe, D 1927 *A Tour thro' the Whole Island of Great Britain*. (1724–6; edition with an introduction by G D H Cole) 2 vols. London: Peter Davies

Dewdney, J (ed.) 1970 *Durham County and City with Teesside*. Durham: British Association for the Advancement of Science

Done, A and Muir, R 2001 'The landscape history of grouse shooting in the Yorkshire Dales'. *Rural History* 12, 195–210

Dumayne, L and Barber, K 1994 'The impact of the Romans on the environment of northern England: pollen data from three sites close to Hadrian's Wall'. *The Holocene* 4.2, 165–73

Durham County Council 2003 *The County Durham Landscape Character Assessment*.

Ellis, S and Crowther, D 1990 *Humberside Perspectives. A Region through the Ages*. Hull: Hull University Press

Faull, M L and Moorhouse, S A (eds) 1981 *West Yorkshire: an archaeological Survey to AD 1500*. 4 vols. Wakefield: West Yorkshire Metropolitan County Council

Fell, C 1964 'The great Langdale stone-axe factory'. *Transactions of the Cumberland and Westmorland Antiquary and Archaeological Society*, new ser 50

Fenton-Thomas, C 2003 *Late Pre-historic and Early Historic Landscapes on the Yorkshire Chalk*. BAR British Series 350. Oxford: Archaeopress

Fleming, A 1998 *Swaledale, Valley of the Wild River*. Edinburgh: Edinburgh University Press

Foster, S and Smout, T C (eds) 1994 *The History of Soils and Field Systems*. Aberdeen: Scottish Cultural Press

Fraser, C M 1955 'The Gilly Corn Rental and the Customary of the Convent of Durham'. *Archaeologia Aeliana*, 4 ser 33, 53

Frodsham, P 2004 *Archaeology in Northumberland National Park*. CBA Research Report 136. York: Council for British Archaeology

Gilpin, W 1768 *Essay on Prints*. London: Frankfurt und Leipzig

Girouard, M 1992 *Town and Country*. New Haven & London: Yale University Press

Godwin, F 1985 *Land*. London: Little Brown

Grady, K 1989 *The Georgian Public Buildings of Leeds and the West Riding*. Leeds: Thoresby Society

Graham, F 1984 *Maps of Newcastle*. Newcastle upon Tyne: Frank Graham

Green, B and Voss, W 2001 *Threatened Landscapes*. London & New York: Spon Press

Hall, M 1973 *The Artists of Northumbria*. Newcastle upon Tyne: Marshall Hall Associates

Hanson, J 'Excavations at Hestlerton, North Yorkshire 1972–82' in Hanson, J and Harding, A F 1981 'Excavations in the prehistoric ritual complex near Millfield in Northumberland'. *Proceedings of the Prehistoric Society* 47, 87–136

Harding, J and Johnstone, R (eds) 2000 *Northern Pasts. Interpretation of the Later Prehistory of Northern England and Southern Scotland*. BAR British Series 302. Oxford: Archaeopress

Harris, H 1969 *The Rural Landscape of the East Riding of Yorkshire 1700–1850*. Wakefield: S R Publishers

Harrison, B and Hutton B 1984 *Vernacular Houses in North Yorkshire and Cleveland*. Edinburgh: J Donald

Harrison, S 2002 *The History of Driffield from the Earliest Times to the Year 2000*. Pickering: Blackthorn

Hedley, G 1982 *The Picturesque Tour in Northumberland and Durham, c.1720–1830*. Newcastle upon Tyne: Tyne & Wear County Council Museums

Hepple, L W 2004 'Reconstruction of a medieval charter boundary at Sturton Grange'. *Archaeologia Aeliana*, 5 ser 33, 89–115

Hepworth, B 1970 *A Pictorial Autobiography*. Bath: Adams & Dart

Hey, D 1986 *Yorkshire from AD 1000*. London & New York: Longman

Higham, N 1986 *The Northern Counties to AD 1000*. London: Longman

Higham, N 1993 *The Kingdom of Northumbria AD 350–1100*. Stroud: Alan Sutton

Hindle, B P 1993 *Roads, Tracks and their Interpretation*. London: Batsford

House, J W (ed.) 1966 *Northern Geographical Essays*. Newcastle upon Tyne: Oriel

Hughes, P 1999 'Staiths (the early river jetties of York, Hull and Howden)'. *Yorkshire Archaeological Journal* 71, 155–84

Hughes, P 1979 *Remains of Elmet: a Pennine sequence*. London: Faber

Illingworth, J L 1970 *Yorkshire's Ruined Castles*. 2nd edn. Wakefield: S R Publishers

James, P (ed.) 1966 *Henry Moore on Sculpture*. London: Macdonald

Jarrett, M and Wrathmell, S 1977 'Sixteenth and seventeenth-century farmsteads: West Whelpington, Northumberland'. *Agricultural History Review*, 25, 108–19

Jenkins, J (ed.) 2002 *Remaking the Landscape: the Changing Face of Britain*. London: Profile Books Ltd

Jennings, B (ed.) 1967 *A History of Nidderdale*. Huddersfield: Advertiser Press

Jennings, B 1999 *Yorkshire Monasteries: Cloister, Land and People*. Otley: Smith Settle

Jewell, H M 1994 *The North-South Divide: the Origins of Northern Consciousness in England*. Manchester: Manchester University Press

Johnson, M 1988 'A medieval harbour at Flamborough'. *Yorkshire Archaeological Journal* 60, 105–12

Johnson, S 1994 *English Heritage Book of Hadrian's Wall*. London: Batsford

Jones, M 2000 *The Making of the South Yorkshire Landscape*. Barnsley: Freepost

Jones, M 2003 *Sheffield's Woodland Heritage*. Rotherham: Green Tree

Jones, N (ed.) 1988 *A Dynamic Estuary: Man, Nature and the Humber*. Hull: Hull University Press

Kappelle, W E 1979 *The Norman Conquest of the North: the Region and its Transformation*. London: Croom Helm

Knight, L 1935 *Painting an Adventure*. London: Nicholson & Watson

Koditschek, T 1990 *Class Formation and Urban Industrial Society: Bradford, 1750–1850*. Cambridge: Cambridge University Press

Langdale, T 1822 *Topographical Dictionary of Yorkshire*. Northallerton: J Langdale

Linsley, S 1998 *Spanning the Tyne: Building the Tyne Bridge, 1926–28*. Newcastle upon Tyne: Newcastle Libraries & Information Service

Linton, D 1956 *Sheffield and its Region*. Sheffield: British Association for the Advancement of Science

Lomas, R A 1982 'A northern farm at the end of the Middle Ages: Elvethall Manor, Durham, 1443–4, 1513–14'. *Northern History* 28

Lomas, R A 1989 'The Black Death in County Durham'. *Journal of Medieval History* 15, 127–40

Lomas, R A 1992 *North-East England in the Middle Ages*. Edinburgh: John Donald

Lomas, R A 1996 *County of Conflict; Northumberland from Conquest to Civil War*. East Linton: Tuckwell Press

Lyte, M 1920–23 *Liber Feodorum 1: 1198–1242*. London: HMSO

Martins, S W 2002 *The English Model Farm*. London: English Heritage

Matless, D 1998 *Landscape and Englishness*. London: Reaktion Books

McCord, N 1979 *North-East England: an Economic and Social History*. London: Batsford

McCord, N and Thompson, R 1998 *The Northern Counties from AD 1000. A Regional History of England*. London: Longman

McDonnell, J 1992 'Pressures on Yorkshire woodland in the later Middle Ages'. *Northern History* **28**

Mellars, P and Dark, P 1998 *Star Carr in Context*. Cambridge: McDonald Institute for Archaeological Research

Mercer, R and Tipping, R 1994 'The prehistory of soil erosion in the northern and eastern Cheviot Hills, Anglo-Scottish Borders' *in* Foster, S and Smout, T C (eds) 1994 *op. cit.*

Miller, I (ed.) 2002 *Steeped in History. The Alum Industry of North-East Yorkshire*. North York Moors National Park

Morris, C (ed.) 1949 *The Journeys of Celia Fiennes*. London: Cresset Press

Muir, R 1997 *The Yorkshire Countryside. A Landscape History*. Keele: Keele University Press

Muir, R 2000 *The New Reading the Landscape*. Exeter: Exeter University Press

Muir, R 2001 *Landscape Detective*. Macclesfield: Windgather Press

Musgrove, F 1990 *The North of England; a History from Roman Times to the Present*. Oxford: Basil Blackwell

Neal, D 1996 *Excavations on the Roman Villa at Beadlam, Yorkshire*. Yorkshire Archaeological Report 2. Leeds: Yorkshire Archaeological Society

Newton, R 1972 *The Northumberland Landscape*. London: Hodder & Stoughton

O'Brien, C 2002 'The early medieval shires of Yeavering, Breamish and Bamburgh'. *Archaeologia Aeliana* 5 ser **30**, 53–73

Page, W (ed.) 1907–13 *The Victoria History of the County of York* (3 vols). London: Constable

Page, W (ed.) 1914–23 *The Victoria History of the County of York: North Riding* (2 vols) London: Constable

Palliser, D M (ed.) 2000 *The Cambridge History of Britain* (Vol. I, 600–1540) Cambridge: Cambridge University Press

Pallister, A F and Pallister, P M J 1978 'A survey of the deserted medieval village of Newsham'. *Transactions of the Architectural and Archaeological Society of Durham and Northumberland*, 2 ser **4**, 8

Penoyre, J and Penroyre J 1978 *Houses in the Landscape. A Regional Study of Vernacular Buildings in England and Wales*. London: Faber & Faber

Pevsner, N 1966 *The Buildings of England: Yorkshire, the North Riding*. London: Penguin

Pevsner, N *et al.* 1967 *The Buildings of England: Yorkshire, the West Riding*. London: Penguin

Pevsner, N *et al.* 1992 *The Buildings of England: Northumberland*. London: Penguin

Pevsner, N *et al.* 2002 *The Buildings of England: County Durham*. New Haven & London: Yale University Press

Powlesland, D 2003 'The Early-Middle Anglo-Saxon Period (AD 400–AD 850)' *in* Butlin, R (ed.) 2003, *op. cit.* 64–7

Powlesland, D with Haughton, C and Hanson, J 1986 'Excavations at Heslerton, North Yorkshire 1972–82'. *Archaeological Journal* **143**, 53–173

Radley, J and Mellars, P 1964 'A Mesolithic structure at Deepcar, Yorkshire, and the affinities of associated industries'. *Proceedings of the Prehistoric Society* **30**, 1–24

Raistrick, A 1967 *Old Yorkshire Dales*. London: David & Charles

Raistrick, A 1968 *The Pennine Dales*. London: Eyre & Spottiswoode

Raistrick, A 1970 *West Riding of Yorkshire*. London: Hodder & Stoughton

Raistrick, A 1978 *Green Roads in the Mid-Pennines*. Buxton: Moorland Publishing Company

Riden, P (ed.) 1980 *The Medieval Town in Britain*, papers from the first Gregynog Seminar in Local History, December 1978, Cardiff Papers in Local History, 1. University College, Cardiff: Department of Extra-Mural Studies

Raistrick, A 1991 *Arthur Raistrick's Yorkshire Dales* (compiled by David Joy). Clapham: Dalesman

Royal Commission on the Historical Monuments of England 1986 *Rural Houses of West Yorkshire 1400–1830*. London

Royal Commission on the Historical Monuments of England 1987 *Houses of the North York Moors*. London

Rennison, R.W. 1979 *Water to Tyneside: a History of the Newcastle and Gateshead Water Company*. Newcastle upon Tyne: The Company

Roberts, B and Wrathmell, S 2000 *An Atlas of Rural Settlement in England*. London: English Heritage

Roberts, B and Wrathmell, S 2002 *Region and Place: a Study of English Rural Settlement*. London: English Heritage

Roberts, B and Austin, D 1975 *A Preliminary Checklist of Rural Clusters in County Durham*. Durham: University of Durham, Department of Geography

Rogers, H C B 1961 *Turnpike to Iron Road*. London: Seeley Service

Ryder, P 1992 'Bastles and bastle-like buildings in Allendale, Northumberland'. *Archaeological Journal* **149**, 351–3

Scammell, G V 1956 *Hugh Du Puisset, Bishop of Durham*. Cambridge: Cambridge University Press

Simmons, I G 1996 *The Environmental Impact of Later Mesolithic Cultures*. Edinburgh: Edinburgh University Press

Sissons, M (ed.) 2001 *A Countryside for All: the Future of Rural Britain*. Ashgate: Vintage

Smailes, A E 1960 *North England*. London & Edinburgh: Thomas Nelson

Smith, C 1990 'Excavations at Dod Law West Hillfort, Northumberland'. *Northern Archaeology* **9** (1988–9), 1–55

Smith, C 1992 'The population of Late Upper Palaeolithic Britain'. *Proceedings of the Prehistoric Society* **58**, 37–40

Smout, T 2000 *Nature Contested: Environmental History in Scotland and Northern England since 1600*. Edinburgh: Edinburgh University Press

Spratt, D A and Harrison, B J D 1996 *The North York Moors. Landscape History*. North York Moors National Park

Steers, J (ed.) 1964 *Field Studies in the British Isles*. London: Nelson

Stoertz, C 1997 *Ancient Landscapes of the Yorkshire Wolds*. Swindon: Royal Commission on the Historical Monuments of England

Swan, G A 1993 *Flora of Northumberland*. Newcastle upon Tyne: Natural History Society of Northumbria

Teasdale, D and Hughes, D 1999 'The glacial history of north-east England', *in* Bridgland, D 1999 *op. sit.*

Thompson, F M L 1963 *English Landed Society in the Nineteenth Century*. London: Routledge & Kegan Paul

Tillott, P M (ed.) 1961 *The Victoria County History of Yorkshire; the City of York*. Oxford: Oxford University Press, for the University of London Institute of Historical Research

Tipping, R 1998 'Towards an environmental history of the Bowmont Valley and the northern Cheviot Hills'. *Landscape History* **20**, 41–50

Tolan-Smith, C (ed.) 1997 *Landscape Archaeology in Tyneside*. Newcastle: Department of Archaeology, University of Newcastle upon Tyne

Tolan-Smith, C and Bonsall, C 1999 'Stone Age Studies in the British Isles: the impact of accelerator dating', *in* Evin, J *et al.* (eds) *14C and Archaeology Acts of 3rd International Symposium* (Lyon 1998) Memoires de la Société Prehistorique Français Tome XXVI, 1999 et supplement 1999 de la Revue d'Archeometrie. Rennes: University de Rennes, 249–57

Tolan-Smith, M 1997 'The Romano British and Late Prehistoric landscape: the deconstruction of a Medieval landscape' *in* Tolan-Smith, C 1997 *op. cit.*

Tomaney, J and Ward, N (eds) 2001 *A Region in Transition: North-East England at the Millenium*. Aldershot: Ashgate

Topping, P 1989 'Early cultivation in Northumberland and the Borders'. *Proceedings of Prehistoric Society* **55**, 161–97

Turnbull, H 1976 *Artists of Yorkshire: A Short Dictionary*. Bedale

Van de Noort, R 2001 'Scaftworth, a Roman bridge and road in the wetlands'. *Current Archaeology* **172** xv, 168–9

Van de Noort, R 2004 *The Humber Wetlands. The Archaeology of a Dynamic Landscape*. Macclesfield: Windgather Press

Van de Noort, R and Ellis, S (eds) 1995 *Wetland Archaeology of Holderness; an Archaeological Survey*. Hull: Wetlands Project, University of Hull

Van de Noort, R and Fletcher, W 2000 'Bronze Age ecodynamics in the Humber Estuary' *in* Bailey, G, Charles, R and Winder, N (eds) *Human Ecodynamics*, Symposia of Association for Environmental Archaeology **19**, 46–54. Oxford: Oxbow Books

Viner, B E 1984 'The excavation of a Neolithic cairn at Street House, Loftus, Cleveland'. *Proceedings of the Prehistoric Society* **50**, 151–95

Waddington, C 1999 *A Landscape Archaeological Study of the Mesolithic-Neolithic in the Millfield Basin, Northumberland*. BAR British Series 291. Oxford: British Archaeological Reports

Waddington, C and Passmore, D 2004 *Ancient Northumberland*. Wooler: Countrystore

Ward, N and Lowe, P 2001 'The "rural" in the "region": towards an inclusive regional policy for the North East', *in* Tomaney, J and Ward, N (eds) 2001, *op. cit.* 18–98

Watkins, P 1989 *Bolton Priory and its Church*. Bolton Priory Church Council

Watts, S J 1975 *From Border to Middle Shire: Northumberland 1586–1625*. Leicester: Leicester University Press

Wheeler, M (ed.) 1995 *Ruskin and Environment: the Storm Cloud of the Nineteenth Century*. Manchester: Manchester University Press

Whellan, F 1894 *History, Topography and Directory of Durham*. London: Eyre Methuen

White, J T 1973 *Scottish Border and Northumberland*. London: Eyre Methuen

White, R 1997 *The Yorkshire Dales*. London: Batsford

White, R and Wilson, P (eds) 2004 *Archaeology and Historic Landscapes of the Yorkshire Dales*. Yorkshire Archaeological Society Occasional Paper 2

Whitworth, A M 2000 *Hadrian's Wall: Some Aspects of its Post-Roman Influence on the Landscape*. BAR British Series 296 Oxford: Archaeopress

Wilson, P 2002 *Cataractonium. Roman Catterick and its Hinterland: Excavations and Research 1958–97*. Council for British Archaeology Research Report 128 and 129. York: York Publishing Services Ltd

Winchester, A 2000 *The Harvest of the Hills. Rural Life in Northern England and the Scottish Borders, 1400–1700*. Edinburgh: Edinburgh University Press

Woodside, R and Crow, J 1999 *Hadrian's Wall: an Historical Landscape*. National Trust

Wrathmell, S 1976 *Deserted and Shrunken Villages in Southern Northumberland*. Unpublished PhD thesis, University of Wales

Wrathmell, S 1980 'Village depopulation in the 17th and 18th centuries: examples from Northumberland'. *Post-Medieval Archaeology* **14**, 113–26

Wrathmell, S 1989 'Peasant houses, farmsteads and villages in North-East England' *in* Aston, M, Austin, D and Dyer, C (eds) *The Rural Settlement of Medieval England*. Oxford: Oxford University Press, 247–67

Index

Picture Credits

Images on the following pages © Crown copyright.NMR or © English Heritage: 12 (NMR 20500/01); 14 (NMR 20498/03); 16 (AA045718); 22t (NMR 17859/24); 22b (NMR 20162/07); 23t (NMR 20062/23); 23b (NMR 20141/19); 24t (NMR 17757/24); 24b (NMR 20217/18); 25 (NMR 17862/04); 26 (NMR 17903/28); 27 (NMR 17914/02); 28 (NMR 17914/16); 38 (NMR 17859/29); 39t (NMR 17393/06); 39b (AA045765); 41 (NMR 12060/06); 43 (NMR 17881/03); 44 (TMG 13889/48); 48 (NMR 17698/30); 50 (NMR 17808/33); 58t (NMR 17862/10); 65 (NMR 17861/05); 68t (NMR 12622/27); 68b (NMR 20062/13); 83t (NMR 20196/24); 84t (AA049249); 84b (AA048550); 85m (AA050439); 85b (AA050434); 88b (AA050338); 92b (NMR 12911/13); 93 (NMR 20216/19); 97 (AA050283); 98 (NMR 12299/17); 99 (NMR 17420/22); 100t (NMR 12324/09); 100b (NMR 20455/20); 101 (NMR 12972/27); 102t (NMR 17009/24); 102b (NMR 4546/28); 103 (NMR 20196/11); 104 (NMR 20217/12); 106t (NMR 20163/10); 106b (AA035536); 107 (NMR 17332/22); 108 (AA017968); 117t (AA050363); 128 (NMR 20162/23); 129tl (NMR 20373/10); 129tr (NMR 17295/15); 129br (NMR 17916/03); 140–1 (NMR 17795/02); 144t (NMR 17930/06); 144b (NMR 17903/06); 145t (NMR 20424/11); 145b (NMR 20216/22); 149 (NMR 17790/010); 150 (NMR 17905/00); 151 (NMR 17607/15); 152t (NMR 20196/02); 159 (NMR 17656/12); 172–3 (AA028527); 178b (NMR 17958/02); 181 (NMR 17753/17); 185 (NMR 17927/01); 186t (NMR 20199/07); 193 (NMR 20197/07); 205t (NMR 17915/00); 206 (NMR 12145/15); 210 (NMR 20120/08); 214 (NMR 17948/14); 216t (NMR 17926/22); 216b (NMR 17925/22); 221 (NMR 17675/23).

English Heritage ground photography was taken by Alun Bull, Derek Kendall and Peter Williams. Additional English Heritage photography by Steve Cole, Patricia Payne and Bob Skingle.

Additional photographs: Alamy: Brian Oxley: 244, Graeme Peacock: 94; with kind permission of the Ashington Group Trustees: 235; Bradford University Libraries: 241tl; Bridgeman Art Library: Bradford Art Galleries and Museums, West Yorkshire, UK: 230b, Yale Center for British Art, Paul Mellon Collection, USA: 232; The British Library: 227; The Trustees of The British Museum: 229, 230t, 231b; *Views on the Newcastle and Carlisle Railway*, by J M Carmichael: 96; Corbis: BBC: 240b, Hulton-Deutsch Collection: 139; County Record Office, Durham: 79; English Nature: Paul Glendell: 32b, Peter Wakely: 34; Thomas Faulkner & Linda Polley: 156t, 160, 163, 166, 168, 178t, 180; courtesy of the Hatton Gallery Collection: 91b, 95c; Tony Hopkins: 58b, 119b; Kingston upon Hull City Libraries: 89, 162; Mike Kipling Photography: 203; courtesy of John Kippin: 238; Laing Art Gallery (Tyne and Wear Museums): 233; photograph by Professor N McCord © University of Newcastle upon Tyne: 95b; Richard Muir: 76, 132t, 143, 136, 186b, 204; National Trust Photo Library: Matthew Antrobus: 240t; courtesy of Newby Hall: 82t, 82b; Philip Nixon: 56; courtesy of Ordnance Survey: 175; A W Purdue: 86; Science and Society Picture Library: National Railway Museum Pictorial Collection: 198, 234; Sheffield Local Studies Library: 174; Sunderland Museum and Winter Gardens (Tyne and Wear Museums): 237; Christopher Tolan-Smith: 33, 37t, 40; Prof. J W R Whitehand, Dept of Geography, University of Birmingham, England: 241tr; The Whitworth Art Gallery, The University of Manchester: 231t, © Estate of Edward Wadsworth 2006. All Rights Reserved, DACS: 236; Dr T W Yellowley: 87, 95t; York Museums Trust (York Art Gallery): 165; Yorkshire Dales National Park Authority: R White: 120, 137, 212.

Aerial survey acknowledgements
New English Heritage aerial photographs were taken by Peter Horne, David Macleod and Jane Stone. The Aerial Reconnaissance team would like to thank the following people for their help: a special note of thanks must go to the skills and patience of the pilots Jon Forsyth, Mark Julian, Jim Loose, Chris Penistone, David Williams, Martin Wood; the aircraft owner Anthony Crawshaw; the NMR cataloguing team Rose Ogle, Katy Groves, Catherine Runciman, Cinzia Bacilieri, Philip Daniels, Geoff Hall; Jon Proudman for all the publication scanning; Sarah Prince for laser copying thousands of aerial photographs to send to the authors; and Kate Bould for post reconnaissance administrative support in York.